RAND McNALLY

S0-AAE-499

Business Traveler's Road Atlas
and Trip Planner

Trip Planning Guide

Major North American Cities Guide

United States Maps

Canada and Mexico Maps

International Travel Information

Photo credits
All photo images on pages 5, 6, 7, 8,
10, 11, 13, 14, 15, 16, 17, 177, 178, 179, 180,
181, 196 and 197 copyright © 1996
PhotoDisc, Inc.; p. 3 © Bruce Ayres/Tony
Stone Images; p. 9 © R. Kord/H.
Armstrong Roberts; p. 18 Seattle,
Washington State Tourism Division; p.
198 © Lonnie Duka/Tony Stone Images;
and p. 199 © Eberhard
Streichan/SuperStock Intl., Inc.
Cover Photo of the Statue of Liberty and
World Trade Center, New York City, NY by
Glen Allison, Tony Stone Worldwide

Introduction

Traveling for business means traveling with a purpose. Time schedules may be tight, allowing little or no opportunity for leisure and sightseeing; prearrangements are of utmost importance. Proper hand-ling of routine details leaves nothing to chance, and this can mean a successful business trip. Choosing the right hotel in the right location is as important as finding the fastest and most direct route to a destination.

The Rand McNally *Business Traveler's Road Atlas* provides all the details, facts, and travel information required by today's succesful business traveler. Information is arranged in four sections. The accurate state, provincial, city and national maps, the city and international directories, and trip planning guide are combined to create an all-in-one guide that takes the business traveler from the planning stage to the destination and home again.

Trip Planning Guide

The Trip Planning Guide provides pertinent information in an easy-to-use format, valuable both while traveling and once the destination has been reached. Mileages and driving times between cities, road condition "hot line" numbers, toll-free telephone numbers for hotel, motel, and car rental firms are provided in handy map and chart formats. Business travelers will also find airline toll-free reservation and frequent flyer numbers, telephone area code information, and commonly used travel telephone numbers included in quick reference formats.

North American travelers will find information about Canadian and Mexican regulations, holidays, and climate. and a table listing hotel/motel amenities to assist in planning meetings and activities in major North American cities.

Major Cities Guide

The Major Cities Guide relates important facts and describes the amenities of more than 95 principal North American cities. Hotels, restaurants and top attractions are selected for their broad appeal to the traveling public. Also provided for each city

are the addresses/telephone numbers for local convention & visitors bureaus, chambers of commerce, and offices of tourism. Forty-one detailed airport maps are included for the major airports serving passenger traffic. Clearly shown is each airport's layout: location of airline terminals, rental car companies, parking, and more. And, a four-color map of each city is included to aid in orienting the first-time visitor and refreshing the memory of the returning traveler.

Atlas Maps

The atlas section includes a United States map and maps of each of the 50 states, Canada, the Canadian provinces, and Mexico. Valuable as aids in routing your trip, these maps also are useful for pinpointing sites referred to in the Trip Planning Guide and for interpreting that section's mileage and climate information. State and provincial maps feature a handy index for ease of use.

International Travel

Today's multinational business environment requires the businessperson to have information about countries in which their firms conduct business. A world political map and maps of the continents orient the North American businessperson to the global environment and international relationships. World air distances, international time zones and weights and measures, plus passport requirements are provided. Hints for doing business in Canada, Mexico, Europe, and Asia and a quick travel data directory of more than 55 countries provide essential information for the traveler.

The quick data directory includes information about language, climate, clothing, entry requirements, holidays, currency name, international dialing code, and city telephone codes for selected major countries. The U.S. consulate telephone number and any travel advisories or special information a person should be aware of during trip planning and travel are also provided in the directory.

North American Mileage and Driving Time Map

Explanation

277   Light italic numerals indicate mileage in statute miles.

7:55   Bold blue numerals indicate driving time.

Driving time shown is approximate under normal conditions. Consideration has been given to topography, number of towns along route, congested urban areas, and the speed limit imposed by each state. Allowances should be made for night driving and unusually fast or slow drivers.

Road Condition "Hot Lines"

United States

Call the following numbers for road conditions and road construction.

Alabama
conditions: 334/242-4378

Alaska
conditions: 907/273-6037, press 1
construction: 907/273-6037, press 3

Arizona
conditions: 602/861-9400, ext. 7623 (recording)
construction: 602/255-6588 weekdays;
602/779-2711 (Northern AZ; recording)

Arkansas
conditions: 501/569-2374 (recording)
construction: 501/569-2227 weekdays

California
conditions: 916/445-7623; 916/445-1534

Colorado
conditions: 303/639-1234 (recording);
303/573-ROAD (recording); 303/639-1111,
press 1
construction: 303/757-9228 weekdays

Connecticut
conditions: 800/443-6817 (CT only);
203/594-2650 weekdays

Delaware
conditions: 800/652-5600 (DE only);
302/739-4313 (limited service)
construction: 302/739-6677 (recording)

District of Columbia
conditions: 202/936-1111 (recording)

Florida
no central source

Georgia
conditions: 800/722-6617 (GA only);
404/624-7890

Hawaii
construction: 808/536-6566 (recording)

Idaho
conditions: 208/336-6600 (recording)
construction: 208/334-8888 (recording)

Illinois
conditions: 312/368-4636 (recording);
217/782-5730 (recording in winter);
800/452-4368 (Nov.-Apr.)
construction: 800/452-4368 (May-Oct.)

Indiana
conditions: 317/232-8298 (recording)
construction: 317/232-5533 (recording)

Iowa
conditions: 515/288-1047 (recording)

Kansas
conditions: 800/585-7623 (KS only);
913/291-3000 (recording)

Kentucky
conditions & construction: 800/459-7623
(recording)

Louisiana
conditions: 504/379-1541 weekdays

Maine
conditions Nov.-Apr. (24 hrs); May-Oct.
weekdays: 207/287-3427
construction: 207/287-2672 weekdays

Maryland
conditions & construction: 800/323-6742
(MD only); 410/333-1122

Massachusetts
conditions: 617/374-1234 (recording)

Michigan
no central source

Minnesota
conditions:800/542-0220 (recording);
612/296-3076 (recording)

Mississippi
conditions: 601/987-1212 24 hours

Missouri
800/222-6400 (recording)

Montana
conditions: 800-332-6171 (recording);
406-444-6339 (recording)

Nebraska
conditions & construction: 402/479-4512
weekdays
conditions (winter):402/471-4533 (recording);
800/906-9069 (NE only)

Nevada
conditions recordings for:
South-Las Vegas: 702/486-3116
Northwest-Reno: 702/793-1313
Northeast-Elko: 702/738-8888

New Hampshire
conditions: 800-918-9993 (NH only);
603/271-6900

New Jersey
conditions for the Turnpike: 908-247-0900
conditions for the Garden State Parkway:
908-727-5929 (recording)

New Mexico
conditions & construction: 800/432-4269
(NM only; recording); 505/827-5154
(recording)

New York
conditions for New York Thruway:
800/847-8929

North Carolina
conditions: 919-549-5100, category 7623
(recording); 919/733-3861

North Dakota
conditions: 800-472-2686 (ND only)
(recording); 701/328-7623(recording)
construction: 701/328-4418 weekdays

Ohio
conditions: 614/466-7170 weekdays

Oklahoma
conditions: 405/425-2385, press 6
construction: 405/521-2554 weekdays

Oregon
conditions: 503/889-3999 (recording)

Pennsylvania
conditions & construction for the Turnpike:
800/331-3414 (PA only); 717/939-9551,
ext. 3060 weekdays
conditions for the Interstate 814/355-7545
weekdays

Rhode Island
construction: 401-277-2468 weekdays

South Carolina
conditions & construction: 803/896-9621
24 hours

South Dakota
conditions & construction: 605/773-3536
24 hours

Tennessee
conditions: 800-858-6349

Texas
conditions: 800-452-9292 weekdays

Utah
conditions: 801/964-6000 (recording)

Vermont
conditions: 802-828-2468 weekdays (longer
hours during storms)

Virginia
conditions & construction: 800/367-7623 (VA
only)

Washington
conditions: Mountain Pass Report (Nov.-Apr.)
206/434-PASS
construction: 360-705-7075 weekdays

West Virginia
conditions: 304/558-2889 (recording)

Wisconsin
conditions (winter) & construction (summer):
800/762-3947 (recording)

Wyoming
conditions: 307/635-9966 (recording)
construction: 307/777-4437 weekdays

Canada

Alberta
conditions: 403/246-5853 (recording)

British Columbia
conditions: 800/663-4997 (BC only;
recording)

Manitoba
conditions: 204/945-3704 (recording in winter)

New Brunswick
conditions: 800-561-4063 (NB only)

Newfoundland
conditions: (weekdays;
24-hour operation in winter)
Clarenville: 709/466-7953
Deer Lake: 709/635-4100
Grand Falls: 709/292-4300

Northwest Territories
Hwys 1-7 conditions: 403/874-2208
(recording)
Hwy 8 conditions: 403/979-2678 (recording)

Nova Scotia
conditions: 902/424-3933 (in winter)

Ontario:
conditions: 800/ONTARIO (in winter)

Prince Edward Island
conditions: 902/368-4770 weekdays;
24 hours in winter

Québec
conditions: 514/873-4121 (in winter)

Saskatchewan
conditions: 306/787-7623 (recording)

Yukon
conditions: 403/667-8215 (recording)

Keys:
weekdays=normal business hours
24 hours=a person answers 24 hours/7 days
per week
recording=available at all times unless noted

Intercity Toll Road Information

State/Province	Road Name	Location	Miles	Auto Toll	Auto/2-Axle Trailer
CANADA					
British Columbia	Coquihalla Highway	Hope (BC 3) to Merritt (BC 5A)	68.4	$7.00*	$7.00*
UNITED STATES					
California	Foothill Transportation Corridor	Portola Pkwy. to Antonio Pkwy., Orange County	7.5	1.00	3.00
	San Joaquin Hills Transportation Corridor	Jambaree Rd. to I-5	14.7	2.00	4.80
Colorado	E-470	1-25 to Parker Rd.	5.0	.25	.50
Delaware	Delaware Route 1	Dover to Smyrna	17.4	1.00	3.00
	Kennedy Memorial Highway	Md. State Line to N.J. State Line	16.3	1.25	2.50
Florida	Airport Expressway (Miami)	NW 42nd Av. to I-95	3.6	.25	.75
	Bee Line Main	Orlando Airport Plaza to FL 520	20	1.00	2.50
	Bee Line East	FL 520 to Cape Canaveral	22	.20	.40
	Bee Line West	I-4 to Co 436 (Semoran Blvd.)	11	.50	1.50
	Central Florida GreenWay	I-4 to US 17/92	50	5.00	13.00
	Crosstown Expressway (Tampa)	Gandy Blvd. (US 92) to I-75	13.9	1.25	2.50
	Dolphin Expressway (Miami)	Le Jeune Road to I-95	4.1	.25	.75
	Don Shula Expressway (Miami)	Homestead Ext. (Florida's Tpk.) to Killian Pkwy.	2.1	.25	.75
	East-West Expressway (Orlando)	Colonial Dr. (east) to Colonial Dr. (west)	22	2.50	6.00
	Everglades Parkway (Alligator Alley)	Naples to Andytown	78	.75	2.00
	Florida's Turnpike	I-75 to Miami	266	14.40	32.30
	Florida's Tpk. (Homestead Ext.)	Miramar to Florida City	47	3.00	9.00
	Gratigny Parkway (Miami)	Palmetto Expwy. to NW 27th Av.	5.2	.25	.75
	Sawgrass Expressway	I-75 to I-95	23	1.50	4.50
	Veterans Expressway	Dale Mabry Hwy. to Courtney Campbell Causeway	15	1.25	3.75
Illinois	Chicago Skyway	I-94, Chicago, to Ind. State Line	7.3	2.00	3.50
	East-West Tollway	I-88, Chicago, to Rock Falls	97	2.70	5.40
	North-South Tollway	I-290, Addison, to I-55, Bolingbrook	17.5	1.00	2.00
	Northwest Tollway	Des Plaines to South Beloit	76	2.00	4.00
	Tri-State Tollway	Ind. State Line to Wis. State Line	83	2.40	4.80
Indiana	Indiana Toll Road	Ohio State Line to Ill. State Line	157	4.65	5.35
Kansas	Kansas Turnpike	Kansas City to Okla. State Line	236	7.75	14.75
Kentucky	Audubon Parkway	Henderson to Owensboro	24.6	.50	1.10
	Cumberland Parkway	Bowling Green to Somerset	88.5	2.00	4.00
	Daniel Boone Parkway	London to Hazard	59.1	1.40	2.80
	William H. Natcher Parkway	Bowling Green to Owensboro	70.7	1.50	3.00
Maine	Maine Turnpike	York to Augusta	100	3.25	4.75
Massachusetts	Massachusetts Turnpike	Boston to N.Y. State Line	135	5.60	7.70
New Hampshire	F.E. Everett Turnpike	Nashua to Concord	44.7	1.50	2.50
	Blue Star Turnpike	Portsmouth to Seabrook	16.1	1.00	1.50
	Spaulding Turnpike	Portsmouth to Milton, N.H.	33.2	1.00	2.00
New Jersey	Atlantic City Expressway	Turnersville to Atlantic City	44	1.25	5.00
	Garden State Parkway	Montvale to Cape May	173	4.20	8.40
	New Jersey Turnpike	Del. Mem. Br. to Washington Br.	148	4.60	15.60
New York	New York Thruway–				
	Eastbound	Pa. State Line to N.Y.C.	496	17.60	32.30
	Westbound	N.Y.C. to Pa. State Line	496	15.10	27.80
	Berkshire Section	Selkirk to Mass. Turnpike	24	1.20	2.15
	New England Section	N.Y.C. to Conn. State Line	15	1.00	2.00
	Niagara Section	Buffalo to Niagara Falls	21	1.00	2.00
Ohio	J. W. Shocknessy Ohio Tpk.	Pa. State Line to Ind. State Line	241.2	6.20	9.50
Oklahoma	Cherokee Turnpike	US 69 to US 59	32.8	2.00	3.75
	Chickasaw Turnpike	Ada to Sulphur	27.1	.50	1.00
	Cimarron Turnpike	I-35 to Tulsa	59.2	2.25	4.00
	Creek Turnpike	US 75 to US 64	7.6	.55	1.05
	H.E. Bailey Turnpike	Oklahoma City to Texas State Line	86.4	3.50	6.50
	Indian Nation Turnpike	Henryetta to Hugo	105.2	4.00	7.00
	Kilpatrick Turnpike	Oklahoma City, OK 74 to I-35/44	9.5	.80	1.55
	Muskogee Turnpike	Tulsa to Webber Falls	53.1	2.25	4.00
	Turner Turnpike	Oklahoma City to Tulsa	86	3.00	6.00
	Will Rogers Turnpike	Tulsa to Mo. State Line	88.5	3.00	6.00

*at January, 1996 rate of exchange

© 1997 Rand McNally & Company

State/Province	Road Name	Location	Miles	Auto Toll	Auto/2-Axle Trailer
Pennsylvania	Amos K. Hutchinson Bypass (PA Tpk. 66)	US 119 to US 22	13	1.00	1.50
	James E. Ross Hwy. (PA Tpk. 60)	Beaver Falls to New Castle	17	1.00	1.50
	James J. Manderino Hwy. (PA Tpk. 43)	I-70 to US 40	5	.50	1.50
	Pennsylvania Turnpike	N.J. State Line to Ohio State Line	359	14.70	21.70
	Pa. Turnpike (N.E. Sect.)	Norristown to Scranton	110	3.60	5.40
Texas	Dallas North Tollway	1-35E, Dallas, to TX 121, Plano	21	1.50	3.00
	Hardy Toll Road	I-45, Houston, to I-610, Houston	21.6	2.00	6.00
	Sam Houston Tollway	US 59, Houston, to I-45	28	3.00	6.00
Virginia	Chesapeake Bay Bridge & Tunnel	US 13, Norfolk/VA Beach to Eastern Shore	17.6	10.00	16.00
	Downtown Expressway (Richmond)	I-195 to I-95	3.4	.35	.55
	Dulles Greenway	VA 28 to Leesburg	14.3	1.00	2.00
	Dulles Toll Road	VA 123 to VA 28	13	.85	1.70
	Powhite Parkway	I-195 to VA 150	2.1	.35	.55
	Powhite Parkway Extension	VA 150 to Old Hundred Rd.	12.5	.75	1.25
West Virginia	West Virginia Turnpike	Charleston to Princeton	88	3.75	6.00
MEXICO	Mexico Highway 1	Tijuana to Ensenada	68	3..33*	**
	Mexico Highway 15	Nogales to Mazatlán	746	18.00*	**
	Mexico Highway 40	Reynosa to Torreón	368	29.73*	**
	Mexico Highway 45	El Paso to Torreón	519	6.53*	**
	Mexico Highway 45-90D	Guadalajara to Querétaro	209	4.93*	**
	Mexico Highway 57	Mexico City to Querétaro	135	4.00*	**
	Mexico Highway 85	Laredo to Monterrey	146	8.00*	**
	Mexico Highway 95D	Mexico City to Acapulco	265	34.00*	**
	Mexico Highway 150D	Mexico City to Veracruz	235	7.20*	**
	Durango-Torreón Toll Road	Durango to Torreón	161	14.93*	**
	Guadalajara-Aguascalientes Toll Rd.	Guadalajara to Aguascalientes	153	14.53*	**
	Guadalajara-Colima Toll Rd.	Guadalajara to Colima	116	2.40*	**
	Mexico City-Aguascalientes Toll Rd.	Mexico City to Aguascalientes	319	10.67*	**
	Mexico City-Oaxaca Toll Rd.	Mexico City to Oaxaca	304	22.00*	**
	Mexico City-Pachuca Toll Rd.	Mexico City to Pachuca	57	1.33*	**
	Torreón-Cuencame Toll Rd.	Torreón to Cuencame	58	4.53*	**

*at January, 1996 rate of exchange   **information not available

Car Rental Toll-Free Numbers

The following selected list of car rental companies provides toll-free "800" reservations numbers good from the United States, Canada and sometimes Mexico. Although these numbers were in effect at press time, Rand McNally cannot be responsible should any of these numbers change. Many companies do not have toll-free reservation numbers; consult your local telephone directory for a regional listing.

Toll-Free Numbers

AAPEX Courtesy Car Rental
800/327-9106 USA and Canada

Alamo Rent-A-Car
800/327-9633 USA and Canada

Allstate Car Rental
800/634-6186 USA and Canada

Avis Reservations Center
800/331-1212 USA (Domestic Res.)
800/331-1084 USA (Intl Res.)
800/879-2847 Canada
95/800/882-8471 Mexico

Avon Rent-A-Car
800/432-2866 USA

Aztec Rent-A-Car
800/231-0400 USA and Canada

Brooks Rent-A-Car
800/ 634-6721 USA and Canada

Budget Rent-A-Car
800/527-0700 USA
800/472-3325 Canada and Mexico

Dollar Rent-A-Car
800/ 800-4000 USA, Canada and Mexico

Enterprise Rent-A-Car
800/325-8007 USA and Canada

Hertz Corporation
800/654-3131 USA and Canada

InterAmerican Car Rental
800/327-1278 USA, Canada and Mexico

National Interrent
800/CAR-RENT USA, Canada and Mexico

Payless Car Rental Intl Inc.
800/PAYLESS USA, Canada and Mexico

Practical/Freedom/AllSTAR Rent-A-Car
800/233-1663 USA

Sears Rent-A-Car
800/527-0770 USA

Thrifty Rent-A-Car
800/367-2277 USA, Canada and Mexico

U-SAVE Auto Rental
800/272-8728 USA and Canada

Value Rent-A-Car
800/GO-VALUE USA and Canada

Limousine Services

The following limousine service companies provide toll-free "800" numbers for making reservations throughout the United States and other parts of North America.

Affordable (R.A.S.) Limousine
800/831-0502 USA and Canada

Carey International
800/336-4646 USA, Canada and Mexico
800/263-9566 Canada

Dav-El Limousine
800/922-0343 USA

Mileage Chart

	Atlanta, GA	Billings, MT	Boston, MA	Charlotte, NC	Chicago, IL	Cincinnati, OH	Cleveland, OH	Dallas, TX	Denver, CO	Detroit, MI	Houston, TX	Indianapolis, IN	Kansas City, MO	Los Angeles, CA	Memphis, TN	Miami, FL	Milwaukee, WI	Minneapolis, MN	New Orleans, LA	New York, NY	Omaha, NE	Philadelphia, PA	Phoenix, AZ	Pittsburgh, PA	Portland, OR	St. Louis, MO	Salt Lake City, UT	San Francisco, CA	Seattle, WA	Tulsa, OK	Washington, DC	Wichita, KS
Albany, NY	991	2086	166	757	836	729	481	1663	1824	655	1751	796	1292	2847	1209	1405	929	1246	1422	156	1284	233	2545	472	2940	1042	2216	2961	2909	1433	361	1482
Albuquerque, NM	1407	993	2225	1641	1335	1391	1603	646	439	1585	894	1284	783	804	1013	1963	1352	1222	1145	2020	868	1940	465	1650	1366	1038	604	1101	1433	649	1885	593
Amarillo, TX	1123	969	1941	1357	1051	1107	1319	362	420	1301	610	1000	603	1088	729	1679	1125	1042	861	1736	651	1656	749	1366	1651	754	878	1385	1718	365	1601	416
Atlanta, GA		1840	1075	240	716	460	712	792	1416	732	802	531	811	2211	394	661	809	1132	473	870	999	772	1859	683	2606	555	1882	2508	2673	807	632	974
Baltimore, MD	669	1965	407	435	715	527	380	1367	1700	534	1455	599	1095	2687	913	1080	808	1125	1126	202	1163	104	2348	251	2819	845	2095	2840	2788	1236	36	1285
Billings, MT	1840		2265	2035	1249	1549	1605	1329	554	1536	1577	1435	1029	1233	1554	2501	1178	843	1828	2071	847	2022	1203	1722	885	1285	544	1178	821	1238	1965	1064
Birmingham, AL	148	1787	1187	388	663	467	719	648	1363	739	671	478	758	2064	247	783	756	1079	342	982	946	887	1715	761	2553	502	1829	2361	2620	653	743	827
Bismarck, ND	1498	416	1788	1554	836	1136	1192	1172	692	1088	1418	1022	757	1574	1204	2153	765	430	1568	1658	611	1609	1453	1309	1258	979	909	1596	1239	998	1516	807
Boise, ID	2184	622	2697	2359	1705	1962	2037	1589	814	1968	1837	1850	1373	842	1904	2845	1744	1467	2088	2503	1234	2454	998	2154	427	1629	339	642	494	1498	2397	1324
Boston, MA	1075	2265		841	1015	869	648	1770	2003	834	1858	941	1437	3026	1316	1486	1108	1425	1529	211	1463	314	2690	593	3119	1187	2395	3140	3088	1582	442	1627
Buffalo, NY	899	1796	463	659	546	439	191	1378	1534	365	1491	506	1002	2557	924	1378	639	956	1244	393	994	384	2255	217	2650	752	1926	2671	2619	1143	391	1192
Charleston, SC	320	2163	968	203	913	615	717	1112	1719	871	1110	726	1114	2573	756	580	1006	1323	781	763	1302	665	2179	650	2909	858	2185	2870	2976	1162	525	1304
Charlotte, NC	240	2035	841		785	487	516	1032	1591	670	1042	598	986	2445	628	721	878	1195	713	636	1174	538	2106	449	2781	730	2057	2742	2848	1034	398	1176
Cheyenne, WY	1449	456	1962	1624	970	1227	1302	875	100	1233	1123	1115	638	1102	1190	2110	1009	879	1374	1768	499	1719	916	1419	1158	894	434	1179	1225	784	1662	610
Chicago, IL	716	1249	1015	785		299	355	928	1011	286	1085	185	530	2034	536	1377	92	409	929	821	471	772	1800	472	2127	297	1403	2148	2072	688	715	720
Cincinnati, OH	460	1549	869	487	299		252	939	1208	272	1052	112	603	2195	485	1121	392	709	805	664	728	584	1856	294	2384	353	1660	2405	2372	744	527	793
Cleveland, OH	712	1605	648	516	355	252		1191	1343	174	1304	319	815	2366	737	1235	448	765	1057	486	803	437	2068	137	2459	565	1735	2480	2428	956	380	1005
Columbus, OH	571	1611	762	433	361	111	142	1050	1279	206	1163	178	674	2266	596	1152	454	771	916	557	792	477	1927	187	2448	424	1724	2469	2434	817	420	864
Dallas, TX	792	1329	1770	1032	928	939	1191		780	1211	246	908	495	1447	454	1317	1002	934	499	1565	672	1470	1067	1233	2011	631	1240	1747	2078	262	1326	365
Davenport, IA	742	1118	1115	907	175	421	496	860	848	427	1011	309	364	1868	550	1397	214	360	943	962	305	913	1554	613	1961	265	1237	1982	1941	620	863	554
Denver, CO	1416	554	2003	1591	1011	1208	1343	780		1274	1028	1101	605	1023	1095	2077	1050	920	1279	1809	540	1757	816	1460	1236	861	512	1257	1303	689	1700	515
Des Moines, IA	976	948	1326	1077	334	591	666	689	675	597	931	479	194	1698	657	1637	373	243	1050	1132	135	1083	1442	783	1791	388	1067	1812	1771	450	1026	384
Detroit, MI	732	1536	834	670	286	272	174	1211	1274		1324	298	793	2297	757	1389	379	696	1077	640	734	591	2050	291	2390	547	1666	2411	2359	938	534	983
Duluth, MN	1137	862	1422	1188	465	765	821	1091	990	752	1333	651	595	1980	960	1856	394	156	1353	1287	536	1238	1768	938	1749	675	1315	2042	1685	851	1188	785
El Paso, TX	1425	1178	2403	1665	1483	1572	1751	633	624	1733	752	1432	931	814	1087	1938	1500	1370	1100	2198	1016	2103	434	1798	1628	1186	866	1193	1695	797	1959	741
Fargo, ND	1369	604	1662	1432	646	946	1002	1089	875	933	1335	832	605	1839	1130	2030	575	240	1523	1468	421	1419	1691	1119	1494	861	1153	1784	1427	810	1362	727
Flagstaff, AZ	1711	1065	2556	1968	1662	1718	1930	973	678	1853	1155	1611	1110	477	1340	2290	1679	1480	1472	2356	1169	2267	136	1955	1226	1362	504	773	1314	976	2169	921
Houston, TX	802	1577	1858	1042	1085	1052	1304	246	1028	1324		1021	737	1566	567	1190	1175	1176	352	1653	918	1558	1186	1346	2259	780	1488	1945	2326	504	1414	611
Indianapolis, IN	531	1435	941	598	185	112	319	908	1101	298	1021		496	2088	472	1192	278	595	816	736	616	656	1749	366	2272	246	1548	2293	2258	637	599	686
Jackson, MS	383	1772	1426	623	749	693	945	409	1223	965	442	685	738	1856	213	908	839	1058	180	1221	926	1126	1476	987	2454	498	1730	2156	2521	534	982	708
Jacksonville, FL	346	2186	1145	380	1062	792	894	1002	1762	1048	875	877	1157	2437	713	341	1155	1478	546	940	1345	842	2057	827	2952	901	2228	2816	3019	1119	702	1293
Kansas City, MO	811	1029	1437	986	530	603	815	495	605	793	737	496		1631	525	1472	569	439	918	1232	188	1152	1248	862	1795	256	1071	1816	1862	255	1095	190
Knoxville, TN	215	1721	933	241	545	247	499	841	1350	519	929	358	745	2204	387	887	638	955	600	733	935	630	1865	496	2542	489	1818	2503	2523	793	484	935
Las Vegas, NV	1987	960	2753	2221	1761	1961	2093	1226	750	2024	1479	1854	1358	275	1593	2543	1800	1670	1725	2559	1290	2510	292	2210	1022	1614	415	568	1122	1229	2465	1173
Lexington, KY	388	1552	932	411	380	82	334	875	1198	354	988	193	593	2179	421	1057	473	790	741	732	783	643	1840	376	2390	337	1666	2411	2354	728	541	783
Little Rock, AR	531	1513	1453	765	655	622	874	319	964	894	432	591	389	1686	137	1165	745	825	441	1248	577	1153	1347	916	2195	351	1471	1983	2262	275	1009	449
Los Angeles, CA	2211	1233	3026	2445	2034	2195	2366	1447	1023	2297	1566	2088	1631		1817	2752	2073	1943	1914	2824	1563	2744	381	2454	967	1842	688	380	1151	1453	2689	1397
Louisville, KY	417	1549	972	484	299	103	355	836	1119	375	949	114	514	2100	382	1078	392	709	702	767	702	687	1761	397	2309	258	1585	2330	2372	649	615	704
Memphis, TN	394	1554	1316	628	536	485	737	454	1095	757	567	472	525	1817		1028	626	845	393	1111	713	1016	1478	779	2326	285	1602	2114	2393	406	872	580
Miami, FL	661	2501	1486	721	1377	1121	1235	1317	2077	1389	1190	1192	1472	2752	1028		1470	1793	861	1281	1660	1183	2372	1168	3267	1216	2543	3131	3334	1434	1043	1608
Milwaukee, WI	809	1178	1108	878	92	392	448	1002	1050	379	1175	278	569	2073	626	1470		338	1019	914	510	865	1817	565	2065	371	1442	2187	2001	762	808	759
Minneapolis, MN	1132	843	1425	1195	409	709	765	934	920	696	1176	595	439	1943	845	1793	338		1238	1231	380	1182	1687	882	1730	619	1312	2057	1666	695	1125	629
Mobile, AL	335	1962	1444	575	923	727	979	599	1413	999	472	738	924	2034	399	718	1016	1244	143	1205	1112	1107	1654	1021	2644	684	1920	2413	2711	724	967	898
Montreal, PQ	1216	1898	324	982	851	836	588	1775	1839	568	1888	862	1358	2862	1321	1630	944	1261	1641	381	1299	458	2615	614	2955	1112	2231	2976	2721	1504	586	1548
Nashville, TN	244	1598	1107	419	474	278	530	664	1174	550	777	289	569	2027	210	905	567	890	527	902	757	807	1688	572	2364	313	1640	2324	2431	616	663	759
New Orleans, LA	473	1828	1529	713	929	805	1057	499	1279	1077	352	816	918	1914	393	861	1019	1238		1324	1106	1229	1534	1099	2510	678	1739	2293	2577	646	1085	864
New York, NY	870	2071	211	636	821	664	486	1565	1809	640	1653	736	1232	2824	1111	1281	914	1231	1324		1269	109	2485	388	2925	982	2201	2946	2894	1382	237	1422
Norfolk, VA	555	2152	577	321	902	662	567	1353	1778	721	1357	725	1173	2716	899	949	995	1312	1028	372	1363	276	2377	438	2968	917	2244	2989	2975	1305	195	1363
Odessa, TX	1153	1224	2091	1386	1234	1293	1467	354	664	1484	551	1183	786	1094	808	1671	1308	1225	853	1928	906	1825	714	1587	1765	937	1003	1475	1832	548	1679	599
Oklahoma City, OK	864	1221	1681	1098	791	847	1059	208	672	1041	454	740	344	1347	470	1498	865	783	707	1476	464	1396	1008	1106	1903	494	1179	1644	1970	105	1342	157
Omaha, NE	999	847	1463	1174	471	728	803	672	540	734	918	616	188	1563	713	1660	510	380	1106	1269		1220	1356	920	1656	444	932	1677	1670	393	1163	310
Orlando, FL	441	2281	1285	520	1157	901	1034	1097	1857	1173	970	972	1252	2532	808	229	1250	1573	641	1080	1440	982	2152	967	3047	996	2323	2911	3114	1214	842	1388
Philadelphia, PA	772	2022	314	538	772	584	437	1470	1757	591	1558	656	1152	2744	1016	1183	865	1182	1229	109	1220		2405	308	2876	902	2152	2897	2845	1293	139	1342
Phoenix, AZ	1859	1203	2690	2106	1800	1856	2068	1067	816	2050	1186	1749	1248	381	1478	2372	1817	1687	1534	2485	1356	2405		2115	1347	1503	658	760	1487	1114	2350	1058
Pittsburgh, PA	683	1722	593	449	472	294	137	1233	1460	291	1346	366	862	2454	779	1168	565	882	1099	388	920	308	2115		2576	612	1852	2597	2545	1003	251	1052
Portland, ME	1176	2366	108	942	1116	970	749	1871	2104	935	1959	1042	1538	3127	1417	1587	1209	1526	1630	312	1564	415	2791	694	3220	1288	2496	3241	3189	1683	543	1728
Portland, OR	2606	885	3119	2781	2127	2384	2459	2011	1236	2390	2259	2272	1795	967	2326	3267	2065	1730	2510	2925	1656	2876	1347	2576		2051	761	636	175	1920	2819	1746
Rapid City, SD	1523	321	1928	1698	912	1212	1268	1071	389	1199	1317	1098	712	1325	1237	2184	841	611	1630	1734	528	1685	1205	1385	1208	968	657	1402	1144	880	1628	706
Reno, NV	2405	956	2918	2580	1926	2183	2258	1671	1035	2189	1924	2071	1594	472	2038	3066	1965	1835	2170	2724	1455	2675	737	2375	579	1850	523	222	763	1622	2618	1545
Roanoke, VA	429	1845	683	193	678	432	429	1099	1548	583	1187	543	943	2462	645	912	771	1088	858	483	1133	380	2123	346	2740	687	2016	2761	2647	1051	236	1133
St. Louis, MO	555	1285	1187	730	297	353	565	631	861	547	780	246	256	1842	285	1216	371	619	678	982	444	902	1503	612	2051		1327	2072	2118	391	845	446
Salt Lake City, UT	1882	544	2395	2057	1403	1660	1735	1240	512	1666	1488	1548	1071	688	1602	2543	1442	1312	1739	2201	932	2152	658	1852	761	1327		745	828	1196	2095	1022
San Antonio, TX	993	1480	2044	1233	1202	1213	1465	274	931	1485	195	1182	814	1372	728	1381	1276	1253	543	1839	934	1744	992	1507	2070	905	1308	1751	2137	536	1600	627
San Diego, CA	2154	1294	3043	2394	2095	2209	2427	1362	1084	2358	1481	2102	1601	124	1816	2667	2134	2004	1829	2838	1624	2758	359	2468	1091	1856	749	504	1275	1467	2688	1411
San Francisco, CA	2508	1178	3140	2742	2148	2405	2480	1747	1257	2411	1945	2293	1816	380	2114	3131	2187	2057	2293	2946	1677	2897	760	2597	636	2072	745		820	1752	2840	1767
Sault St Marie, MI/ON	1056	1283	936	961	461	553	508	1353	1423	350	1507	537	942	2446	958	1680	404	546	1347	974	883	925	2225	625	2170	722	1815	2560	2106	1113	868	1132
Seattle, WA	2673	821	3088	2848	2072	2372	2428	2078	1303	2359	2326	2258	1862	1151	2393	3334	2001	1666	2577	2894	1670	2845	1487	2545	175	2118	828	820		1987	2788	1813
Shreveport, LA	605	1616	1648	845	868	835	1087	187	1067	1107	235	804	583	1634	350	1130	958	1022	320	1443	769	1348	1254	1129	2298	563	1427	1934	2365	350	1204	552
Sioux Falls, SD	1183	667	1587	1354	571	878	927	850	659	858	1096	766	366	1618	811	1847	500	270	1175	1393	184	1344	1472	1044	1554	624	1007	1752	1490	571	1294	488
Spokane, WA	2381	539	2806	2576	1790	2010	2146	1870	1095	2077	2118	1976	1570	1210	2095	3042	1719	1384	2369	2612	1388	2563	1373	2263	346	1826	714	879	282	1779	2506	1605
Springfield, MO	658	1198	1401	862	507	563	775	423	760	757	665	456	169	1634	281	1309	581	605	674	1201	357	1112	1295	822	1964	208	1240	1933	2031	183	1082	287
Tallahassee, FL	270	1989	1234	436	921	692	1022	839	1580	952	712	781	986	2189	550	478	1059	1382	383	1034	1172	929	1894	879	2766	805	2051	2557	2806	956	796	1130
Tampa, FL	458	2298	1343	578	1174	925	1092	1114	1874	1190	987	989	1269	2549	825	270	1267	1590	658	1138	1457	1040	2169	1025	3064	1013	2340	2928	3131	1231	900	1405
Toronto, ON	970	1775	567	766	525	510	298	1449	1513	242	1562	536	1032	2536	995	1485	618	935	1315	528	973	519	2289	324	2629	786	1905	2650	2598	1178	498	1222
Tulsa, OK	775	1178	1582	1034	688	744	956	262	689	938	504	637	255	1453	406	1434	762	695	714	1382	393	1293	1114	1003	1920	391	1196	1752	1987		1263	174
Washington, DC	632	1965	442	398	715	527	380	1326	1700	534	1414	599	1095	2689	872	1043	808	1125	1085	237	1163	139	2350	251	2819	845	2095	2840	2788	1263		1285
Wichita, KS	974	1064	1627	1176	720	793	1005	365	515	983	611	686	190	1397	580	1608	759	629	864	1422	310	1342	1058	1052	1746	446	1022	1767	1813	174	1285	

Mileages Copyright © by Rand McNally—TDM, Inc.

Travel Safety Tips

Hotels and Motels

Room Location   Ask for a room near the elevator or stairs, or reservation office. Hotel rooms on lower floors offer quicker exit in the event of fire. Concierge floors offer an added element of protection, as well as special amenities—for a price.

In-Room Safety   Always keep the door locked and chained when in your room. For an added measure of protection, there are special travel room locks and door stops you can buy. If you do, be sure the gadget is easy to use and that it could be removed quickly in the dark in case an emergency exit is necessary.

Valuables   Do not display valuables or large amounts of cash at check-in. Do not keep valuables in your room—arrange to use the hotel safe.

Fire Safety

Know the building and your floor   Count the number of rooms between your room and the exit; locate the fire alarms and extinguishers nearest your room.

Always assume an alarm is for real   If the alarm sounds:

☐ **Feel the door**   *If it is hot,* call the front desk and stand at your window with a white towel, ready to wave it to attract attention. *If it is cool,* make your exit, taking your key with you.

☐ **Do not use an elevator**   If you are unable to exit by a stairway, try to get to the roof, or return to your room.

☐ **Try to stay calm if you can't exit**   Panic can cause errors in judgment that may make a bad situation worse.

☐ **If your room gets smoky,** *turn off the air conditioner.* Fill the bathtub with water and *put wet towels or sheets over vents and in the cracks along the door* to block the smoke. *Stay close to the floor.* The leading cause of death in hotel/motel fires is smoke inhalation, not the fire itself.

☐ **Don't break a window except as a last resort.**

On The Road

Maintaining safety on the road depends on knowing that your car is in proper working order and contains necessary emergency equipment, as well as following common-sense "rules of the road" for avoiding problems such as theft and carjackings.

Start-up Checks

Whether you own the car you're driving, or are renting it, there are several safety checks you can make just prior to driving that can alert you to potential problems. If you're renting and find a problem during the start-up check, notify the rental personnel and obtain a new car.

✓ Check tires for inflation and wear.
✓ Check the gas gauge.
✓ See that the oil pressure light doesn't remain on.
✓ Check for soft brake action by applying the brakes before engaging the gears.
✓ Check accessories such as lights, turn signals, windshield wipers and horn.
✓ Notice whether the steering is loose or the car pulls to one side when in motion. This should be corrected as soon as possible.

Safety "Rules of the Road"

❍ Keep luggage and valuables out of sight in the car.
❍ Don't leave anything of importance in your car overnight.
❍ Park in the center of a parking lot rather than at the edge.
❍ Know how to reach your destination. Get directions or study a map before getting underway. If you have to recheck a map, do so in a public area; don't simply pull to the side of the road.
❍ Keep car doors locked, even during the day.
❍ Stay on interstates whenever possible.
❍ Choose the center lane where available.
❍ Be especially cautious at night. Don't drive alone if you can help it. Be alert at rest stops, convenience stores, and gas stations. At gas stations in out-of-the-way locations, use the full-service pump if there is one.
❍ Don't pull over for flashing *head*lights. Police and emergency vehicles use auxiliary red or blue flashing lights.
❍ In an isolated area, question *any* flashing lights. If you have any reason to be suspicious of even seemingly official flashing lights, drive directly to the nearest public area before stopping.
❍ If your car gets bumped from behind, don't stop. Drive to the nearest public area and call the police.
❍ If someone signals something is wrong with your car, drive to a service station or populated area before checking it out.

Cellular Phones

Cellular phones are valuable for providing an added measure of safety to your life. If you are lost, you can call for directions from your car rather than chance getting out to phone in a strange neighborhood. Or, if you feel you are being followed or are otherwise at risk, you can call for assistance. For your own and others' peace of mind, use your phone to report delays when someone is expecting your arrival.

On the road, use your cellular phone to call ahead to check road or weather conditions, and to report an accident—your own or others. In the event your car becomes disabled, you can quickly and easily phone your auto club or call for other help.

Although there is not yet a standard nationwide emergency number for cellular phone users, your local carrier can provide you with the emergency number(s) for areas you frequent.

While you are waiting for help to arrive, stay in your car with the doors locked and activate your flashers. In the event you don't have a phone in your car, it is a good idea to carry a windshield sign that alerts other drivers to call the police for you. Should someone stop and offer assistance or to take you to a phone, remain in your car and ask them to call for help for you.

Emergency Equipment

- Spare tire
- Jack
- Lug wrench
- Jumper cables
- Flashlight
- Tool kit
- Road flares
- Empty container for gas
- Can of engine oil
- Spare parts: fan belt, fuses

- First aid kit
- Plus, in winter:
- Ice scraper and snow brush
- Spray can of de-icer
- Shovel
- Traction aids: sand, rock salt, carpet strips, or kitty litter
- Windshield washing solvent
- Blankets

Hotel/Motel Services Guide

This selected list is a handy guide to hotel/motel services and toll-free reservation numbers. The amenities noted for each chain reflect the services that are offered at most, not necessarily all, properties in that particular chain. (The "Airport Transportation" category applies only to properties near airports.) If you require a specific amenity, be sure to ask about its availability when making reservations. The "800" numbers were in effect at press time, however the Atlas cannot be responsible should any of the numbers change. Many establishments do not have toll-free numbers. Consult your local phone directory for a regional listing.

Chain:	US	Canada	Mexico	Toll-Free Reservation Number:	Airport Transportation	Corporate Rates	Weekend Rates
Adam's Mark Hotels	14			800/444-ADAM USA & Canada	•	•	•
Best Western International, Inc.	1,874	124	33	800/528-1234 USA & Canada	•	•	•
Budget Host	179	1		800/BUD-HOST USA & Canada			
Budgetel Inns	1257			800/4-BUDGET USA & Canada	•		
Canadian Pacific Hotels		26		800/441-1414 USA & Canada	•	•	•
Clarion Inns/Hotels/Suites & Resorts	84	8	1	800/CLARION USA & Canada	•	•	•
Comfort Inn & Suites	1,340	117	1	800/228-5150 USA & Canada	•	•	•
Courtyard by Marriott	262			800/321-2211 USA & Canada		•	•
Crowne Plaza	33	3	6	800/2-CROWNE USA & Canada	•	•	•
Days Inn	1,600	47	8	800/DAYS-INN USA & Canada	•	•	•
Delta Hotels & Resorts	2	21		800/268-1133 USA and Canada	•	•	•
Doubletree Hotels ■ Guest Suites	109			800/222-TREE USA & Canada	•	•	•
Drury Inn	84			800/325-8300 USA & Canada	•	•	•
Econo Lodge	728	25		800/55-ECONO USA & Canada	•	•	•
Embassy Suites	116	2	1	800/EMBASSY USA & Canada	•		
Exel Inns of America	26			800/367-3935 Cont'l USA & Canada	•		
Fairfield Inn by Marriott	245			800/228-2800 USA & Canada	•		•
Four Seasons ◆ Regent Hotels & Resorts	17	2	1	800/332-3442 USA; 800/268-6282 Canada	•	•	•
Hampton Inn	541	1	2	800/HAMPTON USA & Canada	•	•	•
Harley Hotels	14			800/321-2323 USA & Canada	•	•	•
Hilton Hotels	222			800/HILTONS USA & Canada	•	•	•
Holiday Inn	1,167	39	19	800/HOLIDAY USA & Canada	•	•	•
Holiday Inn Express	392	16	8	800/HOLIDAY USA & Canada		•	•
Holiday Inn Select	27	3	1	800/HOLIDAY USA & Canada	•	•	•
Homewood Suites	31			800/CALL-HOME USA & Canada	•		•
Howard Johnson	453	34	15	800/I-GO-HOJO USA & Canada	•	•	•
Hyatt Hotels & Resorts	97	1	6	800/233-1234 USA & Canada	•	•	•
La Quinta Inns	240		1	800/531-5900 USA & Canada	•	•	•
Marriott Hotels/Resorts & Suites	219	3	2	800/228-9290 USA & Canada	•	•	•
Motel 6	762			800/4-MOTEL-6 USA & Canada			
Omni Hotels	34		2	800/THE-OMNI USA & Canada		•	•
Park Inn International	46			800/437-PARK USA & Canada	•		•
Passport Inn	15			800/251-1962 USA & Canada			•
Quality Inns/Hotels/Suites & Resorts	416	57	13	800/228-5151 USA & Canada	•	•	•
Radisson Hotels Worldwide	224	15		800/333-3333 USA & Canada	•	•	•
Ramada Inn/Ramada Limited/ Ramada Plaza Hotels	799	33		800/2-RAMADA USA & Canada	•	•	•
Red Carpet Inn	117			800/251-1962 USA & Canada	•		•
Red Lion Hotels & Inns	54			800/547-8010 USA & Canada	•	•	•
Red Roof Inns	234			800/THE-ROOF USA & Canada	•		
Renaissance Hotels and Resorts	35	3		800/HOTELS-1 USA & Canada	•	•	•
Residence Inn by Marriott	200		1	800/331-3131 USA & Canada		•	•
Rodeway Inns	192	4		800/228-2000 USA & Canada	•	•	•
Scottish Inns	131			800/251-1962 USA & Canada	•		•
Sheraton/ITT Sheraton Corp.	235	20	6	800/325-3535 USA & Canada	•	•	•
Shilo Inns	46			800/222-2244 USA & Canada	•	•	•
Signature Inn	23			800/822-5252 USA	•	•	
Sleep Inn	205	2		800/62-SLEEP USA & Canada	•		•
Super 8 Motels, Inc.	1,341	35		800/800-8000 USA & Canada		•	•
Travelodge	425	74	2	800/578-7878 USA & Canada		•	
Vagabond Inns, Inc.	47			800/522-1555 USA & Canada	•	•	
Villager Lodge	37			800/328-7829 USA			
Westin Hotels & Resorts	44	8	7	800/228-3000 USA & Canada		•	•
Wyndham Hotels & Resorts	68			800/WYNDHAM USA & Canada	•	•	•

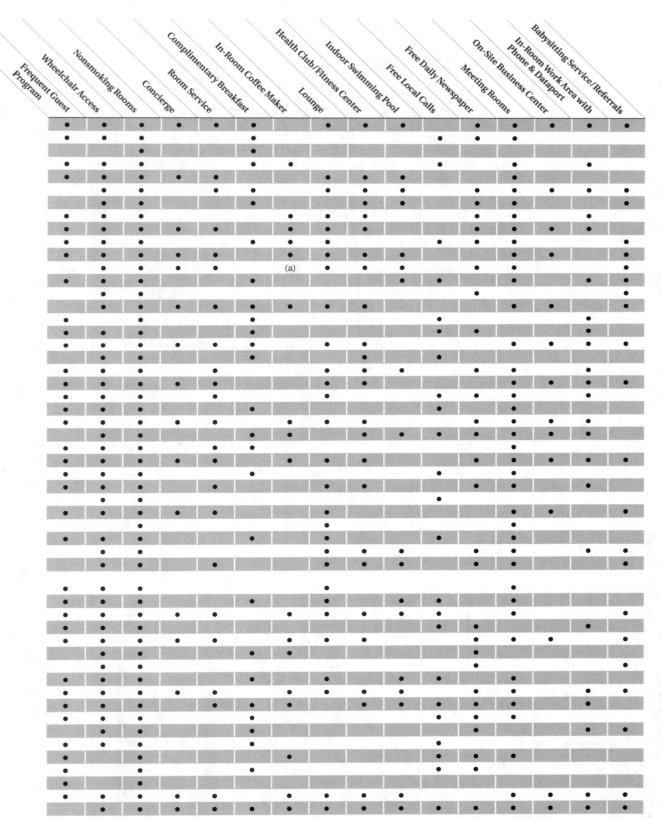

Frequent Guest Program · Wheelchair Access · Nonsmoking Rooms · Concierge · Room Service · Complimentary Breakfast · In-Room Coffee Maker · Health Club/Fitness Center · Lounge · Indoor Swimming Pool · Free Local Calls · Free Daily Newspaper · Meeting Rooms · On-Site Business Center · In-Room Work Area with Phone & Dataport · Babysitting Service/Referrals

(a)

(a) Guest Suites only

Telephone Area Code Map

Time Zone Line		Antiqua & Barbuda	268
Alaska	907	Bahamas	242
Hawaii	808	Barbados	246
Northwest Territories	819, 403	Montserrat	664
Yukon	403	Puerto Rico	787
Bermuda	441	St. Kitts & Nevis	869
Caribbean Islands	809	St. Lucia	758

© Copyright 1997 by Rand McNally

Necessary Business Telephone Numbers

Automated Teller Networks
Cirrus   800/ 4-CIRRUS
Citi bank & Diners Club   800/248-4286
Plus System   800/843-7587

Bus Companies
Greyhound Trailways   800/231-2222

Cablegrams/Telegrams/ Currency Wiring
Western Union   800/325-6000 in the
United States; 800/861-7311: in Montreal
only, and 800/361-1872 throughout the rest
of Canada; in Mexico consult the local
business pages under "Telegraph Office"

Shipping
Federal Express   800/238-5355; or
consult the local business white pages
under "Federal Express"

UPS   800/PICK-UPS; or consult the
local business white pages under "United
Parcel Service"

Trains
Amtrak   800/872-7245 in the United
States and Canada

Via Rail Canada   800/561-3949 in the
United States; in Canada consult the local
business white pages under "Via Rail"

Weather
National Weather Service
301/763-8155

Weather Channel Connection
900/WEATHER

Lost or Stolen Credit Cards
American Express   800/992-3404 in
the United States; in Canada and Mexico,
call collect at 910/333-3211

AT&T Universal Card   800/ 423-4343 in
the United States; in Canada and Mexico,
call collect at 904/ 448-8661

Carte Blanche   800/234-6377 in the
United States: in Canada and Mexico, call
collect at 303/799-1504

Diners Club 800/234-6377 in the United
States; in Canada and Mexico call collect
at 303/799-1504

Discover Card   800/347-2683 in the
United States; in Canada and Mexico,
801/ 568-0205

MasterCard   800/826-2181 in the
United States and Canada; in Mexico, call
collect at 314/275-6690

Visa   800/336-8472 in the United States
and Canada; in Mexico, call collect at
410/581-9994

Airlines Toll-Free Numbers

Airlines	Reservations	Frequent Flyer Customer Service
Aeromexico	800/237-6639	800/247-3737
Air Canada	800/776-3000 (USA) 800/361-8620 (Canada)	800/361-8253 (USA) 800/361-5373 (Canada)
Air France	800/237-2747 (USA and Canada)	same
Alaska Airlines	800/426-0333 (USA and Canada)	800/654-5669
All Nippon Airways	800/ 235-9262 (USA and Canada)	800/262-4653
American	800/433-7300 (USA and Canada)	800/882-8880
America West Airlines	800/235-9292 (USA, Canada and Mexico)	800/247-5691
British Airways	800/247-9297 (USA)	800/955-2748
Canadian Airlines	800/426-7000 (USA) 800/665-1177 (Canada)	800/426-7007 same
China Airlines	800/227-5118 (USA)	800/227-5118 ext. 5
Continental	800/525-0280 (USA, Canada and Mexico)	800/621-7467
Delta	800/221-1212 (USA and Eastern Canada) 800/843-9378 (Western Canada)	
Japan Airlines	800/ 525-3663 (USA and Canada)	800/525-6453
Kiwi International	800/538-5494 (USA)	
KLM Royal Dutch Airlines	800/374-7747	same
Korean Air	800/438-5000 (USA and Canada)	800/525-4480
Lufthansa German Airlines	800/645-3880 (USA)	800/581-6400
Mexicana Airlines	800/531-7921 (USA and Canada)	800/531-7901
Midwest Express Airlines	800/452-2022	same
Northwest	800/225-2525 (USA and Canada) 800/447-4747 (Int'l, includes Mexico)	800/447-3757
Qantas Airways	800/227-4500 (USA and Canada)	
Scandinavian Airlines	800/221-2350 (USA and Canada)	800/437-5807
Southwest	800/435-9792 (USA)	800/445-5764
Swissair	800/221-4750 (USA)	800/221-8125
TWA	800/221-2000 (USA)	800/325-4815
United	800/241-6522 (USA and Canada) 800/538-2929 (Int'l, includes Mexico)	
USAir	800/428-4322 (USA and Canada)	800/872-4738

Lost or Stolen Travelers Checks
When you buy travelers checks, record:

☐ Where you purchased them
☐ The date they were purchased
☐ How you paid for them
☐ The numbers, and denominations, of
all the checks
    As you spend or cash the checks, mark
them off your list along with the date and
place. To report lost or stolen checks:

American Express   800/221-7282 in the
United States and Canada; in Mexico,
call collect at 801/964-6665

Bank of America   800/227-6811 in the
United States and Canada; in Mexico, call
collect at 415/574-7111

Citicorp   800/645-6556 in the United
States and Canada; in Mexico, call collect
at 813/626-4444

Thomas Cook/MasterCard
800/223-7373 in the United States and
Canada; in Mexico, call collect at
609/987-7300

Visa 800/227-6811 in the United States
and Canada; in Mexico, call collect at
410/581-5353

Canada/Mexico Travel Information

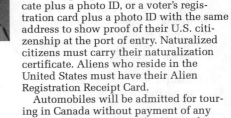

Canadian Tourism Offices

If you wish to obtain information about particular areas, places of interest, activities, or events, contact the provincial or territorial offices directly. General information about Canada is available from Canadian Consulates in major U.S. cities.

Alberta Partnership Tourism
3rd Floor, Commerce Pl.
10155-102 Street
Edmonton, AB T5J 4L6
800/661-8888 (N. Am.)
403/427-4321

Super, Natural **British Columbia**
Parliament Buildings
Victoria, BC V8V 1X4
800/663-6000 (N. Am.)

Travel **Manitoba**
7-155 Carlton St., Dept. RI7
Winnipeg, MB R3C 3H8
800/665-0040 ext. RI7 (N. Am.)
204/945-3777 ext. RI7

Tourism **New Brunswick**
P.O. Box 12345
Fredericton, NB E3B 5C3
800/561-0123 (N. Am.)

Newfoundland and **Labrador** Tourism,
Culture & Recreation
P.O. Box 8730
St. John's, NF A1B 4K2
800/563-6353 (N. Am.)
709/729-2830

Northwest Territories Dept. of Economic
Development & Tourism
Box 1320
Yellow Knife, NT X1A 2L9
800/661-0788 (N. Am.)
403/873-7200

Tourism **Nova Scotia**
P.O. Box 519
Halifax, NS B3J 2R5
800/565-0000 (N. Am. exc AK, HI)
902/424-4247

Ontario Travel
Queen's Park, 900 Bay St.
Toronto, ON M7A 2E1
800/ONTARIO (N. Am.)
416/314-0944

Tourism **PEI (Prince Edward Island**
Box 940
Charlottetown, PE C1A 7M5
800/463-4PEI (N. Am. exc AK, HI)
902/368-4444

Tourisme **Québec**
P.O. Box 979
Montréal, PQ H3C 2W3
800/363-7777 (N. Am.)
514/873-2015

Tourism **Saskatchewan**
500-1900 Albert St.
Regina, SK S4P 4L9
800/667-7191 (N. Am.)
306/787-2300

Tourism **Yukon**
Box 2703
Whitehorse, YT Y1A 2C6
403/667-5340

Canadian Citizens Visiting the United States

Canadian nationals, and aliens having a common nationality with nationals of Canada, are not required to present passports or visas to visit for a period of six months or less, except when arriving from a visit outside the Western Hemisphere. However, such persons should carry evidence of their citizenship. Visitors entering for a period of more than six months and less than one year are required to furnish valid passports.

This article does not attempt to cover all regulations or requirements. Obtain further information from the nearest United States or Canadian immigration office in the U.S., Canada, or a port of entry.

Mexican Citizens Visiting the United States

Mexican citizens who wish to visit the United States are required to present a Mexican passport and a United States visa. For information on obtaining a visa write to:
   The Embassy of the United States
      in Mexico
   Paseo de la Reforma 305
   México, D.F.
   México 06500

United States Citizens Visiting Canada

Passports are not required of native-born United States citizens to enter Canada. They should carry identifying papers such as a passport, certified birth certificate plus a photo ID, or a voter's registration card plus a photo ID with the same address to show proof of their U.S. citizenship at the port of entry. Naturalized citizens must carry their naturalization certificate. Aliens who reside in the United States must have their Alien Registration Receipt Card.

Automobiles will be admitted for touring in Canada without payment of any duty or fee for any period up to twelve months. Vehicle Registration Cards should be carried. Any necessary permits are issued at any port of entry.

Returning motorists must report for inspection. Each U.S. resident, after 48 hours, may bring back articles for personal use valued at up to $400.00 free of duty, provided same has not been claimed in the preceding 30 days.

United States Citizens Visiting Mexico

Passports are not required of native-born U.S. citizens to enter Mexico as tourists. Proof of citizenship should be carried. Naturalized citizens should carry their naturalization certificate to ensure entry into Mexico and re-entry into the United States. Plant and animal products are carefully regulated whether going into or coming out of Mexico.

Tourist cards are valid for any period up to six months, are free of charge, and are required for all persons regardless of age to visit the interior of Mexico. Cards may be obtained from Mexican border authorities, Consuls of Mexico, or Federal Delegates in major cities.

Obtain a $10 (+$1 tax, major credit card only, no cash) automobile permit, good for six months, from the Mexican Customs Office at the border; hold and surrender when leaving Mexico. Carry proof of car ownership or notarized permit for its use. Permits must also be obtained for trailers and boats. Auto insurance policies, other than Mexican, are not valid in Mexico. A short-term liability policy is obtainable at the border.

Each returning U.S. resident may bring back articles for personal use valued at up to $400.00 free of duty.

Mexican Tourism Offices

General information about Mexico is available from Mexican Government Offices of Tourism in major U.S. cities. Information can also be obtained from:
   Mexico City Tourist Bureau
   Amberes No. 54 Esq. Londres
   Zona Rosa Col. Juárez
   06600 México, D.F.
   011-52-5/211-00-99

North American Holidays

The following are religious holidays, national holidays, and other important dates in the United States, Canada, and Mexico. Many are observed by the closing of both businesses and government offices. There may be additional religious and local (state and provincial) holidays.

In cases where the holiday falls on a Saturday or Sunday, commercial establishments may be closed the preceding Friday or the following Monday. This calendar is intended as a working guide only. Confirmation of dates is suggested for business travel planning.

	1996	1997	1998
New Year's Day	Mon., Jan. 1	Wed., Jan. 1	Thurs., Jan. 1
Martin Luther King Day	Mon., Jan. 15	Mon., Jan. 13	Mon,, Jan.19
Constitution Day (Mexico)	Mon., Feb. 5	Wed., Feb. 5	Tues., Feb. 5
Lincoln's Birthday	Mon., Feb. 12	Wed., Feb. 12	Thurs., Feb. 12
Ash Wednesday	Wed., Feb. 21	Wed., Feb. 12	Weds., Feb. 25
St. Valentine's Day	Wed., Feb. 14	Fri., Feb. 14	Sat., Feb. 14
Presidents' Day	Mon., Feb. 19	Mon., Feb. 17	Mon., Feb. 16
Orthodox Lent Begins	Mon., Feb. 26	Mon., Feb. 17	Mon., Mar. 2
Washington's Birthday	Thurs., Feb. 22	Sat., Feb. 22	Sun., Feb. 22
St. Patrick's Day	Sun., Mar. 17	Mon., Mar. 17	Tues., Mar. 17
Benito Juarez Birthday (Mexico)	Thurs., Mar. 21	Fri., Mar. 21	Sat., Mar. 21
Palm Sunday	Sun., Mar. 31	Sun., Mar. 23	Sun., Apr. 5
Good Friday	Fri., Apr. 5	Fri., Mar. 28	Fri., Apr. 10
Easter	Sun., Apr. 7	Sun., Mar. 30	Sun., Apr. 12
Easter Mon. (Canada)	Mon., Apr. 8	Mon., Mar. 31	Mon., Apr. 13
Passover	Thurs., Apr. 4	Tues., Apr. 22	Sat., Apr. 11
Orthodox Easter	Sun., Apr. 14	Sun., Apr. 27	Sun., Apr. 19
Labor Day (Mexico)	Wed., May 1	Thurs., May 1	Fri., May 1
Cinco de Mayo	Sun., May 5	Mon., May 5	Tues., May 5
Mother's Day	Sun., May 12	Sun., May 11	Sun., May 10
Victoria Day (Canada)	Mon., May 20	Mon., May 19	Mon., May 18
Memorial Day	Mon., May 27	Mon., May 26	Mon., May 25
Flag Day	Fri., June 14	Sat., June 14	Sun., June 14
Father's Day	Sun., June 16	Sun., June 15	Sun., June 21
Canada Day	Mon., July 1	Tues., July 1	Weds., July 1
Independence Day	Thurs., July 4	Fri., July 4	Sat., July 4
Labor Day	Mon., Sept. 2	Mon., Sept. 1	Mon., Sept. 7
Grandparents Day	Sun., Sept. 8	Sun., Sept. 7	Sun., Sept. 13
Independence Day (Mexico)	Mon., Sept. 16	Tues., Sept. 16	Weds., Sept. 16
Rosh Hashanah	Sat., Sept. 14	Thurs., Oct. 2	Mon., Sept. 21
Yom Kippur	Mon., Sept. 23	Sat., Oct. 11	Weds., Sept. 30
Columbus Day Observance	Mon., Oct. 14	Mon., Oct. 13	Mon., Oct. 12
Thanksgiving Day (Canada)	Mon., Oct. 14	Mon., Oct. 13	Mon., Oct. 12
Halloween	Thurs., Oct. 31	Fri., Oct. 31	Sat., Oct. 31
Day of the Dead (Mexico)	Fri.–Sat., Nov. 1–2	Sat.–Sun., Nov. 1–2	Sun.-Mon., Nov. 1-2
Election Day	Tues., Nov. 5	Tues., Nov. 4	Tues., Nov. 3
Veterans Day	Mon., Nov. 11	Tues., Nov. 11	Weds., Nov. 11
Remembrance Day (Canada)	Mon., Nov. 11	Tues., Nov. 11	Weds., Nov. 11
Revolution Day (Mexico)	Wed., Nov. 20	Thurs., Nov. 20	Fri., Nov. 20
Thanksgiving Day	Thurs., Nov. 28	Thurs., Nov. 27	Thurs., Nov. 26
Guadalupe Day (Mexico)	Thurs., Dec. 12	Fri., Dec. 12	Sat., Dec. 12
Hanukah	Fri., Dec. 6	Wed., Dec. 24	Mon., Dec. 14
Christmas	Wed., Dec. 25	Thurs., Dec. 25	Fri., Dec. 25
Boxing Day (Canada)	Thurs., Dec. 26	Fri., Dec. 26	Sat., Dec. 26

Climate

State	City	Winter (Dec.–Feb.)				Spring (Mar.–May)				Summer (June–Aug.)				Fall (Sept.–Nov.)			
		Maximum Normal Daily Temp. (F)	Minimum Normal Daily Temp. (F)	Total Precipitation (In)	Total Days with Precipitation	Maximum Normal Daily Temp. (F)	Minimum Normal Daily Temp. (F)	Total Precipitation (In)	Total Days with Precipitation	Maximum Normal Daily Temp. (F)	Minimum Normal Daily Temp. (F)	Total Precipitation (In)	Total Days with Precipitation	Maximum Normal Daily Temp. (F)	Minimum Normal Daily Temp. (F)	Total Precipitation (In)	Total Days with Precipitation
Alabama	Birmingham	56	38	16	32	75	53	15	35	90	70	13	29	76	54	10	23
	Mobile	63	43	15	32	77	57	17	26	90	72	22	42	78	58	12	24
Alaska	Anchorage	23	6	3	26	44	26	2	22	64	48	6	32	42	27	5	33
	Juneau	31	20	12	56	46	31	10	52	63	46	12	50	47	36	19	63
Arizona	Phoenix	67	39	2	12	84	52	1	6	103	74	2	10	87	57	2	8
	Tucson	65	39	2	12	81	50	1	7	97	71	5	21	83	56	2	11
Arkansas	Little Rock	52	31	13	28	71	49	15	30	90	68	10	23	74	49	10	21
California	Los Angeles	67	48	8	16	71	53	3	11	81	62	.07	2	78	58	2	6
	Sacramento	55	39	10	28	72	46	4	17	91	57	.2	2	76	50	3	11
	San Diego	65	47	5	19	68	54	2	14	74	63	.13	1	73	58	2	8
	San Francisco	57	47	12	31	61	49	5	19	64	53	.2	3	67	54	4	13
Colorado	Denver	45	18	2	17	60	34	6	29	84	56	5	27	66	37	3	16
	Grand Junction	40	20	2	20	65	39	2	19	89	61	2	16	67	41	2	17
Connecticut	Hartford	35	18	10	33	58	36	11	33	82	59	11	31	63	41	11	29
Delaware	Wilmington	42	25	9	30	62	42	10	34	84	64	11	28	67	47	9	25
District of Columbia	Washington	45	29	8	28	66	45	10	32	86	67	12	28	69	50	9	23
Florida	Jacksonville	66	45	9	24	79	57	10	24	89	71	21	41	79	61	14	27
	Miami	76	59	6	19	82	67	12	23	89	75	23	48	84	70	20	40
	Tampa	71	51	7	19	82	61	8	19	90	73	23	45	83	65	11	25
Georgia	Atlanta	53	34	13	32	70	50	14	30	86	68	12	31	72	52	9	21
Hawaii	Honolulu	81	66	10	30	83	69	6	28	87	73	2	21	86	71	6	25
Idaho	Boise	40	24	4	34	61	37	3	25	85	55	1	11	64	39	2	20
Illinois	Chicago	33	17	5	32	58	37	9	37	81	59	10	29	63	41	7	29
	Springfield	37	21	6	28	62	42	10	35	85	64	11	27	66	45	9	25
Indiana	Indianapolis	38	22	8	34	61	41	11	37	84	63	11	28	65	44	8	26
	South Bend	33	19	7	43	57	37	10	38	81	60	11	29	62	42	9	31
Iowa	Des Moines	31	15	3	23	58	38	9	31	83	63	11	28	62	42	7	22
Kansas	Wichita	44	24	3	16	67	44	8	26	90	68	12	24	70	47	7	19
Kentucky	Louisville	44	26	10	34	65	44	13	36	86	65	11	29	68	46	9	25
Louisiana	New Orleans	64	45	14	29	78	58	14	24	90	72	17	38	79	60	12	22
	Shreveport	59	39	12	27	76	55	14	27	92	72	9	22	78	56	9	21
Maine	Portland	33	13	11	33	52	32	10	35	77	54	8	28	59	38	11	29
Maryland	Baltimore	43	26	9	28	64	42	10	33	85	64	12	28	68	47	9	23
Massachusetts	Boston	37	24	11	35	56	41	11	34	79	62	9	30	62	48	11	29
Michigan	Detroit	34	21	6	38	56	38	8	37	81	61	9	29	62	45	7	29
	Sault Ste. Marie	24	8	6	53	47	28	7	35	73	50	10	33	52	36	10	43
Minnesota	Duluth	21	2	3	34	47	27	8	34	73	52	12	35	51	34	7	31
	Minneapolis-St. Paul	24	7	2	25	53	33	7	31	80	59	11	32	57	37	6	25
Mississippi	Jackson	60	37	14	30	77	52	15	29	92	69	11	29	79	52	9	23
Missouri	Kansas City	43	26	4	21	64	45	10	30	89	69	11	26	70	48	8	21
	St. Louis	42	25	6	26	65	45	11	33	87	67	11	26	68	48	8	25
Montana	Billings	35	16	2	22	54	33	5	29	81	55	4	24	59	37	3	19
Nebraska	Omaha	36	16	2	20	62	39	9	30	86	64	13	28	66	42	6	19
	Scottsbluff	41	14	1	15	59	32	5	28	85	56	6	26	64	34	2	16
Nevada	Las Vegas	58	34	1	8	78	50	1	6	101	72	1	7	80	53	1	6
	Reno	47	21	3	18	64	31	2	15	87	45	1	8	69	31	1	10
New Hampshire	Concord	33	12	8	32	56	32	9	34	80	54	9	31	61	37	10	29
New Jersey	Atlantic City	43	24	10	31	61	50	10	32	82	62	12	31	66	46	10	29
	Newark	40	25	9	32	60	42	11	34	83	65	11	29	66	48	10	26

*Includes the liquid water equivalent of snowfall–(10″ of snow equals approx. 1″ of liquid water).

State/Province	City	Winter (Dec.–Feb.)				Spring (Mar.–May)				Summer (June–Aug.)				Fall (Sept.–Nov.)			
		Maximum Normal Daily Temp. (F)	Minimum Normal Daily Temp. (F)	Total Precipitation (In)	Total Days with Precipitation	Maximum Normal Daily Temp. (F)	Minimum Normal Daily Temp. (F)	Total Precipitation (In)	Total Days with Precipitation	Maximum Normal Daily Temp. (F)	Minimum Normal Daily Temp. (F)	Total Precipitation (In)	Total Days with Precipitation	Maximum Normal Daily Temp. (F)	Minimum Normal Daily Temp. (F)	Total Precipitation (In)	Total Days with Precipitation
New Mexico	Albuquerque	49	25	1	12	70	41	1	11	90	63	3	22	71	44	2	14
New York	Albany	32	15	7	35	57	35	8	37	81	58	9	31	61	40	8	31
	Buffalo	31	19	8	57	52	36	9	42	77	59	9	31	59	43	10	38
	New York	40	27	9	31	60	43	10	34	83	66	11	30	66	50	10	25
North Carolina	Asheville	49	28	11	31	68	42	12	33	84	61	13	39	68	45	10	28
	Charlotte	53	32	11	30	72	48	11	30	87	67	12	31	72	51	9	21
	Raleigh	52	30	10	29	71	46	10	29	87	65	14	30	72	48	9	23
North Dakota	Bismarck	23	2	1	23	52	29	4	26	81	55	8	29	57	32	3	19
Ohio	Cincinnati	41	26	9	34	64	44	12	37	85	64	11	31	67	47	8	28
	Cleveland	35	22	7	46	57	38	10	43	80	59	10	31	62	44	8	35
	Columbus	38	21	7	38	62	39	11	40	83	60	11	31	65	42	7	28
Oklahoma	Oklahoma City	50	28	4	16	70	48	11	25	91	69	9	22	73	50	7	18
Oregon	Pendleton	43	29	4	37	62	40	3	27	84	57	2	12	63	42	3	23
	Portland	46	34	16	54	60	41	8	43	76	54	3	18	63	44	11	39
Pennsylvania	Harrisburg	39	24	8	32	63	41	10	36	85	63	10	29	66	45	8	24
	Philadelphia	42	26	9	30	63	42	10	33	85	64	12	28	67	47	9	25
	Pittsburgh	37	22	8	47	60	39	11	41	81	59	10	33	63	43	7	32
Rhode Island	Providence	38	22	11	33	56	38	11	34	79	60	9	30	63	44	11	27
South Carolina	Columbia	58	34	10	29	76	51	11	28	91	69	15	33	76	52	9	21
	Greenville	53	34	12	30	71	49	12	32	87	68	12	32	72	51	10	25
South Dakota	Rapid City	37	13	1	20	56	31	6	31	83	56	7	29	62	35	2	16
	Sioux Falls	27	7	2	18	56	34	7	27	83	59	15	29	60	36	9	20
Tennessee	Chattanooga	51	31	16	34	72	47	13	32	89	66	22	33	73	48	10	24
	Memphis	51	33	14	29	71	51	15	30	90	70	10	25	73	51	9	21
	Nashville	49	30	14	33	70	48	13	34	89	67	10	28	72	49	9	24
Texas	Corpus Christi	68	48	5	22	81	62	6	17	93	75	8	17	83	63	9	22
	Dallas	58	36	6	19	75	53	11	24	94	73	7	16	78	56	8	19
	El Paso	59	32	1	11	78	49	1	6	94	68	3	18	77	49	2	12
	Houston	65	43	11	26	79	58	11	25	93	72	13	28	82	58	13	24
Utah	Salt Lake City	40	21	4	28	62	36	5	28	88	57	3	15	65	39	3	18
Vermont	Burlington	28	10	6	41	52	32	7	38	79	56	11	37	58	39	9	37
Virginia	Norfolk	50	33	10	29	67	48	9	31	85	68	15	30	70	53	10	24
	Richmond	49	28	9	28	69	45	9	31	87	65	14	31	71	48	10	23
Washington	Seattle-Tacoma	47	36	14	55	59	42	7	41	73	54	3	20	61	46	10	36
	Spokane	35	23	6	43	56	36	4	29	80	53	2	17	57	38	4	26
West Virginia	Charleston	45	26	10	44	66	43	11	42	84	62	12	35	68	45	8	30
Wisconsin	La Crosse	28	10	3	24	56	36	8	32	81	61	11	30	59	41	7	26
	Milwaukee	30	14	4	31	53	34	8	36	78	57	10	30	59	40	7	28
Wyoming	Casper	36	15	2	22	55	29	4	29	83	52	3	22	60	33	3	20
CANADA																	
Alberta	Edmonton	19	1	2	33	50	26	4	30	72	47	9	41	49	28	3	29
British Columbia	Vancouver	43	34	23	59	57	41	11	43	72	53	5	26	57	44	18	44
Manitoba	Winnipeg	11	−8	3	34	47	24	5	28	76	52	9	32	49	29	5	24
New Brunswick	Saint John	29	13	11	40	45	32	10	39	67	52	10	39	53	40	12	38
Newfoundland	St. John's	30	19	16	47	41	29	12	45	66	49	11	39	52	40	15	47
Nova Scotia	Halifax	33	17	15	46	48	31	14	43	72	53	12	39	57	41	15	39
Ontario	Ottawa	22	5	8	39	50	30	8	34	78	56	10	31	54	37	9	35
	Toronto	31	17	8	41	50	34	8	38	76	57	8	30	56	41	8	36
Québec	Montréal	23	9	10	44	49	33	9	38	76	59	11	36	53	39	11	39
Saskatchewan	Regina	13	−7	1	32	47	23	3	24	76	49	8	32	50	25	3	21

*Includes the liquid water equivalent of snowfall–(10″ of snow equals approx. 1″ of liquid water). © 1997 Rand McNally & Company   1 inch=2.54 centimeters   To compute Centigrade: Subtract 32 from Fahrenheit and divide by 1.8

Major North American Cities Guide

Use the information in this section to acquaint yourself with 97 major cities, including principal United States cities; Mexico City, Cuidad Juárez, Guadalajara, Monterrey, and Tijuana in Mexico; and the Canadian cities of Calgary, Edmonton, Montréal, Ottawa, Toronto, Vancouver, and Winnipeg. The following information is provided:

Population Statistics. Populations of cities, figure followed by (1990C), and their metropolitan areas (figure preceded by an asterisk) are the census figures for the year cited. The U.S. metropolitan areas have been defined by the Bureau of the Census and the U.S. Office of Management and Budget to include one or more major cities and their counties. A metropolitan area may also include additional counties that have strong economic ties to the central county or counties.

Weather Information. Altitude figures and average January and July temper-
atures provide weather information in brief for each city.

Telephone Numbers/Time Zones. Telephone area codes and time zone information help orient you to each new location. Local time and weather numbers are provided where applicable.

Airport Transportation/Maps. Flyers will find useful information in each city listing under Airport Transportation: the distance from each city's airport(s) to downtown and the type of transportation service that is available.

In addition, detailed airport maps locating parking facilities, terminals, and airlines for 41 of the largest cities are included in this section.

Hotels and Restaurants. A listing of selected hotels/motels and restaurants is provided for each city; establishments chosen for their broad appeal to the traveling public.

Attractions. Use the selected list of important local attractions to plan a stop at some of the places of special interest in the city you will be visiting. Addresses and telephone numbers are provided for each attraction listed.

City Maps. Get around each city easily by using the large-scale maps for each city to identify streets, suburbs, freeways, hospitals, airports, points of interest, and more.

Tourist Information Sources. Each city listing also provides information sources for that city. Addresses and/or phone numbers are given for local convention and visitors bureaus, offices of tourism, and chambers of commerce.

Whether you call or write ahead for information, or stop in once you're in town, these offices can provide special information about their city that will enhance your visit and make the most of your sightseeing time.

Major North American Cities

MAJOR CITY DATA Populations of cities, figure followed by (1990C), and their metropolitan areas (figure preceded by an asterisk) are the final census figures for the year cited. A population figure followed by (1991E) is an estimate for the year cited. Metropolitan areas have been defined by the Bureau of the Census and the U.S. Office of Management and Budget to include one or more major cities and their counties. A metropolitan area may also include additional counties that have strong economic and social ties to the central county or counties.

Directory entries for hotels located within approximately two miles of the airport are preceded by the ✈ symbol.

All information in the major city guide has been checked for accuracy at the time of publication. Since changes do occur, the publisher cannot be responsible for any variations from the information printed.

Albuquerque, New Mexico

City map: right
Population: (*542,800) 384,736 (1990C)
Altitude: 4,958 feet
Average Temp.: Jan., 35°F.; July, 79°F.
Telephone Area Code: 505
Time: 505/247-1611 **Weather:** 505/821-1111
Time Zone: Mountain

AIRPORT TRANSPORTATION:
Eight miles to downtown Albuquerque. Taxicab, limousine, and city bus service.

SELECTED HOTELS:
Albuquerque Doubletree, 201 Marquette Ave. NW, 505/247-3344; FAX 505/247-7025
Albuquerque Hilton, 1901 University Blvd. NE, 505/884-2500; FAX 505/889-9118
Albuquerque Marriott, 2101 Louisiana Blvd. NE, 505/881-6800; FAX 505/888-2982
✈ Best Western Airport Inn, 2400 Yale Blvd. SE, 505/242-7022; FAX 505/243-0620
✈ Best Western Fred Harvey Hotel—Albuquerque Int'l Airport, 2910 Yale Blvd. SE, 505/843-7000; FAX 505/843-6307
Best Western Winrock Inn, 18 Winrock Center NE, 505/883-5252; FAX 505/889-3206
Holiday Inn Mountain View, 2020 Menaul Blvd. NE, 505/884-2511; FAX 505/884-5720
Hyatt Regency Albuquerque, 330 Tijeras NW, 505/842-1234; FAX 505/766-6710
La Posada de Albuquerque, 125 2nd St. NW, 505/242-9090; FAX 505/242-8664
Pinnacle Hotel Four Seasons, 2500 Carlisle Blvd. NE, 505/888-3311; FAX 505/881-7452

Pyramid Holiday Inn, 5151 San Francisco Rd. NE, 505/821-3333; FAX 505/828-0230
Ramada Classic Hotel, 6815 Menaul Blvd. NE, 505/881-0000; FAX 505/881-3736
Ramada Inn East, 25 Hotel Circle NE, 505/271-1000; FAX 505/291-9028
Sheraton—Old Town, 800 Rio Grande Blvd. NW, 505/843-6300; FAX 505/842-9863

SELECTED RESTAURANTS:
Allie's American Grill and Bar in the Albuquerque Marriott Hotel, 505/881-6800
The Cooperage, 7220 Lomas Blvd. NE, 505/255-1657
El Pinto, 10500 4th St. NW, 505/898-1771
Firehouse Restuarant at the Tram, 3800 Tramway Loop at the base of Sandia Peak Tramway, 505/856-3473
Garduños, 10551 Montgomery NE, 505/298-5000
La Cascada, in the Albuquerque Doubletree Hotel, 505/247-3344
Luna Mansion, Jct. US 85 & NM 6, 505/865-7333
Maria Teresa Restaurant, 618 Rio Grande Blvd. NW, 505/242-3900
Prairie Star, on Jemez Canyon Rd., 505/867-3327
Rancher's Club, in the Albuquerque Hilton Hotel, 505/884-2500
Seagull Street, 5410 Academy NE, 505/821-0020

SELECTED ATTRACTIONS:
The Albuquerque Museum, 2000 Mountain Rd. NW, 505/242-4600
Cliffs Amusement Park, 4800 Osuna Rd. NE, 505/881-9373

Indian Pueblo Cultural Center, 2401 12th St. NW, 505/843-7270
National Atomic Museum, Wyoming Ave., Kirtland Air Force Base, 505/284-3243
New Mexico Museum of Natural History & Science, 1801 Mountain Rd. NW, 505/841-2800
Petroglyph National Monument, 4735 Unser Blvd. NW, 505/839-4429
Rio Grande Nature Center State Park, 2901 Candelaria NW, 505/344-7240
Sandia Peak Aerial Tramway, #10 Tramway Loop NE, 505/856-7325
Turquoise Trail Scenic and Historic Area, North NM 14, the "Scenic Route" to Santa Fe, and NM 536 to the Sandia Crest, 505/281-5233

INFORMATION SOURCES:
Albuquerque Convention & Visitors Bureau
20 First Plaza NW, Suite 601
P.O. Box 26866
Albuquerque, New Mexico 87102
505/842-9918; 800/284-2282 or 733-9918 (convention services)
Greater Albuquerque Chamber of Commerce
Albuquerque Convention Center
401 2nd St. NW
Albuquerque, New Mexico 87102
505/764-3700

Allentown-Bethlehem, Pennsylvania

City map: page 21
Population: (*559,700)
Allentown 105,090;
Bethlehem 71,428 (1990C)

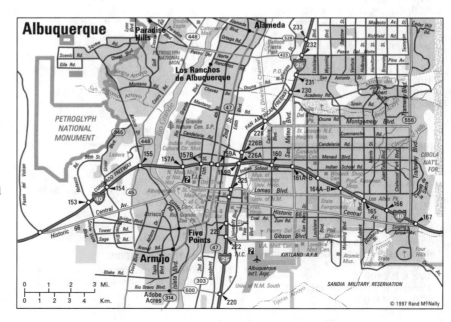

Altitude: Allentown 364 feet; Bethlehem 340 feet
Average Temp.: Jan., 28°F.; July, 74°F.
Telephone Area Code: 610
Time and Weather: 610/797-5900
Time Zone: Eastern

AIRPORT TRANSPORTATION:

Five miles to downtown Allentown; five miles to downtown Bethlehem.
Taxicab, bus, and hotel shuttle service to both towns.

SELECTED HOTELS: ALLENTOWN

Allentown Hilton, 904 Hamilton Mall, 610/433-2221; FAX 610/433-6455
Clarion Hotel, 549 Hamilton St., 6th & Hamilton sts., 610/434-6101; FAX 610/434-6828
Days Inn Conference Center, 1151 Bulldog Dr., 610/395-3731; FAX 610/395-9899
Hampton Inn, 7471 Keebler Way, 610/391-1500; FAX 610/391-0386
Ramada Inn Whitehall, 1500 MacArthur Rd., Whitehall, 610/439-1037; FAX 610/770-1425
✈ Sheraton Inn Jetport, 3400 Airport Rd., 610/266-1000; FAX 610/266-1888

SELECTED RESTAURANTS: ALLENTOWN

Ambassador Restaurant, 3750 Hamilton Blvd., 610/432-2025
Brass Rail, 1137 Hamilton St., 610/434-9383
Captain's Table, 2720 S. Pike Ave., 610/797-3127
King George Inn, 3141 Hamilton Blvd. at Cedar Crest Blvd., 610/435-1723
Teddy's, in the Sheraton Inn Jetport, 610/266-1000
Walp's Restaurant, 911 Union Blvd. at Airport Rd., 610/437-4841

SELECTED ATTRACTIONS: ALLENTOWN

Allentown Art Museum, Fifth & Court sts., 610/432-4333
Dorney Park & Wildwater Kingdom, 3830 Dorney Park Rd., 610/395-3724
Haines Mill Museum, Haines Mill Rd., 610/435-4664
Lehigh County Historical Museum, Old Courthouse, 5th & Hamilton sts., 610/435-4664
Liberty Bell Shrine, 622 Hamilton Mall, 610/435-4232
Lil-Le-Hi Trout Nursery, Fish Hatchery Rd. off of Cedar Crest Blvd., 610/437-7656
Rose & Old-Fashioned Gardens, 2700 Parkway Blvd., 610/437-7628
Trout Hall, 414 Walnut St., 610/435-4664

INFORMATION SOURCES: ALLENTOWN

Lehigh Valley Convention & Visitors Bureau
 2200 Ave. A
 Bethlehem, Pennsylvania 18017
 P.O. Box 20785
 Lehigh Valley, Pennsylvania 18002-0785
 610/882-9200; 800/633-8437
 (meetings & conventions)
Lehigh Valley Visitors Center (Memorial Day to Labor Day)
 I-78 & PA 100 S.
 Fogelsville, Pennsylvania 18051
 610/395-4460

Allentown-Lehigh County Chamber of Commerce
 462 Walnut St.
 Allentown, Pennsylvania 18102
 610/437-9661

SELECTED HOTELS: BETHLEHEM

Comfort Inn—Bethlehem, 3191 Highfield Dr., 610/865-6300; FAX 610/865-6300
✈ Econo Lodge, 2140 Motel Dr., Catasauqua Rd. & Airport Rd. S., 610/867-8681; FAX 610/867-6426
Holiday Inn Hotel & Conference Center, US 22 & PA 512, 610/866-5800; FAX 610/867-9120
Hotel Bethlehem, 437 Main St., 610/867-3711; FAX 610/867-0598

SELECTED RESTAURANTS: BETHLEHEM

The Cafe, 221 W. Broad St., 610/866-1686
Hanoverville Road House, 5001 Hanoverville Rd., 610/837-1122
Inn of the Falcon, 1740 Seidersville Rd., 610/868-6505
Krista's Restaurant, in the Holiday Inn Bethlehem, 610/866-5800
Minsi Trail Inn, 626 Stefko Blvd., 610/691-5613
Sun Inn, 564 Main St., 610/974-9451

SELECTED ATTRACTIONS: BETHLEHEM

Christmas Barn, 4186 Easton Ave., 610/861-0477
18th Century Industrial Quarter, 459 Old York Rd., 610/691-5300
Kemerer Museum of Decorative Arts, 427 N. New St., 610/868-6868
Moravian Museum & Tours, 66 W. Church St., 610/867-0173
1758 Sun Inn, 564 Main St., (tours) 610/866-1758

INFORMATION SOURCES: BETHLEHEM

Lehigh Valley Convention & Visitors Bureau
 2200 Ave. A
 Bethlehem, Pennsylvania 18017
 P. O. Box 20785
 Lehigh Valley, Pennsylvania 18002-0785
 610/882-9200; 800/633-8437
 (meetings & conventions)
Bethlehem Tourism Authority
 52 W. Broad St.
 Bethlehem, Pennsylvania 18018
 610/868-1513; 800/360-8687
Bethlehem Area Chamber of Commerce
 509 Main St.
 Bethlehem, Pennsylvania 18018
 610/867-3788

Anchorage, Alaska

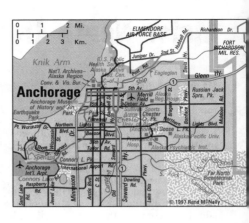

City map: upper right
Population: (*248,400) 226,338 (1990C)
Altitude: 118 feet
Average Temp.: Jan., 12°F.; July, 58°F.
Telephone Area Code: 907
Time: 844 **Weather:** 907/936-2525
Time Zone: Alaskan (one hour earlier than Pacific time)

AIRPORT TRANSPORTATION:

Six miles to downtown Anchorage.
Taxicab, airport limousine, and bus service.

SELECTED HOTELS:

Anchorage Hilton Hotel, 500 W. Third Ave., 907/272-7411; FAX 907/265-7140
✈ Best Western Barratt Inn, 4616 Spenard Rd., 907/243-3131; FAX 907/249-4917
Comfort Inn Ship Creek, 111 W. Ship Creek Ave., 907/277-6887; FAX 907/274-9830
Cusack's Ramada, 598 W. Northern Lights Blvd., 907/561-5200; FAX 907/563-8217
Days Inn, 321 E. Fifth Ave., 907/276-7226; FAX 907/278-6041 & 907/265-5145
Hotel Captain Cook, Fifth Ave. & K St., 907/276-6000; FAX 907/278-5366
Inlet Tower Suites, 1200 L St., 907/276-0110; FAX 907/258-4914
✈ Regal Alaskan Hotel, 4800 Spenard Rd., 907/243-2300; FAX 907/243-8815
Sheraton Anchorage Hotel, 401 E. Sixth Ave., 907/276-8700; FAX 907/276-7561
✈ WestCoast International Inn, 3333 International Airport Rd., 907/243-2233; FAX 907/248-3796
Westmark Anchorage Hotel, 720 W. Fifth Ave., 907/276-7676; FAX 907/276-3615
Westmark Inn Third Avenue (open May through Sept.), 115 E. Third Ave., 907/272-7561; FAX 907/272-3879

SELECTED RESTAURANTS:

Atlasta Deli, 36th & Arctic, 907/563-3354
The Bistro, in the Sheraton Anchorage Hotel, 907/276-8700
Corsair, 944 W. Fifth Ave., 907/278-4502
Crow's Nest, in the Hotel Captain Cook, 907/276-6000
Fletcher's, in the Hotel Captain Cook, 907/276-6000
Josephine's, in the Sheraton Anchorage Hotel, 907/276-8700
La Mex, 900 W. Sixth Ave., 907/274-7678
Romano's, 2415 C St., 907/276-0888
Tony Roma's, 1420 E. Tudor Rd., 907/561-7427

SELECTED ATTRACTIONS:

Alaska Zoo, 4731 O'Malley Rd., 907/346-2133
Anchorage Museum of History and Art, 121 W. Seventh Ave., 907/343-4326
Earthquake Park, about 4 mi. from downtown on W. Northern Lights Blvd.
Elmendorf Air Force Base Wildlife Museum, enter Boniface Gate, about 3 mi. from downtown off Glenn Hwy., 907/552-2282 (tours by appointment)

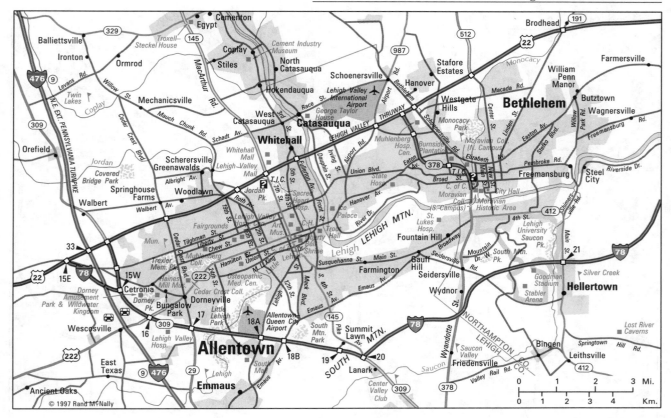

© 1997 Rand McNally

Imaginarium, Science Discovery Center,
737 W. Fifth Ave., 907/276-3179
Oscar Anderson House/Elderberry Park
(open May–September), 420 M St.,
907/274-2336
Portage Glacier/Begich, Boggs Visitor
Center (about 55 mi. south of Anchorage), 907/783-2326 or -3242
TAHETA Art & Culture Group Co-op
(Alaska Native arts & crafts studios),
605 A St., 907/272-5829

INFORMATION SOURCES:

Anchorage Convention & Visitors Bureau
524 W. 4th Ave.
Anchorage Alaska 99501-2212
907/276-4118
Log Cabin Visitor Center
546 W. 4th Ave.
Anchorage, Alaska 99501
907/274-3531
Anchorage Chamber of Commerce
441 W. 5th Ave., Suite 300
Anchorage, Alaska 99501
907/272-7588

Atlanta, Georgia

City map: page 22
Population: (*2,621,100) 394,017 (1990C)
Altitude: 1,050 feet
Average Temp.: Jan., 52°F.; July, 85°F.
Telephone Area Codes: 404, 770
Time: 770/455-7141 **Weather:**
770/486-8834
Time Zone: Eastern

AIRPORT TRANSPORTATION:

See map on page 23.
Eight miles to downtown Atlanta.
Taxicab and limousine bus service.

SELECTED HOTELS:

Atlanta Hilton & Towers, 255 Courtland
St. NE, 404/659-2000;
FAX 404/524-0111
Atlanta Marriott Marquis, 265 Peachtree
Center Ave., 404/521-0000;
FAX 404/586-6299
Best Western American Hotel, 160 Spring
St. NW, 404/688-8600;
FAX 404/658-9458
✈ Holiday Inn—Airport North, 1380
Virginia Ave., 404/762-8411;
FAX 404/767-4963
✈ Howard Johnson Atlanta Airport,
1377 Virginia Ave., East Point,
404/762-5111; FAX 404/762-1277
Hyatt Regency Atlanta, 265 Peachtree St.
NE, 404/577-1234; FAX 404/588-4137
Marriott Perimeter Center, 246 Perimeter
Center Pkwy., Danwoody,
770/394-6500; FAX 770/394-4338
Omni Hotel at CNN Center, 100 CNN
Center, Marietta, between Techwood St.
& Int'l Blvd., 404/659-0000;
FAX 404/525-5050
Radisson Hotel Atlanta, 165 Courtland St.,
404/659-6500; FAX 404/524-1259
Ritz-Carlton Atlanta, 181 Peachtree St.
NE, 404/659-0400; FAX 404/688-0400
Sheraton Colony Square Hotel, 188 14th
St. NE, 404/892-6000;
FAX 404/872-9192

Stone Mountain Park Inn, Robert E. Lee
Blvd. inside Stone Mountain Park,
770/469-3311; FAX 770/498-5691
✈ Stouffer Concourse Hotel, One
Hartsfield Centre Pkwy., 404/209-9999;
FAX 404/209-7031
The Westin Peachtree Plaza, 210
Peachtree St. NW, 404/659-1400;
FAX 404/589-7424
Wyndham Garden Hotel in Buckhead,
3340 Peachtree Rd. NE, 404/231-1234;
FAX 404/231-5236

SELECTED RESTAURANTS:

The Abbey, Piedmont & North aves.,
404/876-8532
Avanzare, in the Hyatt Regency Atlanta,
404/577-1234
Bugatti's, in the Omni Hotel at CNN
Center, 404/659-0000
The Cafe in the Terrace Garden Inn Hotel,
3405 Lenox Rd. NE, 404/261-9250
Coach And Six, 1776 Peachtree St. NW,
404/872-6666
The Crab House, Piedmont & North Ave.
(2nd Level—Rio Mall), 404/872-0011
Dailey's, 17 International Blvd.,
404/681-3303
Dante's Down the Hatch in Buckhead,
3380 Peachtree Rd., 404/266-1600
Garden Terrace, in the Atlanta Hilton &
Towers, 404/659-2000
La Grotta, 2637 Peachtree Rd. NE,
404/231-1368
The Mansion, Piedmont & North Ave.,
404/876-0727
Nikolai's Roof Restaurant, in the Atlanta
Hilton & Towers, 404/659-2000

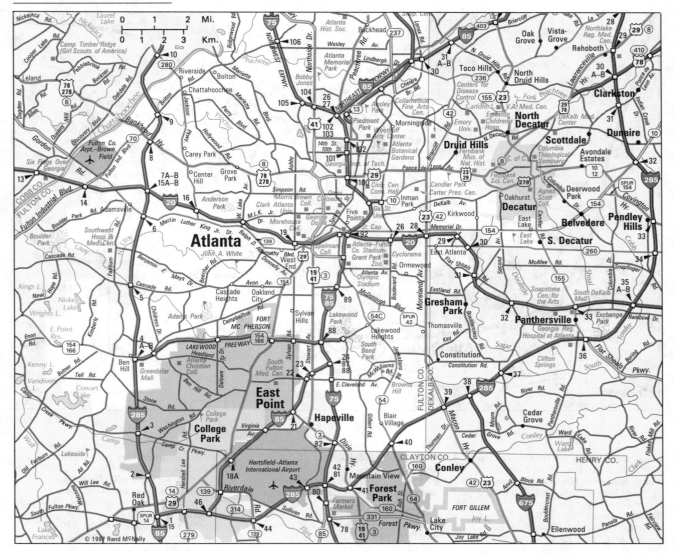

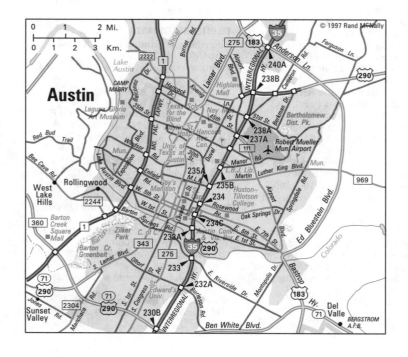

Pano's and Paul's, 1232 W. Paces Ferry
Rd. NW, 404/261-3662
The Restaurant, Ritz-Carlton Hotel,
404/659-0400

SELECTED ATTRACTIONS:
Carter Presidential Center, 1 Copenhill
Ave., 404/420-5110
Fernbank Museum of Natural History, 767
Clifton Rd. NE, 404/378-0127
High Museum of Art, 1280 Peachtree St.
NE, 404/733-4400
Martin Luther King Jr. Historic District,
Auburn Ave. between Jackson &
Randolph sts., (birth home)
404/331-3920, (Ebenezer Baptist
Church) 404/688-7263, Center for Non-
Violent Social Change (grave & exhibit
center) 404/524-1956
The Road to Tara Museum, 659 Peachtree
St. (lower level of the Georgian Terrace,
across from Fox Theatre),
404/897-1939
Stone Mountain Park, US 78, Stone
Mountain, 770/498-5600

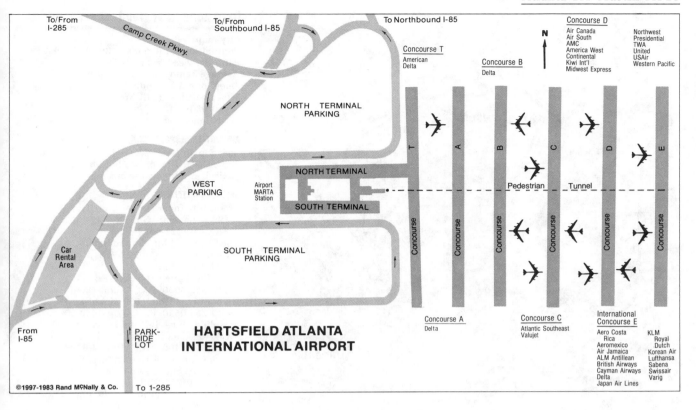

Underground Atlanta, Peachtree St. at Alabama St.

World of Coca-Cola Pavilion, 55 Martin Luther King Jr. Dr., 2 blks. west of State Capitol, 404/676-5151

INFORMATION SOURCES:

Atlanta Convention & Visitors Bureau Suite 2000, 233 Peachtree St. NE Atlanta, Georgia 30303 404/521-6600

Atlanta Chamber of Commerce 235 International Blvd. NW Atlanta, Georgia 30303 404/880-9000

Austin, Texas

City map: page 22
Population: (*631,100) 465,622 (1990C)
Altitude: 501 feet
Average Temp.: Jan., 50°F.; July, 85°F.
Telephone Area Code: 512
Time: 512/476-7744 **Weather:** 512/476-7744
Time Zone: Central

AIRPORT TRANSPORTATION:

Seven-and-a-half miles to downtown Austin.

Taxicab, hotel shuttle, limousine and bus service.

SELECTED HOTELS:

Austin Marriott at the Capitol, 701 E. 11th St., 512/478-1111; FAX 512/478-3700

Doubletree Guest Suites, 303 W. 15th St., 512/478-7000; FAX 512/478-5103

Doubletree Hotel Austin, 6505 I-35N, 512/454-3737; FAX 512/454-6915

Four Points Hotel, 7800 N. Interregional Hwy. (I-35), 512/836-8520; FAX 512/837-0897

Four Seasons Hotel Austin, 98 San Jacinto Blvd., 512/478-4500; FAX 512/478-3117

Hawthorn Suites—Northwest, 8888 Tallwood Dr., 512/343-0008; FAX 512/343-6532

Holiday Inn Austin Airport, 6911 N. Interregional Hwy. (I-35), 512/459-4251; FAX 512/459-9274

Hyatt Regency Austin, 208 Barton Springs Rd., 512/477-1234; FAX 512/480-2069

Radisson Hotel on Town Lake, 111 E. Cesar Chavez St., 512/478-9611; FAX 512/473-8399

✈ Red Lion Hotel, 6121 N. I-35 at US 290, 512/323-5466; FAX 512/371-5269

Wyndham Austin Hotel, 4140 Governor's Row, 512/448-2222; FAX 512/442-8028

SELECTED RESTAURANTS:

Catfish Station, 418 E. Sixth St., 512/477-8875

Chuy's, 1728 Barton Springs Rd., 512/474-4452

County Line on the Hill, 6500 W. Bee C aves, 512/327-1742

County Line on the Lake, 5204 FM 2222, 512/346-3664

Green Pastures, 811 W. Live Oak, 512/444-4747

Hut's Hamburgers, 807 W. Sixth St., 512/472-0693

Matt's El Rancho, 2613 S. Lamar, 512/462-9333

Oasis Cantina Del Lago, 6550 Comanche Trail, 512/266-2442

Shoreline Grill, 98 San Jacinto, 512/477-3300

Threadgill's, 6416 N. Lamar, 512/451-5440

SELECTED ATTRACTIONS:

Center for American History, Sid Richardson Hall, Unit 2, University of Texas campus, 512/495-4515

Elisabet Ney Museum (sculpture), 304 E. 44th St., 512/458-2255

French Legation Museum, 802 San Marcos at E. 7th St., 512/472-8180

Governor's Mansion, 1010 Colorado, 512/463-5516

Huntington Art Gallery, 23rd & San Jacinto, in the Harry Ransom Center, West 21st & Guadalupe, 512/471-7324

Lyndon B. Johnson Presidential Library and Museum, 2313 Red River, University of Texas campus, 512/916-5136

Neill-Cochran House (ca 1855), 2310 San Gabriel, 512/478-2335

State Capitol Building, 11th & Congress, 512/463-0063

Texas Memorial Museum, 2400 Trinity, University of Texas campus, 512/471-1605

Treaty Oak, 503 Baylor

INFORMATION SOURCE:

Austin Convention & Visitors Bureau 201 E. 2nd Austin, Texas 78701 Convention Info. 512/474-5171 Visitor Info. 512/478-0098; 800/926-2282

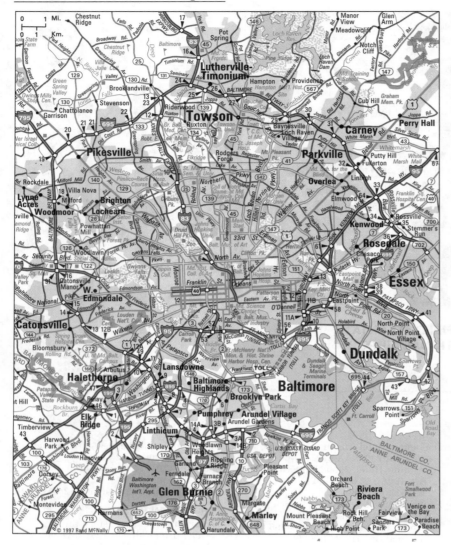

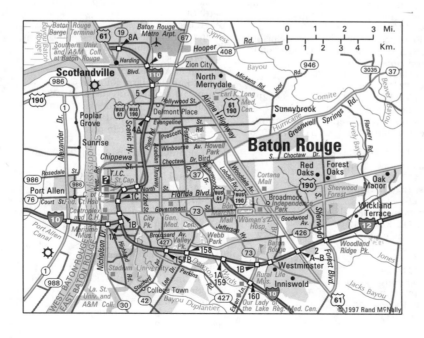

Baltimore, Maryland

City map: left
Population: (*2,045,800) 736,014 (1990C)
Altitude: Sea level to 32 feet
Average Temp.: Jan., 37°F.; July, 79°F.
Telephone Area Code: 410
Time: 410/844-1212 **Weather:**
410/936-1212
Time Zone: Eastern

AIRPORT TRANSPORTATION:

See map on page 25.
Ten miles to downtown Baltimore.
Taxicab and limousine bus service.

SELECTED HOTELS:

Brookshire Inner Harbor Suite Hotel,
120 E. Lombard St., 410/625-1300;
FAX 410/625-0912
The Clarion at Mt. Vernon Square, 612
Cathedral St., 410/727-7101;
FAX 410/789-3312
Cross Keys Inn, 5100 Falls Rd.,
410/532-6900; FAX 410/532-2403
Harbor Court Hotel, 550 Light St.,
410/234-0550; FAX 410/659-5925
✈ Holiday Inn—B-W Int'l Airport, 890
Elkridge Landing Rd., Linthicum,
410/859-8400; FAX 410/684-6778
Holiday Inn Inner Harbor, 301 W.
Lombard St., 410/685-3500;
FAX 410/727-6169
Hyatt Regency Baltimore, 300 Light St.,
410/528-1234; FAX 410/685-3362
Marriott Inner Harbor, 110 S. Eutaw St.,
410/962-0202; FAX 410/625-7832
Marriott's Hunt Valley Inn, 245 Shawan
Rd., Hunt Valley, 410/785-7000;
FAX 410/785-0341
Omni Inner Harbor Hotel, 101 W. Fayette
St., 410/752-1100; FAX 410/752-0832
Pikesville Hilton Inn, 1726 Reisterstown
Rd., 410/653-1100; FAX 410/484-4138
Ramada Hotel, 8 N Howard St. near the
Inner Harbor, 410/539-1188;
FAX 410/539-6411
✈ Sheraton International Hotel—B-W Int'l
Airport, 7032 Elm Rd., 410/859-3300;
FAX 410/859-0565
Stouffer Renaissance Harborplace Hotel,
202 E. Pratt St., 410/547-1200;
FAX 410/539-5780

SELECTED RESTAURANTS:

Bamboo House, Harborplace—Pratt St.,
next to Stouffer Renaissance Harborplace Hotel, 410/625-1191
Chiapparelli's, 237 S. High St.,
410/837-0309
Hampton's, in the Harbor Court Hotel,
410/234-0550
Haussner's Restaurant, 3242 Eastern Ave.,
410/327-8365
Obrycki's Crab House, 1727 E. Pratt St.,
410/732-6399
The Prime Rib, 1101 N. Calvert St., at
Chase St. intersection, 410/539-1804
Tio Pepe Restaurant, 10 E. Franklin St.,
410/539-4675

SELECTED ATTRACTIONS:

B&O Railroad Museum, 901 W. Pratt St.,
410/752-2490
Baltimore Museum of Art, Art Museum
Dr., off the 3100 block of N. Charles St.,
410/396-7101

Baltimore Zoo, Druid Hill Park, 410/366-5466

Fort McHenry National Monument and Historic Shrine, foot of E. Fort Ave. at Locust Point, 410/962-4290

Harbor Cruises, Ltd., 301 Light St., 410/727-3113

Harborplace/The Gallery at Harborplace, 200 E. Pratt St., at Chase St. intersection, 410/332-4191

Lexington Market, Lexington & Eutaw sts., 410/685-6169

Maryland Science Center, 601 Light St., 410/685-5225

National Aquarium in Baltimore, Pier 3, 501 E. Pratt St., 410/576-3800

Top of the World Trade Center, 401 E. Pratt St., 410/837-4515

INFORMATION SOURCE:

Baltimore Area Convention and Visitors Association

100 Light St., 12th Floor
Baltimore, Maryland 21202
410/659-7300; 800/343-3468
Visitor Info. Center 410/837-4636;
800/282-6632 (except Baltimore)

Baton Rouge, Louisiana

City map: page 24
Population: (*464,600) 219,531 (1990C)
Altitude: 58 feet
Average Temp.: Jan., 51°F.; July, 82°F.
Telephone Area Code: 504
Time: 504/387-5411 **Weather:** 504/465-9215
Time Zone: Central

AIRPORT TRANSPORTATION:

Seven miles to downtown Baton Rouge. Taxicab, hotel van, and limousine service.

SELECTED HOTELS:

Baton Rouge Hilton, 5500 Hilton Ave., 504/924-5000; FAX 504/926-8152

Bellemont Hotel, 7370 Airline Hwy., 504/357-8612; FAX 504/357-4974

Courtyard By Marriott, 2421 S. Acadian Thruway, 504/924-6400; FAX 504/923-3041

Holiday Inn—East, 10455 Rieger Rd., 504/293-6880; FAX (same)

Holiday Inn—South, 9940 Airline Hwy., 504/924-7021; FAX (same)

Quality Inn Sherwood Forest, 10920 Mead Rd., 504/293-9370; FAX 504/293-8889

Radisson Hotel & Conference Center, 4728 Constitution Ave., 504/925-2244; FAX 504/930-0140

Ramada Inn Downtown, 1480 Nicholson Dr., 504/387-1111; FAX 504/343-5323

SELECTED RESTAURANTS:

Chalet Brandt, 7655 Old Hammond Hwy., 504/927-604000880001

Don's Seafood & Steakhouse, 6823 Airline Hwy., 504/357-0601

Giamanco's, 4624 Government St., 504/928-5045

Juban's, 3739 Perkins Rd., 504/346-8422

Maison LaCour, 11025 N. Harrell's Ferry Rd., 504/275-3755

Mike Anderson's Seafood, 1031 W. Lee Dr., 504/766-3728

Mulate's Cajun Restaurant, 8322 Bluebonnet Rd., 504/767-4794

Ruth's Chris Steak House, 4836 Constitution, 504/925-0163

SELECTED ATTRACTIONS:

Louisiana Arts & Science Center, 100 S. River Rd., 504/344-5272

Louisiana State Capitol, at the north end of 4th St., 504/342-7317

Louisiana State University (museums, Indian mounds), south of downtown between Highland Rd. and Nicholson Dr., 504/388-3202

LSU Rural Life Museum (19th-century buildings), Essen Ln. at I-10, 504/765-2437

Magnolia Mound Plantation, 2161 Nicholson Dr., 504/343-4955

McGee's Atchafalaya Basin Tours, the Atchafalaya Swamps in Henderson, 504/228-2384

Nottoway Plantation, LA Hwy. 1, White Castle, 504/346-8263

Oak Alley Plantation, LA Hwy. 18, Vacherie, 504/265-2151

Old State Capitol—Louisiana Center for Political & Governmental History, North Blvd. at River Rd., 504/342-0500

USS *Kidd* & Nautical Historic Center, Government St. at River Rd., 504/342-1942

INFORMATION SOURCES:

Baton Rouge Area Convention & Visitors Bureau

730 North Boulevard
Baton Rouge, Louisiana 70802
504/383-1825; 800/LA-ROUGE

The Greater Baton Rouge Chamber of Commerce

564 Laurel St.
P.O. Box 3217
Baton Rouge, Louisiana 70821
504/381-7125

BALTIMORE/WASHINGTON INTERNATIONAL AIRPORT

To/From I-695

LONG TERM PARKING

Pier E
Air Aruba
Air Jamaica
Charters
El Al Israel
Icelandair

Pier D
British Airways
TWA
USAir
USAir Express

UPPER DRIVE
LOWER DRIVE (Arrivals)
(Departures)

PARKING GARAGE AND CAR RENTAL

Pier C
Air Canada
American
America West
Continental
Laker Airways
Northwest
Southwest

(170)

Aviation Blvd.

Elm Rd.

To / From S.R. 295 & I-95

195

SHERATON INT'L HOTEL

PARKING

Pier A
United

Pier B
Delta
United

To/From Dorsey Rd.   ©1997-1985 Rand McNally & Co.

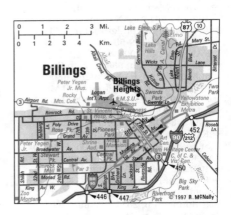

Billings

Billings Heights

Billings, Montana

City map: above
Population: (*100,100) 81,151 (1990C)
Altitude: 3,124 feet
Average Temp.: Jan., 22°F.; July, 72°F.
Telephone Area Code: 406
Time: 976-7651 **Weather:** 406/652-1916
Time Zone: Mountain

AIRPORT TRANSPORTATION:

Three miles to downtown Billings. Taxicab and limousine service.

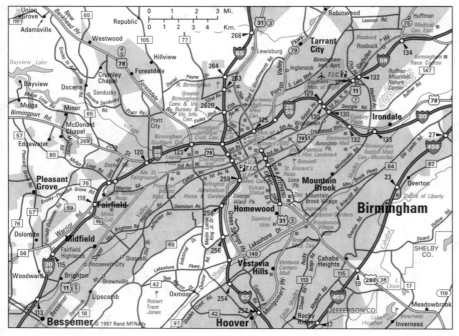

SELECTED HOTELS:

✈ Airport Metra Inn, 403 Main St.,
406/245-6611; FAX (none)
✈ Best Western Ponderosa Inn, 2511 1st
Ave. N., 406/259-5511;
FAX 406/245-8004
✈ The Billings Inn, 880 N. 29th St.,
406/252-6800; FAX 406/252-6800
Billings Plaza Holiday Inn, 5500 Midland
Rd., 406/248-7701; FAX 406/248-8954
Clarion Hotel, 1223 Mullowney Ln.,
406/248-7151; FAX 406/248-2054
✈ Radisson Northern Hotel, 19 N. 28th
St., 406/245-5121; FAX 406/259-9862
Ramada Ltd., 1345 Mullowney Ln.,
406/252-2584; FAX (same)
✈ Sheraton Billings Hotel, 27 N. 27th St.,
406/252-7400; FAX 406/252-2401
War Bonnet Inn, 2612 Belknap Ave.,
406/248-7761; FAX 406/248-7761

SELECTED RESTAURANTS:

The Cattle Company, 300 S. 24th, Rimrock
Mall, 406/656-9090
The Granary, 1500 Poly Dr., 406/259-3488
Jake's, 2701 1st Ave. N., 406/259-9375
Juliano's, 2912 7th Ave. N., 406/248-6400
The Rex, 2401 Montana Ave.,
406/245-7477
Walker's Grill, 301 N. 27th, 406/245-9291

SELECTED ATTRACTIONS:

Boothill Cemetery, east end of Black Otter
Trail, 406/252-4016
Moss Mansion, 914 Division St.,
406/256-5100
Oscar's Dreamland, (pioneer life exhibits),
west on Frontage Rd., then 1 mi. south
of Market Basket, 406/656-0966
Peter Yegen Jr. Yellowstone County
Museum, at Logan Field Airport,
406/256-6811
Pictograph Cave State Park, 5 miles south-
east of Billings off I-90, 406/252-4016

Pompeys Pillar, 28 miles northeast of
Billings, 406/657-6262
Western Heritage Center, 2822 Montana
Ave., 406/256-6809
Yellowstone Art Center, 401 N. 27th St.,
406/256-6804
Zoo Montana, 2100 S. Shiloh Rd.,
406/652-8100

INFORMATION SOURCE:

Billings Convention & Visitors Bureau
Billings Area Chamber of Commerce
815 S. 27th St.
P.O. Box 31177
Billings, Montana 59107
406/245-4111; Visitor Center
800/735-2635

Birmingham, Alabama

City map: above
Population: (*722,700) 265,968 (1990C)
Altitude: 601 feet
Average Temp.: Jan., 46°F.; July, 82°F.
Telephone Area Code: 205
Time: 205/979-8463 **Weather:**
205/945-7000
Time Zone: Central

AIRPORT TRANSPORTATION:

Five miles to downtown Birmingham.
Taxicab, bus and limousine service.

SELECTED HOTELS:

Central Inn Amad, 300 N. 10th St.,
205/328-8560; FAX 205/323-5819
✈ Holiday Inn—Airport, 5000 10th Ave.
N., 205/591-6900; FAX 205/591-2093
Holiday Inn Express, 7941 Crestwood
Blvd., 205/956-8211; FAX 205/956-1234
Holiday Inn—Homewood, 260 Oxmoor
Rd., Homewood, 205/942-2041;
FAX 205/290-9309
Holiday Inn—South, 1548 Montgomery
Hwy., 205/822-4350; FAX 205/822-0350

The Mountain Brook Inn, 2800 US 280,
Mountain Brook, 205/870-3100;
FAX 205/870-5938
Radisson Hotel Birmingham, 808 S. 20th
St. at University Blvd., 205/933-9000;
FAX 205/933-0920
✈ Ramada Inn—Airport, 5216 Airport
Hwy., 205/591-7900; FAX 205/592-6476
The Tutwiler, Park Place at 21st St. N.,
205/322-2100; FAX 205/325-1183
Wynfrey Hotel, 1000 Riverchase Galleria,
205/987-1600; FAX 205/988-4597

SELECTED RESTAURANTS:

Bombay Cafe, 2839 7th Ave. S.,
205/322-1930
Christian's Classic Cuisine, in the
Tutwiler Hotel, 205/323-9822
Highlands, 2011 11th Ave. S.,
205/939-1400
John's Restaurant, 112 N. 21st St.,
205/322-6014
Michael's Sirloin Room, 431 20th St. S.,
205/322-0419
Winston's, in the Wynfrey Hotel,
205/987-1600

SELECTED ATTRACTIONS:

Alabama Jazz Hall of Fame, 17th St. & 4th
Ave. N., 205/254-2720
Alabama Sports Hall of Fame Museum,
22nd St. & Civic Center Blvd.,
205/323-6665
Arlington Antebellum Home and Gardens,
331 Cotton Ave. SW, 205/780-5656
Birmingham Civil Rights Institute, 520
16th St. N., 205/328-9696
Birmingham Museum of Art, 2000 8th
Ave. N., 205/254-2565
Birmingham Zoo, 2630 Cahaba Rd.,
205/879-0408 or -0409
Botanical Gardens, 2612 Lane Park Rd.,
205/879-1227
Five Points South (historic district), 11th
Ave. S. & 20th St., 205/458-8000
Red Mountain Museum (interactive
science center), 2230 22nd St. S.,
205/933-4153
Riverchase Galleria, US 31 South at I-459,
205/985-3039
Sloss Furnaces (iron-making), beside First
Ave.—north viaduct on 32nd St.,
205/324-1911
Vulcan Park (panoramic view from
world's largest cast iron statue), Valley
Ave. at US 31 S., 205/328-6198

INFORMATION SOURCES:

Greater Birmingham Convention and
Visitors Bureau
2200 Ninth Ave. N.
Birmingham, Alabama 35203
205/458-8000; 800/458-8085
Birmingham Area Chamber of Commerce
2027 First Ave. N.
Birmingham, Alabama 35203
205/323-5461

Boise, Idaho

City map: page 27
Population: (*195,600) 125,738 (1990C)
Altitude: 2,726 feet
Average Temp.: Jan., 29°F.; July, 75°F.
Telephone Area Code: 208
Time: 844-8463 **Weather:** 208/342-6569
Time Zone: Mountain

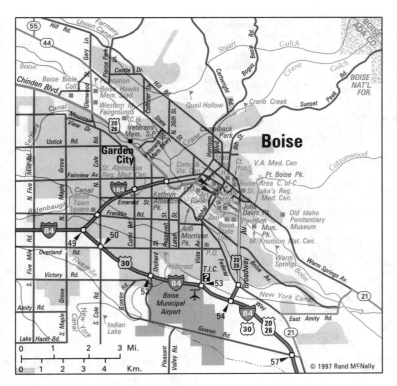

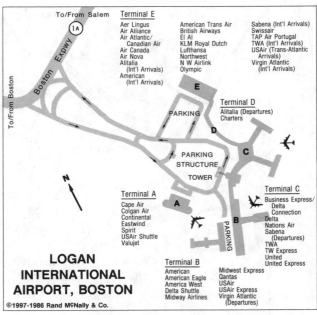

**LOGAN
INTERNATIONAL
AIRPORT, BOSTON**
©1997-1986 Rand McNally & Co.

AIRPORT TRANSPORTATION:

Three miles to downtown Boise.
Taxicab, bus, airport limousine, and hotel
shuttle service.

SELECTED HOTELS:

✈ Best Western Airport Motor Inn, 2660
Airport Way, 208/384-5000;
FAX 208/384-5566
Boisean Motel, 1300 S. Capitol,
208/343-3645; FAX 208/343-4823
Doubletree Club Hotel at ParkCenter, 475
ParkCenter Blvd., 208/345-2002;
FAX 208/345-8354
✈ Holiday Inn Airport, 3300 Vista Ave.,
208/344-8365; FAX 208/343-9635
Plaza Suite Hotel, 409 S. Cole Rd.,
208/375-7666; FAX 208/376-3608
Red Lion Hotel/Riverside, 2900 Chinden
Blvd., 208/343-1871; FAX 208/344-1079
Red Lion Inn/Downtowner, 1800 Fairview
Ave., 208/344-7691; FAX 208/336-3652
Residence Inn by Marriott, 1401 Lusk
Ave., 208/344-1200; FAX 208/384-5354
Shilo Inn—Riverside, 3031 Main St.,
208/344-3521; FAX 208/384-1217
University Inn, 2360 University Dr.,
208/345-7170; FAX 208/345-5118

SELECTED RESTAURANTS:

Angell's, 999 W. Main St., 208/342-4900
Boise Black Angus, 3101 Main,
208/345-7600
Charthouse, 2288 N. Garden St.,
208/336-9370
The Gamekeeper, in the Owyhee Plaza
Hotel, 1109 Main, 208/343-4611
Lock, Stock & Barrel, 4705 Emerald,
208/336-4266

Murphy's Seafood Bar & Grill, 1555
Broadway Ave., 208/344-3691
Pacific Grill & Smokehouse, in the Red
Lion/Riverside, 208/343-1871
Peter Schott's, in the Idanha Hotel, 10th &
Main, 208/336-9100
The Renaissance, 110 S. 5th St.,
208/344-6776
The Sandpiper, 1100 W. Jefferson,
208/344-8911

SELECTED ATTRACTIONS:

The Basque Museum, 611 Grove St.,
208/343-2671
Boise Art Museum, 670 S. Julia Davis Dr.,
208/345-8330
Boise Greenbelt (20-mile riverfront
pathway), Willow Lane Athletic
Complex to Lucky Peak Dam,
208/384-4240
Discovery Center of Idaho (hands-on
science center), 131 Myrtle St.,
208/343-9895
Idaho Botanical Garden, 2355 Old
Penitentiary Rd., 208/343-8649
Idaho Historical Museum, 610 N. Julia
Davis Dr., 208/334-2120
Les Bois Park (horse racing), 5610
Glenwood, 208/376-RACE
Morrison Knudsen Nature Center, 600 S.
Walnut (adjacent to Municipal Park),
208/334-2225
Old Idaho Territorial Penitentiary, 2445
Old Penitentiary Rd., 208/334-2844
World Center for Birds of Prey, Exit 50 off
I-84 at the end of S. Cole Rd.,
208/362-8687
Zoo Boise, in Julia Davis Park,
208/384-4260

INFORMATION SOURCES:

Boise Convention and Visitors Bureau
168 N. 9th, Suite 200
Boise, Idaho 83702
208/344-7777; 800/635-5240
Boise Area Chamber of Commerce
300 N. 6th
P.O. Box 2368
Boise, Idaho 83701
208/344-5515

Boston, Massachusetts

City map: page 28
Population: (*4,171,800) 574,283 (1990C)
Altitude: Sea level to 330 feet
Average Temp.: Jan., 29°F.; July, 72°F.
Telephone Area Code: 617
Time: 617/637-1234 **Weather:**
617/936-1234
Time Zone: Eastern

AIRPORT TRANSPORTATION:

See map at upper right
Three miles to downtown Boston.
Taxicab and limousine bus service.

SELECTED HOTELS:

Boston Harbor Hotel, 70 Rowes Wharf,
617/439-7000; FAX 617/330-9450
Boston Marriott Copley Place, 110
Huntington Ave., 617/236-5800;
FAX 617/236-5885
Boston Park Plaza Hotel, 64 Arlington St.,
617/426-2000; FAX 617/426-5545
The Colonnade, 120 Huntington Ave.,
617/424-7000; FAX 617/424-1717
Copley Plaza Wyndham Hotel, 138 St.
James Ave., 617/267-5300;
FAX 617/375-9648
Four Seasons Hotel, 200 Boylston St.,
617/338-4400; FAX 617/423-0154
✈ Harborside Hyatt Conference Center,
101 Harborside Dr., 617/568-1234;
FAX 617/567-8856

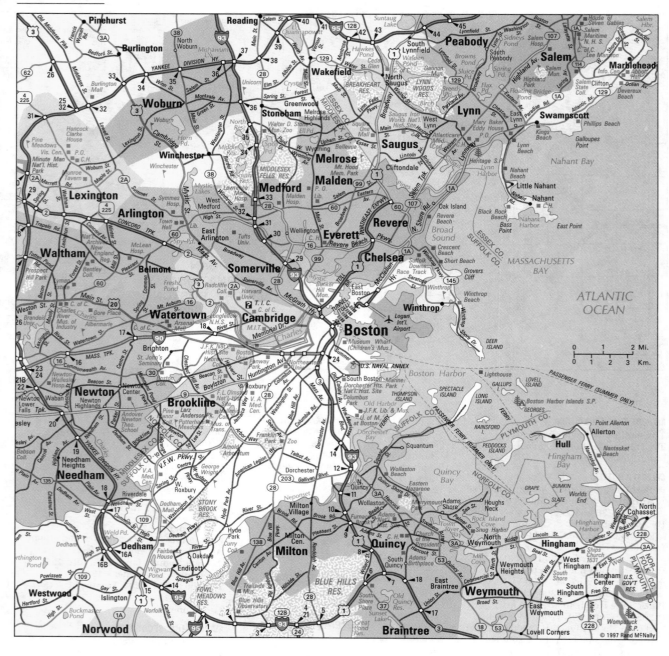

Le Meridien, Boston, 250 Franklin St.,
617/451-1900; FAX 617/423-2844
✈ Logan Airport Hilton, 75 Service Rd., at
Logan International Airport,
617/569-9300; FAX 617/569-3981
Omni Parker House Hotel, 60 School St.,
617/227-8600; FAX 617/742-5729
The Ritz-Carlton, 15 Arlington St.,
617/536-5700; FAX 617/536-1335
Sheraton Boston Hotel & Towers at
Prudential Center, 39 Dalton St.,
617/236-2000; FAX 617/236-1702
The Westin Hotel at Copley Place, 10
Huntington Ave., 617/262-9600;
FAX 617/424-7483

SELECTED RESTAURANTS:

Anthony's Pier 4, 140 Northern Ave.,
617/423-6363

The Cafe Budapest, 90 Exeter St.,
617/266-1979
Caffe Lampara, 916 Commonwealth Ave.,
617/566-0300
Copley's Restaurant, in the Copley Plaza
Hotel, 617/267-5300
Felicia's, 145A Richmond St., up one
flight, 617/523-9885
Hampshire House, 84 Beacon St.,
617/227-9600
Jimmy's Harborside Restaurant, 242
Northern Ave., 617/423-1000
Julien, in Le Meridien Hotel,
617/451-1900
Legal Seafoods, in the Boston Park Plaza
Hotel, 35 Columbus Ave., 617/426-4444
Locke–Ober Cafe, 3 Winter Pl.,
617/542-1340

The Main Dining Room, in The Ritz-
Carlton Hotel, 617/536-5700
Maison Robert, Old City Hall, 45 School
St., 617/227-3370

SELECTED ATTRACTIONS:

Boston Tea Party Ship & Museum,
Congress St. Bridge, 617/338-1773
Cheers!/Bull & Finch Pub, 84 Beacon St.,
617/227-9605
Children's Museum, Museum Wharf, 300
Congress St., 617/426-8855
Faneuil Hall/Faneuil Hall Marketplace,
Congress & North sts., 617/523-1300
The Freedom Trail (self-guided walking
tour, begins at Boston Common;
Tremont, Park & Beacon sts.; stop by
visitors' kiosks for maps), 617/242-5642

Harvard University, Cambridge,
617/495-1000
John F. Kennedy Library & Museum,
Columbia Point, Dorchester,
617/929-4523
Museum of Fine Arts, 465 Huntington
Ave., 617/267-9300
Museum of Science, Science Park, on
Msgr. O'Brien Hwy. between Storrow &
Memorial drives, 617/723-2500
New England Aquarium, Central Wharf
off Atlantic Ave., 617/973-5200
USS Constitution "Old Ironsides" Ship &
Museum, Charlestown Naval Yard,
617/242-5670

INFORMATION SOURCES:
Greater Boston Convention & Visitors
Bureau, Inc.
Prudential Tower, Suite 400
800 Boylston St.
Boston, Massachusetts 02199
617/536-4100; 800/888-5515
Greater Boston Chamber of Commerce
1 Beacon St., 4th Floor
Boston, Massachusetts 02108
617/227-4500

Buffalo, New York

City map: right
Population: (*1,097,600) 328,123 (1990C)
Altitude: 600 feet
Average Temp.: Jan., 26°F.; July, 71°F.
Telephone Area Code: 716
Time and Weather: 716/844-1717
Time Zone: Eastern

AIRPORT TRANSPORTATION:
Nine miles to downtown Buffalo.
Taxicab and limousine bus service.

SELECTED HOTELS:
Best Western Inn Downtown, 510
Delaware Ave., 716/886-8333;
FAX 716/884-3070
Buffalo Hilton, 120 Church St.,
716/845-5100; FAX 716/845-5377
Buffalo Marriott, 1340 Millersport Hwy.,
Amherst, 716/689-6900;
FAX 716/689-0483
Hampton Inn, 10 Flint Rd., Amherst,
716/689-4414; FAX 716/689-4382
✈ Holiday Inn Airport, 4600 Genesee St.,
Cheektowaga, 716/634-6969;
FAX 716/634-0920
Holiday Inn Downtown, 620 Delaware
Ave., 716/886-2121; FAX 716/886-7942
✈ Holiday Inn Express, 6700 Transit Rd.,
Williamsville, 716/634-7500;
FAX 716/634-7502
Holiday Inn Gateway, 601 Dingens St., at
Rossler intersection, Cheektowaga,
716/896-2900; FAX 716/896-3765
Hyatt Regency, 2 Fountain Plaza, at Pearl
& W. Huron sts., 716/856-1234;
FAX 716/852-6157
✈ Quality Inn, 4217 Genesee St.,
Cheektowaga, 716/633-5500;
FAX 716/633-4231
✈ Radisson Hotel & Suites, 4243 Genesee
St., Cheektowaga, 716/634-2300;
FAX 716/632-2387
✈ Ramada Inn Airport, 48 Freeman Rd.,
Williamsville, 716/634-2700;
FAX 716/634-1644

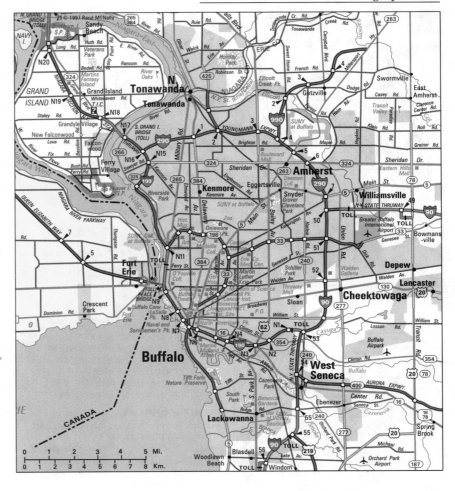

Sheraton Inn Buffalo, 2040 Walden Ave.,
Cheektowaga, 716/681-2400;
FAX 716/681-8067
Williamsville Inn, 5447 Main St.,
Williamsville, 716/634-1111;
FAX 716/631-3367

SELECTED RESTAURANTS:
Anchor Bar, 1047 Main St., 716/886-8920
Asa Ransom House, 10529 Main St.,
Clarence, 716/759-2315
Daffodil's Restaurant, 930 Maple Rd.,
Williamsville, 716/688-5413
E.B. Greens Steakhouse, in the
Hyatt Regency Hotel, 716/856-1539
Grill Ninety-One, 91 Niagara St.,
716/856-8373
Justine's, in the Buffalo Hilton Hotel,
716/845-5100
Lord Chumley's, 481 Delaware Ave.,
between Virginia & Allen sts.,
716/886-2220
Old Red Mill Inn, 8326 Main St.,
Clarence, 716/633-7878
Park Lane Restaurant, 33 Gates Circle, at
Delaware, 716/883-3344

SELECTED ATTRACTIONS:
Albright-Knox Art Gallery, 1285 Elmwood
Ave., 716/882-8700
Buffalo and Erie County Historical
Society Museum, 25 Nottingham Ct.,
716/873-9644

Buffalo Museum of Science, 1020 Humboldt Pkwy., Best St. exit off NY 33,
716/896-5201
Buffalo Naval & Servicemen's Park, 1
Naval Park Cove, 716/847-1773
Buffalo Zoo, 300 Parkside Ave. across
from Delaware Park, 716/837-3900
Miss Buffalo-Niagara Clipper,
716/856-6696
The Original American Kazoo Company,
8703 South Main St., Eden,
716/992-3960

INFORMATION SOURCE:
Greater Buffalo Convention and Visitors
Bureau
107 Delaware Ave.
Buffalo, New York 14202
716/852-0511; 800/283-3256

Calgary, Alberta, Canada

City map: page 30
Population: (*754,033) 710,877 (1991C)
Altitude: 3,439 feet
Average Temp.: Jan., 13°F.; July, 62°F.
Telephone Area Code: 403
Time: 403/266-5314 **Weather:**
403/275-3300
Time Zone: Mountain

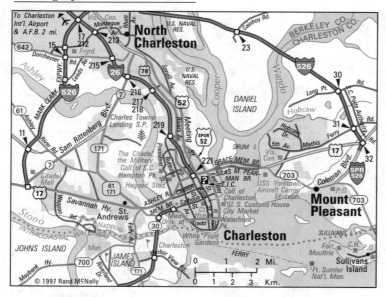

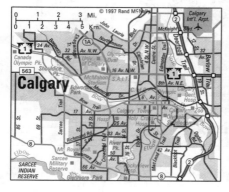

AIRPORT TRANSPORTATION:

Ten miles to downtown Calgary.
Taxicab, airporter shuttle, and limousine
service.

SELECTED HOTELS:

Best Western Hospitality Inn, 135
Southland Dr. SE, 403/278-5050;
FAX 403/278-5050
✈ Best Western Port-O-Call Inn, 1935
McKnight Blvd. NE, 403/291-4600;
FAX 403/250-6827
Blackfoot Inn, 5940 Blackfoot Trail SE,
403/252-2253; FAX 403/252-3574
✈ Canadian Pacific's Calgary's Airport
Hotel, 2001 Airport Rd. NE,
403/291-2600; FAX 403/250-8722
Delta Bow Valley, 209 4th Ave. SE,
403/266-1980; FAX 403/266-0007
The Palliser, 133 9th Ave. SW,
403/262-1234; FAX 403/260-1260
Prince Royal Suites, 618 5th Ave. SW,
403/263-0520; FAX 403/298-4888
Radisson Plaza Hotel Calgary, 110 9th
Ave. SE, 403/266-7331;
FAX 403/262-8442
Ramada Hotel Downtown Calgary, 708 8th
Ave. SW, 403/263-7600;
FAX 403/237-6127

Sandman Hotel Calgary, 888 7th Ave. SW,
403/237-8626; FAX 403/290-1238
Sheraton Cavalier, 2620 32nd Ave. NE,
403/291-0107; FAX 403/291-2834
The Westin Hotel, 320 4th Ave. SW,
403/266-1611; FAX 403/233-7471

SELECTED RESTAURANTS:

Atrium Terrace, in the Chateau Airport
Hotel, 403/291-2600
Caesar's, 512 4th Ave. SW, 403/264-1222
Hy's Steak House, 316 4th Ave. SW,
403/263-2222
Japanese Village, 302 4th Ave. SW,
403/262-2738
La Caille on the Bow, 100 La Caille Pl.,
7th St. & 1st. Ave. SW, 403/262-5554
La Chaumiere, 139 17th Ave. SW,
403/228-5690
La Dolce Vita, 916 1st Ave. NE,
403/263-3445
Owl's Nest Dining Room, in the Westin
Hotel, 403/266-1611
Panorama Room, atop the Calgary Tower,
101 9th Ave. SW, 403/266-7171
Rimrock Room, in the Palliser Hotel,
403/262-1234

SELECTED ATTRACTIONS:

Alberta Science Centre/Centennial
Planetarium, 701 11th St. SW,
403/221-3700
Calaway Park, 10 km. west on the
Trans-Canada Hwy., 403/240-3822
Calgary Tower, 9th Ave. and Centre St.,
403/266-7171
Calgary Zoo, Botanical Gardens &
Prehistoric Park, Memorial Dr. west of
Deerfoot Trail, 403/232-9372
Canada Olympic Park, on the western city
limits along the Trans-Canada Hwy.,
403/286-2632
Eau Claire Market & IMAX Theatre, 2nd
St. & 2nd Ave., 403/264-6450
Fort Calgary, 750 9th Ave. SE,
403/290-1875
Glenbow Museum, 130 9th Ave. SE,
403/268-4100

Heritage Park (turn-of-the-century village),
Heritage Dr. & 14th St. SW,
403/259-1900
Inglewood Bird Sanctuary, south of 9th
Ave. & Sanctuary Rd. SE, 403/269-6688
Museum of Movie Art, #9 3600 21st St.
NE, 403/250-7588

INFORMATION SOURCES:

Calgary Convention & Visitors Bureau
237 8th Ave. SE, Suite 200
Calgary, Alberta, Canada T2G 0K8
403/263-8510; 800/661-1678
The Calgary Chamber of Commerce
517 Centre St. S.
Calgary, Alberta, Canada T2G 2C4
403/750-0400

Charleston, South Carolina

City map: left
Population: (*416,400) 80,414 (1990C)
Altitude: 118 feet
Average Temp.: Jan., 49°F.; July, 80°F.
Telephone Area Code: 803
Time: 803/572-8463 **Weather:**
803/744-3207
Time Zone: Eastern

AIRPORT TRANSPORTATION:

Twelve miles to downtown Charleston.
Taxicab, airport shuttle, hotel van, and
limousine service.

SELECTED HOTELS:

Best Western King Charles Inn, 237
Meeting St., 803/723-7451;
FAX 803/723-2041
Best Western Northwoods Atrium Inn,
7401 Northwoods Blvd., N. Charleston,
803/572-2200; FAX 803/863-8316
Charleston Hilton, 4770 Goer Dr., N.
Charleston, 803/747-1900;
FAX 803/744-2530
Comfort Inn Riverview, 144 Bee St.,
803/577-2224; FAX 803/77-9001
Econo-Lodge, 3668 Dorchester Rd.,
Charleston Heights, 803/747-0961;
FAX 803/747-3230
✈ Hampton Inn Charleston, 4701 Saul
White Blvd., N. Charleston,
803/554-7154; FAX 803/566-9299
Hampton Inn—Historic District, 345
Meeting St., 803/723-4000;
FAX 803/722-3725
Hawthorn Suites, 181 Church St.,
803/577-2644; FAX 803/577-2697
Holiday Inn Mt. Pleasant, 250 Johnnie
Dodds Blvd. (SC 17 Bypass), Mt.
Pleasant, 803/884-6000;
FAX 803/881-1786
Holiday Inn—Riverview, 301 Savannah
Hwy., 803/556-7100; FAX 803/556-6176
Mills House Hotel, 115 Meeting St.,
803/577-2400; FAX 803/722-0623
Omni Hotel at Charleston Place, 130
Market St., 803/722-4900;
FAX 803/722-0728
Radisson Inn, 5991 Rivers Ave., N.
Charleston, 803/744-2501;
FAX 803/744-2501
Sheraton Charleston Hotel, 170 Lockwood
Dr., 803/723-3000; FAX 803/720-0844

SELECTED RESTAURANTS:

Ashley's, Sheraton Charleston Hotel,
803/723-3000

Barbadoes Room, in the Mills House
   Hotel, 803/577-2400
Carolina's, 10 Exchange St., 803/724-3800
French Quarter, in the Lodge Alley Inn,
   195 E. Bay St., 803/722-1611
The Palmetto Cafe, in the Omni Hotel at
   Charleston Place, 803/722-4900
Papillon, 32 North Market St.,
   803/723-3614
Shem Creek Bar & Grill, 508 Mill St., Mt.
   Pleasant, 803/884-8102

SELECTED ATTRACTIONS:

Audubon Swamp Garden, Hwy. 61, 10 mi.
   NW of city. Enter at Magnolia Plantation
   & Gardens, 803/571-1266
The Charleston Museum, 360 Meeting St.,
   803/722-2996
Charles Towne Landing 1670, 1500 Old
   Town Rd., 803/852-4200
Drayton Hall Plantation, 3380 Ashley
   River Rd., 803/766-0188
Fort Moultrie, 1214 Middle St. on
   Sullivan's Island, 803/883-3123
Fort Sumter Tours (leave from locations at
   the City Marina & Patriot's Point com-
   plex), 803/722-1691
Gibbes Museum of Art, 135 Meeting St.,
   803/722-2706
Heyward-Washington House, 87 Church
   St., 803/722-0354
Magnolia Plantation & Gardens, Hwy. 61,
   10 mi. NW of city, 803/571-1266
Patriots Point Naval & Maritime Museum,
   40 Patriots Point Rd., Mt. Pleasant,
   803/884-2727

INFORMATION SOURCES:

Charleston Area Convention & Visitors
Bureau
   81 Mary St.
   P.O. Box 975
   Charleston, South Carolina 29402
   803/853-8000; 800/868-8118
Visitor Reception & Transportation Center
   375 Meeting St.
   Charleston, South Carolina 29402-0975
   803/853-8000
Charleston Metro Chamber of Commerce
   P.O. Box 975
   Charleston, South Carolina 29402-0975
   803/577-2510

Charlotte, North Carolina

City map: upper right
Population: (*598,400) 395,934 (1990C)
Altitude: 700 feet
Average Temp.: Jan., 52°F.; July, 88°F.
Telephone Area Code: 704
Time and Weather: 704/375-6711
Time Zone: Eastern

AIRPORT TRANSPORTATION:

See map at right.
Ten miles to downtown Charlotte.
Taxicab and hotel shuttle service.

SELECTED HOTELS:

Adam's Mark, 555 S. McDowell St.,
   704/372-4100; FAX 704/348-4645
Charlotte Marriott City Center, 100 W.
   Trade St., 704/333-9000;
   FAX 704/342-3419
✈ Comfort Inn Airport, 4040 S. I-85,
   704/394-4111; FAX 704/394-4111

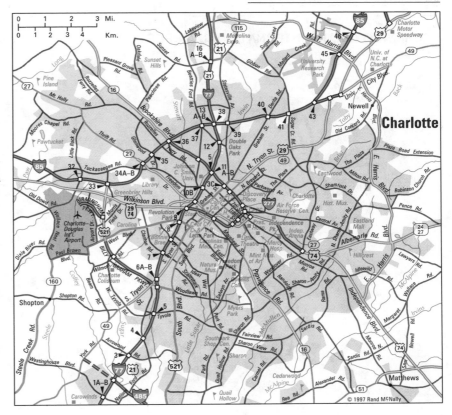

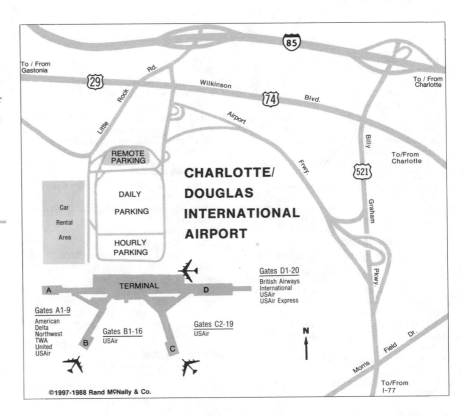

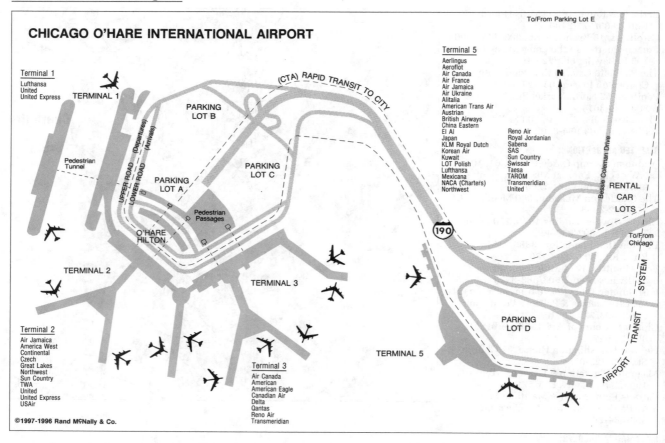

CHICAGO O'HARE INTERNATIONAL AIRPORT

Terminal 1
Lufthansa
United
United Express

TERMINAL 1

PARKING LOT B

(CTA) RAPID TRANSIT TO CITY

To/From Parking Lot E

Terminal 5
Aerlingus
Aeroflot
Air Canada
Air France
Air Ukraine
Alitalia
American Trans Air
Austrian
British Airways
China Eastern
El Al
Japan
KLM Royal Dutch
Korean Air
Kuwait
LOT Polish
Lufthansa
Mexicana
NACA (Charters)
Northwest

Reno Air
Royal Jordanian
Sabena
SAS
Sun Country
Swissair
Taesa
TAROM
Transmeridian
United

N

Pedestrian Tunnel

UPPER ROAD (Departures)
LOWER ROAD (Arrivals)

PARKING LOT A

PARKING LOT C

Pedestrian Passages

O'HARE HILTON

TERMINAL 2

TERMINAL 3

190

RENTAL CAR LOTS

To/From Chicago

Bessie Coleman Drive

PARKING LOT D

TERMINAL 5

AIRPORT TRANSIT SYSTEM

Terminal 2
Air Jamaica
America West
Continental
Czech
Great Lakes
Northwest
Sun Country
TWA
United
United Express
USAir

Terminal 3
Air Canada
American
American Eagle
Canadian Air
Delta
Qantas
Reno Air
Transmeridian

©1997-1996 Rand McNally & Co.

Embassy Suites, 4800 S. Tryon St.,
704/527-8400; FAX 704/527-7035
✈ Holiday Inn Airport, 2707 Little Rock
Rd. & I-85, 704/394-4301;
FAX 704/394-1844
Holiday Inn Express, 5301 N. I-85, 4
Sugar Creek Rd., 704/596-9390;
FAX 704/596-9390 ext. 299
Holiday Inn Independence, 3501 E.
Independence Blvd., 704/537-1010;
FAX 704/531-2439
Omni Charlotte Hotel, 222 E. 3rd St.,
704/377-6664; FAX 704/377-4143
Radisson Plaza Hotel, 101 S. Tryon St.,
704/377-0400; FAX 704/347-0649

SELECTED RESTAURANTS:
Azalea's, in the Radisson Plaza Hotel,
704/377-0400
Epicurean, 1324 East Blvd., 704/377-4520
Hereford Barn Steak House, 4320 N. I-85
Service Rd., 704/596-0854
J.W. Steakhouse, Charlotte Marriott City
Center Hotel, 704/333-9000
The Lamplighter, 1065 E. Morehead St.,
704/372-5343
Ranch House, 5614 Wilkinson Blvd.,
704/399-5411
The 30th Edition, 2 First Union Tower,
30th Floor, 704/372-7778

SELECTED ATTRACTIONS:
Charlotte Motor Speedway, 5555 Hwy. 29
N., Concord, 704/455-3200
Discovery Place (science museum,
Omnimax Theatre & Planetarium), 301
N. Tryon St., 704/372-6261

Mint Museum of Art, 2730 Randolph Rd.,
704/337-2000
Paramount's Carowinds (theme park), I-77
& Carowinds Blvd. (exit 90),
704/588-2606
Reed Gold Mine State Historic Site, 9621
Reed Mine Rd., Stanfield, 20 mi. east of
Charlotte off Albemarle Rd. (NC 24/27),
704/786-8337

INFORMATION SOURCES:
Charlotte Convention & Visitors Bureau
122 E. Stonewall St.
Charlotte, North Carolina 28202-1838
704/334-2282
Info Charlotte
330 S. Tryon St.
Charlotte, North Carolina 28202
704/331-2700 or -2701; 800/231-4636
Charlotte Chamber of Commerce
330 S. Tryon St.
P. O. Box 32785
Charlotte, North Carolina 28232
704/378-1300

Chicago, Illinois

City map: page 33
Population: (*7,835,300) 2,783,726
(1990C)
Altitude: 596 feet
Average Temp.: Jan., 27°F.; July, 75°F.
Telephone Area Codes: 312, 773
Time: 976-1616 **Weather:** 976-1212
Time Zone: Central

AIRPORT TRANSPORTATION:
See map above.
Nineteen miles from O'Hare to downtown
Chicago; 10 miles from Midway to
downtown Chicago.
Taxicab, bus/rapid transit, and limousine
bus service from both airports.

SELECTED HOTELS:
The Ambassador West, 1300 N. State
Pkwy, 312/787-3700; FAX 312/740-2967
Chicago Marriott Downtown, 540 N.
Michigan Ave., 312/836-0100;
FAX 312/836-6139
Chicago Marriott O'Hare, 8535 W. Higgins
Rd., 773/693-4444; FAX 773/714-4297
Courtyard by Marriott Downtown, 30 E.
Hubbard, 312/329-2500;
FAX 312/329-0293
Days Inn on Lake Shore Drive, 644 N.
Lake Shore Dr., 312/943-9200;
FAX 312/255-4411
The Drake, 140 E. Walton Place,
312/787-2200; FAX 312/951-5803
The Fairmont Hotel—Chicago, 200 N.
Columbus Dr. at Illinois Center,
312/565-8000; FAX 312/856-1032
Holiday Inn Mart Plaza, 350 N. Orleans
St., 312/836-5000; FAX 312/222-9508
Hotel Nikko, 320 N. Dearborn,
312/744-1900; FAX 312/527-2650
Hyatt Regency Chicago, 151 E. Wacker Dr.,
312/565-1234; FAX 312/565-2966
✈ Hyatt Regency O'Hare, 9300 W. Bryn
Mawr Ave., Rosemont, 847/696-1234;
FAX 847/698-0139

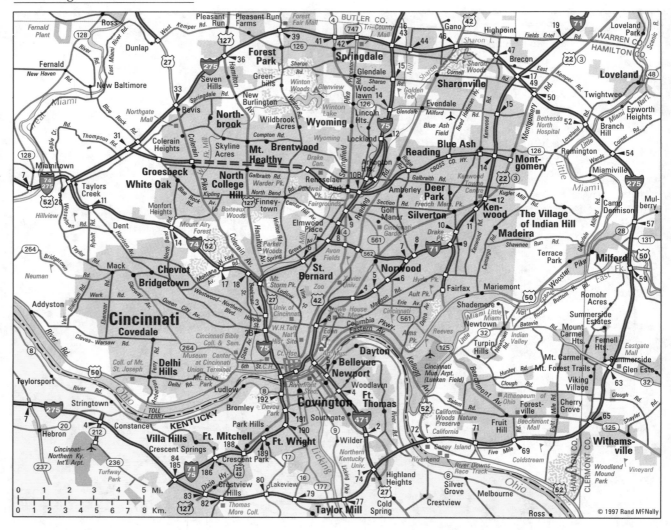

© 1997 Rand McNally

✈ O'Hare Hilton, at O'Hare International Airport, 773/686-8000; FAX 773/601-2873

Omni Ambassador East, 1301 N. State Pkwy., 312/787-7200; FAX 312/787-4760

Palmer House Hilton, 17 E. Monroe St., 312/726-7500; FAX 312/263-2556

Park Hyatt Chicago, 800 N. Michigan Ave., 312/280-2222; FAX 312/280-1963

The Ritz-Carlton, Chicago, 160 E. Pearson St., 312/266-1000; FAX 312/266-1194

Swissotel Chicago, 323 E. Wacker Dr., 312/565-0565; FAX 312/565-0540

The Tremont Hotel, 100 E. Chestnut St., 312/751-1900; FAX 312/751-8691

The Westin Hotel, 909 N. Michigan Ave., 312/943-7200; FAX 312/649-7447

SELECTED RESTAURANTS:

Biggs Restaurant, 1150 N. Dearborn, 312/787-0900

Cafe Gordon, in The Tremont Hotel, 312/751-1900

Cape Cod Room, in the Drake Hotel, 312/787-2200

Gordon Restaurant, 500 N. Clark, 312/467-9780

House of Hunan, 535 N. Michigan Ave., 312/329-9494

Jaxx, in the Park Hyatt Chicago Hotel, 312/280-2222

Lawry's The Prime Rib, 100 E. Ontario St., 312/787-5000

Michael Jordan's—The Restaurant, 500 N. La Salle, 312/644-3865

Nick's Fishmarket, 1 First National Plaza, Monroe at Dearborn, 312/621-0200

Pizzeria Uno, 29 E. Ohio St., 312/321-1000

Planet Hollywood, 633 N. Wells, 312/266-7827

The Pump Room, in the Omni Ambassador East Hotel, 312/266-0360

Signature Room at the Ninety-Fifth, 172 E. Chestnut, in the John Hancock Center, 312/787-9596

Su Casa, 49 E. Ontario St., 312/943-4041

SELECTED ATTRACTIONS:

Adler Planetarium, 1300 S. Lake Shore Dr., 312/322-0300

Art Institute, Michigan Ave. at Adams St., 312/443-3600

Brookfield Zoo, 31st St. & 1st Ave., Brookfield, 708/485-0263

Field Museum of Natural History, Roosevelt Rd. at S. Lake Shore Dr., 312/922-9410

John G. Shedd Aquarium, 1200 S. Lake Shore Dr., 312/939-2438

Lincoln Park Zoo, Fullerton Ave. & N. Lake Shore Dr., 312/742-2000

The "Magnificent Mile" (shopping), N. Michigan Ave.

Museum of Science & Industry, 57th St. & S. Lake Shore Dr., 312/684-1414

Sears Tower, 233 S. Wacker Dr., 312/875-9696

Spertus Museum of Judaica, 618 S. Michigan Ave., 312/322-1747

INFORMATION SOURCES:

Chicago Convention & Tourism Bureau, Inc.
McCormick Place
2301 S. Lake Shore Dr.
Chicago, Illinois 60616-1490
312/567-8500

Chicago Office of Tourism
78 E. Washington
Chicago, Illinois 60602
312/744-2400

Chicagoland Chamber of Commerce
330 N. Wabash
Chicago, Illinois 60611
312/494-6700

Cincinnati, Ohio

City map: page 34
Population: (*1,547,700) 364,040 (1990C)
Altitude: 683 feet
Average Temp.: Jan., 35°F.; July, 78°F.
Telephone Area Code: 513
Time: 513/721-1700 **Weather:**
    513/241-1010
Time Zone: Eastern

AIRPORT TRANSPORTATION:

See map at right.
Thirteen miles to downtown Cincinnati.
Taxicab and limousine bus service.

SELECTED HOTELS:

Cincinnati Marriott, 11320 Chester Rd.,
    513/772-1720; FAX 513/772-6466
Comfort Inn, 11440 Chester Rd.,
    513/771-3400; FAX 513/771-6340
Crowne Plaza, 15 W. 6th St.,
    513/381-4000; FAX 513/381-5158
Harley Hotel of Cincinnati, 8020
    Montgomery Rd., 513/793-4300;
    FAX 513/793-1413
Holiday Inn I-275 North, 3855 Hauck Rd.,
    513/563-8330; FAX 513/563-9679
Hyatt Regency, 151 W. 5th St.,
    513/579-1234; FAX 513/579-0107
Imperial House Hotel, 5510 Rybolt Rd.,
    513/574-6000; FAX 513/574-6566
Omni Netherland Plaza, 35 W. 5th St.,
    513/421-9100; FAX 513/421-4291
Ramada Hotel Central, 8001 Reading Rd.,
    513/821-5111; FAX 513/821-4972
Regal Cincinnati Hotel, 150 W. 5th St.,
    513/352-2100; FAX 513/352-2148
Vernon Manor Hotel, 400 Oak St.,
    513/281-3300; FAX 513/281-8933
The Westin Hotel, Fountain Square, 5th &
    Vine, 513/621-7700; FAX 513/852-5670

SELECTED RESTAURANTS:

Celestial, 1071 Celestial St., 513/241-4455
La Normandie Grill, 118 E. 6th St.,
    513/721-2761
The Longhorn, 713 Vine, 513/421-9696
Maisonette, 114 E. 6th St., 513/721-2260
Montgomery Inn at the Boathouse, 925
    Eastern Ave., 513/721-7427
Orchids at the Palm Court, in the Omni
    Netherland Plaza, 513/421-9100
The Palace Restaurant, in the
    Cincinnatian Hotel, 601 Vine St.,
    513/381-3000
Rookwood Pottery, 1077 Celestial St.,
    513/721-5456
Windjammer, 11330 Chester Rd.,
    Sharonville, 513/771-3777

SELECTED ATTRACTIONS:

Children's Museum of Cincinnati,
    Longworth Hall, 700 W. Pete Rose Way,
    513/421-5437
Cincinnati Fire Museum, 315 W. Court St.,
    513/621-5553
Cincinnati Zoo, 3400 Vine St. (auto en-
    trance on Dury), 513/281-4700

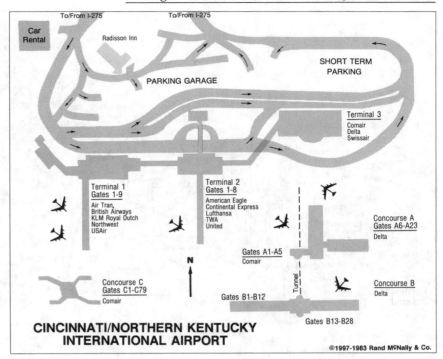

CINCINNATI/NORTHERN KENTUCKY INTERNATIONAL AIRPORT

©1997-1983 Rand M\u1d9cNally & Co.

The Museum Center (Museum of Natural
    History, Cincinnati Historical Society &
    Omnimax Theatre), 1301 Western Ave.,
    513/287-7000 or 800/733-2077
Paramount's Kings Island (theme park),
    Kings Island, 513/241-5600
Showboat Majestic (live stage and musical
    shows), foot of Broadway, 513/241-6550
    (April–Oct.)
Tower Place at the Carew Tower
    (shopping), 4th & Race sts.,
    513/241-7700
William Howard Taft National Historic
    Site, 2038 Auburn Ave., 513/684-3262

INFORMATION SOURCES:

Greater Cincinnati Convention and
Visitors Bureau
    300 W. 6th St.
    Cincinnati, Ohio 45202
    513/621-2142
    Visitor Info. 800/246-2987
Greater Cincinnati Chamber of Commerce
    300 Carew Tower
    441 Vine St.
    Cincinnati, Ohio 45202
    513/579-3100

Ciudad Juárez, Chihuahua, Mexico

City map: page 46
Population: El Paso-Ciudad Juárez
    (*1,211,300) 789,522 (1990C)
Altitude: 3,842 feet
Average Temp.: Jan., 44°F.; July, 82°F.
Telephone Code: 011/52/16
Time: 03 **Weather:** (none)
Time Zone: Central

AIRPORT TRANSPORTATION:

Ten miles to downtown Juárez from El
    Paso International Airport (U.S.); 12

miles from Abraham Gonzales Interna-
    tional Airport (Mexico).
Taxicab service from El Paso Interna-
    tional. Taxicab and van service from
    Abraham Gonzales International
    Airport.

SELECTED HOTELS:

Colonial las Fuentes Motel, Avenida de
    las Américas & Avenida Lincoln,
    011/52/16/13-50-50
Holiday Inn Express, Paseo del Triunfo de
    la República 3745, 011/52/16/29-60-00
Lucerna Hotel, Paseo Triunfo de la
    República 3976, 011/52/16/11-29-11
Plaza Juárez, Avenida Lincoln &
    Coyoacán, 011/52/16/13-13-10
Villa del Sol Hotel, Paseo Triunfo de la
    República 339, 011/52/16/17-24-24

SELECTED RESTAURANTS:

Ajua, Avenida Lincoln & Coyoacán
Chihuahua Charlie's, Avenida Paseo
    Triunfo de la República & Avenida
    Lincoln
Los Arcos, Avenida Paseo Triunfo de la
    República & Avenida de Las Américas
Paso del Norte, Avenida Hermanos
    Escobar 3650

SELECTED ATTRACTIONS:

FONART (national arts and crafts gallery),
    Avenida Lincoln & Coyoacán
Guadalupe Mission, Avenida 16 de
    Septiembre & Plaza Central
Juárez Sports Book & Racetrack, Avenida
    Prop. Vincente Guererro
Mercado Juárez, Avenida 16 de
    Septiembre & Melgar
Pueblito Mexicano (shopping), Avenida
    Lincoln & Zempoala

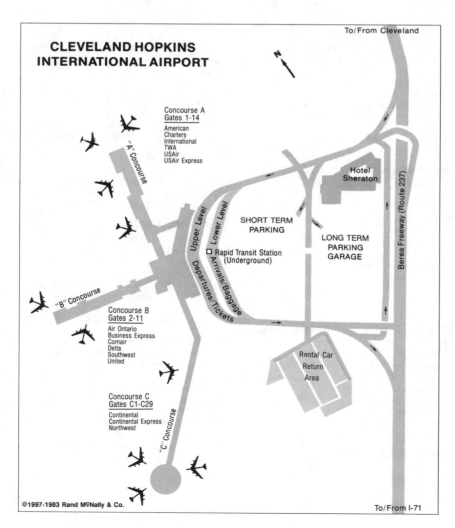

CLEVELAND HOPKINS INTERNATIONAL AIRPORT

To/From Cleveland

N

Concourse A
Gates 1-14
American
Charters
International
TWA
USAir
USAir Express

"A" Concourse

Hotel
Sheraton

SHORT TERM
PARKING

LONG TERM
PARKING
GARAGE

Berea Freeway (Route 237)

Upper Level
Lower Level
Departures/Tickets

Rapid Transit Station
(Underground)

Arrivals/Baggage

"B" Concourse

Concourse B
Gates 2-11
Air Ontario
Business Express
Comair
Delta
Southwest
United

Rental Car
Return
Area

Concourse C
Gates C1-C29
Continental
Continental Express
Northwest

"C" Concourse

©1997-1983 Rand McNally & Co.

To/From I-71

INFORMATION SOURCE:
Tourism Office
Eje Vial Juan Gabriel & Aserraderos
011/52/16/29-33-00

Cleveland, Ohio

City map: above
Population: (*2,142,100) 505,616 (1990C)
Altitude: 570 to 1,050 feet
Average Temp.: Jan., 29°F.; July, 74°F.
Telephone Area Code: 216
Time and Weather: 216/931-1212
Time Zone: Eastern

AIRPORT TRANSPORTATION:
See map at left.
Twelve miles from Hopkins to downtown
  Cleveland.
Taxicab, train, and limousine bus service.

SELECTED HOTELS:
Cleveland Airport Marriott, 4277 W. 150th
  St., 216/252-5333; FAX 216/251-1508
Cleveland Marriott East, 3663 Park East
  Dr., I-271 & Chagrin Blvd., Beachwood,
  216/464-5950; FAX 216/464-6539
Harley Hotel Cleveland East, 6051 S.O.M.
  Center Rd., Willoughby, 216/944-4300;
  FAX 216/944-5344
Harley Hotel Cleveland West, 17000
  Bagley Rd., Middleburg Heights,
  216/243-5200; FAX 216/243-5240
Hilton Inn Cleveland, 6200 Quarry Ln. at
  I-77 & Rockside Rd., Independence,
  216/447-1300; FAX 216/642-9334
Holiday Inn Lakeside, 1111 Lakeside Ave.,
  216/241-5100; FAX 216/241-7437
Renaissance Cleveland Hotel, 24 Public
  Sq., 216/696-5600; FAX 216/696-0432

The Ritz-Carlton, 1515 W. 3rd St.,
216/623-1300; FAX 216/623-1492
✈ Sheraton Airport Hotel, 5300 Riverside
Dr. at the airport, 216/267-1500;
FAX 216/265-3177
Sheraton Cleveland City Centre, 777 St.
Clair Ave., 216/771-7600;
FAX 216/566-0736

SELECTED RESTAURANTS:

Brasserie, in the Renaissance Cleveland
Hotel, 216/696-5600
Cafe Sausilito, in the Galleria Mall, E. 9th
St., 216/696-2233
Flat Iron Cafe, 1114 Center St.,
216/696-6968
Great Lakes Brewing Company, 2516 Mar-
ket St., 216/771-4404
Hickerson's at the Hanna, 1422 Euclid
Ave., 216/771-1818
Sammy's, 1400 W. 10th St., 216/523-5560
Samurai Japanese Steak House, 23611
Chagrin Blvd., Beachwood,
216/464-7575
That Place on Bellflower, 11401
Bellflower Rd., 216/231-4469

SELECTED ATTRACTIONS:

Cleveland Children's Museum, 10730
Euclid Ave., 216/791-7114
Cleveland Museum of Art, 11150 E.
Boulevard, on University Circle,
216/421-7340
Cleveland Museum of Natural History,
University Circle, 216/231-4600
The Galleria (shopping), East 9th at St.
Clair, 216/621-9999
Geauga Lake Amusement Park, 1060
Aurora Rd., Aurora, 216/562-7131
Health Museum, 8911 Euclid Ave.,
216/231-5010
Metroparks Zoo, 3900 Brookside Park Dr.,
216/661-6500
NASA Visitor Center, 21000 Brookpark
Rd., 216/433-4000
Sea World of Ohio, 1100 Sea World Dr.,
Aurora, 216/562-8101
Trolley Tours of Cleveland, 216/771-4484

INFORMATION SOURCES:

Convention and Visitors Bureau of Greater
Cleveland
3100 Terminal Tower
Cleveland, Ohio 44113
216/621-4110; 800/321-1001
Greater Cleveland Growth Association
200 Tower City Center
50 Public Square
Cleveland, Ohio 44113-2291
216/621-3300

Columbus, Ohio

City map: upper right
Population: (*1,085,700) 632,910 (1990C)
Altitude: 685 to 893 feet
Average Temp.: Jan., 31°F.; July, 76°F.
Telephone Area Code: 614
Time and Weather: 614/469-1010
Time Zone: Eastern

AIRPORT TRANSPORTATION:

Eight miles to downtown Columbus.
Taxicab and limousine bus service.

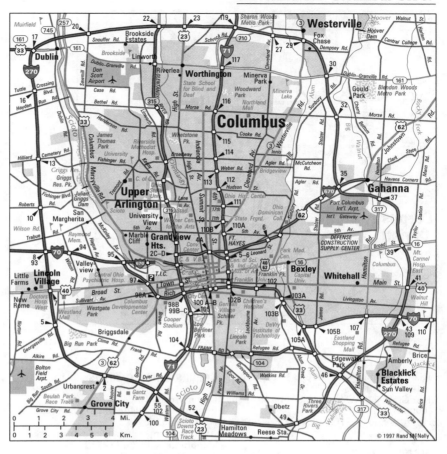

SELECTED HOTELS:

Adam's Mark Hotel, 50 N. 3rd. St. (due to
open Spring of 1997)
Best Western North, 888 E. Dublin-
Granville Rd., 614/888-8230;
FAX 614/846-5347
Best Western University, 3232 Olentangy
River Rd., 614/261-7141; FAX (same)
Clarion Hotel, 7007 N. High St., Worthing-
ton, 614/436-0700; FAX 614/436-1208
Columbus Marriott North, 6500
Doubletree Ave., 614/885-1885;
FAX 614/885-7222
✈ Concourse Hotel, 4300 International
Gateway, 614/237-2515;
FAX 614/237-6134
Harley Hotel of Columbus, 1000 E.
Dublin-Granville Rd., 614/888-4300;
FAX 614/888-3477
✈ Holiday Inn Airport, 750 Stelzer Rd.,
614/237-6360; FAX 614/237-2978
Holiday Inn Columbus East I-70, 4560
Hilton Corporate Dr., 614/868-1380;
FAX 614/863-3210
Holiday Inn on the Lane, 328 W. Lane
Ave., 614/294-4848; FAX 614/294-3390
Hyatt Regency Columbus, 350 N. High St.,
614/463-1234; FAX 614/463-9161

✈ Radisson Airport Hotel & Conference
Center, 1375 N. Cassidy Ave.,
614/475-7551; FAX 614/476-1476
Ramada Inn Columbus, 2124 S. Hamilton
Rd., 614/861-7220; FAX 614/866-9067
Westin Hotel Columbus, 310 S. High St.,
614/228-3800; FAX 614/228-7666

SELECTED RESTAURANTS:

The Clarmont, 684 S. High St.,
614/443-1125
Fifty-five on the Boulevard, 55
Nationwide Blvd., 614/228-5555
Handke's Cuisine, 520 S. Front St.,
614/621-2500
Hoster Brewing Co., 550 S. High St.,
614/228-6066
Hyde Park Grille, 1615 Old Henderson
Rd., 614/442-3310
Jai Lai, 1421 Olentangy River Rd.,
614/421-7337
Kahiki, 3583 E. Broad St., 614/237-5425
Morton's of Chicago, Two Nationwide
Plaza, 614/464-4442
One Nation, One Nationwide Plaza, 38th
Floor, 614/221-0151
The Refectory, 1092 Bethel Rd.,
614/451-9774

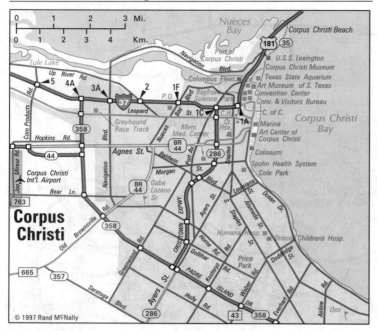

Corpus Christi

© 1997 Rand McNally

Rigsby's Cuisine Volatile, 698 N. High St., 614/461-7888
River Club, 679 W. Long St., 614/469-0000
Schmidt's Sausage Haus, 240 E. Kossuth St., 614/444-6808

SELECTED ATTRACTIONS:

Columbus Museum of Art, 480 E. Broad St., 614/221-6801
Columbus Zoo, 9990 Riverside Dr., Powell, 614/645-3400
COSI (science & industry museum), 280 E. Broad St., 614/228-COSI
Franklin Park Conservatory, 1777 E. Broad St., 614/645-3000
German Village Meeting House, 588 S. 3rd St., 614/221-8888
Ohio Historical Center/Ohio Village, 17th Ave. & I-71, 614/297-2300
Ohio Statehouse, Capitol Square, 614/752-9777
Santa Maria (ship replica), Battelle Riverfront Park, 614/645-8760
Wexner Center for the Arts, N. High St. at 15th Ave., 614/292-0330
Wyandot Lake (water & amusement park), 10101 Riverside Dr., 614/889-9283

INFORMATION SOURCES:

Greater Columbus Convention & Visitors Bureau
    10 W. Broad St., Suite 1300
    Columbus, Ohio 43215
    614/221-6623; 800/345-4FUN
Columbus Visitor Center
    Columbus City Center, Second Level, (walk-in tourist info.)
Greater Columbus Chamber
    37 N. High St.
    Columbus, Ohio 43215
    614/221-1321

Corpus Christi, Texas

City map: above
Population: (*294,000) 257,453 (1990C)
Altitude: 35 feet
Average Temp.: Jan., 56°F.; July, 85°F.
Telephone Area Code: 512
Time: 512/884-8463 **Weather:** 512/289-1861
Time Zone: Central

AIRPORT TRANSPORTATION:

Nine miles to downtown Corpus Christi. Taxicab, airport shuttle, and hotel shuttle service.

SELECTED HOTELS:

Best Western Sandy Shores Resort, 3200 Surfside Blvd., 512/883-7456; FAX 512/883-1437
Corpus Christi Marriott Bayfront, 900 N. Shoreline Blvd., 512/887-1600; FAX 512/887-6715
Holiday Inn Airport, 5549 Leopard St., 512/289-5100; FAX 512/289-6209
Holiday Inn Emerald Beach, 1102 S. Shoreline Blvd., 512/883-5731; FAX 512/883-9079
Howard Johnson Marina Hotel, 300 N. Shoreline Blvd., 512/883-5111; FAX 512/883-7702
La Quinta Inn South, 6225 S. Padre Island Dr., 512/991-5730; FAX 512/993-1578
Ramada Hotel Bayfront, 601 N. Water St., 512/882-8100; FAX 512/888-6540
Sheraton Corpus Christi Bayfront, 707 N. Shoreline Blvd., 512/882-1700; FAX 512/882-3113

SELECTED RESTAURANTS:

Catfish Charlie's, in Crossroads Shopping Village, Airline & McArdle, 512/993-0363
Edelweiss, No. 10 Crossroads Shopping Village, Airline & McArdle, 512/993-1901

Elmo's Staples St. Grille and Oyster Bar, 5253 S. Staples, 512/992-3474
The Lighthouse, 444 N. Shoreline, Lawrence St. T-Head, 512/883-3982
Water Street Seafood Company, 309 N. Water, 512/882-8683
Windows By the Bay, atop the Howard Johnson Hotel, 512/883-5111

SELECTED ATTRACTIONS:

Art Museum of South Texas, 1902 N. Shoreline, 512/884-3844
The Asian Cultures Museum & Education Center, Sunrise Mall (upper level), 5858 South Padre Island Dr., 512/993-3963
Centennial House, 411 Upper N. Broadway, 512/992-6003
The Columbus Fleet (*Niña, Pinta, Santa Maria* replicas), 1900 N. Chaparral, 512/883-4118
Corpus Christi Botanical Gardens, on S. Staples past Oso Creek, 512/852-2100
Corpus Christi Museum of Science & History, 1900 N. Chaparral, 512/883-2862
Hans A. Suter Wildlife Refuge, on Ennis Joslin overlooking Oso Bay
Heritage Park (restored houses), bordered by N. Chaparral & Mesquite sts., 512/883-0639
International Kite Museum, in the Best Western Sandy Shores, 3200 Surfside Blvd., 512/883-7456
Texas State Aquarium, 2710 N. Shoreline Blvd., underneath Harbor Bridge on Corpus Christi Beach, 512/881-1200
USS *Lexington* Museum on the Bay, off Corpus Christi Beach, 512/888-4873

INFORMATION SOURCES:

Corpus Christi Area Convention & Visitors Bureau
    1201 N. Shoreline
    P.O. Box 2664
    Corpus Christi, Texas 78403-2664
    512/881-1888; 800/678-OCEAN
Greater Corpus Christi Business Alliance
    1201 N. Shoreline
    P.O. Box 640
    Corpus Christi, Texas 78403
    512/881-1888

Dallas-Fort Worth, Texas

City map: pages 40–41
Population: (*3,606,600) Dallas 1,006,877; Fort Worth 447,619 (1990C)
Altitude: 463 to 750 feet
Average Temp.: Jan., 44°F.; July, 86°F.
Telephone Area Code: (Dallas) 214, 972 (Fort Worth) 817
Time: 817/844-6611 **Weather:** 817/787-1111
Time Zone: Central

AIRPORT TRANSPORTATION:

See map on page 39.
About 17 miles to downtown Dallas or Fort Worth.
Taxicab and limousine bus service.

SELECTED HOTELS: DALLAS

The Adolphus Hotel, 1321 Commerce St., 214/742-8200; FAX 214/651-3561

Courtyard by Marriott Las Colinas, 1151 W. Walnut Hill, Irving, 214/550-8100; FAX 214/550-0764

Dallas Grand Hotel, 1914 Commerce St., 214/747-7000; FAX 214/747-1342

Fairmont Hotel, 1717 N. Akard St., 214/720-2020; FAX 214/720-5269

Hyatt Regency Dallas, 300 Reunion Blvd., 214/651-1234; FAX 214/742-8126

✈ Hyatt Regency—Dallas-Fort Worth Airport, International Pkwy., 214/453-1234; FAX 214/456-8668

Le Meridien, 650 N. Pearl St., 214/979-9000; FAX 214/953-1931

The Mansion on Turtle Creek, 2821 Turtle Creek Blvd., 214/559-2100; FAX 214/528-4187

Omni Mandalay Hotel, 221 E. Las Colinas Blvd., Irving, 214/556-0800; FAX 214/556-0729

Quality Hotel Market Center, 2015 Market Center Blvd., 214/741-7481; FAX 214/747-6191

Renaissance Dallas Hotel, 2222 N. Stemmons Frwy., 214/631-2222; FAX 214/634-9319

Sheraton Park Central Hotel, 12720 Merit Dr., 214/385-3000; FAX 214/991-4557

Westin Hotel Galleria—Dallas, 13340 Dallas Pkwy., 214/934-9494; FAX 214/851-2869

Wyndham Anatole Hotel, 2201 Stemmons Frwy., 214/748-1200; FAX 214/748-7474

SELECTED RESTAURANTS: DALLAS

Beau Nash, Hotel Crescent Court, 400 Crescent Ct., 214/871-3200

Butcher Shop, 808 Munger Ave., 214/720-1032

Il Sorrento, 8616 Turtle Creek Blvd., 214/352-8759

Nana Grill, in the Wyndham Anatole Hotel, 214/748-7474

Old Warsaw, 2610 Maple Ave., 214/528-0032

The Pyramid Room, in the Fairmont Hotel, 214/720-5249

Sam's Cafe, 100 Crescent Ct. #140, 214/855-2233

650 North, Le Meridien Hotel, 214/979-9000

Sonny Bryan's Smokehouse II, 302 N. Market St., 214/744-1610

SELECTED ATTRACTIONS: DALLAS

Biblical Arts Center, 7500 Park Lane, 214/691-4661

Dallas Arboretum & Botanical Gardens, 8525 Garland Rd., 214/327-8263

Dallas Museum of Art, 1717 N. Harwood St., 214/922-1200

Dallas Zoo, in Marsalis Park, 621 E. Clarendon, 214/670-5656

Fair Park (museums), 214/670-8400

The Meadows Museum (14th-20th century Spanish art), Meadows School of the Arts, Bishop Blvd., Southern Methodist University campus, 214/768-2516

Old City Park (museum village), 1717 Gano, 214/421-5141

The Sixth Floor Museum (President John F. Kennedy educational exhibit), Houston & Elm St., 214/653-6666

West End Historic District, on the west end of Dallas' central business district

INFORMATION SOURCES: DALLAS

Dallas Convention & Visitors Bureau
  1201 Elm St., Suite 2000
  Dallas, Texas 75270
  214/746-6677

Greater Dallas Chamber of Commerce Information Department
  1201 Elm St., Suite 2000
  Dallas, Texas 75270
  214/746-6700

SELECTED HOTELS: FORT WORTH

Best Western Mid-Cities Inn, 125 NE. Loop I-820, Hurst, 817/284-9461; FAX 817/284-2126

Courtyard by Marriott, 3150 Riverfront Dr., 817/335-1300; FAX 817/336-6926

Green Oaks Inn, 6901 W. Freeway, 817/738-7311; FAX 817/377-1308

Hampton Inn Fort Worth West, 2700 Cherry Lane, 817/560-4180; FAX 817/560-8032

Holiday Inn Fort Worth Center, 2000 Beach St., 817/534-4801; FAX 817/534-2761

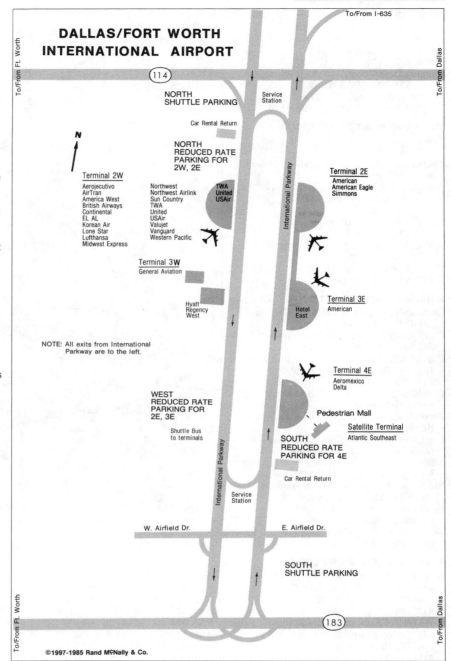

DALLAS/FORT WORTH INTERNATIONAL AIRPORT

To/From I-635

To/From Ft. Worth

To/From Dallas

114

NORTH SHUTTLE PARKING

Service Station

Car Rental Return

NORTH REDUCED RATE PARKING FOR 2W, 2E

N

Terminal 2W
Aerojecutivo
AirTran
America West
British Airways
Continental
EL AL
Korean Air
Lone Star
Lufthansa
Midwest Express

Northwest
Northwest Airlink
Sun Country
TWA
United
USAir
Valujet
Vanguard
Western Pacific

TWA
United
USAir

Terminal 2E
American
American Eagle
Simmons

International Parkway

Terminal 3W
General Aviation

Hyatt Regency West

Terminal 3E
American

Hotel East

NOTE: All exits from International Parkway are to the left.

WEST REDUCED RATE PARKING FOR 2E, 3E

Shuttle Bus to terminals

Terminal 4E
Aeromexico
Delta

Pedestrian Mall

Satellite Terminal
Atlantic Southeast

SOUTH REDUCED RATE PARKING FOR 4E

Car Rental Return

International Parkway

Service Station

W. Airfield Dr.

E. Airfield Dr.

SOUTH SHUTTLE PARKING

To/From Ft. Worth

To/From Dallas

183

©1997-1985 Rand McNally & Co.

Holiday Inn Fort Worth South, 100 Alta
Mesa E. Blvd., 817/293-3088;
FAX 817/551-5877

Radisson Plaza, 815 Main St.,
817/870-2100; FAX 817/882-1300

Ramada Downtown, 1701 Commerce St.,
817/335-7000; FAX 817/335-3333

Worthington Hotel, 200 Main St.,
817/870-1000; FAX 817/338-9176

SELECTED RESTAURANTS: FORT WORTH

The Balcony, 6100 Camp Bowie Blvd.,
817/731-3719

Cactus Bar & Grill, in the Radisson Plaza,
817/870-2100

Juanita's, 115 W. 2nd St., 817/335-1777

Prego's Pasta House, 301 Main St.,
817/870-1908

Riscky's Bar-B-Q, 300 Main St.,
817/877-3306

Rodeo Steakhouse, 1309 Calhoun St.,
817/332-1288

7th St. Cafe, 3500 W. 7th St.,
817/870-1672

SELECTED ATTRACTIONS: FORT WORTH

Botanic Gardens, 3220 Botanic Garden
Blvd., 817/871-7686

Cattleman's Museum, 1301 W. Seventh
St., 817/332-7064

Fort Worth Museum of Science and
History, 1501 Montgomery St.,
817/732-1631

Fort Worth Zoo, 1989 Colonial Pkwy.,
817/871-7050 or -7051

Kimbell Art Museum, 3333 Camp Bowie
Blvd., 817/332-8451

Log Cabin Village, on University across
from the zoo, 817/926-5881

Modern Art Museum of Fort Worth, 1309
Montgomery St., 817/738-9215

Sid Richardson Collection of Western Art,
309 Main St., 817/332-6554

Stockyard Station Market, 130 E.
Exchange, 817/625-9715

Tarantula Train, 140 E. Exchange,
817/625-RAIL

INFORMATION SOURCES: FORT WORTH

Fort Worth Convention & Visitors Bureau
415 Throckmorton St.
Fort Worth, Texas 76102
817/336-8791; 800/433-5747

Fort Worth Chamber of Commerce
777 Taylor, Suite 900
Fort Worth, Texas 76102-4997
817/336-2491

Dayton, Ohio

City map: page 42
Population: (*780,000) 182,044 (1990C)
Altitude: 757 feet
Average Temp.: Jan., 26°F.; July, 74°F.
Telephone Area Code: 973
Time and Weather: 973/499-1212
Time Zone: Eastern

AIRPORT TRANSPORTATION:

Seven miles to downtown Dayton.
Taxicab and limousine service.

SELECTED HOTELS:

Crowne Plaza Hotel, 33 E. 5th St.,
973/224-0800; FAX 973/224-3913

Days Inn Downtown, 330 W. 1st St.,
973/223-7131; FAX (same)

✈ Dayton Airport Inn, at Dayton Int'l.
Airport, Vandalia, 973/898-1000;
FAX 973/898-3761

Dayton Marriott, 1414 S. Patterson Blvd.,
973/223-1000; FAX 973/223-7853

Radisson Hotel & Suites, 111 S. Ludlow
St., 973/461-4700; FAX 973/224-9160

Radisson Inn North Dayton, 2401
Needmore Rd. at I-75, 973/278-5711;
FAX 973/278-6148

Ramada Inn, 800 N. Broad St., Fairborn,
973/879-3920; FAX 973/879-3896

Ramada Inn North, 4079 Little York Rd.,
973/890-9500; FAX 973/890-8525

SELECTED RESTAURANTS:

Jay's Seafood, 225 E. 6th St., 973/222-2892

King Cole Restaurant, in the Kettering
Tower, 2nd & Main sts., 973/222-6771

L'Auberge. 4120 Far Hills Ave.,
973/299-5536

Peerless Mill Inn, 319 S. 2nd St.,
Miamisburg, 973/866-5968

The Pine Club, 1926 Brown St.,
973/228-7463

Windows, in the Crowne Plaza Hotel,
973/224-0800

SELECTED ATTRACTIONS:

Aviation Trail (self-guided driving tour),
973/443-0793

Carriage Hill Farm (1880s living history
farm), 7800 Shull Rd., 973/879-0461

The Citizens Motorcar Company, A
Packard Museum, 420 S. Ludlow St.,
973/226-1917

Dayton Art Institute, 456 Belmont Park N.,
973/223-5277

Dayton Museum of Natural History, 2600
DeWeese Pkwy., 973/275-7431

International Women's Air and Space
Museum, 26 N. Main St., Centerville,
973/433-6766

SunWatch (archaeological Indian site),
2301 W. River Rd., 973/268-8199

United States Air Force Museum/IMAX
Theatre, Springfield & Harshman,
973/255-3284

Wright Cycle Company/Dayton Aviation
Heritage National Historical Park (open
daily Memorial Day–Labor Day; weekends year-round or by appointment) 22
S. Williams St., 973/225-7705

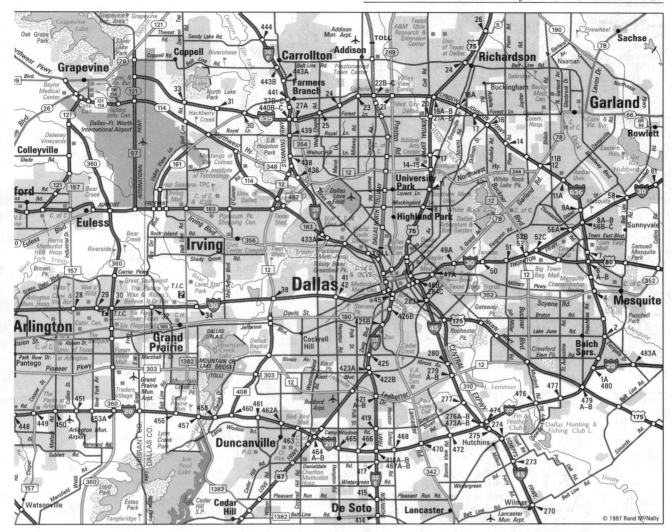

INFORMATION SOURCES:

Dayton/Montgomery County Convention
and Visitors Bureau
  1 Chamber Plaza, Suite A
  Dayton, Ohio 45402-2400
  973/226-8211
  800/221-8234 (Ohio)
  800/221-8235 (Elsewhere)
Dayton Area Chamber of Commerce
  1 Chamber Plaza
  Dayton, Ohio 45402-2400
  973/226-1444

Denver, Colorado

City map: page 42
Population: (*1,617,900) 467,610 (1990C)
Altitude: 5,280 feet
Average Temp.: Jan., 31°F.; July, 74°F.
Telephone Area Code: 303
Time and Weather: 303/337-2500
Time Zone: Mountain

AIRPORT TRANSPORTATION:

See map on page 43.
Twenty-three miles to downtown Denver.
Bus, taxicab, and limousine bus service.

SELECTED HOTELS:

Adam's Mark Hotel, 1550 Court Pl.,
  303/893-3333; FAX 303/892-0521
The Brown Palace Hotel, 321 17th St.,
  303/297-3111; FAX 303/293-9204
The Burnsley All Suite Hotel, 1000 Grant
  St., 303/830-1000; FAX 303/830-7676
Denver Marriott—City Center, 1701
  California St., 303/297-1300;
  FAX 303/298-7474
Denver Marriott Southeast, 6363 E.
  Hampden Ave., 303/758-7000;
  FAX 303/691-3418
Doubletree Hotel, 13696 E. Iliff Pl.,
  Aurora, 303/337-2800;
  FAX 303/752-0296
Holiday Inn Denver Downtown, 1450
  Glenarm Pl., 303/573-1450;
  FAX 303/572-1113
Hyatt Regency Denver, 1750 Welton St.,
  303/295-1200; FAX 303/292-2472
Oxford Hotel, 1600 17th St.,
  303/628-5400; FAX 303/628-5413
The Red Lion Hotel, 3203 Quebec St.,
  303/321-3333; FAX 303/329-9179
Stapleton Plaza Hotel, 3333 Quebec St.,
  303/321-3500; FAX 303/322-7343

SELECTED RESTAURANTS:

Ellyngton's, in The Brown Palace Hotel,
  303/297-3111
European Café, 1515 Market,
  303/825-6555
Marlowe's, Glenarm & 16th St.,
  303/595-3700
Normandy French Restaurant, 1515
  Madison St., 303/321-3311
Palace Arms, in The Brown Palace Hotel,
  303/297-3111
Racine's, 850 Bannock, 303/595-0418
Strings, 1700 Humboldt, 303/831-7310
Tante Louise, 4900 E. Colfax Ave.,
  303/355-4488

SELECTED ATTRACTIONS:

Baby Doe's Matchless Mine, 2520 W. 23rd
  Ave., 303/433-3386
Buffalo Bill's Grave and Museum, top of
  Lookout Mountain, 303/526-0747
Children's Museum of Denver, 2121
  Children's Museum Dr., 303/433-7444
Colorado Railroad Museum, 17155 W.
  44th Ave., Golden, 303/279-4591
Coors Brewing Company (tours), 13th &
  Ford sts., Golden, 303/277-BEER

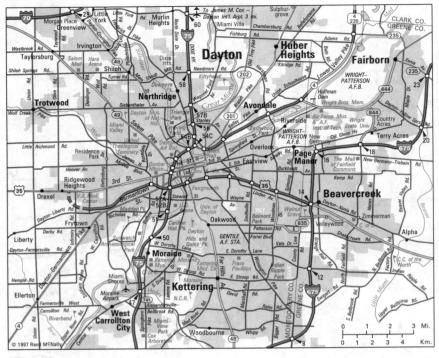

Denver Center for the Performing Arts,
14th & Curtis sts., 303/893-4100
Denver Museum of Natural History, 20th
& Colorado Blvd. in City Park,
303/322-7009
Denver's Zoo, 23rd and Steele St., north of
City Park, 303/331-4110
Larimer Square (restored Victorian-era
section of Denver), 1400 block of
Larimer
Molly Brown House Museum, 1340
Pennsylvania, 303/832-4092
United States Mint, 320 W. Colfax Ave.,
303/844-3582

INFORMATION SOURCES:

Denver Metro Convention and Visitors
Bureau
 Visitor Center
 225 W. Colfax Ave.
 Denver, Colorado 80202
 303/892-1112; 800/645-3446
Denver Metro Chamber of Commerce
 1445 Market St.
 Denver, Colorado 80202
 303/534-8500

Des Moines, Iowa

City map: page 43
Population: (*338,200) 193,187 (1990C)
Altitude: 803 feet
Average Temp.: Jan., 21°F.; July, 76°F.
Telephone Area Code: 515
Time: 515/244-5611 **Weather:**
 515/270-2614
Time Zone: Central

AIRPORT TRANSPORTATION:

Six miles to downtown Des Moines.
Taxicab and limousine service.

SELECTED HOTELS:

Best Western Bavarian Inn, 5220 NE 14th
 St., 515/265-5611; FAX 515/265-1669
✈ Best Western Des Moines International,
 1810 Army Post Rd., 515/287-6464;
 FAX 515/287-5818
Best Western Des Moines—West, 11040
 Hickman Rd., Clive, 515/278-5575;
 FAX 515/278-4078
Best Western Inn—Ankeny, 133 SE
 Delaware, Ankeny, 515/964-1717;
 FAX 515/964-8781
Best Western Starlite Village, 929 3rd St.,
 515/282-5251; FAX 515/282-6871
Des Moines Marriott, 700 Grand Ave.,
 515/245-5500; FAX 515/245-5567
Executive Inn, 3530 Westown Pkwy., West
 Des Moines, 515/225-1144;
 FAX 515/225-6463
✈ Hampton Inn, 5001 Fleur Dr.,
 515/287-7300; FAX 515/287-6343
✈ Holiday Inn Airport, 6111 Fleur Dr.,
 515/287-2400; FAX 515/287-4811
Holiday Inn Downtown, 1050 6th Ave.,
 515/283-0151; FAX (same)
Holiday Inn—Merle Hay, 5000 Merle Hay
 Rd., 515/278-0271; FAX 515/276-8172
Holiday Inn—University Park, 1800 50th
 St., West Des Moines, 515/223-1800;
 FAX 515/223-0894

SELECTED RESTAURANTS:

Aunt Butch's Bistro, 1700 Woodland Ave.,
 515/244-3365

Bavarian Haus, in the Best Western
  Bavarian Inn, 515/266-1173
801 Steak & Chop House, 801 Grand Ave.,
  Suite 200, 515/288-6000
The Gotham Club, in the Hotel Fort Des
  Moines, 10th & Walnut, 515/243-1161
The Mandarin Chinese Restaurant, 3520
  Beaver, 515/277-6263
Quenelles, in the Des Moines Marriott
  Hotel, 515/245-5500
Tokyo Steak House, 2900 University, in
  Clocktower Square, West Des Moines,
  515/225-3325
Waterfront Seafood Market, 2900
  University Ave., in Clocktower Square,
  West Des Moines, 515/223-5106

SELECTED ATTRACTIONS:

Adventureland Theme Park, Jct. I-80 & US
  65, Altoona, 515/266-2121
Blank Park Zoo (open May through Oct.),
  7401 SW 9th St., 515/285-4722
Des Moines Art Center, 4700 Grand Ave.,
  515/277-4405
Living History Farms, 2600 NW 111th St.,
  515/278-5286
Prairie Meadows (horse track), 1 Prairie
  Meadows Dr., Altoona, 515/967-1000
Salisbury House (museum: weekday tours
  by appointment), 4025 Tonawanda Dr.,
  515/279-9711
Science Center of Iowa, 4500 Grand Ave.,
  515/274-4138
Terrace Hill (mansion), 2300 Grand Ave.,
  515/281-3604
White Water University (water park), 5401
  E. University, 515/265-4904

INFORMATION SOURCES:

Greater Des Moines Convention & Visitors
Bureau
  Ruan II, Suite 222
  601 Locust
  Des Moines, Iowa 50309
  515/286-4960; 800/451-2625
Greater Des Moines Chamber of
Commerce Federation
  601 Locust, Suite 100
  Des Moines, Iowa 50309
  515/286-4950

Detroit, Michigan

City map: page 45
Population: (*4,348,100) 1,027,974
  (1990C)
Altitude: 573 to 672 feet
Average Temp.: Jan., 26°F.; July, 73°F.
Telephone Area Code: 313
Time: 313/472-1212 **Weather:**
  313/941-7192
Time Zone: Eastern

AIRPORT TRANSPORTATION:

See map on page 44.
Nineteen miles from Metropolitan Airport
  to downtown Detroit.
Taxicab and limousine bus service.

SELECTED HOTELS:

✈ Clarion Inn—Metro Airport, 31200
  Industrial Expy., Romulus,
  313/728-2800; FAX 313/728-2260
Crowne Plaza Pontchartrain, 2
  Washington Blvd., 313/965-0200;
  FAX 313/965-9464

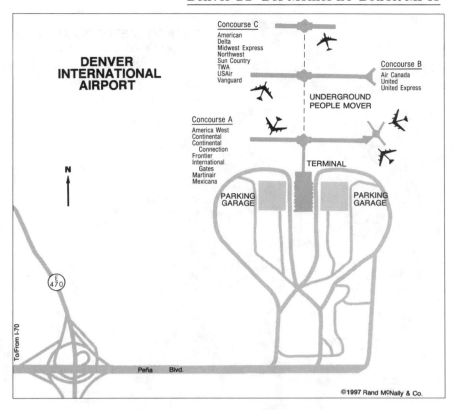

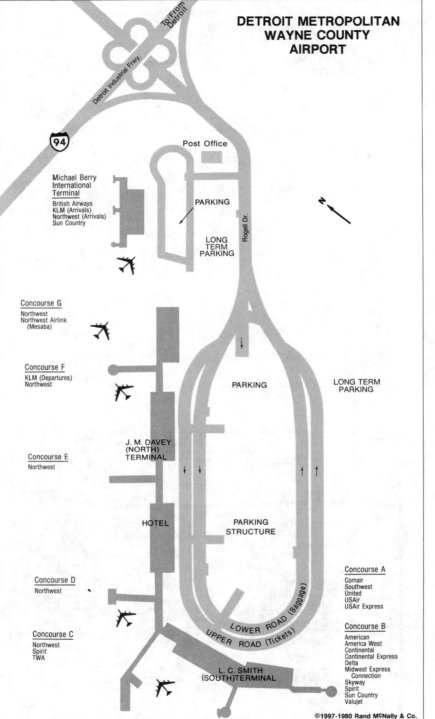

DETROIT METROPOLITAN WAYNE COUNTY AIRPORT

To/From Detroit

Detroit Industrial Frwy.

94

Post Office

Michael Berry International Terminal
British Airways
KLM (Arrivals)
Northwest (Arrivals)
Sun Country

PARKING

Rogell Dr.

LONG TERM PARKING

Concourse G
Northwest
Northwest Airlink
(Mesaba)

Concourse F
KLM (Departures)
Northwest

PARKING

LONG TERM PARKING

J. M. DAVEY
(NORTH)
TERMINAL

Concourse E
Northwest

HOTEL

PARKING STRUCTURE

Concourse D
Northwest

Concourse A
Comair
Southwest
United
USAir
USAir Express

LOWER ROAD (Baggage)
UPPER ROAD (Tickets)

Concourse B
American
America West
Continental
Continental Express
Delta
Midwest Express
Connection
Skyway
Spirit
Sun Country
Valujet

Concourse C
Northwest
Spirit
TWA

L. C. SMITH
(SOUTH)TERMINAL

©1997-1980 Rand McNally & Co.

Hotel St. Regis, 3071 W. Grand Blvd.,
313/873-3000; FAX 313/873-2574
Hyatt Regency Dearborn, Fairlane Town
Center Dr., Dearborn, 313/593-1234;
FAX 313/593-3366
Northfield Hilton, 5500 Crooks Rd., Troy,
810/879-2100; FAX 810/879-6054
Omni International, 333 E. Jefferson Ave.,
313/222-7700; FAX 313/222-6509
The Plaza, 16400 J.L. Hudson Dr.,
Southfield, 810/559-6500;
FAX 810/559-3625
Royce Hotel, 31500 Wick Rd., Romulus,
313/467-8000; FAX 313/721-8870
The Westin Hotel Renaissance,
Renaissance Center, 313/568-8000;
FAX 313/568-8146

SELECTED RESTAURANTS:
Carl's Chop House, 3020 Grand River
Ave., 313/833-0700
Caucus Club, 150 W. Congress St.,
313/965-4970
Charley's Crab, 5498 Crooks Rd., Troy,
810/879-2060
The Golden Mushroom, 18100 W. 10 Mile
Rd., Southfield, 810/559-4230
Joe Muer's Sea Food, 2000 Gratiot Ave.,
313/567-1088
Mario's Restaurant, 4222 2nd Ave.,
313/832-1616
Opus One, 565 E. Larned, 313/961-7766
St. Regis Restaurant, in the St. Regis
Hotel, 3071 W. Grand Blvd.,
313/873-3000
The Summit, in the Westin Hotel
Renaissance, 313/568-8000
Van Dyke Place, 649 Van Dyke Ave.,
313/821-2620

SELECTED ATTRACTIONS:
Cranbrook Art Museum, 1221 N. Wood-
ward, Bloomfield Hills,
810/645-3312 or 810/645-3323
Detroit Institute of Arts, 5200 Woodward
Ave., 313/833-7900
Detroit Zoological Park, 8450 W. Ten Mile
Rd., Royal Oak, 810/398-0900
Edsel & Eleanor Ford House, 1100
Lakeshore Rd., Grosse Pointe Shores,
313/884-3400 or 313/884-4222
Henry Ford Estate-Fair Lane, University of
Michigan—Dearborn campus, west side
of Evergreen between Ford Rd. &
Michigan Ave., Dearborn, 313/593-5590
Henry Ford Museum & Greenfield Village,
20900 Oakwood Blvd., Dearborn,
313/271-1620
Motown Museum, 2648 W. Grand Blvd.,
313/875-2264

INFORMATION SOURCES:
Metropolitan Detroit Convention &
Visitors Bureau
Suite 1900, 100 Renaissance Center
Detroit, Michigan 48243
313/259-4333; 800/DETROIT
Metropolitan Detroit Visitor Information
Center
Suite 1900, 100 Renaissance Center
Detroit, Michigan 48243
800/338-7648
Greater Detroit Chamber of Commerce
600 W. Lafayette
P.O. Box 33840
Detroit, Michigan 48232-0840
313/964-4000

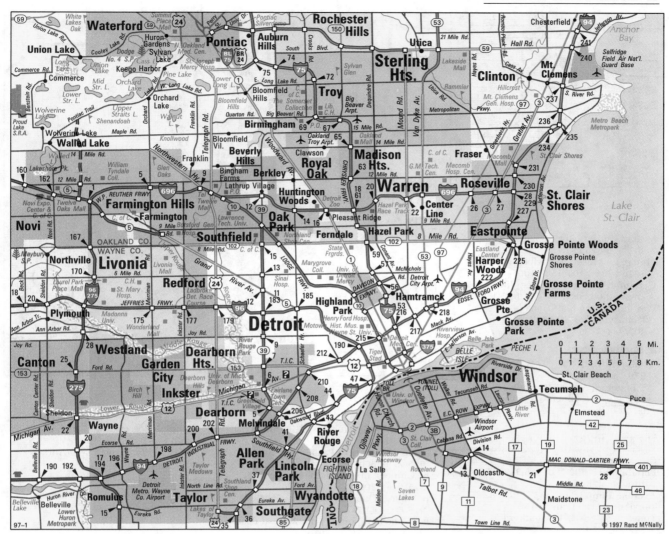

Edmonton, Alberta, Canada

City map: page 46
Population: (*839,924) 616,741 (1991C)
Altitude: 2,192 feet
Average Temp.: Jan., 6°F.; July, 62°F.
Telephone Area Code: 403
Time and Weather: 403/449-4444
Time Zone: Mountain

AIRPORT TRANSPORTATION:

Eighteen miles from Edmonton International to downtown Edmonton; three miles from Edmonton Municipal to downtown Edmonton.
Taxicab; Airporter bus to and from Edmonton International; shuttle service between Edmonton International and Edmonton Municipal.

SELECTED HOTELS:

Best Western Westwood Inn, 18035 Stony Plain Rd., 403/483-7770;
   FAX 403/486-1769
Convention Inn, 4404 Calgary Trail, 403/434-6415; FAX 403/436-9247
Crowne Plaza Chateau Lacombe, 10111 Bellamy Hill, 403/428-6611;
   FAX 403/425-6564
Delta Edmonton Centre Suite Hotel, 10222 102nd St., 403/429-3900;
   FAX 403/428-1566
Edmonton Hilton, 10235 101st St., 403/428-7111; FAX 403/441-3098
Edmonton Inn, 11830 Kingsway Ave., 403/454-9521; FAX 403/453-7360
Edmonton Renaissance Hotel, 10155 105th St., 403/423-4811;
   FAX 403/423-3204
Howard Johnson Plaza Hotel, 10010 104th St., 403/423-2450; FAX 403/426-6090
✈ Nisku Inn, 4th St. & 11th Ave., across from International Airport,
   403/955-7744; FAX 403/955-7743
The Westin Hotel, 10135 100th St., 403/426-3636; FAX 403/428-1454

SELECTED RESTAURANTS:

Boulevard Café, in the Edmonton Renaissance Hotel, 403/423-4811
The Carvery, in the Westin Hotel, 403/426-3636
Claude's, 9797 Jasper Ave., in the Convention Center, 403/429-2900
Earl's Tin Palace, 11830 Jasper Ave., 403/488-6582
Hard Rock Cafe, 1638 Bourbon St., in West Edmonton Mall, 403/444-1905
Japanese Village, 10126 100th St., 403/422-6083
La Ronde, in the Crowne Plaza Chateau Lacombe, 403/428-6611
The Mill, 8109 101st St., 403/432-1838
Top of the Inn, in the Convention Inn Hotel, 403/434-6415

SELECTED ATTRACTIONS:

Alberta Railway Museum (not open in winter), 24215 34th St. NE, 403/472-6229
Edmonton Space & Science Centre, 11211 142nd St., 403/451-7722
Elk Island National Park, 35 mi. east on Hwy. 16, 403/992-2950
Fort Edmonton Park, Whitemud & Fox drs., 403/496-8787

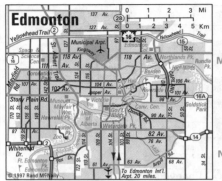

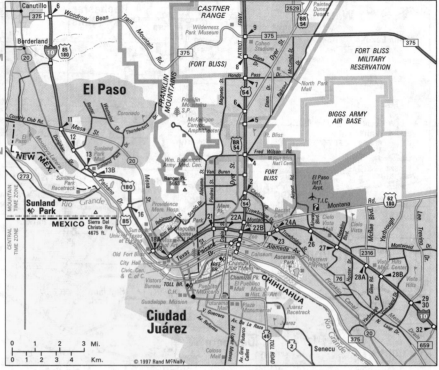

Muttart Conservatory, 9626 96 A St.,
403/496-8755
Provincial Museum of Alberta, 128th St. &
102nd Ave., 403/453-9100
Ukrainian Cultural Heritage Village, 35
km. east on Hwy. 16, 403/662-3640
West Edmonton Mall/Canada
Fantasyland, 8770 170th St.,
403/444-5200

INFORMATION SOURCE:
Edmonton Tourism
9797 Jasper Ave.
Edmonton, Alberta, Canada T5J 1N9
403/426-4715; 800/463-4667
(Cont'l USA)

El Paso, Texas

City map: upper right
Population: (*592,100) 515,342 (1990C)
Altitude: 3,762 feet
Average Temp.: Jan., 44°F.; July, 82°F.
Telephone Area Code: 915
Time: 915/585-7276 **Weather:**
915/562-4040
Time Zone: Mountain

AIRPORT TRANSPORTATION:
Eight miles to downtown El Paso.
Taxicab, airporter shuttle, and hotel
shuttle service.

SELECTED HOTELS:
✈ Best Western Airport Inn, 7144
Gateway East, 915/779-7700;
FAX 915/772-1920
Camino Real Paso del Norte, 101 S. El
Paso St., 915/534-3000;
FAX 915/534-3014
✈ El Paso Airport Hilton, 2027 Airway
Blvd., 915/778-4241; FAX 915/772-6871
✈ El Paso Marriott, 1600 Airway Blvd.,
915/779-3300; FAX 915/772-0915
✈ Embassy Suites, 6100 Gateway East,
915/779-6222; FAX 915/779-8846
✈ Holiday Inn Airport, 6655 Gateway
West, 915/778-6411; FAX 915/778-6517
Holiday Inn Park Place, 325 N. Kansas,
915/533-8241; FAX 915/544-9979
La Quinta El Paso West, 7550 Remcon
Circle, 915/833-2522;
FAX 915/581-9303

SELECTED RESTAURANTS:
Bella Napoli Ristorante, 6331 N. Mesa,
915/584-3321

Bombay Bicycle Club, 6080 Gateway East,
915/778-4251
Chatfield's, in the El Paso Marriott,
915/779-3300
The Cinders, in the International Hotel,
915/544-3300
Doc's Bar-B-Que, 8220 Gateway East,
915/593-DOCS
The Dome Grill, in the Camino Real Paso
del Norte, 915/534-3010
El Rancho Escondido, 14549 Montana,
915/857-1184
Forti's Mexican Elder, 321 Chelsea,
915/772-0066
Seafarer Seafood, 1711 Lee Trevino,
915/593-8388
Windows, 21st floor of the State National
Bank, 221 N. Kansas, 915/534-3084

SELECTED ATTRACTIONS:
Americana Museum, 5 Civic Center Plaza,
915/542-0394
El Paso Museum of Art, 1211 Montana,
915/541-4040
El Paso Museum of History, 12901
Gateway W., 915/858-1928
El Paso Zoo, 4001 E. Paisano,
915/544-1928
Fort Bliss Museums, Pleasanton Rd.,
Building 5000 & Buildings 5051-5054,
915/568-7345
Historic missions: San Elizario Presidio,
Socorro Mission, Ysleta Mission,
915/534-0630
Insights-El Paso Science Museum, 505 N.
Santa Fe St., 915/534-0000
Juarez trolley tour, El Paso-Juarez Trolley
Co., One Civic Center Plaza,
915/544-0061
Magoffin Home, 1120 Magoffin,
915/533-5147

Tigua Indian Reservation, 119 S. Old
Pueblo Rd., 915/859-7913
Wet 'n' Wild Waterworld, I-10 Anthony
Exit "0", 915/886-2222

INFORMATION SOURCES:
El Paso Convention & Visitors Bureau
One Civic Center Plaza
El Paso, Texas 79901
915/534-0696; 800/351-6024
El Paso Chamber of Commerce
10 Civic Center Plaza
El Paso, Texas 79901
915/534-0500

Fargo, North Dakota

City map: page 47
Population: (*125,400) 74,111 (1990C)
Altitude: 900 feet
Average Temp.: Jan., 6°F.; July, 71°F.
Telephone Area Code: 701
Time: (none) **Weather:** 701/235-2600
Time Zone: Central

AIRPORT TRANSPORTATION:
Two miles to downtown Fargo.
Taxicab and hotel shuttle service.

SELECTED HOTELS:
✈ Airport Dome Days Inn, 1507 19th Ave.
N., 701/232-0000; FAX 701/237-4464
Best Western Doublewood Inn, 3333 13th
Ave. S., 701/235-3333;
FAX 701/280-9482
Comfort Inn East, 1407 35th St. S.,
701/280-9666; FAX 701/235-0948
Country Suites by Carlson, 3316 13th Ave.
S., 701/234-0565; FAX (same)
Holiday Inn, 3803 13th Ave. S.,
701/282-2700; FAX 701/281-1240

Holiday Inn Express, 1040 40th St. S.,
701/282-2000; FAX 701/282-4721
Madison Hotel, 600 30th Ave. S.,
Moorhead, 218/233-6171;
FAX 218/233-0945
Radisson Hotel Fargo, 201 5th St. N.,
701/232-7363; FAX 701/298-9134
Ramada Plaza Suites, 1635 42nd St. SW,
701/232-7000; FAX 701/281-7145
River Inn, 301 3rd Ave. N.,
701/232-8851; FAX 701/235-8701
✈ Select Inn of Fargo, 1025 38th St. SW,
701/282-6300; FAX 701/282-6308

SELECTED RESTAURANTS:
The Dakota Grill, in the Best Western
Doublewood Inn, 701/235-3333
Fargo Cork, 3301 S. University Dr.,
701/237-6790
Gallery Terrace & Cafe, in the Holiday Inn,
701/282-2700
The Grainery, in West Acres Shopping
Center, 42nd St. & 13th Ave.,
701/282-6262
Old Broadway, 22 Broadway,
701/237-6161
Passages, in the Radisson Hotel,
701/232-7363
Tree Top, 403 Center Ave., Moorhead,
218/233-1393

SELECTED ATTRACTIONS:
Bonanzaville (pioneer village & museum),
W. Main Ave., West Fargo,
701/282-2822
Children's Museum at Yunker Farm,
University Dr. & 28th Ave. N.,
701/232-6102
Comstock House, 506 8th St. S.,
Moorhead, MN, 218/233-0848
Hjemkomst Center/Clay County Historical
Society, 202 First Ave. N., Moorhead,
MN, 218/233-5604
Planetarium, Moorhead State University-
Bridges Hall, Rm. 167, 11th St. & 8th
Ave. S., Moorhead, MN, 218/236-3982
Roger Maris Museum, West Acres
Shopping Mall, I-29 & 13th Ave. S.,
701/282-2222
Trollwood Park, Trollwood Dr. between N.
Broadway & Elm St., 701/241-8160

INFORMATION SOURCES:
Fargo-Moorhead Convention & Visitors
Bureau
2001 44th St. SW
Fargo, North Dakota 58103
701/282-3653; 800/235-7654
Fargo Chamber of Commerce
321 N. 4th St.
P.O. Box 2443
Fargo, North Dakota 58108
701/237-5678

Fresno, California

City map: upper right
Population: (*515,000) 354,202 (1990C)
Altitude: 296 feet
Average Temp.: Jan., 45°F.; July, 81°F.
Telephone Area Code: 209
Time: 767-8900 **Weather:** 209/291-1068
Time Zone: Pacific

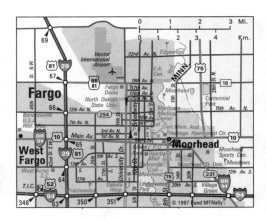

AIRPORT TRANSPORTATION:
Seven miles to downtown Fresno.
Taxicab, city bus, and hotel shuttle
service.

SELECTED HOTELS:
Best Western Tradewinds, 2141 N.
Parkway Dr., 209/237-1881;
FAX 209/237-9719
Courtyard by Marriott, 140 E. Shaw Ave.,
209/221-6000; FAX 209/221-0368
Fresno Hilton Inn, 1055 Van Ness St.,
209/485-9000; FAX 209/485-3210
✈ Holiday Inn—Airport, 5090 E. Clinton
Ave., 209/252-3611; FAX 209/456-8243
Holiday Inn—Fresno Centre Plaza, 2233
Ventura Ave., 209/268-1000;
FAX 209/486-6625
Piccadilly Inn—University, 4961 N. Cedar
Ave., 209/224-4200; FAX 209/227-2382
Ramada Inn, 324 E. Shaw Ave.,
209/224-4040; FAX 209/222-4017
The San Joaquin Hotel, 1309 W. Shaw
Ave., 209/225-1309; FAX 209/225-6021
Sheraton Smuggler's Inn, 3737 N.
Blackstone Ave., 209/226-2200;
FAX 209/222-7147

SELECTED RESTAURANTS:
Daily Planet, 1211 N. Wishon,
209/266-4259
Gaslight Steak House, in the Best Western
Tradewinds, 209/237-1881
Harland's, 722 W. Shaw, 209/225-7100
Nicola's, 3075 N. Maroa, 209/224-1660
The Old Spaghetti Factory, 1610 E. Shaw,
209/222-1066
Pizzetta's, in the Holiday Inn—Fresno
Centre Plaza, 209/268-1000
The Remington, 927 S. Clovis Ave.,
209/251-8228
Richard's, 1609 E. Belmont, 209/266-4077
Stuart Anderson's Black Angus, 1737 E.
Shaw, 209/224-2205

SELECTED ATTRACTIONS:
Blackbeard's Family Entertainment
Center, 4055 N. Chestnut, 209/292-4554
The Blossom Trail (Feb.-March),
209/233-0836
Chaffee Zoo, in Roeding Park, 894 W.
Belmont, 209/498-2671
Forestiere Underground Gardens (closed
in winter), 5021 W. Shaw Ave.,
209/271-0734
Fresno Art Museum, 2233 N. First St.,
209/441-4221
Fresno Metropolitan Museum of Art,
History & Science, 1515 Van Ness Ave.,
209/441-1444
Kearney Mansion Museum, in Kearney
Park, 209/441-0862
Meux Home, Tulare & "R" sts.,
209/233-8007
Simonian Farms, 2629 S. Clovis Ave.,
209/237-2294
Wild Water Adventures Water Park, 11413
E. Shaw Ave., Clovis, 209/297-6500
Yosemite Mountain Sugar Pine Railroad,
56001 CA 41, 2 miles south of Fish
Camp, 209/683-7273

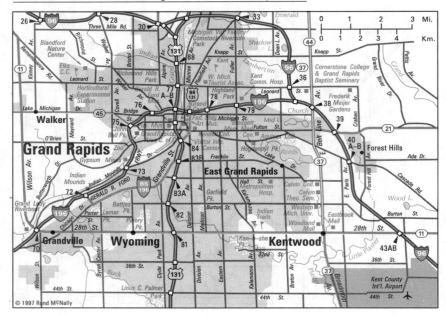

INFORMATION SOURCES:

Fresno Convention & Visitors Bureau
808 "M" St.
Fresno, California 93721
209/233-0836; 800/788-0836
Fresno Chamber of Commerce
2331 Fresno St.
Fresno, California 93721
209/495-4800

Grand Rapids, Michigan

City map: above
Population: (*570,200) 189,126 (1990C)
Altitude: 657 feet
Average Temp.: Jan., 23°F.; July, 72°F.
Telephone Area Code: 616
Time and Weather: 616/776-1234
Time Zone: Eastern

AIRPORT TRANSPORTATION:

Sixteen miles to downtown Grand Rapids.
Taxicab service.

SELECTED HOTELS:

✈ Airport Hilton Inn, 4747 28th St. SE,
616/957-0100; FAX 616/957-2977
Amway Grand Plaza, 187 Monroe Ave.,
616/774-2000; FAX 616/776-6489
Best Western Midway Hotel, 4101 28th St.
SE, 616/942-2550; FAX 616/942-2446
✈ Crowne Plaza, 5700 28th St. SE,
616/957-1770; FAX 616/957-0629
✈ Days Inn, 5500 28th St. SE,
616/949-8400; FAX (same)
Fairfield Inn, 3930 Stahl Dr. SE,
616/940-2700; FAX (same)
✈ Hampton Inn, 4981 28th St. SE,
616/956-9304; FAX 616/956-6617
Harley Hotel, 4041 Cascade Rd. SE,
616/949-8800; FAX 616/949-4303
Holiday Inn—North, 270 Ann St. NW,
616/363-9001; FAX 616/363-0670
Lexington Hotel Suites, 5401 28th St.
Court SE, 616/940-8100;
FAX 616/940-0914

SELECTED RESTAURANTS:

Cascade Roadhouse, 6817 Cascade SE,
616/949-1540
Charley's Crab, 63 Market St. SW,
616/459-2500
Curly's Corner, 740 Michigan NE,
616/451-2767
Cygnus, in the Amway Grand Plaza Hotel,
616/774-2000
Duba's, 420 E. Beltline NE, 616/949-1011
Gibson's, 1033 Lake Drive SE,
616/774-8535
The Hoffman House, in the Best Western
Midway Hotel, 616/942-2550
K. J. Cashmere's, 29 Pearl NW,
616/454-0299
The Legend, 420 Stocking NW,
616/459-6655
The 1913 Room, in the Amway Grand
Plaza Hotel, 616/774-2000
Pietro's Ristorante, 2780 Birchcrest SE,
616/452-3228
Sayfee's, 3555 Lake Eastbrook Blvd. SE,
616/949-5750

SELECTED ATTRACTIONS:

Blandford Nature Center, 1715 Hillburn
NW, 616/453-6192
First (Park) Congregational Church
(Tiffany windows), 10 E. Park Pl. NE,
616/459-3203
Frederik Meijer Gardens—Michigan
Botanic Garden/Meijer Sculpture Park,
3411 Bradford NE, 616/957-1580
Gerald R. Ford Museum, 303 Pearl St.
NW, 616/451-9290
Heritage Hill Historic District, Crescent to
Pleasant-Union to Lafayette,
616/459-8950
John Ball Zoo, Fulton & Valley,
616/336-4301
Roger B. Chaffee Planetarium, Pearl St. at
Front Ave., 616/456-3663
Van Andel Museum Center, Pearl St. at
Front Ave., 616/456-3977
Voigt House, 115 College SE,
616/456-4600

INFORMATION SOURCES:

Grand Rapids/Kent County Convention &
Visitors Bureau
140 Monroe Center NW, Suite 300
Grand Rapids, Michigan 49503-2832
616/459-8287; 800/678-9859
Grand Rapids Area Chamber of Commerce
111 Pearl St. NW
Grand Rapids, Michigan 49503-2831
616/771-0300

Guadalajara, Jalisco, Mexico

City map: page 49
Population: (*2,430,000) 1,650,042
(1990C)
Altitude: 5,012 ft.
Average Temp.: Jan., 59°F.; July, 70°F.
Telephone Code: 011/52/3
Time: (none) **Weather:**
011/52/3/616-4937
Time Zone: Central

AIRPORT TRANSPORTATION:

Twelve miles to downtown Guadalajara
from Miguel Hidalgo Int'l Airport.
Taxicab and van service.

SELECTED HOTELS:

Continental Plaza, Av. de las Rosas 2933,
011/52/3/678-0505;
FAX 011/52/3/678-0511
Crowne Plaza Guadalajara, Av. López Ma-
teos Sur 2500, 011/52/3/634-1034;
FAX 011/52/3/631-9393
De Mendoza, Venustiano Carranza 16,
011/52/3/613-4646;
FAX 011/52/3/613-7310
Fenix, Av. Corona 160,
011/52/3/614-5714;
FAX 011/52/3/613-4005
Fiesta Americana, Aurelio Aceves 225,
011/52/3/625-3434;
FAX 011/52/3/630-3725
Fiesta Inn, Av. Mariana Otero 1550,
011/52/3/669-3032;
FAX 011/52/3/647-6776
Holiday Inn Select, Av. Niños Héroes
3089, 011/52/3/122-2020;
FAX 011/52/3/647-7778
Hyatt Regency, Av. López Mateos Sur &
Moctezuma, 011/52/3/678-1234;
FAX 011/52/3/678-1222

SELECTED RESTAURANTS:

Copenhagen, Marcos Castellanos 140
La Pianola, Av. Mexico 3220
La Trattoria, Av. Niños Héroes 3051
La Troje, Av. Américas 1311
Pierrot, Justo Sierra 2355
Río Viejo, Av. de las Américas 302
Suehiro, Av. La Paz 1701

SELECTED ATTRACTIONS:

Bullfights, held in Plaza Nuevo Progreso,
Calzada Independencia Nte.
Catedral, Av. Alcalde between Av. Hidalgo
& Calle Morelos
Instituto Cultural Cabañas, Calle Caban-
nas 8 (at the Plaza Tapatía)
Mercado Libertad (enclosed traditional
marketplace), Calzada Independencia
Sur & Av. Javier Mina
Museo Regional de Guadalajara, Av.
Hidalgo & Calle Liceo
Palació de Gobierno (State Capitol build-
ing), Av. Corona at Morelos

Pargue Agua Azul, Calzada Independencia Sur & Calzada Gonzales Gallo

Teatro Degollado (orchestra, opera and dance theater) Calle Degollado & Av. Hidalgo

Tlaquepaque (arts & crafts center), 5 mi. southeast of downtown Guadalajara

Zoo and Planetarium, in Huentitan Park, Calzada Independencia Nte. & Calzada Ricardo Flores Magon, 20 min. north of downtown

INFORMATION SOURCES:

Jalisco State Tourism Ministry
  102 Morelos (on Plaza Tapatia)
  011/52/3/658-2222; 011/52/3/614-8686, ext. 114; or 011/52/3/613-0306

Convention & Visitors Office
  4095 Av. Vallarta at Niño Obrero
  011/52/3/122-8711

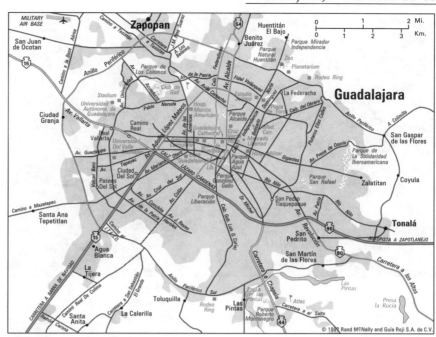

Hartford, Connecticut

City map: lower right
Population: (*1,085,900) 139,739 (1990C)
Altitude: 10 to 290 feet
Average Temp.: Jan., 28°F.; July, 74°F.
Telephone Area Code: 860
Time: 860/524-8123 **Weather:** 936-1212
Time Zone: Eastern

AIRPORT TRANSPORTATION:

Thirteen miles to downtown Hartford. Taxicab and limousine bus service.

SELECTED HOTELS:

The Goodwin Hotel, 1 Haynes St., 860/246-7500; FAX 860/247-4576

Hartford Marriott Farmington, 15 Farm Springs Rd., Farmington, 860/678-1000; FAX 860/677-8849

✈ Holiday Inn Airport, 16 Ella Grasso Tpk., Windsor Locks, 860/627-5171; FAX 860/627-7029

Holiday Inn—Downtown, 50 Morgan St., 860/549-2400; FAX 860/527-2746

Ramada Hotel, 100 E. River Dr., E. Hartford, 860/528-9703; FAX 860/289-4728

Sheraton Hartford Hotel, 315 Trumbull St., 860/728-5151; FAX 860/240-7247

SELECTED RESTAURANTS:

Avon Old Farms Inn, 1 Knott Rd. at Hwy. 44 & Rte. 10, 860/677-2818

The Blacksmith's Tavern, 2300 Main St., Glastonbury, 860/659-0366

Carbone's, 588 Franklin Ave., 860/296-9646

Gaetano's, One Civic Center Plaza, 860/249-1629

Hot Tomato's, 1 Union Place, at Asylum Ave., 860/249-5100

Main & Hopewell, 2 Hopewell Rd., S. Glastonbury, 860/633-8698

93 Church St., Sheraton Hartford Hotel, 860/728-5151

Pierpont's, The Goodwin Hotel, 860/246-7500

The Village Green, Hartford Marriott Farmington, 860/678-1000

SELECTED ATTRACTIONS:

Bushnell Park Carousel Society (hand-carved carousel), 860/246-7739

Butler-McCook Homestead (1782), 396 Main St., 860/522-1806

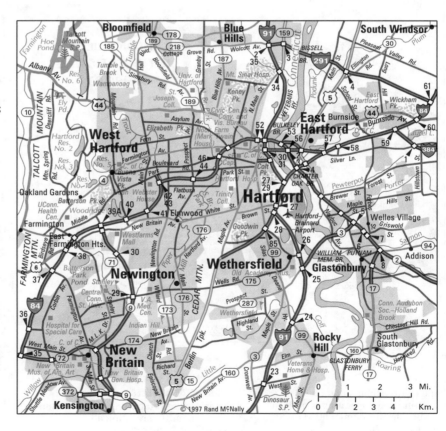

Center Church & The Ancient Burying Ground, Main & Gold sts., 860/249-5631

Elizabeth Park (rose garden), Prospect & Asylum aves.

Harriet Beecher Stowe House, Visitor Center, 71 Forest St., at the corner of Farmington Ave., 860/525-9317

Mark Twain House, 351 Farmington Ave. between Woodland & Forest sts., 860/493-6411

Old State House, 800 Main St., 860/522-6766

Honolulu

PACIFIC OCEAN

© 1997 Rand McNally

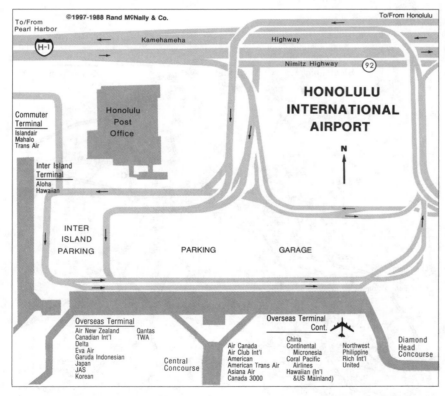

©1997-1988 Rand McNally & Co.

HONOLULU INTERNATIONAL AIRPORT

Wadsworth Atheneum (oldest continuously operating American public art museum), 600 Main St., 860/278-2670

INFORMATION SOURCES:
Greater Hartford Convention & Visitors Bureau, Inc. (conventions)
One Civic Center Plaza
 Hartford, Connecticut 06103
 860/728-6789; 800/446-7811

Greater Hartford Tourism District (tourism)
 One Civic Center Plaza
 Hartford, Connecticut 06103
 860/520-4480; 800/793-4480;
 Visitor Information: 860/275-6456
Old Statehouse Information Center
 800 Main St.
 (brochures only; self-service)
Greater Hartford Chamber of Commerce
 250 Constitution Plaza
 Hartford, Connecticut 06103-1882
 860/525-4451

Honolulu, Hawaii

City map: left
Population: (*836,200) 365,272 (1990C)
Altitude: 18 feet
Average Temp.: Jan., 72°F.; July, 80°F.
Telephone Area Code: 808
Time: 808/983-3211 **Weather:** 808/973-4381
Time Zone: Hawaiian (Two hours earlier than Pacific standard time)

AIRPORT TRANSPORTATION:
See map at lower left.
Nine miles to Waikiki.
Taxicab and limousine bus service.

SELECTED HOTELS:
Halekulani, 2199 Kalia Rd., 808/923-2311; FAX 808/926-8004
Hawaiian Regent, 2552 Kalakaua Ave., 808/922-6611; FAX 808/921-5255
Hilton Hawaiian Village, 2005 Kalia Rd., 808/949-4321; FAX 808/947-7898
Hyatt Regency Waikiki, 2424 Kalakaua Ave., 808/923-1234; FAX 808/926-3415
The Ilikai Hotel Nikko Waikiki, 1777 Ala Moana Blvd., 808/949-3811; FAX 808/947-4523
Kahala Mandarin Oriental Hawaii, 5000 Kahala Ave., 808/739-8888; FAX 808/739-8800
The Outrigger Waikiki, on the Beach, 2335 Kalakaua Ave., 808/923-0711; FAX 808/921-9749
Queen Kapiolani, 150 Kapahulu Ave., 808/922-1941; FAX 808/922-2694
Royal Hawaiian, 2259 Kalakaua Ave., 808/923-7311; FAX 808/924-7098
Sheraton Moana Surfrider, 2365 Kalakaua Ave., 808/922-3111; FAX 808/923-0308
Sheraton Waikiki, 2255 Kalakaua Ave., 808/922-4422; FAX 808/923-8785

SELECTED RESTAURANTS:
Canoes at the Ilikai, in the Ilikai Hotel Nikko Waikiki, 808/949-3811
Castagnola's Italian Lanai, in the Inn on the Park, 1920 Ala Moana Blvd., 808/949-6277
Furusato, 2500 Kalakaua Ave., 808/922-5502
Golden Dragon Room (Chinese), in the Hilton Hawaiian Village, 808/949-4321
The Hanohano Room, in the Sheraton Waikiki, 808/922-4422
Michel's, in the Colony Surf Hotel, 2895 Kalakaua Ave., 808/923-6552
Pikake Terrace, in the Sheraton Princess Kaiulani Hotel, 120 Kaiulani Ave., 808/922-5811
The Plantation Cafe, in the Ala Moana Hotel, 410 Atkinson Dr., 808/955-4811

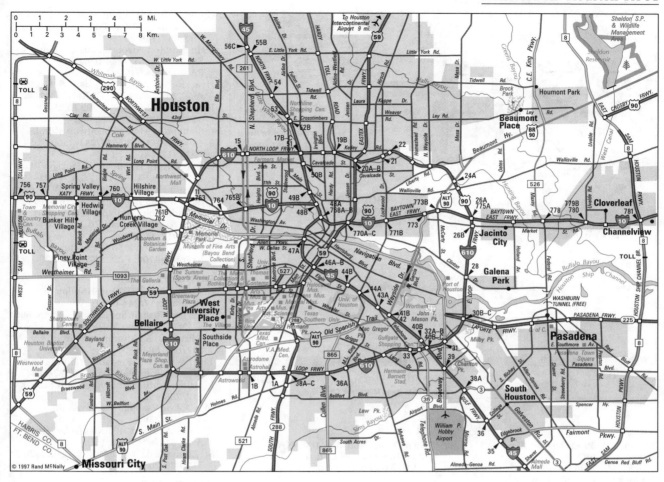

SELECTED ATTRACTIONS:
Bernice P. Bishop Museum & Planetarium, 1525 Bernice St., 808/847-3511
Foster Botanical Garden, 50 N. Vineyard Blvd., 808/522-7065
Honolulu Academy of Arts, 900 S. Beretania St., 808/532-8701
Honolulu Zoo, Kapahulu & Kalakaua aves., 808/971-7171
National Memorial Cemetery of the Pacific, overlooking Honolulu, 808/566-1430
Pearl Harbor/The U.S.S. Arizona Memorial, 808/422-0561
Polynesian Cultural Center, 55-370 Kam Hwy., Laie, 808/293-3333
Sea Life Park, Makapuu Point, 808/259-7933
Waikiki Aquarium, 2777 Kalakaua Ave., 808/923-9741
Waimea Falls Park, 59-864 Kam Hwy. on the north shore of Oahu, 808/638-8511

INFORMATION SOURCES:
Hawaii Visitors Bureau
2270 Kalakaua Ave., 8th Floor
Honolulu, Hawaii 96815
808/923-1811; 800/GO-HAWAII
The Chamber of Commerce of Hawaii
1132 Bishop St., Suite 200
Honolulu, Hawaii 96813
808/522-8800

Houston, Texas

City map: above
Population: (*3,327,800) 1,630,553 (1990C)
Altitude: Sea level to 50 feet
Average Temp.: Jan., 59°F.; July, 82°F.
Telephone Area Code: 281, 713
Time: 713/222-8463 **Weather:** 713/529-4444
Time Zone: Central

AIRPORT TRANSPORTATION:
See map on page 52.
Twenty miles from Intercontinental Airport to downtown Houston; 10 miles from Hobby Airport to downtown.
Taxicab, limousine, coach bus, and helicopter service.

SELECTED HOTELS:
Adam's Mark, 2900 Briarpark Dr. at Westheimer, 713/978-7400; FAX 713/735-2727
Doubletree Guest Suites Galleria West, 5353 Westheimer Rd., 713/961-9000; FAX 713/877-8835
Doubletree Hotel at Allen Center, 400 Dallas St., 713/759-0202; FAX 713/759-1166
✈Doubletree at Houston Intercontinental Airport, 15747 JFK Blvd., 713/442-8000; FAX 713/590-8461

Four Seasons Hotel Houston, 1300 Lamar St., 713/650-1300; FAX 713/650-8169
Hyatt Regency Houston, 1200 Louisiana St., 713/654-1234; FAX 713/951-0934
Omni Houston Hotel, 4 Riverway Dr., 713/871-8181; FAX 713/871-0719
Ramada Hotel Astrodome, 2100 S. Braeswood, 713/797-9000; FAX 713/799-8362
Renaissance Houston Hotel, 6 Greenway Plaza E., 713/629-1200; FAX 713/629-4702
✈Sheraton Crown Hotel & Conference Center, 15700 JFK Blvd., 713/442-5100; FAX 713/987-9130
Sheraton Grand Hotel by the Galleria, 2525 W. Loop South, 713/961-3000; FAX 713/961-1490
The Westin Galleria, 5060 W. Alabama St., 713/960-8100; FAX 713/960-6553
The Westin Oaks, 5011 Westheimer Rd., 713/960-8100; FAX 713/960-6554
The Wyndham Warwick, 5701 Main St., 713/526-1991; FAX 713/639-4545

SELECTED RESTAURANTS:
Brennan's, 3300 Smith St., 713/522-9711
De Ville, in the Four Seasons Hotel Houston, 713/650-1300
The Great Caruso, 10001 Westheimer Rd., 713/780-4900
La Tour d'Argent, 2011 Ella Blvd., 713/864-9864

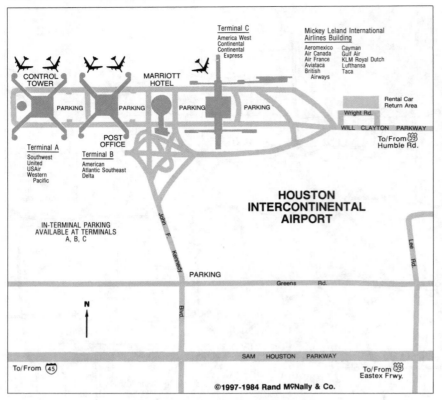

Terminal C
America West
Continental
Continental
Express

Mickey Leland International
Airlines Building
Aeromexico   Cayman
Air Canada   Gulf Air
Air France   KLM Royal Dutch
Aviataca   Lufthansa
British   Taca
Airways

CONTROL
TOWER

MARRIOTT
HOTEL

PARKING   PARKING   PARKING   PARKING

Rental Car
Return Area

Wright Rd.

WILL CLAYTON PARKWAY

POST
OFFICE

Terminal A
Southwest
United
USAir
Western
Pacific

Terminal B
American
Atlantic Southeast
Delta

To/From 59
Humble Rd.

IN-TERMINAL PARKING
AVAILABLE AT TERMINALS
A, B, C

HOUSTON
INTERCONTINENTAL
AIRPORT

John F. Kennedy Blvd.

Lee Rd.

N

PARKING

Greens   Rd.

SAM   HOUSTON   PARKWAY

To/From 45

To/From 59
Eastex Frwy.

©1997-1984 Rand McNally & Co.

Maxim's, 3755 Richmond Ave.,
713/877-8899
The Rivoli, 5636 Richmond Ave., one half
block west of Chimney Rock,
713/789-1900
Tony's, 1801 Post Oak Blvd.,
713/622-6778
Vargo's, 2401 Fondren Rd., 713/782-3888

SELECTED ATTRACTIONS:
Battleship Texas, in San Jacinto
Battleground State Historic Park, 22
miles east of Houston off TX 225 East,
713/479-2411
Bayou Bend (residence/museum of
American decorative arts/gardens), 1
Westcott, (reservations required for
tours of residence) 713/639-7750
The Contemporary Arts Museum, 5216
Montrose Blvd., 713/526-3129
The Galleria (shopping, dining,
entertainment), Loop 610 at
Westheimer, 713/621-1907
Houston Museum of Natural Science, One
Hermann Circle Dr., Hermann Park,
713/639-4600
Houston Zoo, in Hermann Park, off the
6300 block of Fannin St., 713/523-5888
The Menil Collection (art museum), 1515
Sul Ross, 713/525-9400
Museum of Fine Arts, 1001 Bissonnet,
713/639-7375
San Jacinto Monument & Museum of
History, in San Jacinto Battleground
State Historic Park, 22 miles east of
Houston off Texas Highway 225 East,
713/479-2421

Space Center Houston, 1601 NASA Rd. 1,
25 miles south of Houston,
713/244-2100

INFORMATION SOURCES:
Greater Houston Convention & Visitors
Bureau
801 Congress St.
Houston, Texas 77002
713/227-3100; 800/365-7575
Greater Houston Partnership
1200 Smith, 7th Floor
Houston, Texas 77002-4309
713/651-2100

Indianapolis, Indiana

City map: page 53
Population: (*1,154,500) 731,327 (1990C)
Altitude: 717 feet
Average Temp.: Jan., 29°F.; July, 76°F.
Telephone Area Code: 317
Time and Weather: 317/635-5959
Time Zone: Eastern standard all year

AIRPORT TRANSPORTATION:
Eight miles to downtown Indianapolis.
Taxicab and limousine bus service.

SELECTED HOTELS:
Adam's Mark Indianapolis, 2544
Executive Drive, 317/248-2481;
FAX 317/381-6159
Comfort Inn Downtown, 530 S. Capitol
Ave., 317/631-9000; FAX 317/631-9999
Courtyard by Marriott Downtown, 501 W.
Washington St., 317/635-4443;
FAX 317/687-0029

Crowne Plaza at Union Station, 123 W.
Louisiana, 317/631-2221;
FAX 317/236-7474
Holiday Inn Airport, 2501 S. High
School Rd., 317/244-6861;
FAX 317/243-1059
Hyatt Regency Indianapolis, 1 S. Capitol
Ave., 317/632-1234; FAX 317/231-7569
Indianapolis Marriott, 7202 E. 21st St.,
317/352-1231; FAX (same)
Indianapolis Motor Speedway Motel,
4400 W. 16th St., 317/241-2500;
FAX 317/241-2133
Omni Severin Hotel, 40 W. Jackson Pl.,
317/634-6664; FAX 317/767-0003
Radisson Hotel City Center, 31 W. Ohio
St., 317/635-2000; FAX 317/638-0782
Ramada Hotel Indianapolis Airport,
2500 S. High School Rd., 317/244-3361;
FAX 317/241-9202
The Westin Hotel, 50 S. Capitol Ave.,
317/262-8100; FAX 317/231-3928

SELECTED RESTAURANTS:
Chanteclair Sur Le Toit, Holiday Inn
Airport, 317/244-6861
Chez Jean Restaurant Francais & Inn, 8821
S. IN 67, Camby, 317/831-0870
Del Frisco's, 55 Monument Circle,
317/687-8888
The Eagle's Nest Restaurant, in the Hyatt
Regency Indianapolis, 317/632-1234
Fireside South, 522 E. Raymond St.,
317/788-4521
Max & Erma's, 8930 Wesleyan Rd.,
317/872-2300
Old Point Tavern, 401 Massachusetts
Ave., 317/634-8943
St. Elmo Steak House, 127 S. Illinois St.,
317/635-0636

SELECTED ATTRACTIONS:
Children's Museum of Indianapolis, 3000
Illinois, 317/924-5431
Conner Prairie Pioneer Settlement, 13400
Allisonville Rd., Fishers, 317/776-6000
Eiteljorg Museum of American Indians
and Western Art, 500 W. Washington
St., 317/636-9378
Indiana State Museum & Historic Sites,
202 N. Alabama St., 317/232-1637
Indianapolis "500" Motor Speedway and
Hall of Fame Museum, 4790 W. 16th St.,
317/484-6747
Indianapolis Museum of Art, 1200 W.
38th St., 317/923-1331
Indianapolis Zoo, 1200 W. Washington
St., 317/630-2030
Union Station Festival Marketplace,
Meridian between South St. & W.
Jackson Place

INFORMATION SOURCES:
Indianapolis Convention and Visitors
Association
1 RCA Dome, Suite 100
Indianapolis, Indiana 46225
317/639-4282;
Visitor Info. 800/323-INDY;
Convention Info. 800/642-INDY
Indianapolis Chamber of Commerce
320 N. Meridian St., Suite 200
Indianapolis, Indiana 46204
317/464-2200

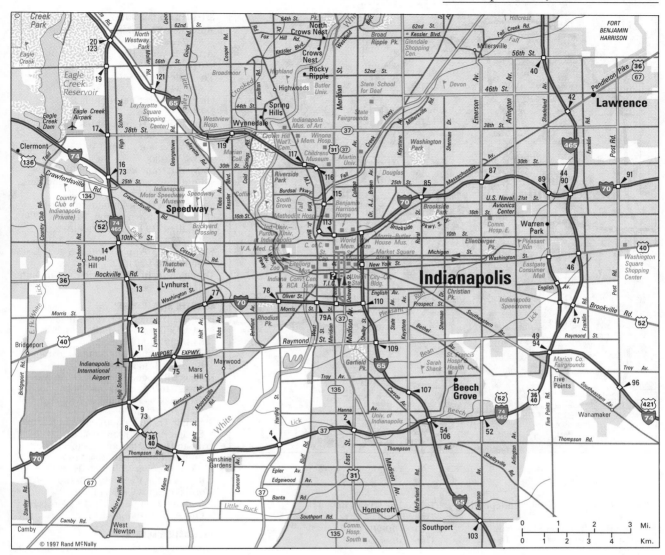

© 1997 Rand McNally

Indianapolis City Center
201 S. Capitol
Indianapolis, Indiana 46225
317/237-5200

Jacksonville, Florida

City map: page 54
Population: (*777,100) 635,230 (1990C)
Altitude: 19 feet
Average Temp.: Jan., 55°F.; July, 80°F.
Telephone Area Code: 904
Time: 904/358-1212 **Weather:**
  904/741-4311
Time Zone: Eastern

AIRPORT TRANSPORTATION:

Fifteen miles to downtown Jacksonville.
Taxicab and limousine service.

SELECTED HOTELS:

Adeeb Sea Turtle Inn, 1 Ocean Blvd.,
  Atlantic Beach, 904/249-7402;
  FAX 904/241-7439

Best Western of Orange Park, 300 Park
  Ave. N., Orange Park, 904/264-1211;
  FAX 904/269-6756
Comfort Inn South, 3233 Emerson St.,
  904/398-3331; FAX 904/398-3331
  ext. 243
Days Inn Oceanfront Resort, 1031 S. First
  St., Jacksonville Beach, 904/249-7231;
  FAX 904/249-7924
Fairfield Inn, 8050 Baymeadows Circle W,
  904/739-0739; FAX 904/739-0739
✈Hampton Inn—Airport, 1170 Airport
  Entrance Rd., 904/741-4980;
  FAX 904/741-4186
✈Holiday Inn North, I-95 at Airport Rd.,
  904/741-4404; FAX 904/741-4907
Holiday Inn Orange Park, 150 Park Ave.,
  Orange Park, 904/264-9513;
  FAX 904/264-9513 ext. 486
Omni Jacksonville Hotel, 245 Water St.,
  904/355-6664; FAX 904/350-0359
Radisson Riverwalk Hotel, 1515 Pruden-
  tial Dr., 904/396-5100;
  FAX 904/396-7154

Ramada Inn Conference Center, 5685
  Arlington Expy., 904/724-3410;
  FAX 904/727-7606

SELECTED RESTAURANTS:

Alhambra Dinner Theatre, 12000 Beach
  Blvd., 904/641-1212
Crawdaddy's, 1643 Prudential Dr.,
  904/396-3546
Gene's Seafood, 6132 Merrill Rd.,
  904/744-2333
Nero's Italian, 3607 N. University Blvd.,
  904/743-3141
Ruby Tuesdays, 2 Independent Dr.,
  904/358-7737
The Wine Cellar, 1314 Prudential Dr.,
  904/398-8989

SELECTED ATTRACTIONS:

Alhambra Dinner Theatre, 12000 Beach
  Blvd., 904/641-1212
Anheuser-Busch Brewery (tours), 111
  Busch Dr., 904/751-8117 or -8118
Cummer Museum of Art & Gardens, 829
  Riverside Ave., 904/356-6857

© 1997 Rand McNally

The Jacksonville Landing, 2 Independent
    Dr., 904/353-1188
Jacksonville Museum of Contemporary
    Art, 4160 Boulevard Center Dr.,
    904/398-8336
Jacksonville Zoo, 8605 Zoo Dr. (Exit 124A
    on I-95), 904/757-4463
Kathryn Abby Hanna Park, 500
    Wonderwood Dr., 904/249-2317
Mayport Naval Station (weekend tours),
    Mayport, 904/270-NAVY
Museum of Science & History, 1025
    Museum Circle, 904/396-7062
The Riverwalk, 1515 Prudential Dr.,
    904/396-4900

INFORMATION SOURCES:
Jacksonville & the Beaches Convention &
Visitors Bureau
    3 Independent Dr.
    Jacksonville, Florida 32202-5092
    904/798-9148; 800/733-2668
Jacksonville Chamber of Commerce
    3 Independent Dr.
    Jacksonville, Florida 32202
    904/366-6600

Kansas City, Missouri

City map: page 55
Population: (*1,388,600) 435,146 (1990C)
Altitude: 800 feet
Average Temp.: Jan., 30°F.; July, 81°F.

Telephone Area Code: 816
Time: 816/844-1212 **Weather:**
    816/540-6021
Time Zone: Central

AIRPORT TRANSPORTATION:
See map on page 56.
Eighteen miles to downtown Kansas City.
Taxicab and limousine bus service.

SELECTED HOTELS:
Adam's Mark Kansas City, 9103 E. 39th
    St., 816/737-0200; FAX 816/737-4712
Crowne Plaza, 4445 Main St.,
    816/531-3000; FAX 816/531-3007
✈Doubletree Hotel at KC International
    Airport, 8801 NW. 112th St.,
    816/891-8900; FAX 816/891-8030
Hyatt Regency Crown Center, 2345 McGee
    St., 816/421-1234; FAX 816/435-4190
✈Kansas City Airport Marriott, 775
    Brasilia, 816/464-2200;
    FAX 816/464-5915
Marriott Downtown, 200 W. 12th St.,
    816/421-6800; FAX 816/855-4418
Park Place Hotel, 1601 N. Universal Ave.,
    816/483-9900; FAX 816/231-1418
The Ritz Carlton, Kansas City, 401 Ward
    Pkwy., 816/756-1500;
    FAX 816/756-1635
The Westin Crown Center, 1 Pershing Rd.,
    816/474-4400; FAX 816/391-4438
Wyndham Garden Hotel, One E. 45th St.
    at Main St., (due to open late 1996)

SELECTED RESTAURANTS:
American Restaurant, 2500 Grand,
    816/426-1133
Arthur Bryant's Barbeque, 1727 Brooklyn,
    816/231-1123
The Golden Ox, 1600 Genessee,
    816/842-2866
Harry Starkers, 200 Nichols Rd.,
    816/753-3565
The Hereford House, 20th & Main,
    816/842-1080
Jasper's Restaurant, 405 W. 75th St.,
    816/363-3003
La Mediterranee, Glenwood Shopping
    Center, 91st & Metcalf, Overland Park,
    816/561-2916
Peppercorn Duck Club, in the Hyatt
    Regency Crown Center, 816/421-1234
Plaza III, 4749 Pennsylvania Ave.,
    816/753-0000
Stephenson's Apple Farm, US 40 & Lee's
    Summit Rd., 816/373-5400
Trader Vic's, in The Westin Crown Center,
    816/391-4444

SELECTED ATTRACTIONS:
Harry S. Truman Library & Museum, US
    24 & Delaware St., Independence,
    816/833-1400
Kansas City Museum, 3218 Gladstone
    Blvd., 816/483-8300
Kansas City Zoo, 6700 Zoo Dr. in Swope
    Park, 816/871-5701 or -5700
Nelson-Atkins Museum of Art, 4525 Oak
    St., 816/561-4000
Starlight Theater, 4600 Starlight Rd. in
    Swope Park, 816/363-7827
Truman Home National Historic Site,
    Independence, 816/254-7199
Watkins Woolen Mill State Historic Site,
    6 mi. east of Kearney, 816/296-3357
Worlds of Fun/Oceans of Fun
    (theme/water parks), 4545 Worlds of
    Fun Ave., 816/454-4545

INFORMATION SOURCES:
Convention and Visitors Bureau of Greater
Kansas City
    City Center Square, 1100 Main St.
    Suite 2550
    Kansas City, Missouri 64105
    816/221-5242; 800/767-7700
    Visitor Info. Recording:
    816/691-3800
Greater Kansas City Chamber of
Commerce
    911 Main St., Suite 2600
    Kansas City, Missouri 64105
    816/221-2424

Knoxville, Tennessee

City map: page 56
Population: (*600,800) 165,121 (1990C)
Altitude: 889 feet
Average Temp.: Jan., 39°F.; July, 78°F.
Telephone Area Code: 423
Time: (none) **Weather:** (none)
Time Zone: Eastern

AIRPORT TRANSPORTATION:
Thirteen miles to downtown Knoxville.
Taxicab, limousine and hotel shuttle
    service.

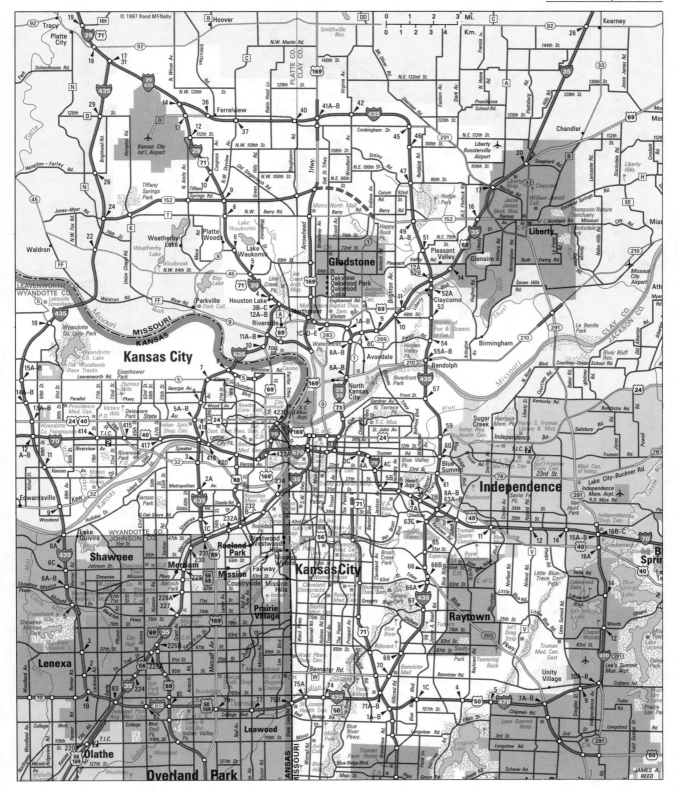

© 1997 Rand McNally

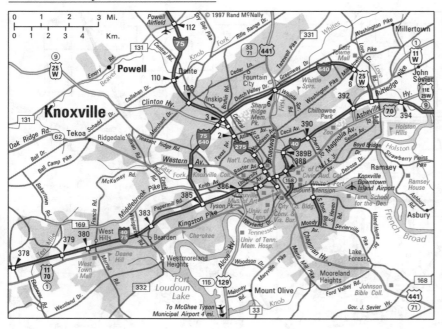

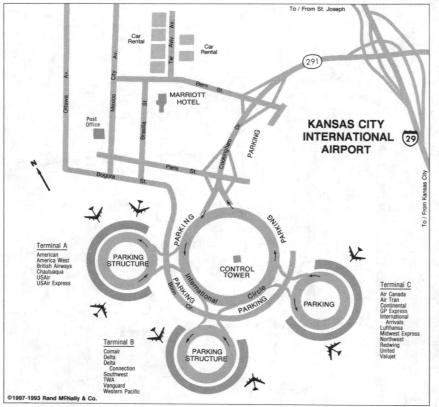

SELECTED HOTELS:

Campus Inn, 1706 W. Cumberland Ave., 423/521-5000; FAX (same)

Comfort Inn, 5334 Central Ave. Pike, 423/688-1010; FAX (same)

✈Hampton Inn, 148 Int'l. Ave., Alcoa, 423/983-1101; FAX 423/984-0110

Holiday Inn Cedar Bluff, 304 N. Cedar Bluff Rd., 423/693-1011; FAX 423/694-0253

Holiday Inn Select, 525 Henley St., 423/522-2800; FAX 423/523-0738

Holiday Inn West, 1315 Kirby Rd., 423/584-3911; FAX 423/588-0920

Howard Johnson's Lodge North, 118 Merchants Dr., 423/688-3141; FAX 423/687-4645

Hyatt Regency Knoxville, 500 Hill Ave. SE, 423/637-1234; FAX 423/522-5911

✈Knoxville Airport Hilton, 2001 Alcoa Hwy., Alcoa, 423/970-4300; FAX 423/984-7080

Knoxville Hilton, 501 W. Church St., 423/523-2300; FAX 423/525-6532

✈Quality Inn Airport, 2306 Airport Hwy., 423/970-3140; FAX (same)

Quality Inn West, 7621 Kingston Pike, 423/693-8111; FAX (none)

Radisson Hotel Knoxville, 401 Summit Hill Dr., 423/522-2600; FAX 423/523-7200

Ramada Inn Cedar Bluff, 323 Cedar Bluff Rd., 423/693-7330; FAX 423/693-7383

✈Ramada Inn Knoxville Airport, 2962 Alcoa Hwy., Alcoa, 423/970-3060; FAX 423/970-2641

SELECTED RESTAURANTS:

Chesapeake's, 500 Henley St., 423/673-3433

Copper Cellar, 1807 Cumberland Ave., 423/673-3411

Copper Cellar & Cappuccino's, 7316 Kingston Pike, 423/673-3422

The Country Garden, in the Hyatt Regency Knoxville Hotel, 423/637-1234

The Orangery, 5412 Kingston Pike, 423/588-2964

Regas, 318 N. Gay St., 423/637-9805

Ruby Tuesday, East Towne Mall, Mall Rd. & Millertown Pike, 423/524-1237

SELECTED ATTRACTIONS:

Blount Mansion, 200 W. Hill Ave., 423/525-2375

James White Fort, 205 E. Hill Ave., 423/525-6514

Knoxville Museum of Art, 1050 World's Fair Park Dr., 423/525-6101

Knoxville Zoo, off I-40 East, exit 392, 423/637-5331

Museum of Appalachia, on US 61, 1 mi. off I-75, Norris, 423/494-7680

INFORMATION SOURCES:

Knoxville Convention & Visitors Bureau
The Sunsphere
810 Clinch Ave.
Knoxville, Tennessee 37902
423/523-7263; 800/727-8045

Greater Knoxville Chamber of Commerce
301 E. Church Ave.
Knoxville, Tennessee 37915
423/637-4550

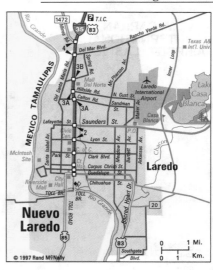

Laredo, Texas

City map: upper right
Population: (*342,200) Laredo-Nuevo Laredo Metro Area) 122,899 (1990C)
Altitude: 420 feet
Average Temp.: Jan., 46°F.; July, 96°F.
Telephone Area Code: 210
Time: 210/725-2345 **Weather:** (none)
Time Zone: Central

AIRPORT TRANSPORTATION:

Five miles to downtown Laredo from Laredo International Airport.
Taxicab and bus service to downtown Laredo.

SELECTED HOTELS:

Family Gardens Inn, 5830 San Bernardo, 210/723-5300; FAX 210/791-8842
Holiday Inn Civic Center, 800 Garden, 210/727-5800; FAX 210/727-0278
Holiday Inn Rio Grande, 1 S. Main, 210/722-2411; FAX 210/722-4578
La Posada Hotel/Suites, 1000 Zaragoza, 210/722-1701; FAX 210/722-4758
La Quinta Inn, 3600 Santa Ursula, 210/722-0511; FAX 210/723-6642

SELECTED RESTAURANTS:

Charlie's Corona of Laredo, 3902 San Bernardo Ave., 210/725-8227
De Soto, in La Posada Hotel, 210/722-1701
Laredo Bar & Grill, 102 Del Court, 210/717-0090
Pelican's Wharf, 4119 San Dario, 210/727-5070
The Unicorn, 3810 San Bernardo Ave., 210/727-4663

SELECTED ATTRACTIONS:

Capitol Building of the Republic of the Rio Grande, 1009 Zaragoza, San Agustin Plaza
El Mercado (marketplace), 500 Flores, in El Mercado Historic District
The Laredo Center for the Arts, 500 St. Agustin Ave., 210/725-1715
The Laredo Children's Museum, west end of Washington St., at Laredo Community College campus, 210/725-2299
Ortiz House, 915 Zaragoza
Saint Augustine Church, east side of San Agustin Plaza
San Bernardo Street (Mexican & Central American wholesale shops)
Zaragoza Street (shopping)

INFORMATION SOURCE:

Laredo Convention & Visitors Bureau
P.O. Box 579
501 San Agustin
Laredo, Texas 78042-0579
210/712-1230; 800/361-3360

Las Vegas, Nevada

City map: lower right
Population: (*720,900) 258,295 (1990C)
Altitude: 2,020 feet
Average Temp.: Jan., 44°F.; July, 90°F.
Telephone Area Code: 702
Time: 702/364-8463 **Weather:** 702/248-4800
Time Zone: Pacific

AIRPORT TRANSPORTATION:

See map on page 58.
Eight miles to downtown Las Vegas.
Taxicab and limousine service.

SELECTED HOTELS:

Caesars Palace, 3570 Las Vegas Blvd. S., 702/731-7110; FAX 702/731-6636
Days Inn Downtown, 707 E. Fremont St., 702/388-1400; FAX 702/388-9622
Excalibur Hotel/Casino, 3850 Las Vegas Blvd. S., 702/597-7777; FAX 702/597-7009
Golden Nugget Hotel & Casino, 129 E. Fremont St., 702/385-7111; FAX 702/386-8362
Hacienda Resort Hotel & Casino, 3950 Las Vegas Blvd. S., 702/739-8911; FAX 702/798-8289
Imperial Palace Hotel & Casino, 3535 Las Vegas Blvd. S., 702/731-3311; FAX 702/735-8578
Jackie Gaughan's Plaza Hotel, 1 Main St., 702/386-2110; FAX 702/382-8281
Las Vegas Hilton, 3000 Paradise Rd., 702/732-5111; FAX 702/794-3611
Luxor Hotel/Casino, 3900 Las Vegas Blvd. S., 702/262-4000; FAX 702/262-4405
✈MGM Grand Hotel/Casino, 3799 Las Vegas Blvd. S., 702/891-1111; FAX 702/891-3036
The Mirage, 3400 Las Vegas Blvd. S., 702/791-7111; FAX 702/791-7414
Sahara Hotel & Casino, 2535 Las Vegas Blvd. S., 702/737-2111; FAX 702/737-1017
Sands Hotel & Casino, 3355 Las Vegas Blvd. S., 702/733-5000; FAX 702/733-5624
Sheraton Desert Inn Resort & Casino, 3145 Las Vegas Blvd. S., 702/733-4444; FAX 702/733-4774
Treasure Island at the Mirage, 3300 Las Vegas Blvd. S., 702/894-7111; FAX 702/894-7414
✈Tropicana Resort/Casino, 3801 Las Vegas Blvd. S., 702/739-2222; FAX 702/736-1883

SELECTED RESTAURANTS:

Bacchanal, in Caesars Palace Hotel, 702/731-7110
Georges La Forge's Pamplemousse Restaurant, 400 E. Sahara Ave., 702/733-2066
Golden Steer Steak House, 308 W. Sahara Ave., 702/384-4470
The House of Lords, in the Sahara Hotel & Casino, 702/737-2111
Nero's, in Caesars Palace Hotel, 702/731-7110
Palace Court, in Caesars Palace Hotel, 702/731-7110
Portofino Room, in the Sheraton Desert Inn Resort & Casino, 702/733-4444
Regency, in the Sands Hotel & Casino, 702/733-5000
The Rikshaw, in the Riviera Hotel, 2901 Las Vegas Blvd. S., 702/734-5110

SELECTED ATTRACTIONS:

Belz Factory Outlet World Mall, Las Vegas Blvd. S. & Warm Springs Rd., 702/896-5599

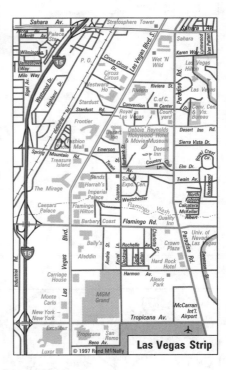

Las Vegas Strip

The Forum Shops at Caesars, Las Vegas Blvd. S., adjacent to Caesars Palace Hotel, 702/893-4800
Gambling and Entertainment, at casinos and hotels throughout Las Vegas
Grand Slam Canyon (amusement park), 2880 Las Vegas Blvd. S., 702/794-3912
Hoover Dam, 30 miles east of Las Vegas on US 93, 702/293-1081
Liberace Museum, 1775 E. Tropicana Ave., 702/798-5595
Valley of Fire State Park, 55 miles northeast of Las Vegas off I-15, 702/397-2088

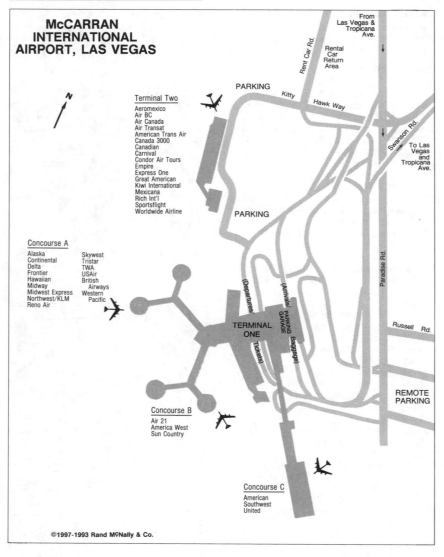

McCARRAN INTERNATIONAL AIRPORT, LAS VEGAS

N

Terminal Two
Aeromexico
Air BC
Air Canada
Air Transat
American Trans Air
Canada 3000
Canadian
Carnival
Condor Air Tours
Empire
Express One
Great American
Kiwi International
Mexicana
Rich Int'l
Sportsflight
Worldwide Airline

Concourse A
Alaska
Continental
Delta
Frontier
Hawaiian
Midway
Midwest Express
Northwest/KLM
Reno Air
Skywest
Tristar
TWA
USAir
British Airways
Western Pacific

Concourse B
Air 21
America West
Sun Country

Concourse C
American
Southwest
United

TERMINAL ONE

(Departures/Tickets)

(Arrivals/Baggage)

PARKING GARAGE

PARKING

PARKING

From Las Vegas & Tropicana Ave.

Rent Car Rd.

Kitty Hawk Way

Rental Car Return Area

Swanson Rd.

To Las Vegas and Tropicana Ave.

Paradise Rd.

Russell Rd.

REMOTE PARKING

©1997-1993 Rand McNally & Co.

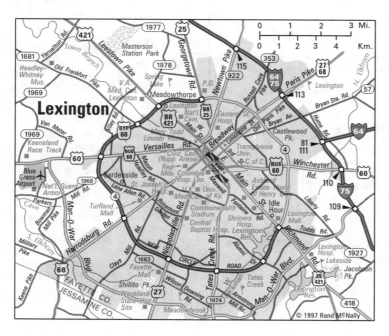

Lexington

(map labels:)
421 1681 Headley-Whitney Mus. 1969 Old Frankfort Pike Yarnallton Rd. Town Branch Leestown Pike 421 1977 25 Masterson Station Park Georgetown Rd. 1978 Spring Lake 353 115 922 P.O. 27 68 64 75 Paris Pike Lexington 113 57 N. Elkhorn Bryan Sta. Rd. Van Meter Rd. 1969 BYP 60 BR 421 Lexington Nat'l Cem. BR 25 Eastern State Hosp. Broadway Old Paris Pike Bryan Av. Castlewood Pk. Hume Rd. 64 Keeneland Race Track BUS 60 Mary Todd Lincoln Home Versailles Rd. Manson Rd. Main St. Civic Cen. (Rupp Arena) Transylvania Univ. S.C. of C. 81 111 BUS 60 Winchester Rd. 60 Blue Grass Airport Nat'l Guard Armory 1968 Gardenside Headley Rd. St. Joseph Hosp. Lane Allen Rd. Red Mile Columbia Hosp. Lex. U.K. Med. Center of Ky. 3rd St. Maxwell E. Main 4 110 109 75 Parkers Lake Bowman Mill Rd. S. Elkhorn Turfland Mall Rosemont Gdn. Gilkey Rd. Commonwealth Stadium Shriners Hosp. Fontaine Rd. Liberty Rd. Lexington Mall Idle Hour Lexington Res. Man-O-War Blvd. Harrodsburg Rd. 4 Nicholasville Rd. Central Baptist Hosp. Alumni Dr. Richmond Rd. Todds Rd. Lexington Hosp. Lakeside Jacobson Pk. 1927 68 Keene Pike Military Pike Clays Mill Rd. New CIRCLE Tates Creek Rd. 1683 Fayette Mall Shillito Pk. 27 ROAD Wilson Downing Rd. Tates Creek 1974 Armand Mill Rd. Man-O-War Blvd. 25 421 Lexington Res. 418 FAYETTE CO. JESSAMINE CO. Waveland State Hist'l. Site Meadowbrook

Scale: 0 1 2 3 Mi. / 0 1 2 3 4 Km.

© 1997 Rand McNally

INFORMATION SOURCES:

Las Vegas Convention and Visitors Authority
  Convention Center
  3150 Paradise Rd.
  Las Vegas, Nevada 89109
  702/892-0711
Las Vegas Chamber of Commerce
  711 E. Desert Inn
  Las Vegas, Nevada 89109
  702/735-1616

Lexington, Kentucky

City map: lower left
Population: (*281,300) 225,366 (1990C)
Altitude: 983 feet
Average Temp.: Jan., 33°F.; July, 76°F.
Telephone Area Code: 606
Time: 606/259-2333 **Weather:** 606/293-9999
Time Zone: Eastern

AIRPORT TRANSPORTATION:

Eight miles to downtown Lexington.
Taxicab and limousine service.

SELECTED HOTELS:

Campbell House Inn, 1375 Harrodsburg Rd., 606/255-4281; FAX 606/254-4368
Continental Inn, 801 New Circle Rd. NE, 606/299-5281; FAX 606/293-5905
Harley Hotel of Lexington, 2143 N. Broadway, 606/299-1261; FAX 606/293-0048
Holiday Inn—North, 1950 Newtown Pike, 606/233-0512; FAX 606/231-9285
Hyatt Regency Lexington, 400 W. Vine St., 606/253-1234; FAX 606/233-7974
Marriott's Griffin Gate Resort, 1800 Newtown Pike, 606/231-5100; FAX 606/255-9944
Radisson Plaza Hotel, 369 W. Vine St., 606/231-9000; FAX 606/281-3737
Ramada Hotel, 1938 Stanton Way, 606/259-1311; FAX 606/233-3658
Residence Inn by Marriott, 1080 Newtown Pike, 606/231-6191; FAX (same)

SELECTED RESTAURANTS:

Cafe by the Park, in the Radisson Plaza Hotel, 606/231-9000
The Coach House, 855 S. Broadway, 606/252-7777
Fifth Quarter, 2305 Nicholasville Rd., 606/276-5223
The Glass Garden, in the Hyatt Regency Lexington, 606/253-1234
J. W. Steak House, in the Marriott's Griffin Gate Resort, 606/231-5100
The Mansion at Griffin Gate, 1720 Newtown Pike, 606/288-6142
Nagasaki Inn, 2013 Regency Rd., 606/278-8782
The Springs Inn, 2020 Harrodsburg Rd., 606/277-5751

SELECTED ATTRACTIONS:

Ashland (Henry Clay's home), Richmond Rd. at Sycamore, 606/266-8581
The Hunt-Morgan home, 201 N. Mill St. in Gratz Park, 606/233-3290
Kentucky Horse Park/International Museum of the Horse, 4089 Iron Works Pike, 606/233-4303

Lexington Cemetery, 833 W. Main St., 606/255-5522

Mary Todd Lincoln House, 578 W. Main St., 606/233-9999

Old Fort Harrod State Park, US 27 & US 68, Harrodsburg, 606/734-3314

Shaker Village at Pleasant Hill, 7 miles northeast of Harrodsburg off US 68, 606/734-5411

Waveland State Historic Site, 225 Higbee Mill Rd. off US 27 south, 606/272-3611

INFORMATION SOURCES:

Greater Lexington Convention and Visitors Bureau
301 E. Vine St.
Lexington, Kentucky 40507
606/233-1221; 800/848-1224

Lexington Chamber of Commerce
330 E. Main St.
Lexington, Kentucky 40507
606/254-4447

Little Rock, Arkansas

City map: right
Population: (*401,200) 175,795 (1990C)
Altitude: 330 feet
Average Temp.: Jan., 40,°F.; July, 82°F.
Telephone Area Code: 501
Time and Weather: 501/376-4400
Time Zone: Central

AIRPORT TRANSPORTATION:

Four miles to downtown Little Rock.
Taxicab, bus and hotel shuttle service.

SELECTED HOTELS:

Capital Hotel, 111 W. Markham, 501/374-7474; FAX 501/370-7091

Comfort Inn, 8219 I-30, 501/562-4448; FAX (same)

Doubletree Hotel, 424 W. Markham at Broadway, 501/372-4371; FAX 501/372-0518

Downtown Masters Economy Inn, 707 I-30, 501/372-4392; FAX 501/372-1732

Excelsior Hotel, 3 Statehouse Plaza, 501/375-5000; FAX 501/375-4721

Holiday Inn City Center, 617 S. Broadway, 501/376-2071; FAX 501/376-7733

Holiday Inn North, 111 W. Pershing Blvd., North Little Rock, 501/758-1440; FAX 501/758-2094

Ramada Inn, 120 W. Pershing Blvd., North Little Rock, 501/758-1851; FAX 501/758-5616

Riverfront Hilton Inn, 2 Riverfront Place, 501/371-9000; FAX (same)

SELECTED RESTAURANTS:

Alouette's, 11401 Rodney Parham Rd., 501/225-4152

Cafe Saint Moritz, 225 E. Markham, 501/372-0411

Ciao's Italian Restaurant, 405 W. 7th St., 501/372-0238

Josephine's, in the Excelsior Hotel, 501/375-5000

Landry's at the Wharf, 2400 Cantrell Rd., 501/375-5351

La Scala, 2721 Kavanaugh Blvd., 501/663-1196

SELECTED ATTRACTIONS:

Arkansas Aerospace Education Center, 3301 E. Roosevelt Rd., 501/376-IMAX

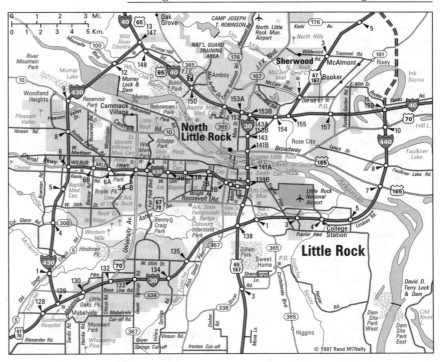

Arkansas Arts Center, MacArthur Park, 9th and Commerce, 501/372-4000

Arkansas State Capitol, Woodlawn and Capitol, for guided tours: 501/682-5080

Little Rock Zoo, 1 Jonesboro Dr., 501/666-2406

Old State House, 300 W. Markham, 501/324-9685

Quapaw Quarter Historic District, (tours) 501/371-0075

INFORMATION SOURCES:

Little Rock Convention & Visitors Bureau
P.O. Box 3232
Little Rock, Arkansas 72203
501/376-4781; 800/844-4781

Greater Little Rock Chamber of Commerce
101 S. Spring St., Suite 200
Little Rock, Arkansas 72201
501/374-4871

Los Angeles, California

City map: pages 60–61
Population: (*11,705,000) 3,485,398 (1990C)
Altitude: Sea level to 330 feet
Average Temp.: Jan., 55°F.; July, 73°F.
Telephone Area Code: 213, 310, 562
Time: 213/853-1212 **Weather:** 213/554-1212
Time Zone: Pacific

AIRPORT TRANSPORTATION:

See map on page 62.
Seventeen miles to downtown Los Angeles.
Taxicab, limousine bus and city bus service.

SELECTED HOTELS:

Biltmore Hotel, 506 S. Grand Ave., 213/624-1011; FAX 213/612-1628

Crowne Plaza Los Angeles Downtown, 3540 S. Figueroa St., 213/748-4141; FAX 213/746-3255

Holiday Inn—Hollywood, 1755 N. Highland Ave., 213/462-7181; FAX 213/466-9072

Hotel Bel-Air, 701 Stone Canyon Rd., 310/472-1211; FAX 310/476-5890

Hyatt Regency Los Angeles, 711 S. Hope St., 213/683-1234; FAX 213/629-3230

Kawada Hotel, 200 S. Hill St., 213/621-4455; FAX 213/687-4455

Le Parc, 733 N. West Knoll Dr., W. Hollywood, 310/855-8888; FAX 310/659-7812

✈Los Angeles Airport Marriott, 5855 W. Century Blvd., 310/641-5700; FAX 310/337-5358

The New Otani Hotel & Garden, 120 S. Los Angeles St., 213/629-1200; FAX 213/622-0980

Omni Los Angeles Hotel and Centre, 930 Wilshire Blvd., 213/688-7777; FAX 213/612-3989

Sheraton Universal Hotel, 333 Universal Terrace Pkwy., Universal City, 818/980-1212; FAX 818/985-4980

The Westin Bonaventure Hotel and Suites, 404 S. Figueroa St., 213/624-1000; FAX 213/612-4800

Westin Century Plaza Hotel & Tower, 2025 Avenue of the Stars, Century City, 310/277-2000; FAX 310/551-3355

✈Wyndham Hotel at Los Angeles Airport, 6225 W. Century Blvd., 310/670-9000; FAX 310/670-8110

SELECTED RESTAURANTS:

Bernard's, in the Biltmore Hotel, 213/612-1580

Epicentre Restaurant, in the Kawada Hotel, 213/625-0000

Lawry's Prime Rib, 100 N. La Cienega
   Blvd., 310/652-2827
L'Orangerie, 903 N. La Cienega Blvd.,
   310/652-9770
Madame Wu's Garden, 2201 Wilshire
   Blvd., 310/828-5656
Pacific Dining Car, 1310 W. 6th St.,
   213/483-6000
Stepps, 330 S. Hope St., 213/626-0900

SELECTED ATTRACTIONS:

Disneyland, 1313 S. Harbor Blvd.,
   Anaheim, 714/781-4000
El Pueblo de Los Angeles State Historic
   Monument, bounded by Cesar Chavez &
   Alameda, Arcadia and Main St.,
   213/628-1274
Farmer's Market & Shopping Village, 6333
   W. 3rd St., 213/933-9211
Griffith Park Observatory, 2800 E.
   Observatory Rd., 213/664-1191
Knott's Berry Farm, 8039 Beach Blvd.,
   Buena Park, 714/220-5200
Los Angeles Zoo, 5333 Zoo Dr.,
   213/664-1100
Mann's Chinese Theatre (movie stars'
   hand and foot prints), 6925 Hollywood
   Blvd., 213/461-3331
Queen Mary, 1126 Queens Hwy., Long
   Beach, 213/435-3511
Rodeo Drive (shopping), Beverly Hills
Universal Studios, 100 Universal City
   Plaza, Universal City, 818/622-3801

INFORMATION SOURCES:

Los Angeles Convention & Visitors Bureau
   633 W. 5th St., Suite 6000
   Los Angeles, California 90071
   213/624-7300; 800/228-2452
Los Angeles Area Chamber of Commerce
   350 S. Bixel St.
   Los Angeles, California 90017
   213/580-7500

Louisville, Kentucky

City map: page 63
Population: (*887,600) 269,063 (1990C)
Altitude: 462 feet
Average Temp.: Jan., 35°F.; July, 78°F.
Telephone Area Code: 502
Time: 502/585-5961 **Weather:**
   502/585-1212
Time Zone: Eastern

AIRPORT TRANSPORTATION:

Five miles to downtown Louisville.
Taxicab, limousine, and bus service.

SELECTED HOTELS:

Breckinridge Inn, 2800 Breckinridge Lane,
   502/456-5050; FAX 502/451-1577
The Camberley Brown, 335 W. Broadway,
   502/583-1234; FAX 502/587-7006
✈Executive Inn Motor Hotel, 978 Phillips
   Ln., 502/367-6161; FAX 502/363-1880
✈Executive West Hotel, 830 Phillips Ln.,
   502/367-2251; FAX 502/363-2087
Fairfield Inn, 9400 Blairwood Rd.,
   502/339-1900; FAX (same)
The Galt House, 140 N. 4th St.,
   502/589-5200; FAX 502/589-3444
Holiday Inn Downtown, 120 W.
   Broadway, 502/582-2241;
   FAX 502/584-8591

Holiday Inn Southwest, 4110 Dixie Hwy.,
   502/448-2020; FAX 502/448-0808
Hurstbourne Hotel & Conference Center,
   9700 Bluegrass Pkwy., 502/491-4830;
   FAX 502/499-2893
Hyatt Regency Louisville, 320 W. Jefferson
   St., 502/587-3434; FAX 502/581-0133
The Seelbach Hotel, 500 Fourth Ave.,
   502/585-3200; FAX 502/585-9239

SELECTED RESTAURANTS:

The Atrium, 1028 Barret Ave.,
   502/456-6789
Bristol Bar & Grille, 1321 Bardstown Rd.,
   502/456-1702
Cafe Metro, 1700 Bardstown Rd.,
   502/458-4830
Dell Frisco's, 4107 Oechsli Ave.,
   502/897-7077
Mama Grisanti's, 3938 DuPont Circle,
   502/893-0141
New Orleans House East, 9424 Shel-
   byville Rd., 502/426-1577
Oak Room, in The Seelbach Hotel,
   502/585-3200
The Spire, in the Hyatt Regency
   Louisville, 502/587-3434

SELECTED ATTRACTIONS:

Actors Theatre of Louisville, 316 W. Main
   St., 502/584-1205
Churchill Downs, 700 Central Ave.,
   502/636-4400
Farmington Historic Home, 3033
   Bardstown Rd., 502/452-9920
Hillerich & Bradsby (Louisville Slugger
   factory), 800 W. Main, 502/585-5226
J.B. Speed Art Museum, 2035 S. Third St.,
   502/636-2920
Kentucky Center for the Arts, W. Main St.
   between 5th & 6th, 502/584-7777
Kentucky Derby Museum, 704 Central
   Ave., 502/637-1111
Locust Grove Historic Home, 561
   Blankenbaker Ln., 502/897-9845
Louisville Science Center/IMAX Theater,
   727 W. Main St., 502/561-6100
Louisville Zoo, 1100 Trevilian Way,
   502/459-2181

INFORMATION SOURCES:

Louisville and Jefferson County
Convention & Visitors Bureau
   400 S. 1st
   Louisville, Kentucky 40202
   502/584-2121; 800/626-5646
Louisville Tourist Information
   400 S. 1st
   Louisville, Kentucky 40202
   800/792-5595
Louisville Area Chamber of Commerce
   600 W. Main St.
   Louisville, Kentucky 40202
   502/625-0000

Memphis, Tennessee

City map: page 63
Population: (*951,500) 610,337 (1990C)
Altitude: 264 feet
Average Temp.: Jan., 43°F.; July, 80°F.
Telephone Area Code: 901
Time and Weather: 901/522-8888
Time Zone: Central

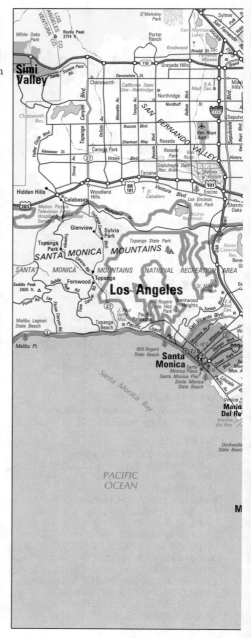

AIRPORT TRANSPORTATION:

See map on page 63.
Ten miles to downtown Memphis.
Taxicab and limousine bus service.

SELECTED HOTELS:

Adam's Mark Hotel, 939 Ridge Lake Blvd.,
   901/684-6664; FAX 901/762-7411
Brownestone Hotel, 300 N. Second St.,
   901/525-2511; FAX (same)
✈Comfort Inn Airport, 2411 Winchester
   Rd., at the Airport, 901/332-2370;
   FAX 901/398-4085
Crowne Plaza, 250 N. Main St.,
   901/527-7300; FAX 901/526-1561
✈Four Points Hotel, 2240 Democrat Rd.,
   901/332-1130; FAX 901/398-5206

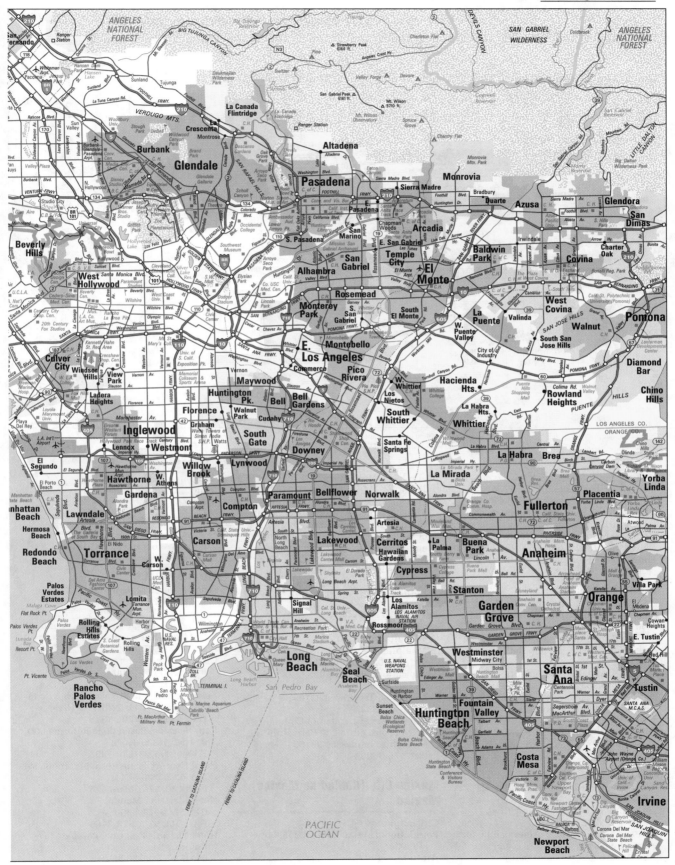

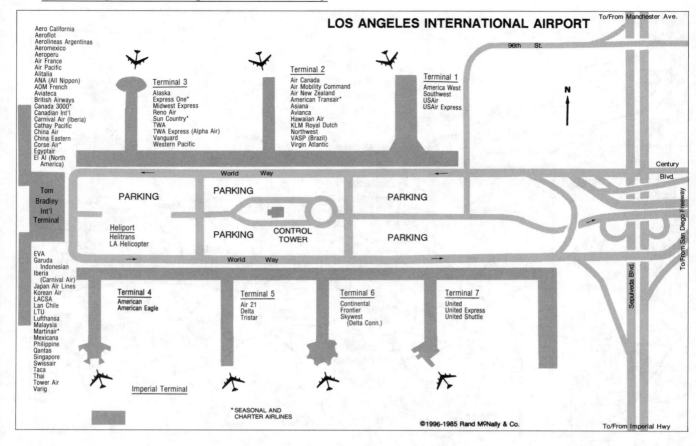

LOS ANGELES INTERNATIONAL AIRPORT

To/From Manchester Ave.

96th St.

Terminal 3
Alaska
Express One*
Midwest Express
Reno Air
Sun Country*
TWA
TWA Express (Alpha Air)
Vanguard
Western Pacific

Terminal 2
Air Canada
Air Mobility Command
Air New Zealand
American Transair*
Asiana
Avianca
Hawaiian Air
KLM Royal Dutch
Northwest
VASP (Brazil)
Virgin Atlantic

Terminal 1
America West
Southwest
USAir
USAir Express

Aero California
Aeroflot
Aerolineas Argentinas
Aeromexico
Aeroperu
Air France
Air Pacific
Alitalia
ANA (All Nippon)
AOM French
Aviateca
British Airways
Canada 3000*
Canadian Int'l
Carnival Air (Iberia)
Cathay Pacific
China Air
China Eastern
Corse Air*
Egyptair
El Al (North America)

Tom Bradley Int'l Terminal

EVA
Garuda Indonesian
Iberia (Carnival Air)
Japan Air Lines
Korean Air
LACSA
Lan Chile
LTU
Lufthansa
Malaysia
Martinair*
Mexicana
Philippine
Qantas
Singapore
Swissair
Taca
Thai
Tower Air
Varig

N

Century Blvd.

World Way

PARKING
PARKING
PARKING

Heliport
Helitrans
LA Helicopter

PARKING
CONTROL TOWER
PARKING

World Way

Terminal 4
American
American Eagle

Terminal 5
Air 21
Delta
Tristar

Terminal 6
Continental
Frontier
Skywest
(Delta Conn.)

Terminal 7
United
United Express
United Shuttle

Imperial Terminal

* SEASONAL AND CHARTER AIRLINES

Sepulveda Blvd.

To/From San Diego Freeway

©1996-1985 Rand M°Nally & Co.

To/From Imperial Hwy.

Holiday Inn International Airport, 1441 E. Brooks Rd., 901/398-9211; FAX (same)
Holiday Inn Midtown/Medical Center, 1837 Union Ave., 901/278-4100; FAX 901/272-3810
Memphis Marriott, 2625 Thousand Oaks Blvd., 901/362-6200; FAX 901/360-8836
The Peabody Memphis, 149 Union Ave., 901/529-4000; FAX 901/529-3600

SELECTED RESTAURANTS:

Anderton's, 1901 Madison, 901/726-4010
Benihana of Tokyo, 912 Ridgelake, 901/683-7390
Corky's, 5259 Poplar, 901/685-9744
Folk's Folly, 551 S. Mendenhall, 901/762-8200
Grisanti's, 220 S. Claybrook St., 901/722-9363
Justine's, 919 Coward Pl., 901/527-3815
Paulette's, 2110 Madison Ave., 901/726-5128
The Pier, 100 Wagner Pl., 901/526-7381
The Rendezvous, 52 S. 2nd St., 901/523-2746

SELECTED ATTRACTIONS:

Beale Street (birthplace of the blues), 901/529-0999
Graceland, 3734 Elvis Presley Blvd., 901/332-3322
Heritage Tours (African-American history tours), 901/527-3427
Liberty Land (amusement park), Mid-South Fairgrounds, 901/274-1776

Memphis Motor Sports Park, 5500 Taylor Forge Rd., Millington, 901/358-7223
Memphis Pink Palace Museum, Planetarium & IMAX Theater, 3050 Central Ave., 901/320-6320
Memphis Queen Line, 901/527-5694
Memphis Zoo & Aquarium, 2000 Gallaway, in Overton Park, 901/726-4787
National Civil Rights Museum, 450 Mulberry, 901/521-9699

INFORMATION SOURCES:

Memphis Convention & Visitors Bureau
47 Union Ave.
Memphis, Tennessee 38103
901/543-5300; 800/873-6282
Visitor Information Center
340 Beale St.
Memphis, Tennessee 38103
901/543-5333
Memphis Area Chamber of Commerce
22 N. Front, Suite 200 Falls Building
Memphis, Tennessee 38103
901/575-3500

Mexico City (Ciudad de México), Mexico

City map: page 64
Population: (*14,100,000) 8,235,744 (1990C)
Altitude: 7,450 ft.
Average Temp.: Jan., 54°F.; July, 64°F.

Telephone Code: 011/52/5
Time & Weather: None
Time Zone: Central

AIRPORT TRANSPORTATION:

See map on page 64.
Four miles to downtown Mexico City.
Taxicab and limousine service.

SELECTED HOTELS:

Aristos, Paseo de la Reforma 276, 011/52/5/211-0112; FAX 011/52/5/514-8005
Camino Real, Av. Mariano Escobedo 700, 011/52/5/203-2121; FAX 011/52/5/250-6897
Crowne Plaza, Reforma 1, 011/52/5/128-5000; FAX 011/52/5/125-5050
Fiesta Americana Reforma, Paseo de la Reforma 80, 011/52/5/705-1515; FAX 011/52/5/705-1313
Four Seasons, Paseo de la Reforma 500, 011/52/5/230-1818; FAX 011/52/5/230-1808
Hotel Century Zona Rosa, Liverpool 152, 011/52/5/726-9911; FAX 011/52/5/525-7475
Hotel Majestic, Madero 73, 011/52/5/521-8600; FAX 011/52/5/518-3466
Hotel Marquis Reforma, Paseo de la Reforma 011/52/5/465, 011/52/5/211-3600; FAX 011/52/5/211-5561

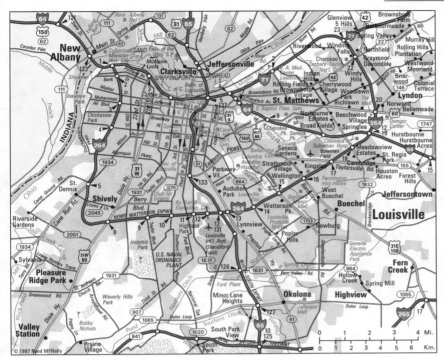

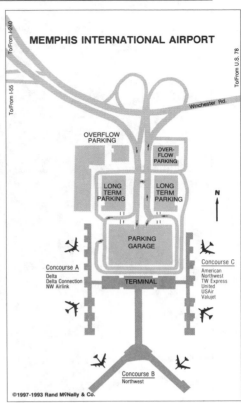

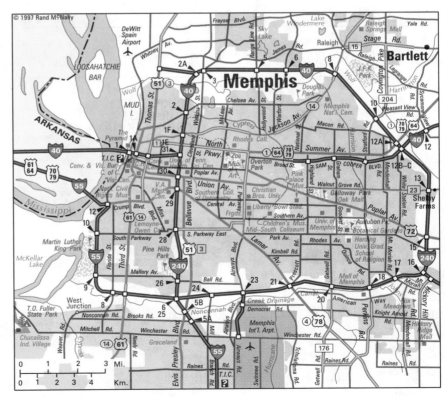

Hotel Nikko, Campos Eliseos 204,
011/52/5/280-1111;
FAX 011/52/5/280-9191
Krystal Rosa, Liverpool 155,
011/52/5/228-9928;
FAX 011/52/5/511-3490
Maria Cristina Hotel, Rio Lerma 31,
011/52/5/566-9688;
FAX 011/52/5/566-9194
Presidente Inter-Continental, Campos
Eliseos 218, 011/52/5/327-7700;
FAX 011/52/5/327-7783
Radisson Paraiso Hotel, Cúspide 53,
011/52/5/606-4211;
FAX 011/52/5/606-4006
Royal Pedregal Hotel, Periférico Sur 4363,
011/52/5/726-9036;
FAX 011/52/5/645-7964
Sheraton Maria Isabel Hotel & Towers,
Paseo de la Reforma 325,
011/52/5/207-3933;
FAX 011/52/5/207-0684
Westin Galeria Plaza, Hamburgo 195,
011/52/5/211-0014;
FAX 011/52/5/207-5867

SELECTED RESTAURANTS:

Anderson's, Paseo de la Reforma 382
Antigua Hacienda de Tlalpan, Calz de
Tlalpan 4619
Azulejos, in the Camino Real Hotel
Bellinghausen, Londres 95
Chalet Suizo, Niza 37
Champs Elysees, Paseo de la Reforma 316
El Parador, Niza 17
Focolare, Hamburgo 87 Zona Rosa
Fonda del Refugio, Liverpool 166
Fouquets de Paris, in the Camino Real
Hotel
La Cava, Insurgentes Sur 2465

La Hacienda de los Morales, Vázquez de
    Mella 525
Les Moustaches, Rio Sena 88
Loredo, Insurgentes Sur 635
Maxims, in the Presidente Inter-
    Continental Hotel
Mesón del Caballo Bayo, Av. Conscripción
    360
Prendes, 16 de Septiembre
Restaurant del Lago, Chapultepec Park
    2nd Section
Rincón Argentina, Presidente Masaryk
    177
San Angel Inn, Diego Rivera 50

SELECTED ATTRACTIONS:

Ballet Folklórico, at the Palace of Fine
    Arts on Av. Juárez
Chapultepec Castle, at the entrance to
    Chapultepec Park
Diego Rivera Museum, Plaza Solidaridad
Floating Gardens of Xochimilco
Frida Kahlo Museum, Londres 247,
    Coyoacán
Hipodromo de las Americas (horseracing)
National Museum of Anthropology, in
    Chapultepec Park
National Palace
Pyramids of Teotihuacán (light and sound
    show)
Rufino Tamayo Museum (art), in
    Chapultepec Park on the west side of
    Reforma
Templo Mayor (Aztec temple remains),
    northeast corner of the Zocalo

INFORMATION SOURCES:

Mexico City Tourist Bureau
    Amberes No. 54 Esq. Londres
    Zona Rosa Col. Juárez
    06600 México, D.F.
    011/52/5/211-00-99
Federal District Chamber of Commerce
    Paseo de la Reforma No. 42
    Delegación Cuauhtémoc
    06048 México, D.F.
    011/52/5/592-26-77
Mexican Government Tourism Office
    405 Park Avenue, Suite 1401
    New York, New York 10022
    212/755-7261 or 212/421-6655
    800/446-3942

Miami, Florida

City map: page 65
Population: (*3,456,600) 358,548 (1990C)
Altitude: Sea level to 30 feet
Average Temp.: Jan., 69°F.; July, 82°F.
Telephone Area Code: 305
Time: 305/324-8811 **Weather:**
    305/229-4522
Time Zone: Eastern

AIRPORT TRANSPORTATION:

See map on page 66.
Five miles to downtown Miami.
Taxicab and limousine bus service.

SELECTED HOTELS:

Best Western Marina Park Hotel, 340
    Biscayne Blvd., 305/371-4400;
    FAX 305/372-2862
Biscayne Bay Marriott Hotel & Marina,
    1633 N. Bayshore Dr., 305/374-3900;
    FAX 305/375-0597

MEXICO CITY,
JUAREZ
INTERNATIONAL
AIRPORT

PARKING STRUCTURE
Overhead Ramps
HOTEL
PARKING
Car Rental
TERMINAL
PARKING
TERMINAL BUILDING

Ground Level			Second Level Gates 1-17	
Aero California	British Airways	Malaysian Airline	Aero California	Canadian Airlines Int'l	Mexicana
Aeroflot	Continental	Mexicana	Aeroflot	Continental	Taca
Aerolineas Argentinas	Cubana Airlines	Taca	Aerolineas Argentinas	Cubana Airlines	United
Aeromar	Canadian Airlines Int'l	Taesa	Aeromar	Delta	USAir
Aeromexico	Delta	United	Aeromexico	Iberia	Varig
Aeroperu	Iberia	USAir	Aeroperu	Japan Air Lines	
Air France	Japan Air Lines	Varig	Air France	KLM	
American	KLM		American	LACSA	
America West	LACSA		America West	Lloyd Aereo Boliviano	
Aviacsa	Lufthansa		Avianca	Lufthansa	
Avianca	Lloyd Aereo Boliviano		Aviateca	Malaysian Airline	
Aviateca			British Airways		

©1997-1996 Rand McNally & Co.

Crowne Plaza Miami, 1601 Biscayne
Blvd., 305/374-0000; FAX 305/374-0020
Don Shula's Hotel & Golf Club, 15255 Bull
Run Rd., Miami Lakes, 305/821-1150;
FAX 305/820-8190
Doubletree Hotel at Coconut Grove, 2649
S. Bayshore Dr., 305/858-2500;
FAX 305/858-5776
Fontainebleau Hilton Resort & Towers,
4441 Collins Ave., Miami Beach,
305/538-2000; FAX 305/531-9274
Hyatt Regency Miami, 400 SE. 2nd Ave.,
305/358-1234; FAX 305/358-0529
✈Miami Airport Hilton & Towers, 5101
Blue Lagoon Dr., 305/262-1000;
FAX 305/267-0038
✈Miami Airport Marriott, 1201 NW.
LeJeune Rd., 305/649-5000;
FAX 305/642-3369
The Omni Colonnade, 180 Aragon Ave.,
Coral Gables, 305/441-2600;
FAX 305/445-3929
✈Ramada Hotel—Miami International
Airport, 3941 NW. 22nd St.,
305/871-1700; FAX 305/871-4830
Sheraton Biscayne Bay, 495 Brickell Ave.,
305/373-6000; FAX 305/374-2279
Travelodge Inn at the Civic Center, 1170
NW 11th St., 305/324-0800;
FAX 305/547-1820

SELECTED RESTAURANTS:

Bay 61, 9561 E. Bay Harbor Dr.,
305/866-8779
Centro Vasco, 2235 SW. 8th St.,
305/643-9606
The Chart House, 51 Charthouse Dr.,
Coconut Grove, 305/856-9741
The Dining Galleries, in the
Fontainebleau Hilton, 305/538-2000
Joe's Stone Crab, 227 Biscayne St., Miami
Beach, 305/673-0365
La Paloma, 10999 Biscayne Blvd.,
305/891-0505

SELECTED ATTRACTIONS:

Ancient Spanish Monastery, in St.
Bernard's Church, 16711 W. Dixie Hwy.,
North Miami Beach, 305/945-1461
Biscayne National Park Tour Boats,
Biscayne National Park Headquarters,
9 mi. east of Homestead, 305/230-1100
Fairchild Tropical Garden, 10901 Old
Cutler Rd., Coral Gables, 305/667-1651
Miami Metrozoo, 12400 SW 152nd St.,
305/251-0400
Miami Museum of Science & Space
Transit Planetarium, 3280 S. Miami
Ave., 305/854-4247
Miami Seaquarium, 4400 Rickenbacker
Causeway, 305/361-5705
Miccosukee Indian Village & Airboat
Tours, 30 miles west of Miami on US
41, 305/223-8380 (weekdays)
Monkey Jungle, 14805 SW 216th St.,
305/235-1611
Parrot Jungle & Gardens, 11000 SW 57th
Ave., 305/666-7834
Vizcaya Museum and Gardens, 3251 S.
Miami Ave., 305/250-9133

INFORMATION SOURCE:

Greater Miami Convention and Visitors
Bureau
701 Brickell Ave., Suite 2700
Miami, Florida 33131
305/539-3000; 800/283-2707

Milwaukee, Wisconsin

City map: page 66
Population: (*1,407,200) 628,088 (1990C)
Altitude: 634 feet
Average Temp.: Jan., 21°F.; July, 71°F.
Telephone Area Code: 414
Time: 414/844-1414 **Weather:**
414/936-1212
Time Zone: Central

AIRPORT TRANSPORTATION:

Eight miles to downtown Milwaukee.
Taxicab, bus, and limousine bus service.

SELECTED HOTELS:

✈The Grand Milwaukee Hotel, 4747
S. Howell Ave., 414/481-8000;
FAX 414/481-8065
Hyatt Regency Milwaukee, 333 W.
Kilbourn Ave., 414/276-1234;
FAX 414/276-6338
Milwaukee Hilton, 509 W. Wisconsin
Ave., 414/271-7250; FAX 414/271-1039
Milwaukee River Hilton Inn, 4700 N. Port
Washington Rd., Glendale,
414/962-6040; FAX 414/962-6166
The Pfister Hotel, 424 E. Wisconsin Ave.,
414/273-8222; FAX 414/273-5025
Sheraton Milwaukee Mayfair, 2303
N. Mayfair, Wauwatosa, 414/257-3400;
FAX 414/257-0900
Wyndham Milwaukee Center, 139 E.
Kilbourn Ave., 414/276-8686;
FAX 414/276-8007

SELECTED RESTAURANTS:

Benson's, in the Milwaukee Hilton,
414/271-7250
The English Room, in The Pfister Hotel,
414/273-8222
Grenadier's, 747 N. Broadway,
414/276-0747

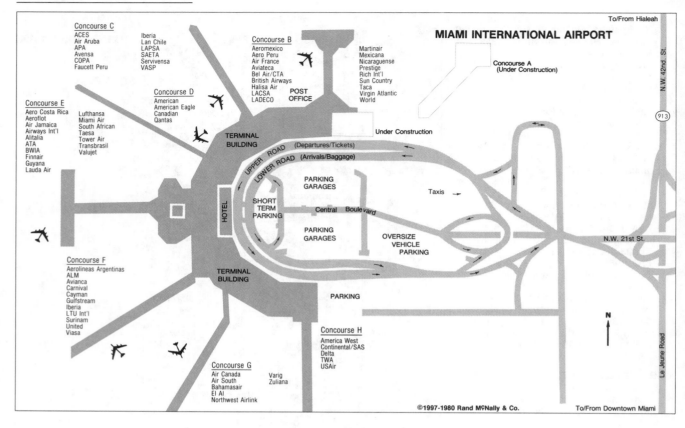

MIAMI INTERNATIONAL AIRPORT

Concourse C
ACES
Air Aruba
APA
Avensa
COPA
Faucett Peru

Iberia
Lan Chile
LAPSA
SAETA
Servivensa
VASP

Concourse B
Aeromexico
Aero Peru
Air France
Aviateca
Bel Air/CTA
British Airways
Halisa Air
LACSA
LADECO

Martinair
Mexicana
Nicaraguense
Prestige
Rich Int'l
Sun Country
Taca
Virgin Atlantic
World

Concourse A
(Under Construction)

Concourse D
American
American Eagle
Canadian
Qantas

POST OFFICE

Concourse E
Aero Costa Rica
Aeroflot
Air Jamaica
Airways Int'l
Alitalia
ATA
BWIA
Finnair
Guyana
Lauda Air

Lufthansa
Miami Air
South African
Taesa
Tower Air
Transbrasil
Valujet

TERMINAL BUILDING

Under Construction

UPPER ROAD (Departures/Tickets)
LOWER ROAD (Arrivals/Baggage)

HOTEL

SHORT TERM PARKING

PARKING GARAGES

Central Boulevard

PARKING GARAGES

Taxis

OVERSIZE VEHICLE PARKING

N.W. 21st St.

Concourse F
Aerolineas Argentinas
ALM
Avianca
Carnival
Cayman
Gulfstream
Iberia
LTU Int'l
Surinam
United
Viasa

TERMINAL BUILDING

PARKING

Concourse H
America West
Continental/SAS
Delta
TWA
USAir

Concourse G
Air Canada
Air South
Bahamasair
El Al
Northwest Airlink

Varig
Zuliana

To/From Hialeah

N.W. 42nd St.

913

N

Le Jeune Road

©1997-1980 Rand McNally & Co.

To/From Downtown Miami

John Ernst's, Ogden at Jackson, 414/273-1878

Karl Ratzsch's, 320 E. Mason St., 414/276-2720

Mader's German Restaurant, 1037 N. Old World 3rd St., 414/271-3377

Pieces of Eight, 550 N. Harbor Dr., 414/271-0597

Whitney's, in the Milwaukee Marriott, 375 S. Moorland Rd., Brookfield, 414/786-1100

SELECTED ATTRACTIONS:

Miller Brewing Company, 4251 W. State St., 414/931-BEER

Milwaukee Art Museum, 750 N. Lincoln Memorial Dr., 414/224-3200

Milwaukee County Zoo, 10001 W. Bluemound Rd., 414/771-3040

Milwaukee Public Museum, 800 W. Wells St., 414/278-2702

Mitchell Park Horticultural Conservatory (The Domes), 524 S. Layton Blvd., 414/649-9830

Pabst Brewing Company, 915 W. Juneau Ave., 414/223-3709

Pabst Mansion, 2000 W. Wisconsin Ave., 414/931-0808

Potawatomi Bingo, 1721 W. Canal St., 414/645-6888

INFORMATION SOURCES:

Greater Milwaukee Convention & Visitors Bureau
510 W. Kilbourn Ave.
Milwaukee, Wisconsin 53203
414/273-3950; 800/231-0903

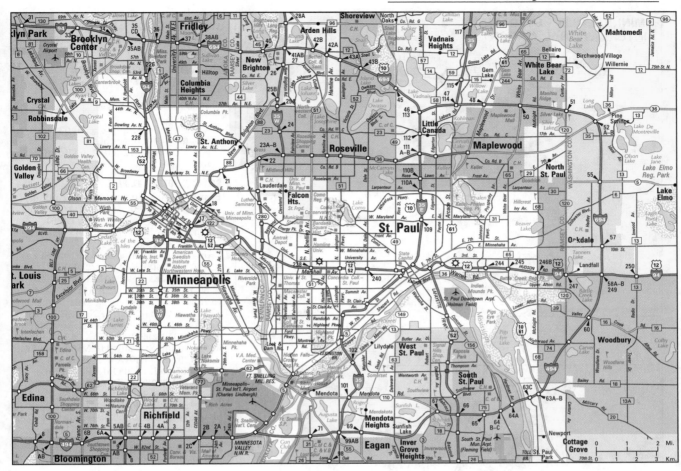

Metropolitan Milwaukee Association of
Commerce
 756 N. Milwaukee St.
 Milwaukee, Wisconsin 53202
 414/287-4100

Minneapolis-St. Paul, Minnesota

City map: above
Population: (*2,332,100) Minneapolis
 368,383; St. Paul 272,235 (1990C)
Altitude: Minneapolis 840 feet;
 St. Paul 874 feet
Average Temp.: Jan., 15°F.; July, 74°F.
Telephone Area Code: 612
Time: 612/224-8463 **Weather:**
 612/361-6680
Time Zone: Central

AIRPORT TRANSPORTATION:

See map on page 68.
About 8 miles to downtown Minneapolis
 or St. Paul.
Taxicab, bus, and limousine bus service to
 Minneapolis and St. Paul.

SELECTED HOTELS: MINNEAPOLIS

Crowne Plaza Northstar Hotel, 618 2nd
 Ave. S., 612/338-2288;
 FAX 612/338-2288

Holiday Inn International Airport #2,
 5401 Green Valley Dr., Bloomington,
 612/831-8000; FAX 612/831-8426
Hotel Sofitel, 5601 W. 78th St.,
 612/835-1900; FAX 612/835-2696
Hyatt Regency Minneapolis, 1300 Nicollet
 Mall, 612/370-1234; FAX 612/370-1463
Mall of America Grand Hotel, 7901 24th
 Ave. S., Bloomington, 612/854-2244;
 FAX 612/854-4421
Minneapolis Hilton & Towers, 1001
 Marquette Ave., 612/376-1000;
 FAX 612/397-4875
Minneapolis Marriott Bloomington, 2020
 E. 79th St., Bloomington, 612/854-7441;
 FAX 612/854-7671
Minneapolis Marriott City Center, 30 S.
 7th St., 612/349-4000;
 FAX 612/332-7165
Radisson Hotel Metrodome, 615
 Washington Ave. SE, 612/379-8888;
 FAX 612/379-8682
Radisson Hotel South & Plaza Tower, 7800
 Normandale Blvd., Bloomington,
 612/835-7800; FAX 612/893-8419
✈Sheraton Airport Inn, 2500 E. 79th St.,
 Bloomington, 612/854-1771;
 FAX 612/854-5898
Wyndham Garden Hotel, 4460 W. 78th St.
 Circle, Bloomington, 612/831-3131;
 FAX 612/831-6372

SELECTED RESTAURANTS: MINNEAPOLIS

The Anchorage Restaurant, 1330
 Industrial Blvd., 612/379-4444
Goodfellow's, 800 Nicollet Mall, 4th floor,
 612/332-4800
Gustino's, in the Minneapolis Marriott
 City Center, 612/349-4000
Lord Fletcher's of the Lake, 3746 Sunset
 Dr., Spring Park, 612/471-8513
Taxxi Restaurant, in the Hyatt Regency
 Minneapolis, 612/370-1234

SELECTED ATTRACTIONS: MINNEAPOLIS

American Swedish Institute, 2600 Park
 Ave., 612/871-4907
Bell Museum (Minnesota flora and fauna
 in natural habitat), University of
 Minnesota, 17th Ave. & University Ave.
 SE, 612/624-7083
Frederick R. Weisman Art Museum, 333
 E. River Rd., University of Minnesota
 campus, 612/625-9494
Guthrie Theatre, 725 Vineland Pl.,
 612/377-2224
The Mall of America, MN 77 & I-494,
 Bloomington, 612/883-8800
Minneapolis Institute of Arts, 2400 Third
 Ave. S., 612/870-3046
Minneapolis Planetarium, inside the
 Public Library, 300 Nicollet Mall,
 612/372-6644

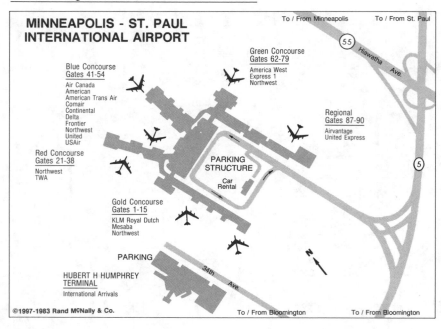

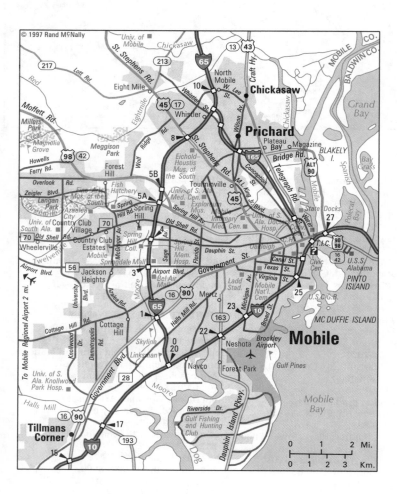

Nicollet Mall, downtown Minneapolis
Walker Art Center/Minneapolis Sculpture
   Garden, 725 Vineland Pl., 612/375-7577
   or -7600

INFORMATION SOURCE: MINNEAPOLIS

Greater Minneapolis Convention &
Visitors Association
   4000 Multifoods Tower
   33 S. 6th St.
   Minneapolis, Minnesota 55402
   612/661-4700 (meetings &
   conventions); 612/348-7000 (tourist
   information)

SELECTED HOTELS: ST. PAUL

Best Western Kelly Inn, 161 St. Anthony
   Ave., 612/227-8711; FAX 612/227-1698
Country Inn by Carlson, 4940 US 61,
   White Bear Lake, 612/429-5393;
   FAX 612/429-6342
Crown Sterling Suites, 175 E. 10th St.,
   612/224-5400; FAX 612/224-0957
Holiday Inn Express, 1010 Bandana Blvd.
   W., 612/647-1637; FAX 612/647-0244
Holiday Inn St. Paul/East, 2201 Burns
   Ave., 612/731-2220; FAX 612/731-0243
Radisson Hotel St. Paul, 11 E. Kellogg
   Blvd., 612/292-1900; FAX 612/224-8999
Radisson Inn St. Paul, 411 Minnesota St.,
   612/291-8800; FAX 612/292-8845
Ramada Hotel, 1870 Old Hudson Rd.,
   612/735-2333; FAX 612/735-1953
The St. Paul Hotel, 350 Market St.,
   612/292-9292; FAX 612/228-9506
Sheraton Midway, 400 N. Hamline Ave.,
   612/642-1234; FAX 612/642-1126

SELECTED RESTAURANTS: ST. PAUL

Bali Hai, 2305 White Bear Ave. and MN
   36, Maplewood, 612/777-5500
The Carrousel, in the Radisson Hotel,
   612/292-1900
Forepaugh's Restaurant, 276 S. Exchange
   St., 612/224-5606
Gallivan's, 354 Wabasha St., 612/227-6688
McGovern's Pub, 225 W. 7th St.,
   612/224-5821
Venetian Inn, 2814 Rice St., 612/484-7215

SELECTED ATTRACTIONS: ST. PAUL

Alexander Ramsey House, 265 S.
   Exchange St., 612/296-8760
Como Park Zoo and Conservatory,
   Midway Pkwy. & Kaufman Dr.,
   612/488-5571 or -4041
Historic Fort Snelling, Fort Rd. at MN
   Hwys. 5 & 55, 612/725-2413
James J. Hill House, 240 Summit Ave.,
   612/297-2555
Jonathan Padelford & Josiah Snelling
   Riverboats, Harriet Island,
   612/227-1100
Minnesota Children's Museum, 10 W. 7th
   St., 612/225-6000
Minnesota History Center, 345 Kellogg
   Blvd. W., 612/296-6126
Minnesota Museum of American Art, in
   Landmark Center, 75 W. 5th St.,
   612/292-4355
Minnesota State Capitol, Cedar & Aurora
   sts., 612/297-3521 (recorded info.);
   612/296-2881 (tour reservations)
Science Museum of Minnesota/William L.
   McKnight Omnitheater, Exchange &
   Wabasha sts., 612/221-9454

INFORMATION SOURCES: ST. PAUL

St. Paul Convention & Visitors Bureau
102 Norwest Center
55 E. 5th St.
St. Paul, Minnesota 55101
612/297-6985; 800/627-6101;
FAX 612/297-6879
Minnesota Office of Tourism
101 Metro Square Building
121 7th Place E.
St. Paul, Minnesota 55101-2112
612/296-5029; 800/657-3700
St. Paul Area Chamber of Commerce
101 Norwest Center
55 E. 5th St.
St. Paul, Minnesota 55101
612/223-5000

Mobile, Alabama

City map: page 68
Population: (*375,800) 196,278 (1990C)
Altitude: 7 feet
Average Temp.: Jan., 51°F.; July, 82°F.
Telephone Area Code: 334
Time: 334/660-0044 **Weather:**
334/223-7460
Time Zone: Central

AIRPORT TRANSPORTATION:

Twelve miles to downtown Mobile.
Taxicab and limousine bus service.

SELECTED HOTELS:

Adam's Mark Hotel—Riverview Plaza, 64
S. Water St., 334/438-4000;
FAX 334/415-3060
Clarion Hotel, 3101 Airport Blvd.,
334/476-6400; FAX 334/476-9360
Holiday Inn I-10, 6527 US 90 West,
334/666-5600; FAX 334/666-2773
Holiday Inn I-65, 850 S. Beltline Hwy.,
334/342-3220; FAX 334/342-8919
Malaga Inn, 359 Church St.,
334/438-4701; FAX 334/438-4701
ext. 123
Radisson Admiral Semmes Hotel, 251
Government St., 334/432-8000;
FAX 334/432-8000
Ramada Conference Center, 600 S.
Beltline Hwy., 334/344-8030;
FAX 334/344-8055

SELECTED RESTAURANTS:

La Louisiana, 2400 Airport Blvd.,
334/476-8130
Mayme's Restaurant, Malaga Inn,
334/438-4701
Nautilus, Hwys. 98 & 90, Daphne,
334/626-0783
The Pillars, 1757 Government St.,
334/478-6341
Port City Brewery, 225 Dauphin St.,
334/438-2739
Ruth's Chris Steak House, 271 Glenwood
St., 334/476-0516

SELECTED ATTRACTIONS:

Battleship USS *Alabama* Memorial Park,
Hwy. 98, off I-10, 334/433-2703
Bellingrath Gardens and Home, 12401
Bellingrath Gardens Rd., Theodore,
334/973-2217
Bragg-Mitchell Mansion, 1906 Spring Hill
Ave., 334/471-6364

The Exploreum, 1906 Spring Hill Ave.,
334/471-5923
Fort Condé, 150 S. Royal St.,
334/434-7658
Museum of the City of Mobile, 355
Government St., 334/434-7569
Oakleigh Mansion, 350 Oakleigh Pl.,
334/432-1281
The Phoenix Fire Museum, 203 S.
Claiborne St., 334/434-7554
Richards DAR House, 256 N. Joachim St.,
334/434-7320

INFORMATION SOURCES:

Mobile Convention & Visitors Corporation
1 S. Water St.
Mobile, Alabama 36602
334/415-2000; 800/5MOBILE
City of Mobile Fort Condé Welcome
Center
150 S. Royal St.
Mobile, Alabama 36602
334/434-7304
Mobile Area Chamber of Commerce
451 Government
Mobile, Alabama 36602
334/433-6951

Monterrey, Nuevo Leon, Mexico

City map: above
Population: (*2,015,000) 1,068,996
(1990C)
Altitude: 1,270 ft.
Average Temp.: Jan., 58°F.; July, 81°F.
Telephone Code: 011/52/8
Time & Weather: 011/52/8/369-0950
Time Zone: Central

AIRPORT TRANSPORTATION:

Fifteen miles to downtown Monterrey
from Mariano Escobedo Int'l Airport.
Taxicab service.

SELECTED HOTELS:

Best Western Safi, Pino Suárez Sur 444,
011/52/8/399-7000;
FAX 011/52/8/342-2388
Camino Real Ambassador, Hidalgo Ote.
310, 011/52/8/342-2040;
FAX 011/52/8/345-1984
Crowne Plaza Monterrey, Av. Constitucion
Ote. 300, 011/52/8/319-6000;
FAX 011/52/8/344-3007
Fiesta Americana, Av. Vasconcelos Ote.
300, 011/52/8/368-6000;
FAX 011/52/8/368-6040
Fiesta Inn Valle, Av. Lazaro Cardenas Ote.
327, 011/52/8/399-1500;
FAX 011/52/8/399-1501
Gran Hotel Ancira, Plaza Hidalgo,
011/52/8/345-7575;
FAX 011/52/8/344-5226
Holiday Inn Convention Center, Av.
Fundidora 100, 011/52/8/369-6000;
FAX 011/52/8/369-6048
Holiday Inn Norte, Av. Universidad Nte.
101, 011/52/8/376-2302;
FAX 011/52/8/332-0565
Howard Johnson Suites Hotel, Corregidora
Ote. 519, Zona Rosa, 011/52/8/319-0900;
FAX 011/52/8/319-0990
Quinta Real Monterrey, Diego Rivera 500,
011/52/8/368-1000;
FAX 011/52/8/368-1070
Royal Courts, Av. Universidad 314,
011/52/8/376-2710; FAX (same)

SELECTED RESTAURANTS:

Casa Grande, Vasconcelos Pte. 152, Garza
Garcia
El Rey del Cabrito, Av. Constitución 817
Galeria del Gourmet, Av. San Pedro Nte.
117
Le Pavillon, in the Camino Real Ambas-
sador Hotel
Luisiana, Av. Hidalgo Ote. 530

© 1997 Rand McNally and Guía Roji S.A. de C.V.

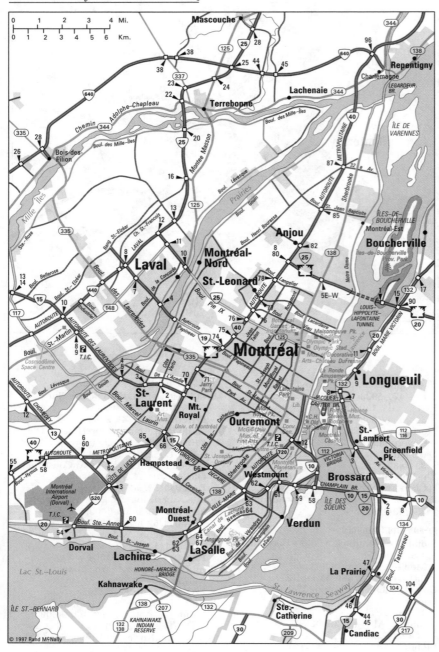

INFORMATION SOURCE:
Direccion Estatal de Turismo
  Av. Zaragosa 1300 Sur
  Level A1, Suite 137
  Monterrey, N.L.
  011/52/8/344-4343 or 340-1080
  (800/235-2438 in the U.S.)

Montréal, Québec, Canada

City map: left
Population: (*3,127,242) 1,017,666
  (1991C)
Altitude: 50 ft.
Average Temp.: Jan., 16°F.; July, 71°F.
Telephone Area Code: 514
Time: (none) **Weather:** 514/283-4006
Time Zone: Eastern

AIRPORT TRANSPORTATION:
See map on page 71.
Fourteen miles from Dorval Airport to
  downtown Montréal, 34 miles from
  Mirabel Airport.
Taxicab and bus service.
Transit service between Dorval and
  Mirabel airports.

SELECTED HOTELS:
Grand Hotel, 777 University St.,
  514/879-1370; FAX 514/879-1761
Hotel le Westin Mont-Royal, 1050
  Sherbrooke St. W., 514/284-1110;
  FAX 514/845-3025
Le Centre Sheraton, 1201 René-Lévesque
  Blvd. W., 514/878-2000;
  FAX 514/878-3958
Le Meridien Montréal, 4 Complexe
  Desjardins at Jeanne Mance St.,
  514/285-1450; FAX 514/285-1243
Marriott Chateau Champlain, 1050 De
  Gauchetiere, corner of Peel St.,
  514/878-9000; FAX 514/878-6761
✈Montréal Aeroport Hilton—Dorval,
  12505 Cote de Liesse Rd.,
  514/631-2411; FAX 514/631-0192
Montréal Hilton Bonaventure, 1 Place
  Bonaventure, 514/878-2332;
  FAX 514/878-1442
Queen Elizabeth Hotel, 900 Blvd.
  René-Lévesque W., 514/861-3511;
  FAX 514/954-2256
The Ritz-Carlton Hotel, 1228 Sherbrooke
  St. W., 514/842-4212; FAX 514/842-3383
Ruby Foo's Hotel, 7655 Decarie Blvd.,
  514/731-7701; FAX 514/731-7158

SELECTED RESTAURANTS:
Beaver Club, Queen Elizabeth Hotel,
  514/861-3511
Café de Paris, Ritz-Carlton Hotel,
  514/842-4212
Chez la Mère Michel, 1209 Guy,
  514/934-0473
Desjardins, 1175 Mackay, 514/866-9741
Le Castillon, Montréal Hilton Bonaven-
  ture Hotel, 514/878-2332
Les Halles, 1450 Crescent St.,
  514/844-2328
Le Vieux Auberge St. Gabriel, 426 Rue St.,
  Gabriel, 514/878-3561

SELECTED ATTRACTIONS:
Biodôme, 4777 Pierre-de-Coubertin Ave.,
  514/868-3000
Botanical Gardens, 4101 Sherbrooke St.
  E., 514/872-1400

Quinta La Noria, Gómez Morin 265
Regio, Av. Universidad Nte. 801
Residence, Degollado Sur 605 at
  Matamoros

SELECTED ATTRACTIONS:
Alfa Cultural Center (science museum,
  planetarium/Omnimax theater), 1000
  Av. Roberto Garza Sada Sur
Cañon de Huasteca (Huasteca Canyon),
  Hwy. 40 to Santa Catarina, then 2
  miles south on Huasteca
Church of the Immaculate Conception
  (Iglesia de la Purisma), Serafin Peña &
  Av. Hidalgo Pte.
Cuauhtemoc Moctezuma Brewery Com-
  plex, 202 Av. Universidad Nte.

El Obispado/Regional Museum of Nuevo
  Leon, west side of town atop Cerro de
  Chepe Vera
Gran Plaza (Macro Plaza), between
  Washington, Constitucion, Zaragoza &
  Dr. Coss
Grutas de Garcia (Garcia Caverns), 28
  miles from Monterrey off Hwy. 40
Museo de Arts Contemporaneo, Gran
  Plaza at Calle Dr. Coss & Ocampo
Museo de Historia Mexicana, 455 Calle
  Dr. Coss, on Gran Plaza
Palacio de Gobierno (Statehouse),
  Zaragoza & 5 de Mayo
Plaza Hidalgo Shopping District, off
  Zaragoza between Moreles & Hidalgo

Canadian Centre for Architecture, 1920
  Baile St., 514/939-7000
Contemporary Art Museum, 185
  Ste-Catherine St. W., 514/847-6212
Insectarium, in the Botanical Gardens,
  4101 Sherbrooke St. E., 514/872-0663
Jet boating on the Lachine Rapids, the Old
  Port at the foot of Berri St. & de la
  Commune St., 514/284-9607
Montréal Museum of Fine Arts, 1379 &
  1380 Sherbrooke St. W., 514/285-1600
Notre Dame Basilica 424 St. Sulpice St.,
  in front of Place d'Armes, Old Montréal,
  514/842-2925
Olympic Park and Tower, 3200 Viau,
  514/252-8687
The Underground City, Ste-Catherine St.
  Downtown

INFORMATION SOURCES:
Greater Montréal Convention & Tourism
Bureau
  1555 Peel St., Suite 600
  Montréal, Québec H3A 1X6
  514/844-5400; 800/363-7777 (tourism
  information)
Canadian Consulate General
  1251 Avenue of the Americas
  New York, New York 10020-1175
  212/596-1600

Nashville, Tennessee

City map: page 72
Population: (*985,026) 487,969 (1990C)
Altitude: 440 feet
Average Temp.: Jan., 38°F.; July, 80°F.
Telephone Area Code: 615
Time and Weather: 615/259-2222
Time Zone: Central

AIRPORT TRANSPORTATION:
See map on page 72.
Seven miles to downtown Nashville.
Taxicab, limousine and bus service.

SELECTED HOTELS:
Courtyard by Marriott, 103 East Park Dr.,
  Brentwood, 615/371-9200;
  FAX 615/371-0832
✈Days Inn, 1 International Plaza, Briley
  Pkwy., 615/361-7666;
  FAX 615/399-0283
Doubletree Hotel, 315 4th Ave. N.,
  615/244-8200; FAX 615/747-4894
The Hermitage Suite Hotel, 231 6th Ave.
  N., 615/244-3121; FAX 615/254-6909
Holiday Inn Express, 981 Murfreesboro
  Rd., 615/367-9150; FAX 615/361-4865
✈Holiday Inn Select., 2200 Elm Hill Pike,
  615/883-9770; FAX 615/391-4521
Nashville Marriott Hotel, 600 Marriott Dr.,
  615/889-9300; FAX 615/889-9315
Opryland Hotel, 2800 Opryland Dr.,
  615/889-1000; FAX 615/871-7741
Quality Inn Hall of Fame, 1407 Division
  St., 615/242-1631; FAX 615/244-9519
Ramada Inn Airport, 709 Spence Ln.,
  615/361-0102; FAX 615/361-4765
Regal Maxwell House, 2025 MetroCenter
  Blvd., 615/259-4343; FAX 615/313-1327
Renaissance Nashville Hotel, 611 Com-
  merce St., 615/255-8400;
  FAX 615/255-8202

MONTRÉAL DORVAL
INTERNATIONAL AIRPORT
©1997-1983 Rand McNally & Co.

SELECTED RESTAURANTS:
Arthur's of Nashville, in the Union
  Station Hotel, 1001 Broadway,
  615/255-1494
The Capital Grill, in The Hermitage Suite
  Hotel, 615/244-3121
JD's Chop House, in the Regal Maxwell
  House, 615/259-4343
Mario's, 2005 Broadway, 615/327-3232
New Orleans Manor, 1400 Murfreesboro
  Rd., 615/367-2777
Old Hickory, in the Opryland Hotel,
  615/889-1000
Praline's, in the Regal Maxwell House,
  615/259-4343
Ruth's Chris Steak House, 204 21st Ave.
  S., 615/320-0163
Stockyard, 901 2nd Ave. N., 615/255-6464
Union Street Grill, in the Doubletree
  Hotel, 615/244-8200

SELECTED ATTRACTIONS:
Belle Meade Plantation, 5025 Harding
  Rd., 615/356-0501
Cheekwood, 1200 Forest Park Dr.,
  615/356-8000
Country Music Hall of Fame, 4 Music
  Square E., 615/256-1639
Cumberland Science Museum, 800 Fort
  Negley Blvd., 615/862-5160
General Jackson Showboat, Exit 11 on
  Briley Pkwy., 615/889-6611
Grand Ole Opry, in Opryland USA Park,
  615/889-6611
The Hermitage, 4580 Rachel's Lane,
  Hermitage, 615/889-2941
Opryland USA, 2802 Opryland Dr.,
  615/889-6600

The Parthenon, West End & 25th aves., in
  Centennial Park, 615/862-8431
Tennessee State Museum, Polk Cultural
  Center, 505 Deaderick St., 615/741-2692

INFORMATION SOURCES:
Nashville Convention & Visitors Bureau
  161 4th Ave. N.
  Nashville, Tennessee 37219
  615/259-4730; Tourist Line
  615/259-4700
Nashville Area Chamber of Commerce
  161 4th Ave. N.
  Nashville, Tennessee 37219
  615/259-4755

New Orleans, Louisiana

City map: page 73
Population: (*1,147,300) 496,938 (1990C)
Altitude: -5 to 25 feet
Average Temp.: Jan., 55°F.; July, 82°F.
Telephone Area Code: 504
Time: 504/529-6111 **Weather:**
  504/465-9212
Time Zone: Central

AIRPORT TRANSPORTATION:
See map on page 73.
Eleven miles to downtown New Orleans.
Taxicab, airport shuttle, and limousine
  bus service.

SELECTED HOTELS:
Chateau Sonesta, 800 Iberville St.,
  504/586-0800; FAX 504/586-1987
Dauphine Orleans Hotel, 415 Dauphine
  St., 504/586-1800; FAX 504/586-1409

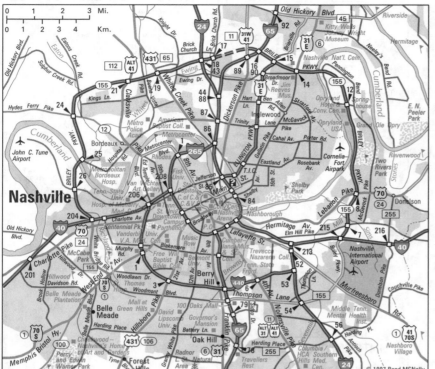

Fairmont Hotel, 123 Baronne St.,
504/529-7111; FAX 504/522-2303
Hotel Inter-Continental New Orleans, 444
St. Charles Ave., 504/525-5566;
FAX 504/523-7310
Hyatt Regency New Orleans, 500 Poydras
Plaza, 504/561-1234; FAX 504/587-4141
The Monteleone Hotel, 214 Royal St.,
504/523-3341; FAX 504/528-1019
New Orleans Hilton Riverside, 2 Poydras
St. at the Mississippi River,
504/561-0500; FAX 504/568-1721
New Orleans Marriott Hotel, 555 Canal
St., 504/581-1000; FAX 504/523-2755
Omni Royal Orleans, 621 St. Louis St.,
504/529-5333; FAX 504/523-5046
The Pontchartrain Hotel, 2031 St. Charles
Ave., 504/524-0581; FAX 504/529-1165
Radisson Hotel, 1500 Canal St.,
504/522-4500; FAX 504/525-2644
Royal Sonesta Hotel, 300 Bourbon St.,
504/586-0300; FAX 504/586-0335
Wyndham Riverfront Hotel—New
Orleans, 701 Convention Center Dr.,
504/524-8200; FAX 504/524-0600

SELECTED RESTAURANTS:

Arnaud's, 813 Bienville, 504/523-5433
Brennan's, 417 Royal St., 504/525-9711
Caribbean Room, in The Pontchartrain
Hotel, 504/524-0581
Commander's Palace Restaurant, 1403
Washington Ave., 504/899-8221
Copeland's, 1001 S. Clearview Pkwy.,
504/733-7843
Galatoire's Restaurant, 209 Bourbon St.,
504/525-2021
Kabby's, in the New Orleans Hilton
Riverside, 504/561-0500
Louis XVI French Restaurant, in the St.
Louis Hotel, 730 Bienville,
504/581-7000
Praline Connection, 542 Frenchman St.,
504/943-3934
Rib Room, in the Omni Royal Orleans
Hotel, 504/529-5333
Sazerac Restaurant, in the Fairmont Hotel,
504/529-7111

SELECTED ATTRACTIONS:

Aquarium of the Americas, 1 Canal St.,
504/565-3033, ext. 549 (information)
Audubon Zoo, 6500 Magazine St.,
504/861-2537
French Quarter, 78-block area bounded by
the Mississippi River, Esplanade Ave.,
Rampart St., & Canal St.
New Orleans Centre, 1400 Poydras St.,
504/568-0000
New Orleans Museum of Art, Lelong Ave.
in City Park, 504/488-2631
New Orleans Paddlewheels (cruises),
504/529-4567
New Orleans Steamboat Company
(cruises), 504/586-8777
Riverwalk (festival marketplace),
1 Poydras St., 504/522-1555

INFORMATION SOURCES:

New Orleans Metropolitan Convention &
Visitors Bureau
1520 Sugar Bowl Dr.
New Orleans, Louisiana 70112
504/566-5011

The Chamber/New Orleans and the River Region
Pan American Building
601 Poydras, Suite 1700
New Orleans, Louisiana 70130
504/527-6900

New York, New York

City map: page 75
Population: (*17,310,800) 7,322,564 (1990C)
Altitude: Sea level to 30 feet
Average Temp.: Jan., 33°F.; July, 75°F.
Telephone Area Code: 212
Time: 212/976-1000 **Weather:** 212/976-1212
Time Zone: Eastern

AIRPORT TRANSPORTATION:
See maps on pages 74 and 76.
Fifteen miles to Manhattan from JFK Airport; 8 miles from La Guardia Airport to Manhattan; 10 miles from Newark Airport to Manhattan.
Taxicab; limousine bus service to and from JFK, La Guardia, and Newark airports and East Side Airlines Terminal. Also JFK Express Subway/bus service from Manhattan to JFK Airport.

SELECTED HOTELS:
The Carlyle, 35 E. 76th St. at Madison Ave, 212/744-1600; FAX 212/717-4682
The Lowell Hotel, 28 E. 63rd St., 212/838-1400; FAX 212/319-4230
Marriott Marquis, 1535 Broadway at 46th St., 212/398-1900; FAX 212/704-8930
The New York Hilton & Towers, 1335 Avenue of the Americas, 212/586-7000; FAX 212/315-1374
The New York Palace, 455 Madison Ave., 212/888-7000; FAX 212/303-6000
The Peninsula New York, 700 5th Ave., 212/247-2200; FAX 212/903-3949
The Pierre, 2 E. 61st St. at 5th Ave., 212/838-8000; FAX 212/940-8109
The Plaza, 768 5th Ave. at 59th St., 212/759-3000; FAX 212/759-3167
The Regency Hotel, 540 Park Ave., 212/759-4100; FAX 212/826-5674
Sheraton New York, 811 7th Ave. at 52nd St., 212/581-1000; FAX 212/841-6466
United Nations Plaza at 44th St., 1 U.N. Plaza, 212/758-1234; FAX 212/702-5051
Waldorf–Astoria, 301 Park Ave. at E. 50th St., 212/355-3000; FAX 212/872-7272

SELECTED RESTAURANTS:
The Four Seasons, 99 E. 52nd St., 212/754-9494
Fraunces Tavern Restaurant, Pearl & Broad sts., 212/269-0144
Gallagher's Steak House, 228 W. 52nd, 212/245-5336
Hurley's Steak & Seafood, 1240 Avenue of the Americas at 49th St., 212/765-8981
La Côte Basque, 60 W. 55th St., 212/688-6525
La Reserve, 4 W. 49th St., 212/247-2993
Lutèce, 249 E. 50th St., 212/752-2225
Mitsukoshi, 465 Park Ave., 212/935-6444
The Russian Tea Room, 150 W. 57th, 212/265-0947
Sardi's, 234 W. 44th, 212/221-8440

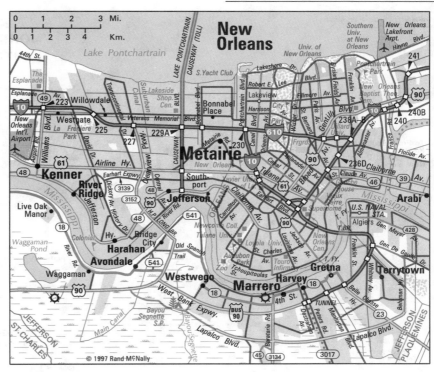

Stage Delicatessen, 834 7th Ave., 212/245-7850
Toots Shor, 233 W. 33rd, 212/630-0333
"21" Club, 21 W. 52nd St., 212/582-7200

SELECTED ATTRACTIONS:
American Museum of Natural History, 79th & Central Park W., 212/769-5100
Empire State Building, Fifth Ave. & 34th St., 212/736-3100
Guggenheim Museum, Fifth Ave. at 88th St., 212/423-3600
Intrepid Sea-Air-Space Museum, W. 46th St. & 12th Ave., 212/245-0072

Metropolitan Museum of Art (in Central Park), Fifth Ave. & 82nd St., 212/535-7710
Museum of Modern Art, 53rd St., between 5th & 6th aves., 212/708-9480
NBC Tours, 30 Rockefeller Plaza, at 49th St., 212/664-7174
South Street Seaport, Water & Fulton sts., 212/732-7678
Statue of Liberty & Ellis Island Tours, National Park Service, 212/363-3200
World Trade Center Observation Deck, 2 World Trade Center, 212/323-2340

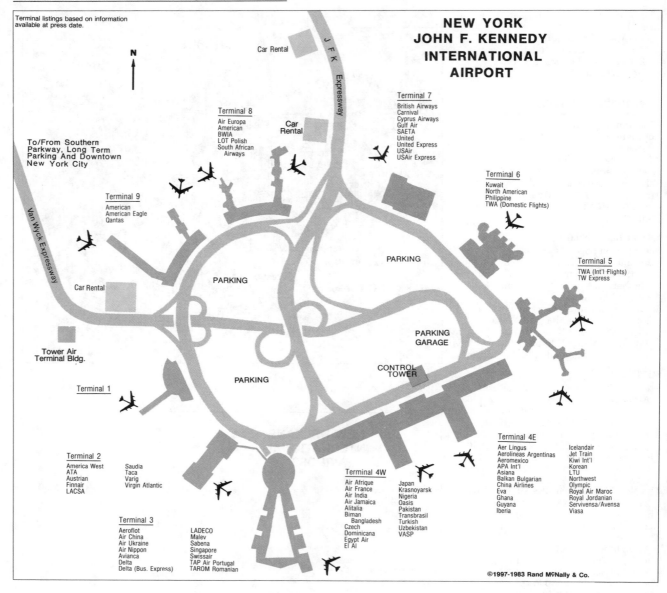

Terminal listings based on information available at press date.

NEW YORK JOHN F. KENNEDY INTERNATIONAL AIRPORT

N

Car Rental

J F K Expressway

Terminal 7
British Airways
Carnival
Cyprus Airways
Gulf Air
SAETA
United
United Express
USAir
USAir Express

Terminal 8
Air Europa
American
BWIA
LOT Polish
South African
Airways

Car Rental

Terminal 6
Kuwait
North American
Philippine
TWA (Domestic Flights)

To/From Southern Parkway, Long Term Parking And Downtown New York City

Van Wyck Expressway

Terminal 9
American
American Eagle
Qantas

Terminal 5
TWA (Int'l Flights)
TW Express

PARKING

Car Rental

PARKING

PARKING GARAGE

Tower Air Terminal Bldg.

PARKING

CONTROL TOWER

Terminal 1

Terminal 4E
Aer Lingus
Aerolineas Argentinas
Aeromexico
APA Int'l
Asiana
Balkan Bulgarian
China Airlines
Eva
Ghana
Guyana
Iberia

Icelandair
Jet Train
Kiwi Int'l
Korean
LTU
Northwest
Olympic
Royal Air Maroc
Royal Jordanian
Servivensa/Avensa
Viasa

Terminal 2
America West
ATA
Austrian
Finnair
LACSA

Saudia
Taca
Varig
Virgin Atlantic

Terminal 4W
Air Afrique
Air France
Air India
Air Jamaica
Alitalia
Biman
  Bangladesh
Czech
Dominicana
Egypt Air
El Al

Japan
Krasnoyarsk
Nigeria
Oasis
Pakistan
Transbrasil
Turkish
Uzbekistan
VASP

Terminal 3
Aeroflot
Air China
Air Ukraine
Air Nippon
Avianca
Delta
Delta (Bus. Express)

LADECO
Malev
Sabena
Singapore
Swissair
TAP Air Portugal
TAROM Romanian

©1997-1983 Rand McNally & Co.

INFORMATION SOURCE:

New York Convention and Visitors Bureau, Inc.
  Two Columbus Circle
  New York City, New York 10019
  212/397-8200; 800/692-8474

Norfolk-Virginia Beach, Virginia

City map: page 77
Population: (*962,300 Norfolk-Virginia Beach-Newport News Metro Area) Norfolk 261,229; Virginia Beach 393,069 (1990C)
Altitude: Sea level to 12 feet
Average Temp.: Jan., 41°F.; July, 77°F.
Telephone Area Code: 757
Time: 757/622-9311 **Weather:** 757/853-3013
Time Zone: Eastern

AIRPORT TRANSPORTATION:

Ten miles to downtown Norfolk; twenty-two miles to downtown Virginia Beach.
Taxicab, limousine and bus service to Norfolk; taxicab and airport limousine service to Virginia Beach.

SELECTED HOTELS: NORFOLK

✈Airport Hilton, 1500 N. Military Hwy., 757/466-8000; FAX 757/466-8000
Best Western Center Inn, 235 N. Military Hwy., 757/461-6600; FAX 757/466-9093
Comfort Inn, 6360 Newtown Rd., 757/461-1081; FAX 757/461-4390
Doubletree Club Hotel 880 N. Military Hwy., 757/461-9192; FAX 757/461-8290
Hampton Inn, 8501 Hampton Blvd., 757/489-1000; FAX 757/489-4509

Marriott Waterside, 235 E. Main St., 757/627-4200; FAX 757/628-6466
Omni Waterside Hotel, 777 Waterside Dr., 757/622-6664; FAX 757/625-8271
Ramada Madison Hotel, 345 Granby St., 757/622-6682; FAX 757/623-5949

SELECTED RESTAURANTS: NORFOLK

The Dumb Waiter, 117 W. Tazewell St., 757/623-3663
Elliot's, 1421 Colley Ave., 757/625-0259
Freemason Abbey, 209 W. Freemason St., 757/622-3966
La Galleria, 120 College Pl., 757/623-3939
Lockhart's Seafood Restaurant, 8440 Tidewater Dr., 757/588-0405
Riverwalk Cafe, in the Omni Waterside Hotel, 757/622-6664
San Antonio Sam's, 1501 Colley Ave., 757/623-0233
The Ship's Cabin Seafood Restaurant, 4110 E. Ocean View Ave., 757/362-2526

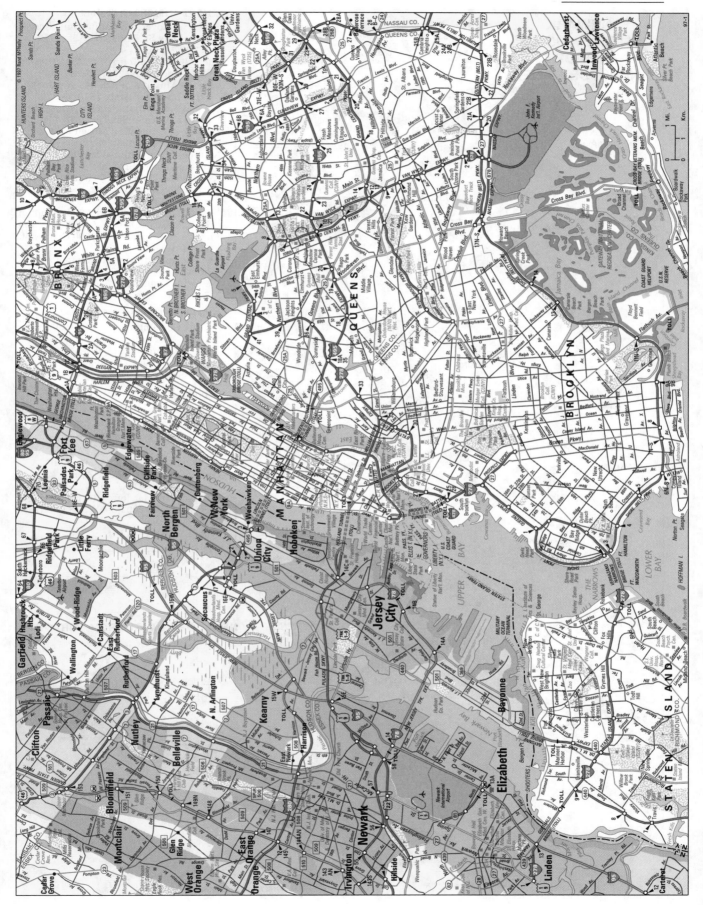

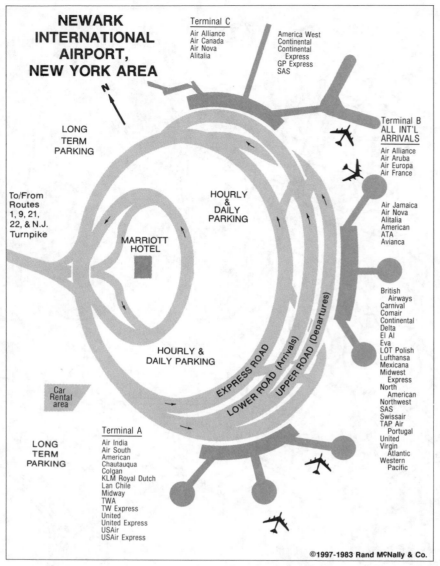

NEWARK INTERNATIONAL AIRPORT, NEW YORK AREA

N

Terminal C
Air Alliance
Air Canada
Air Nova
Alitalia

America West
Continental
Continental Express
GP Express
SAS

LONG TERM PARKING

Terminal B ALL INT'L ARRIVALS
Air Alliance
Air Aruba
Air Europa
Air France

Air Jamaica
Air Nova
Alitalia
American
ATA
Avianca

To/From Routes 1, 9, 21, 22, & N.J. Turnpike

MARRIOTT HOTEL

HOURLY & DAILY PARKING

British Airways
Carnival
Comair
Continental
Delta
El Al
Eva
LOT Polish
Lufthansa
Mexicana
Midwest Express
North American
Northwest
SAS
Swissair
TAP Air Portugal
United
Virgin Atlantic
Western Pacific

HOURLY & DAILY PARKING

EXPRESS ROAD
LOWER ROAD (Arrivals)
UPPER ROAD (Departures)

Car Rental area

LONG TERM PARKING

Terminal A
Air India
Air South
American
Chautauqua
Colgan
KLM Royal Dutch
Lan Chile
Midway
TWA
TW Express
United
United Express
USAir
USAir Express

SELECTED ATTRACTIONS: NORFOLK

American Rover Tall Sailing Ship Tours end of Bay St., Portsmouth, 757/627-SAIL
Carrie B. Harbor Tours, 333 Waterside Dr., Waterside Marina, 757/393-4735
Chrysler Museum of Art, 245 W. Olney Rd. & Mowbray Arch, 757/664-6200
Douglas MacArthur Memorial Museum, City Hall Ave. & Bank St., 757/441-2965
Hermitage Foundation Museum, 7637 N. Shore Rd., 757/423-2052
Nauticus—The National Maritime Center, west end of Main St. at the Waterfront, 757/664-1000 or 800/664-1080
Norfolk Botanical Gardens, Azalea Garden Rd., 757/441-5830
Norfolk Naval Base (tour), 9079 Hampton Blvd., adjacent to Gate 5, 757/444-7955
Virginia Zoological Park, 3500 Granby St., 757/441-2706
The Waterside (festival marketplace), 333 Waterside Dr., 757/627-3300
Waterside Live!, 333 Waterside Dr., 757/625-LIVE

INFORMATION SOURCES: NORFOLK

Norfolk Convention and Visitors Bureau 232 E. Main St.
Norfolk, Virginia 23510
757/664-6620; 800/368-3097
Hampton Roads Chamber of Commerce P.O. Box 327
420 Bank St.
Norfolk, Virginia 23501
757/622-2312

SELECTED HOTELS: VIRGINIA BEACH

Colonial Inn, 2809 Atlantic Ave., 757/428-5370; FAX 757/422-5902
Comfort Inn, 2800 Pacific Ave., 757/428-2203; FAX 757/422-6043
Courtyard by Marriott, 5700 Greenwich Rd., 757/490-2002; FAX 757/490-0169

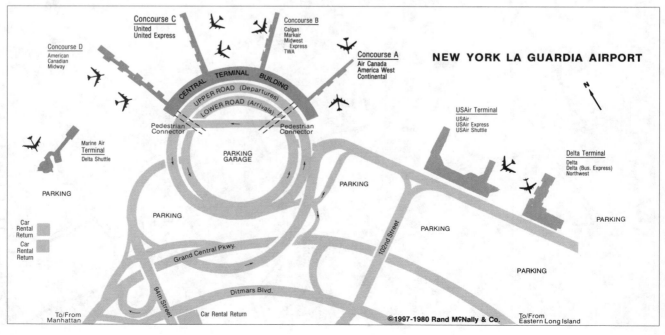

Concourse D
American
Canadian
Midway

Concourse C
United
United Express

Concourse B
Calgan
Markair
Midwest Express
TWA

Concourse A
Air Canada
America West
Continental

CENTRAL TERMINAL BUILDING

UPPER ROAD (Departures)
LOWER ROAD (Arrivals)

Pedestrian Connector

Pedestrian Connector

NEW YORK LA GUARDIA AIRPORT

N

USAir Terminal
USAir
USAir Express
USAir Shuttle

Marine Air Terminal
Delta Shuttle

PARKING GARAGE

Delta Terminal
Delta
Delta (Bus. Express)
Northwest

PARKING

PARKING

PARKING

PARKING

PARKING

PARKING

PARKING

PARKING

Car Rental Return

Car Rental Return

Grand Central Pkwy.

102nd Street

94th Street

Ditmars Blvd.

Car Rental Return

To/From Manhattan

To/From Eastern Long Island

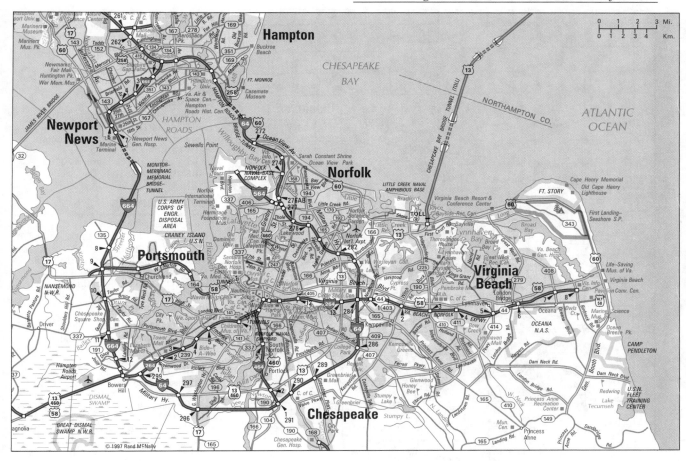

© 1997 Rand McNally

→Days Inn, 5708 Northampton Blvd.,
 757/460-2205; FAX 757/363-8089
Founders Inn & Conference Center, 5641
 Indian River Rd., 757/424-5511;
 FAX 757/366-0613
→Holiday Inn Airport, 5725 Northampton
 Blvd., 757/464-9351; FAX 757/363-8569
Holiday Inn Executive Center, 5655
 Greenwich Rd., 757/499-4400;
 FAX 757/473-0517
Holiday Inn Sunspree Resort, 3900 At-
 lantic Ave., 757/428-1711;
 FAX 757/425-5742
Quality Inn Pavilion, 716 21st St.,
 757/422-3617; FAX 757/428-7434
Radisson Hotel Virginia Beach, 1900
 Pavilion Dr., 757/422-8900;
 FAX 757/425-8460

SELECTED RESTAURANTS: VIRGINIA BEACH

Beach Pub, 1001 Laskin Rd.,
 757/422-8817
Belle Monte Cafe, 134 Hilltop E.,
 757/425-6290
Bennigan's, 757 Lynnhaven Pkwy.,
 757/463-7100
Casual Clam, 3157 Virginia Beach Blvd.,
 757/463-5106
Olive Garden, 683 Lynnhaven Pkwy.,
 757/486-8234
Szechuan Garden, 2720 N. Mall Dr.,
 757/463-1680
Three Ships Inn, 3800 Shore Dr.,
 757/460-0055

SELECTED ATTRACTIONS: VIRGINIA BEACH

Adam Thoroughgood House
 (17th-century), 1636 Parish Rd.,
 757/460-0007
Association for Research & Enlightenment
 (headquarters for the work of psychic
 Edgar Cayce), 67th St. & Atlantic Ave.,
 757/428-3588
Atlantic Fun Center, 25th St. & Atlantic
 Ave., 757/422-1742
Back Bay National Wildlife Refuge, 4005
 Sandpiper Rd., 757/721-2412
Christian Broadcasting Network, I-64 at
 Exit 286B, 757/579-2745
First Landing Cross, Fort Story,
 757/422-7305
Lynnhaven House (circa 1725), 4405
 Wishart Rd., 757/460-1688
Ocean Breeze Fun Park, 849 General
 Booth Blvd., 757/422-4444 or -0718
Seashore State Park, 2500 Shore Dr.,
 757/481-4836 or -2131
Virginia Marine Science Museum, 717
 General Booth Blvd., 757/437-4949 or
 757/425-FISH (recording)

INFORMATION SOURCES: VIRGINIA BEACH

Virginia Beach Convention & Visitor
Development
 2101 Parks Ave., Suite 500
 Virginia Beach, Virginia 23451
 757/437-4700

Virginia Beach Visitor Information Center
 2100 Parks Ave.
 Virginia Beach, Virginia 23451
 757/437-4888; 800/446-8038
Hampton Roads Chamber of Commerce
 4512 Virginia Beach Blvd.
 Virginia Beach, Virginia 23462
 757/490-1223

Oklahoma City, Oklahoma

City map: page 78
Population: (*850,900) 444,719 (1990C)
Altitude: 1,243 feet
Average Temp.: Jan., 37°F.; July, 82°F.
Telephone Area Code: 405
Time: 405/599-1234 **Weather:**
 405/360-5928
Time Zone: Central

AIRPORT TRANSPORTATION:

Ten miles to downtown Oklahoma City.
Taxicab, limousine bus service.

SELECTED HOTELS:

Clarion Hotel & Comfort Inn, 4345 N.
 Lincoln Blvd., 405/528-2741;
 FAX 405/525-8185
Days Inn Northwest, 2801 NW. 39th St.,
 405/946-0741; FAX 405/942-0181
Days Inn South, 2616 S. I-35,
 405/677-0521; FAX (same)

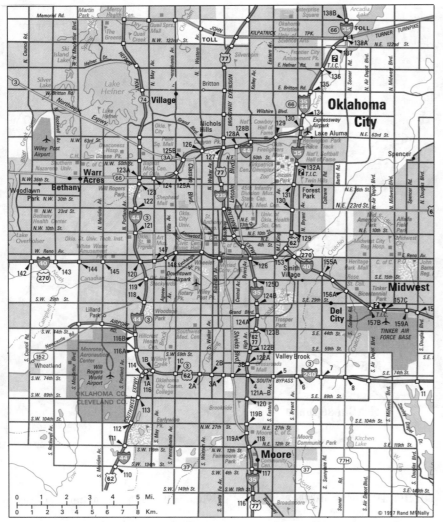

© 1997 Rand McNally

Oklahoma City Zoo, NE 50th & Martin
Luther King Blvd., 405/424-3344
Remington Park (racetrack), One
Remington Pl., 405/424-9000

INFORMATION SOURCES:

Oklahoma City Convention & Visitors
Bureau
123 Park Ave.
Oklahoma City, Oklahoma 73102
405/297-8912; 800/225-5652
Oklahoma City Chamber of Commerce
123 Park Ave.
Oklahoma City, Oklahoma 73102
405/297-8900

Omaha, Nebraska

City map: page 79
Population: (*571,100) 335,795 (1990C)
Altitude: 1,040 feet
Average Temp.: Jan., 23°F.; July, 77°F.
Telephone Area Code: 402
Time: 402/342-8463 **Weather:**
402/392-1111
Time Zone: Central

AIRPORT TRANSPORTATION:

Three miles to downtown Omaha.
Taxicab, bus and hotel limousine service.

SELECTED HOTELS:

Best Western Central, 3650 S. 72nd.,
402/397-3700; FAX 402/397-8362
Best Western Omaha Inn, 4706 S. 108th
St., 402/339-7400; FAX 402/339-5155
Best Western Regency West, 909 S. 107th
St., 402/397-8000; FAX (same)
Embassy Suites, 7270 Cedar St.,
402/397-5141; FAX 402/397-3266
Holiday Inn Central, 3321 S. 72nd St.,
402/393-3950; FAX 402/393-8718
Holiday Inn Express, 3001 Chicago St.,
402/345-2222; FAX 402/345-2501
New Tower Inn, 7764 Dodge St.,
402/393-5500; FAX (same)
Omaha Marriott, 10220 Regency Circle,
402/399-9000; FAX 402/399-0223
Omaha Sheraton Inn, 4888 S. 118th St.,
402/895-1000; FAX 402/896-9247
Ramada Hotel Central, 7007 Grover St.,
402/397-7030; FAX 402/397-8449
✈Ramada Inn Airport, 2002 E. Locust St.,
402/342-5100; FAX (same)
Red Lion Inn Omaha, 1616 Dodge St.,
402/346-7600; FAX 402/346-5722

SELECTED RESTAURANTS:

Anthony's, 7220 F St., 402/331-7575
Cascio, 1620 S. 10th St., 402/345-8313
Chardonnay, in the Omaha Marriott,
402/399-9000
French Cafe, 1017 Howard St.,
402/341-3547
Gallagher's, 10730 Pacific, 402/393-1421
Gorats Steak House, 4917 Center St.,
402/551-3733
Johnny's Cafe, 4702 S. 27th St.,
402/731-4774
Maxine's, in the Red Lion Inn Omaha
Hotel, 402/346-7600
Neon Goose, 1012 S. 10th St.,
402/341-2063

✈Embassy Suites, 1815 S. Meridian,
405/682-6000; FAX 405/682-9835
Hilton Inn Northwest, 2945 NW. Expwy.,
405/848-4811; FAX 405/843-4829
Holiday Inn East, 5701 Tinker Diagonal,
Midwest City, 405/737-4481;
FAX 405/732-5706
Oklahoma City Marriott, 3233 NW.
Expwy., 405/842-6633;
FAX 405/842-3152
Oklahoma City Medallion Hotel, One N.
Broadway Ave., 405/235-2780;
FAX 405/232-8752
Radisson Inn, 401 S. Meridian Ave.,
405/947-7681; FAX 405/947-4253
The Waterford Hotel, 6300 Waterford
Blvd., 405/848-4782; FAX 405/843-9161

SELECTED RESTAURANTS:

Applewoods, 4301 SW. 3rd, 405/947-8484
Eddy's Steak House, 4227 N. Meridian
Ave., 405/787-2944
Greybill's, in the Oklahoma City Medal-
lion Hotel, 405/235-2780
Harry's, 5705 Mosteller Dr., 405/840-9912

Oklahoma County Line, 1226 NE. 63rd,
405/478-4955
Shorty Small's, Meridian & Reno,
405/947-0779
Shorty's Dockside, 23rd & Meridian,
405/946-1421
Sleepy Hollow, 1101 NE. 50th,
405/424-1614
Texanna Red's, 4600 W. Reno Ave.,
405/947-8665

SELECTED ATTRACTIONS:

Enterprise Square, 2501 E. Memorial Rd.,
405/425-5030
Frontier City (theme park), 11501 NE
Expressway, 405/478-2414
Horse Shows (year-round), at the State
Fairgrounds, 405/948-6700
Kirkpatrick Center Complex, 2100 NE
52nd, 405/427-5461
Myriad Botanical Gardens/Crystal Bridge,
Reno & Robinson, 405/297-3995
National Cowboy Hall of Fame & Western
Heritage Center, 1700 NE 63rd St.,
405/478-2250

Ross' Steak House, 909 S. 72nd St.,
402/393-2030
V. Mertz, 1022 Howard, 402/345-8980

SELECTED ATTRACTIONS:

AKsarben Thoroughbred Racetrack, 63rd
& Shirley, 402/444-4000
Belle Riverboat Cruises, 1515 Abbott Dr.,
Miller's Landing, 402/292-BOAT
Boys Town, W. Dodge Rd. between 132nd
& 144th, 402/498-1140
Fun Plex, 70th & Q sts., 402/331-8436
Gene Leahy Mall (park land), 14th & Far-
nam, 402/444-5955
Heartland of America Park & Fountain,
8th & Douglas
Henry Doorly Zoo/Lied Jungle, 3701 S.
10th, 402/733-8400 or -8401
Joslyn Art Museum, 22nd & Dodge,
402/342-3300
Old Market, 10th to 13th, Harney to
Jackson
Strategic Air Command (SAC) Museum,
2510 SAC Pl., Bellevue, 402/292-2001

INFORMATION SOURCES:

Greater Omaha Convention & Visitors
Bureau
6800 Mercy Rd., Suite 202
Omaha, Nebraska 68106-2627
402/444-4660; 800/332-1819
Greater Omaha Chamber of Commerce
1301 Harney St.
Omaha, Nebraska 68102
402/346-5000

Orlando, Florida

City map: page 80
Population: (*900,400) 164,693 (1990C)
Altitude: 106 feet
Average Temp.: Jan., 62°F.; July, 82°F.
Telephone Area Code: 407
Time: 407/646-3131 **Weather:**
407/851-7510
Time Zone: Eastern

AIRPORT TRANSPORTATION:

See map on page 80.
Fifteen miles to downtown Orlando.
Taxicab, limousine and bus service.

SELECTED HOTELS:

Delta Orlando Resort, 5715 Major Blvd.,
407/351-3340; FAX 407/345-2872
Holiday Inn—Central Park, 7900 S.
Orange Blossom Trail, 407/859-7900;
FAX 407/859-7442
Holiday Inn Express, 3330 W. Colonial
Dr., 407/299-6710; FAX 407/296-4005
Holiday Inn at the Orlando Arena, 304 W.
Colonial Dr., 407/843-8700;
FAX 407/841-4978
Howard Johnson Centroplex Arena, 929
W. Colonial Dr., 407/843-1360;
FAX 407/839-3333
✈Hyatt Regency Orlando Airport, 9300
Airport Blvd., 407/825-1234;
FAX 407/856-1672

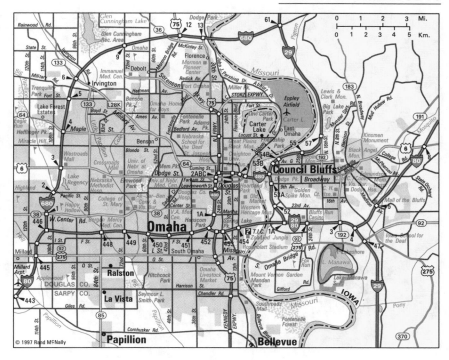

Marriott Orlando International Drive,
8001 International Dr., 407/351-2420;
FAX 407/345-5611
Marriott Orlando World Center, 8701
World Center Dr., 407/239-4200;
FAX 407/238-8777
Peabody Orlando, 9801 International Dr.,
407/352-4000; FAX 407/351-9177
Ramada Hotel Resort Florida Center, 7400
International Dr., 407/351-4600;
FAX 407/354-5729
✈Renaissance Hotel—Airport, 5445
Forbes Pl., 407/240-1000;
FAX 407/240-1005
Renaissance Orlando Resort, 6677 Sea
Harbor Dr., 407/351-5555;
FAX 407/351-9991
Sheraton World Resort, 10100 Interna-
tional Dr., 407/352-1100;
FAX 407/352-3679

SELECTED RESTAURANTS:

Cafe on the Park, in the Harley Hotel of
Orlando, 151 E. Washington,
407/841-3220
Charlie's Lobster House, 8445
International Dr., 407/352-6929
Christini's, 7600 Dr. Phillips Blvd.,
407/345-8770
Church Street Station, 129 W. Church St.,
407/422-2434
4th Fighter Group, 494 Rickenbacker Dr.,
407/898-4251
Maison et Jardin, 430 S. Wymore Rd.,
407/862-4410

Ming Court, 9188 International Dr.,
407/351-9988

SELECTED ATTRACTIONS:

Church Street Station (dining, shopping,
entertainment), 129 W. Church St.,
407/422-2434
Cypress Gardens, 2641 S. Lake Summit
Dr., near Winter Haven, 813/324-2111
Florida Citrus Tower, Clermont,
904/394-4061
Gatorland, 14501 S. Orange Blossom
Trail, 407/855-5496
Kennedy Space Center, 407/452-2121
Ripley's Believe It or Not Museum, 8201
International Dr., 407/363-4418
Sea World of Florida, 7007 Sea World Dr.,
407/351-3600
Universal Studios Florida, off I-4 Exit
30B, 407/363-8000
Walt Disney World, Lake Buena Vista,
407/824-4321

INFORMATION SOURCES:

Orlando/Orange County Convention and
Visitors Bureau
6700 Forum Dr., Suite 100
Orlando, Florida 32821
407/363-5800; 800/643-9492
Greater Orlando Chamber of Commerce
75 S. Ivanhoe Blvd.
Orlando, Florida 32802
407/425-1234

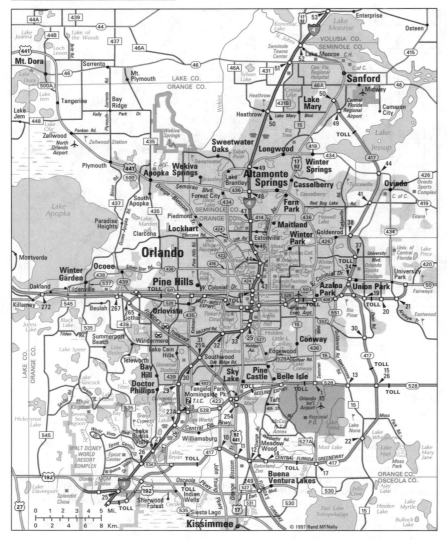

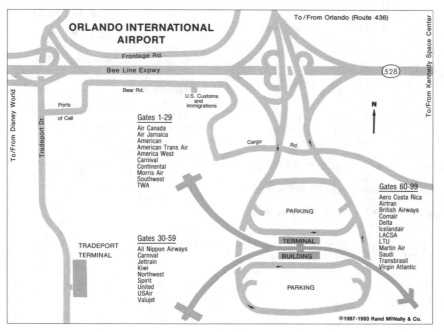

Ottawa, Ontario, Canada

City map: page 81
Population: (*920,857) 313,987 (1991C)
Altitude: 374 ft.
Average Temp.: Jan., 12°F.; July, 70°F.
Telephone Area Code: 613
Time: 613/745-1576 **Weather:**
  613/998-3439
Time Zone: Eastern

AIRPORT TRANSPORTATION:

Fifteen miles to downtown Ottawa.
Taxicab, limousine, and hotel shuttle bus
  service.

SELECTED HOTELS:

Best Western Barons Hotel, 3700
  Richmond Rd., 613/828-2741;
  FAX 613/596-4742
Best Western Macies Hotel, 1274 Carling,
  613/728-1951; FAX 613/728-1955
Chateau Laurier, 1 Rideau St.,
  613/241-1414; FAX 613/241-2958
Chimo Hotel, 1199 Joseph Cyr St.,
  613/744-1060; FAX 613/744-7845
Citadel Inn Ottawa, 101 Lyon St.,
  613/237-3600; FAX 613/237-2351
Delta Ottawa Hotel & Suites, 361 Queen
  St., 613/238-6000; FAX 613/238-2290
Holiday Inn Ottawa Centre, 350
  Dalhousie St., 613/241-1000;
  FAX 613/241-4804
Howard Johnson Hotel, 140 Slater St.,
  613/238-2888; FAX 613/235-8421
Radisson Hotel Ottawa Centre, 100 Kent
  St., 613/238-1122; FAX 613/783-4229
Sheraton Ottawa Hotel & Towers, 150
  Albert St., 613/238-1500;
  FAX 613/235-2723
WelcomINNS, 1220 Michael St.,
  613/748-7800; FAX 613/748-0499
The Westin Hotel, 11 Colonel By Dr.,
  613/560-7000; FAX 613/234-5396

SELECTED RESTAURANTS:

The Courtyard Restaurant, 21 George St.,
  613/241-1516
Friday's Roast Beef House, 150 Elgin St.,
  613/237-5353
Hy's Steakhouse, 170 Queen St., Metropolitan Life Building, 613/234-4545
Leone's Ristorante, 412 Preston St.,
  613/230-6021
Marble Works, 14 Waller St.,
  613/241-6764
Nick & Jerry's Simply Seafood, 253 Slater,
  613/232-4895
The Siam Bistro, 1268 Wellington St.,
  613/728-3111
Wilfrid's, in the Chateau Laurier Hotel,
  613/241-1414

SELECTED ATTRACTIONS:

Bytown Museum-Ottawa Locks, 50 Canal
  Ln., take stairs next to Chateau Laurier
  Bridge, 613/234-4570
Canadian Museum of Civilization, 100
  Laurier St., Hull, 819/776-7002
Canadian Museum of Contemporary
  Photography, 1 Rideau Canal,
  613/991-4896
Canadian Museum of Nature, Metcalfe St.
  at McLeod, 613/996-3102
Canadian War Museum, 330 Sussex Dr.,
  819/776-8600

Currency Museum, 245 Sparks St.,
613/782-8914

Laurier House, 335 Laurier Ave. E., corner
of Chapel St., 613/992-8142

National Aviation Museum, 1 Aviation
Pkwy., 613/993-2010

National Gallery of Canada, 380 Sussex
Dr., 613/990-1985

National Museum of Science &
Technology, 1867 St. Laurent Blvd.,
613/991-3044

Rideau Hall (Governor General's
residence), 1 Sussex Dr., 613/998-7113

Royal Canadian Mint, 320 Sussex Dr.,
613/993-3500 or 800/268-6468

INFORMATION SOURCES:

Ottawa Tourism and Convention
Authority
130 Albert St., Suite 1800
Ottawa, Ontario K1P 5G4
613/237-5150; 800/363-4465

Canadian Consulate General
1251 Avenue of the Americas
New York, New York 10020-1175
212/596-1600

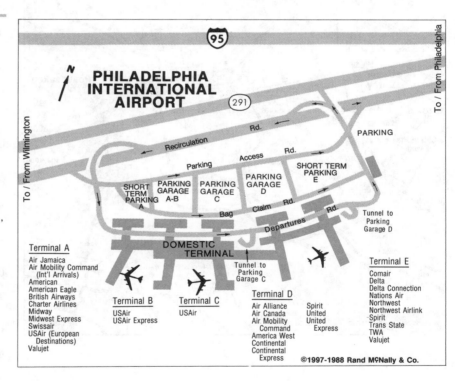

Philadelphia, Pennsylvania

City map: page 82
Population: (*5,529,600) 1,585,577
(1990C)
Altitude: 45 feet
Average Temp.: Jan., 35°F.; July, 78°F.
Telephone Area Code: 215
Time: 215/846-1212 **Weather:**
215/936-1212
Time Zone: Eastern

AIRPORT TRANSPORTATION:

See map at right.
Eight miles to downtown Philadelphia.
Taxicab, limousine bus, and rail line
service.

SELECTED HOTELS:

Adam's Mark, City Ave. & Monument Rd.,
215/581-5000; FAX 215/581-5089

✈Airport Hilton Hotel, 4509 Island Ave.,
215/365-4150; FAX 215/937-6382

The Barclay Hotel, 237 S. 18th St.,
215/545-0300; FAX 215/545-2896

The Bellevue Hotel, 1415 Chancellor Ct.,
Broad & Walnut sts., 215/893-1776;
FAX 215/732-8518

The Four Seasons, 18th St. & Benjamin
Franklin Pkwy., 215/963-1500;
FAX 215/963-9506

The Latham Hotel, 135 S. 17th St. at
Walnut St., 215/563-7474;
FAX 215/568-0110

Penn Tower Hotel, 34th St. & Civic Center
Blvd., 215/387-8333; FAX 215/386-8304

Philadelphia Marriott, 1201 Market St.,
215/625-2900; FAX 215/625-6000

Radisson Hotel & Conference Center of
Bucks County, 2400 Old Lincoln Hwy.,
Trevose, 215/638-8300;
FAX 215/638-4377

Sheraton Society Hill, 1 Dock St.,
215/238-6000; FAX 215/922-2709

The Warwick Hotel, 1701 Locust St.,
215/735-6000; FAX 215/790-7766

Wyndham Franklin Plaza, 17th & Race
sts., 215/448-2000; FAX 215/448-2864

SELECTED RESTAURANTS:

Deux Cheminees, 1221 Locust St.,
215/790-0200

Di Lullo Centro, 1407 Locust,
215/546-2000

The Garden, 1617 Spruce St.,
215/546-4455

Harry's Bar and Grill, 22 S. 18th St.,
215/561-5757

La Famiglia, 8 S. Front St., 215/922-2803

Le Bec Fin, 1523 Walnut St.,
215/567-1000

The Monte Carlo Living Room, 150 South
St. at 2nd, 215/925-2220

Old Original Bookbinders, 125 Walnut St.,
215/925-7027

The Palm Restaurant, 200 S. Broad St. at
Walnut, 215/546-7256

Zanzibar Blue, 305 S. 11th St.,
215/829-0300

SELECTED ATTRACTIONS:

Academy of Natural Sciences, 19th &
Benjamin Franklin Pkwy., 215/299-1000

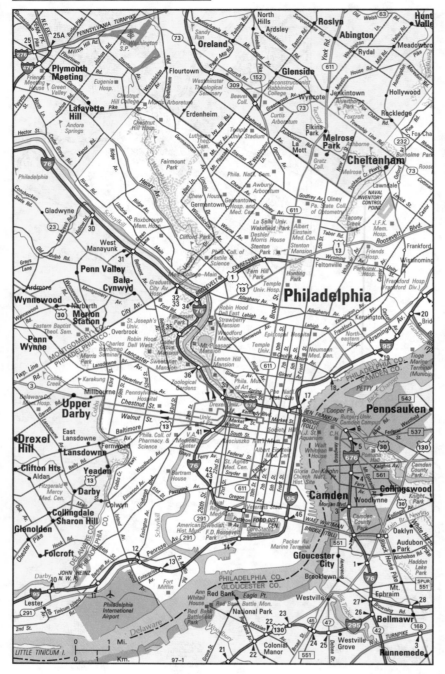

Philadelphia Visitors Center
16th St. & JFK Blvd.
Philadelphia, Pennsylvania 19102
215/636-1666; 800/537-7676
Greater Philadelphia Chamber of Commerce
1234 Market St., 18th Floor
Philadelphia, Pennsylvania 19107
215/545-1234

Phoenix, Arizona

City map: page 83
Population: (*2,124,900) 983,403 (1990C)
Altitude: 1,090 feet
Average Temp.: Jan., 51°F.; July, 85.9°F.
Telephone Area Code: 602
Time and Weather: 602/265-5550
Time Zone: Mountain Standard all year

AIRPORT TRANSPORTATION:

See map on page 83.
Four miles to downtown Phoenix.
Taxicab, bus, and limousine bus service.

SELECTED HOTELS:

Arizona Biltmore, 24th St. & Missouri
Ave., 602/955-6600; FAX 602/381-7600
Crowne Plaza, 100 N. 1st St.,
602/257-1525; FAX 602/254-7926
✈Embassy Suites Thomas Road—Airport
West, 2333 E. Thomas Rd.,
602/957-1910; FAX 602/955-2861
Hyatt Regency Phoenix, 122 N. 2nd St.,
602/252-1234; FAX 602/254-9472
Orange Tree Golf & Conference Resort,
10601 N. 56th St., Scottsdale,
602/948-6100; FAX 602/483-6074
✈Phoenix Airport Hilton, 2435 S. 47th
St., 602/894-1600; FAX 602/894-0326
The Pointe Hilton Resort at Squaw Peak,
7677 N. 16th St., 602/997-2626;
FAX 602/997-2391
Quality Hotel and Resort, 3600 N. 2nd
Ave., 602/248-0222; FAX 602/265-6331
Ritz-Carlton, 2401 E. Camelback Rd.,
602/468-0700; FAX 602/468-9883

SELECTED RESTAURANTS:

Arizona Cafe & Grill, 3113 Lincoln Dr.,
602/957-0777
Compass, in the Hyatt Regency Phoenix,
602/252-1234
The Copper Creek, in the Wyndham
Metrocenter Hotel, 10220 N. Metro
Pkwy. E., 602/997-5900
Don & Charlie's, 7501 E. Camelback,
Scottsdale, 602/990-0900
Etienne's Different Pointe of View, 11111
N. 7th St., 602/863-0912
Ruth's Chris Steak House, 7001 N.
Scottsdale Rd., Scottsdale,
602/991-5988
Wright's, in the Arizona Biltmore Hotel,
602/954-2507

SELECTED ATTRACTIONS:

Blackhawk Ranch Trail Rides, one quarter
mile south of Thunderbird on 7th St.,
602/993-1356
Champlin Fighter Aircraft Museum, in-
side Falcon Field Airfield, 4636 Fighter
Aces Dr., Mesa, 602/830-4540
Desert Botanical Gardens, 1201 N. Galvin
Pkwy., 602/941-1217

Afro-American Historical & Cultural
Museum, NW corner of 7th & Arch sts.,
215/574-0380
Betsy Ross House, 239 Arch St.,
215/627-5343
Franklin Institute-Futures Center &
Omniverse Theater, 20th & Benjamin
Franklin Pkwy., 215/448-1208
Independence National Historical Park,
3rd & Chestnut (Vistors Center),
215/597-8974
The New Jersey State Aquarium at
Camden, 1 Riverside Dr., Camden, New
Jersey, 609/365-3300

Philadelphia Museum of Art, 26th &
Benjamin Franklin Pkwy., 215/763-8100
Philadelphia Zoo, 34th & W. Girard Ave.,
215/243-1100
Please Touch Museum for Children, 210
N. 21st St., 215/963-0666
U.S. Mint, 5th & Arch sts., 215/597-7353

INFORMATION SOURCES:

Philadelphia Convention & Visitors
Bureau
1515 Market St., Suite 2020
Philadelphia, Pennsylvania 19102
215/636-3300; 800/225-5745

Dolly's Steamboat (Canyon Lake tours), 602/827-9144

Frank Lloyd Wright's Taliesin West, Scottsdale, 602/860-8810

Gila River Arts & Crafts Center, 30 miles south, off I-10 Exit 175, 602/963-3981

Hall of Flame Museum, between Center Pkwy. & Van Buren St. on Project Dr., 602/275-3473

The Heard Museum, 22 E. Monte Vista, 602/252-8840

Pueblo Grande Museum, 4619 E. Washington, 602/495-0901

Rawhide (recreated 1880s Western town), Scottsdale Rd. 4 mi. north of Bell Rd., Scottsdale, 602/563-1880

INFORMATION SOURCE:

Phoenix & Valley of the Sun Convention & Visitors Bureau
One Arizona Center
400 E. Van Buren St., Suite 600
Phoenix, Arizona 85004-2290
602/254-6500
Visitor Info. Hotline 602/252-5588;
Meeting Planners Line 800/535-8898

Pittsburgh, Pennsylvania

City map: page 84
Population: (*2,062,000) 369,879 (1990C)
Altitude: 760 feet
Average Temp.: Jan., 33°F.; July, 75°F.
Telephone Area Code: 412
Time: 412/391-9500 **Weather:** 412/936-1212
Time Zone: Eastern

AIRPORT TRANSPORTATION:

See map on page 84.
Seventeen miles to downtown Pittsburgh.
Taxicab and limousine bus service.

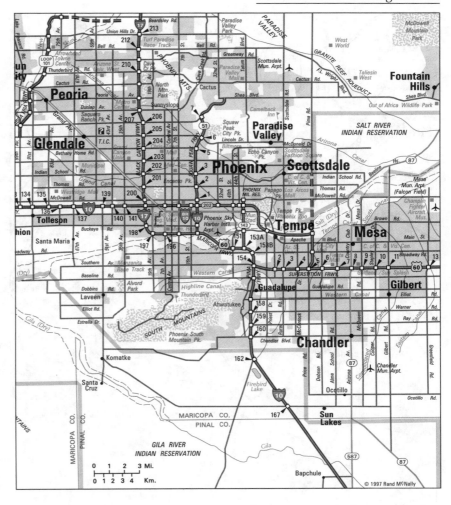

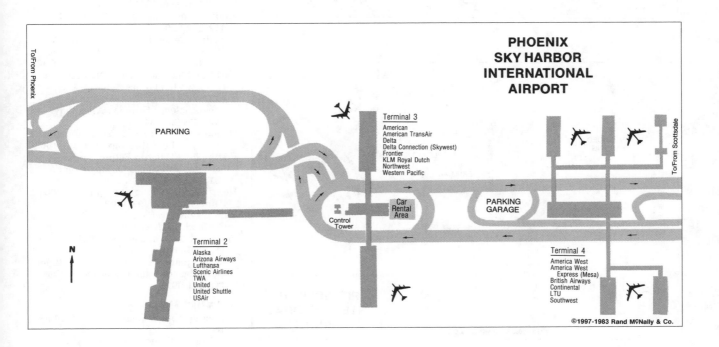

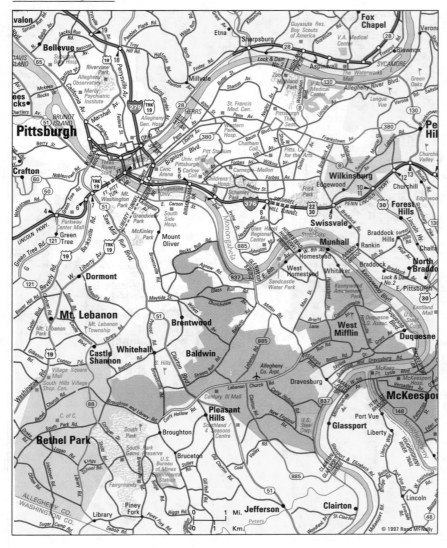

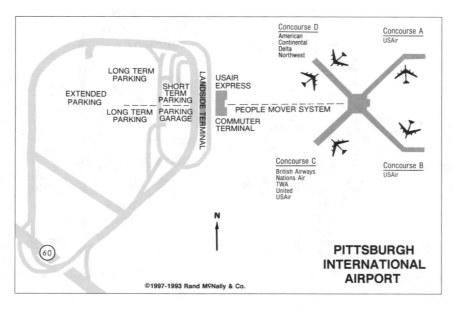

Concourse D
American
Continental
Delta
Northwest

Concourse A
USAir

LONG TERM PARKING

EXTENDED PARKING

SHORT TERM PARKING

LONG TERM PARKING

PARKING GARAGE

LANDSIDE TERMINAL

USAIR EXPRESS

PEOPLE MOVER SYSTEM

COMMUTER TERMINAL

Concourse C
British Airways
Nations Air
TWA
United
USAir

Concourse B
USAir

N

60

©1997-1993 Rand McNally & Co.

PITTSBURGH INTERNATIONAL AIRPORT

SELECTED HOTELS:

Best Western Parkway Center Inn, 875 Greentree Rd., 412/922-7070; FAX 412/922-4949

Clairion—Royce Hotel, 1160 Thorn Run Rd., Coraopolis, 412/262-2400; FAX 412/264-9373

Doubletree Hotel, 1000 Penn Ave. 412/281-3700; FAX 412/227-4500

Green Tree Marriot, 101 Marriot Dr., 412/922-8400; FAX 412/922-8981

Holiday Inn Airport, 1406 Beers School Rd., Coraopolis, 412/262-3600; FAX 412/262-3600

Hyatt Regency, 112 Washington Pl., 412/471-1234; 412/FAX 412/355-0315

The Pittsburgh Hilton & Towers, 600 Commonwealth Pl., Gateway Center, 412/391-4600; FAX 412/594-5161

Sheraton Hotel Station Sq., 7 Station Sq. Dr., 412/261-2000; FAX 412/261-2932

The Westin William Penn, 530 William Penn Pl., 412/281-7100; FAX 412/553-5252

SELECTED RESTAURANTS:

Christopher's, 1411 Grandview Ave., 412/381-4500

Colony, Greentree & Cochran rds., 412/561-2060

Common Plea, 310 Ross St., 412/281-5140

D'Imperio's, 3412 Wm. Penn Hwy., 412/823-4800

Grand Concourse, 1 Station Sq., 412/261-1717

Le Mont Restaurant, 1114 Grandview Ave., 412/431-3100

Tambellini, 860 Saw Mill Run Rd., 412/481-1118

The Terrace Room, in the Westin William Penn, 412/281-7100

Top of the Triangle, 600 Grant St., 62nd Floor, 412/471-4100

SELECTED ATTRACTIONS:

Andy Warhol Museum, 117 Sandusky St., 412/237-8300

Benedum Center for the Performing Arts, 7th St. between Penn & Liberty aves., 412/456-2600

Carnegie Museum of Art & Natural History, 4400 Forbes Ave., 412/622-3172

Carnegie Science Center, 1 Allegheny Ave., 412/237-3400

Duquesne Incline Cable Car, W. Carson St., below Ft. Pitt Bridge, 412/381-1665

Frank Lloyd Wright's Fallingwater, between Mill Run & Ohiopyle on PA 381, 412/329-8501

Heinz Hall (Pittsburgh Symphony), 600 Penn Ave., 412/392-4800

Phipps Conservatory, Schenley Park, Oakland, 412/622-6914

Pittsburgh Zoo, in Highland Park, 412/665-3639

Station Square, W. Carson St. & Smithfield St. Bridge, near the Duquesne Incline, 412/261-9911

INFORMATION SOURCE:

Greater Pittsburgh Convention & Visitors Bureau
4 Gateway Center, 18th Floor
Pittsburgh, Pennsylvania 15222
412/281-7711; 800/366-0093

Portland, Oregon

City map: right
Population: (1,391,700) 437,319 (1990C)
Altitude: Sea level to 1,073 feet
Average Temp.: Jan., 40°F.; July, 69°F.
Telephone Area Code: 503
Time and Weather: 503/236-7575
Time Zone: Pacific

AIRPORT TRANSPORTATION:

Nine miles to downtown Portland.
Taxicab, limousine bus service and public
  mass transit system

SELECTED HOTELS:

The Benson Hotel, 309 SW. Broadway,
  503/228-2000; FAX 503/226-4603
✈Best Western Fortniter Motel, 4911 NE.
  82nd Ave., 503/255-9771;
  FAX 503/255-9774
The Heathman Hotel, 1001 SW. Broadway,
  503/241-4100; FAX 503/790-7110
✈Holiday Inn Airport, 8439 NE. Columbia
  Blvd., 503/257-5000; FAX 503/257-4742
Holiday Inn Portland Downtown, 1021
  NE. Grand Ave., 503/235-2100;
  FAX 503/238-0132
Portland Hilton, 921 SW. 6th Ave.,
  503/226-1611; FAX 503/220-2565
Portland Marriott, 1401 SW. Front Ave.,
  503/226-7600; FAX 503/221-1789
Red Lion Coliseum, 1225 N. Thunderbird
  Way, 503/235-8311; FAX 503/232-2670
Red Lion Hotel Columbia River, 1401 N.
  Hayden Island Dr., 503/283-2111;
  FAX 503/283-4718
Red Lion Jantzen Beach, 909 N. Hayden
  Island Dr., 503/283-4466;
  FAX 503/283-4743
Red Lion Hotel Portland Downtown, 310
  SW. Lincoln St., 503/221-0450;
  FAX 503/226-6260
✈Sheraton Portland Airport Hotel, 8235
  NE. Airport Way, 503/281-2500;
  FAX 503/249-7602

SELECTED RESTAURANTS:

Alexander's, atop Portland Hilton,
  503/226-1611
Brickstone's Restaurant, in the Red Lion
  Hotel Columbia River, 503/283-2111
Couch Street Fish House, 105 NW. 3rd
  Ave., 503/223-6173
Harbor Side, 0309 SW. Montgomery St.,
  503/220-1865
Huber's, 411 SW. 3rd., 503/228-5686
Jake's Famous Crawfish Restaurant, 401
  SW. 12th Ave., 503/226-1419
The London Grill, in The Benson Hotel,
  503/228-2000
Opus Too, 33 NW. 2nd, 503/222-6077
Ringside, 2165 W. Burnside St.,
  503/223-1513

SELECTED ATTRACTIONS:

International Rose Test Gardens, in
  Washington Park
Japanese Gardens, in Washington Park,
  503/223-1321
Metro Washington Park Zoo, 4001 SW.
  Canyon Rd., 503/226-1561
Oregon Historical Society's Library &
  Museum, 1200 SW. Park Ave.,
  503/222-1741
Oregon Museum of Science & Industry,
  1945 SE. Water Ave., 503/797-4000

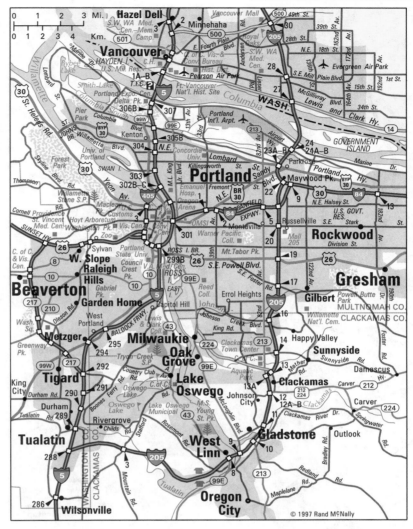

© 1997 Rand McNally

Pittock Mansion, 3229 NW. Pittock Dr.,
  503/823-3624
Portland Art Museum, 1219 SW. Park
  Ave., 503/226-2811
Sanctuary of Our Sorrowful Mother (the
  "Grotto"), NE. 85th & Sandy Blvd.,
  503/254-7371
World Forestry Center, 4033 SW. Canyon
  Rd. in Washington Park, 503/228-1367

INFORMATION SOURCES:

Portland/Oregon Visitors Association
  Marketing, Tourism & Conventions
  26 SW. Salmon St.
  Portland, Oregon 97204
  503/275-9750; Visitor Information
  503/222-2223
Portland Metropolitan Chamber of
Commerce
  221 NW. 2nd Ave.
  Portland, Oregon 97209
  503/228-9411

Providence, Rhode Island

City map: page 86
Population: (*979,300) 160,728 (1990C)
Altitude: 24 feet
Average Temp.: Jan., 29°F.; July, 72°F.
Telephone Area Code: 401
Time and Weather: 401/976-1212
Time Zone: Eastern

AIRPORT TRANSPORTATION:

Nine miles to downtown Providence.
Taxicab and airport limousine service.

SELECTED HOTELS:

Days Hotel on the Harbor, 220 India St.,
  401/272-5577; FAX 401/272-5577
Holiday Inn at the Crossing, 801
  Greenwich Ave., Warwick,
  401/732-6000; FAX 401/732-4839
Holiday Inn Downtown, 21 Atwells Ave.,
  401/831-3900; FAX 401/751-0007
Providence Biltmore, Kennedy Plaza,
  10 Dorrance St., 401/421-0700;
  FAX 401/455-3050
Providence Marriott, Charles & Orms sts.,
  401/272-2400; FAX 401/273-2686
✈Sheraton Tara Airport Hotel, 1850 Post
  Rd., Warwick, 401/738-4000;
  FAX 401/738-8206
The Westin Hotel—Providence, 1 W.
  Exchange St., 401/598-8000;
  FAX 401/598-8200

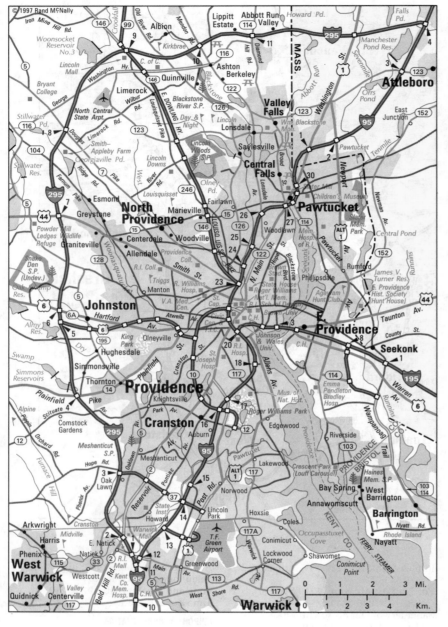

© 1997 Rand McNally

Greater Providence Chamber of Commerce
30 Exchange Terrace
Providence, Rhode Island 02903
401/521-5000

Raleigh, North Carolina

City map: page 87
Population: (*452,400) 207,951 (1990C)
Altitude: 363 feet
Average Temp.: Jan., 42°F.; July, 78°F.
Telephone Area Code: 919
Time: 919/976-2511 **Weather:**
  919/515-8225
Time Zone: Eastern

AIRPORT TRANSPORTATION:

See map on page 87.
Fifteen miles to downtown Raleigh.
Taxicab and airport limousine service.

SELECTED HOTELS:

Brownstone Hotel, 1707 Hillsborough St.,
  919/828-0811; FAX 919/834-0904
Days Inn North, 2805 Highwoods Blvd.,
  919/872-3500; FAX 919/872-3500
✈Holiday Inn Airport, I-40 Exit 282 at
  Page Rd., Research Triangle Park,
  919/941-6000; FAX 919/941-6030
Holiday Inn—Downtown, 320
  Hillsborough St., 919/832-0501;
  FAX 919/833-1631
Holiday Inn Raleigh—North, 2815 Capital
  Blvd., 919/872-7666; FAX 919/872-3915
North Raleigh Hilton, 3415 Wake Forest
  Rd., 919/872-2323; FAX 919/876-0890
The Plantation Inn Resort, 6401 Capital
  Blvd., 919/876-1411; FAX 919/790-7093
Radisson Plaza Hotel Raleigh, 421 S.
  Salisbury St., 919/834-9900;
  FAX 919/833-1217
Raleigh Marriott Crabtree Valley, 4500
  Marriott Dr., 919/781-7000;
  FAX 919/781-3059
Ramada Inn South/Apex, on US 1 at Hwy.
  55, 919/362-8621; FAX 919/362-9383
✈Sheraton Imperial Hotel & Convention
  Center, 4700 Emperor Blvd., Research
  Triangle Park, 919/941-5050;
  FAX 919/941-5156
Sheraton Inn Raleigh at Crabtree Valley,
  4501 Creedmoor Rd., 919/787-7111;
  FAX 919/783-0024
The Velvet Cloak Inn, 1505 Hillsborough
  St., 919/828-0333; FAX 919/828-2656

SELECTED RESTAURANTS:

Angus Barn Ltd., 9401 Glenwood Ave.,
  Hwy. 70, 919/787-3505
42nd St. Oyster Bar, 508 W. Jones St.,
  919/831-2811
Fox & Hound, 107 Edinburgh S.,
  MacGregor Village Shopping Center,
  Cary, 919/380-0080
Greenshields Brewery & Pub, 214 E.
  Martin St., 919/829-0214
Jacqueline's, in The Plantation Inn Resort,
  919/876-1411
JW's Steakhouse, in the Raleigh Marriott
  Crabtree Valley Hotel, 919/781-7000
Top of the Tower, in the Holiday
  Inn—Downtown, 919/832-0501

SELECTED ATTRACTIONS:

Artspace, 201 E. Davie St., 919/821-2787
City Cemetery (1798), S. East & Hargett sts.

SELECTED RESTAURANTS:

Camille's, 71 Bradford St., 401/751-4812
Capriccio, Dyer and Pine sts.,
  401/421-1320
Old Grist Mill Tavern, 390 Fall River Ave.,
  Seekonk, MA, 508/336-8460
Raphael's, 345 S. Water, 401/421-4646
Stacey's, in the Providence Marriott,
  401/272-2400

SELECTED ATTRACTIONS:

The Arcade, 66 Weybosset St.,
Benefit Street ("Mile of History"), The
  Preservation Society, 401/831-7440
First Baptist Meeting House, 75 N. Main
  St., 401/454-3418
Governor Stephen Hopkins House, Benefit
  & Hopkins sts., 401/421-0694
John Brown House, 52 Power St.,
  401/331-8575

Lippitt House, 199 Hope St.,
  401/453-0688
Museum of Art, Rhode Island School of
  Design, 224 Benefit St., 401/454-6507
Roger Williams National Memorial, 282 N.
  Main St., 401/521-7266
State House (tours), 82 Smith St.,
  401/277-2357
WaterPlace (riverwalk area), Francis St. &
  Memorial Blvd.

INFORMATION SOURCES:

Greater Providence Convention & Visitors
Bureau
  30 Exchange Terrace
  Providence, Rhode Island 02903
  401/274-1636; 800/233-1636 (out of
  state)

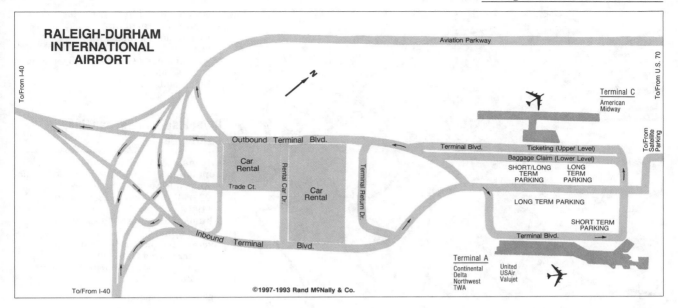

RALEIGH-DURHAM INTERNATIONAL AIRPORT

©1997-1993 Rand McNally & Co.

Executive Mansion, 301 N. Blount St.,
  (Visitor Center, for tours) 919/733-3456
Hardee's Walnut Creek Amphitheatre,
  3801 Rock Quarry Rd., 919/831-6400
Mordecai Historic Park, 1 Mimosa St.,
  919/834-4844
North Carolina Museum of Art, 2110 Blue
  Ridge Rd., 919/839-6262
North Carolina Museum of History, 5 E.
  Edenton St., 919/715-0200
Oakwood Cemetery (1866), Oakwood Ave.
  at Watauga St.
State Capitol, bounded by Wilmington,
  Edenton, Salisbury, and Morgan sts.,
  919/733-4994
Wakefield (oldest dwelling in Raleigh),
  Hargett & St. Mary's sts., 919/833-3431

INFORMATION SOURCES:

Greater Raleigh Convention & Visitors
Bureau
  225 Hillsborough St., Suite 400
  P.O. Box 1879
  Raleigh, North Carolina 27602
  919/834-5900
  800/849-8499
Greater Raleigh Chamber of Commerce
  800 S. Salisbury St.
  P.O. Box 2978
  Raleigh, North Carolina 27602
  919/664-7000

Richmond, Virginia

City map: page 88
Population: (*785,300) 203,056 (1990C)
Altitude: 150 feet
Average Temp.: Jan., 38°F.; July, 78°F.
Telephone Area Code: 804
Time: (none) **Weather:** 804/268-1212
Time Zone: Eastern

AIRPORT TRANSPORTATION:

Ten miles to downtown Richmond.
Taxicab and limousine service.

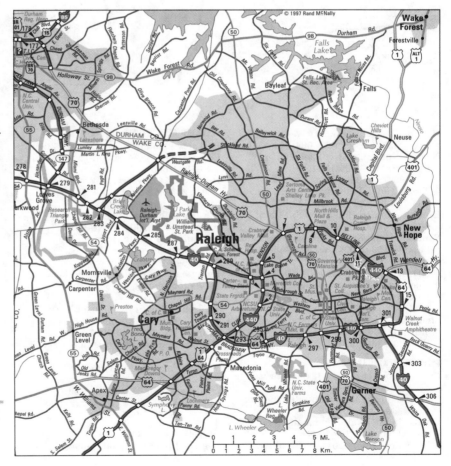

© 1997 Rand McNally

SELECTED HOTELS:

Commonwealth Park Suites Hotel, 9th &
  Bank sts., 804/343-7300;
  FAX 804/343-1025

Courtyard by Marriott, 6400 W. Broad St.,
  804/282-1881; FAX 804/288-2934
Embassy Suites, 2925 Emerywood Pkwy.,
  804/672-8585; FAX 804/672-3749

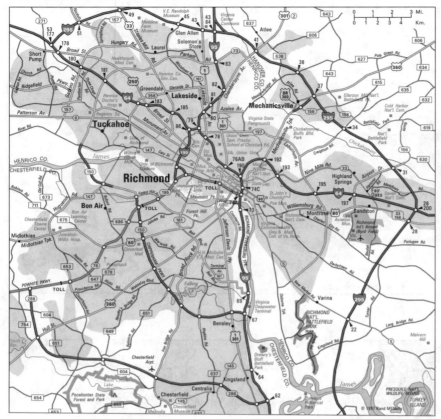

Metro Richmond Visitors Center
1710 Robin Hood Rd.
Richmond, Virginia 23220
804/358-5511

Metro Richmond Chamber of Commerce
201 E. Franklin
Richmond, Virginia 23219
804/648-1234

Riverside-San Bernardino, California

City map: above
Population: (*1,205,800—San Bernardino-Riverside Metro Area) Riverside 226,505; San Bernardino 164,164 (1990C)
Altitude: Riverside 858 feet; San Bernardino 1,049 feet
Average Temp.: Jan., 46°F.; July, 74°F.
Telephone Area Code: 909
Time: 909/853-1212 **Weather:** (none)
Time Zone: Pacific

AIRPORT TRANSPORTATION:

Sixteen miles from Ontario International to downtown Riverside; twenty-four miles to downtown San Bernardino from Ontario International

Taxicab, bus and airport shuttle service to Riverside. Taxicab, limousine, and van service to San Bernardino.

SELECTED HOTELS: RIVERSIDE

Courtyard by Marriott, 1510 University Ave., 909/276-1200; FAX 909/787-6783
Dynasty Suites, 3735 Iowa Ave., 909/369-8200; FAX 909/341-6486
Econolodge, 1971 University Ave., 909/684-6363; FAX 909/684-9228
The Hampton Inn, 1590 University Ave., 909/683-6000; FAX 909/782-8052
Holiday Inn Riverside, 3400 Market St., 909/784-8000; FAX 909/369-7127
✈Marriott Airport Hotel, 2200 E. Holt Blvd., Ontario, 909/986-8811; FAX 909/391-6151
Mission Inn, 3649 Mission Inn Ave. 909/784-0300; FAX 909/683-1342
✈Red Lion Inn, 222 N. Vineyard Ave., Ontario, 909/983-0909; FAX 909/983-8851

SELECTED RESTAURANTS: RIVERSIDE

Carlos O'Brien's, 3667 Riverside Plaza, 909/686-5860
Cask 'N Cleaver, 1333 University Ave., 909/682-4580
C.J.'s Fine Dining, in the Holiday Inn Riverside, 909/784-8000
El Gato Gordo, 1360 University Ave., 909/787-8212
Mario's Place, 1725 Spruce St., 909/684-7755
Mission Inn Restaurant, at the Mission Inn, 909/784-0300
Riverside Brewing Company, 3397 Mission Inn Ave., 909/784-2739

SELECTED ATTRACTIONS: RIVERSIDE

California Citrus State Historic Park, 9400 Dufferin Ave., 909/780-6222
California Museum of Photography, 3824 Main St., 909/787-4787

Historic District Hotel, 301 W. Franklin St., 804/644-9871; FAX 804/344-4380
Hyatt Richmond at Brookfield, 6624 W. Broad St., 804/285-1234; FAX 804/288-3961
Jefferson Hotel, Franklin & Adams sts., 804/788-8000; FAX 804/225-0334
Omni Richmond Hotel, 100 S. 12th St., 804/344-7000; FAX 804/648-6704
Radisson Hotel Richmond, 555 East Canal St., 804/788-0900; FAX 804/788-0791
Richmond Marriott, 500 E. Broad St., 804/643-3400; FAX 804/788-1230
✈Sheraton Airport Inn, 4700 S. Laburnum Ave., 804/226-4300; FAX 804/226-6516
Sheraton Park South, 9901 Midlothian Turnpike, 804/323-1144; FAX 804/320-5255

SELECTED RESTAURANTS:

Byram's Lobster House, 3215 W. Broad St., 804/355-9193
Gallego's Steakhouse, Omni Richmond Hotel, 804/344-7000
Hugo's, in the Hyatt Richmond at Brookfield, 804/285-1234
Julian's Restaurant, 2617 W. Broad St., 804/359-0605
Kabuto—Japanese House of Steaks, 8052 W. Broad St., 804/747-9573
Sal Federico's, 1808 Staples Mill Rd., 804/358-9111
Tropics, Embassy Suites Hotel, 804/672-8585

SELECTED ATTRACTIONS:

Berkeley Plantation, Rte. 5, 804/829-6018
Edgar Allan Poe Museum, 1914 E. Main St., 804/648-5523
Hollywood Cemetery, Albemarle & Cherry sts., 804/648-8501
Maymont House and Park (turn-of-the-century estate), 1700 Hampton St., 804/358-7166
Museum and White House of the Confederacy, 12th & Clay sts., 804/649-1861
Richmond National Battlefield Park (Visitor Center), 3215 E. Broad St., 804/226-1981
St. John's Church ("Give me Liberty or give me death" speech site), 24th & E. Broad sts., 804/648-5015
Shockoe Slip (historic district), Cary St. between 12th & 14th sts.
Virginia Aviation Museum, 5701 Huntsman Rd. next to Richmond International Airport, 804/236-3622
Virginia Museum of Fine Arts, 2800 Grove Ave., 804/367-0844

INFORMATION SOURCES:

Metropolitan Richmond Convention & Visitors Bureau
550 E. Marshall St.
Richmond, Virginia 23219
804/782-2777; 800/365-7272

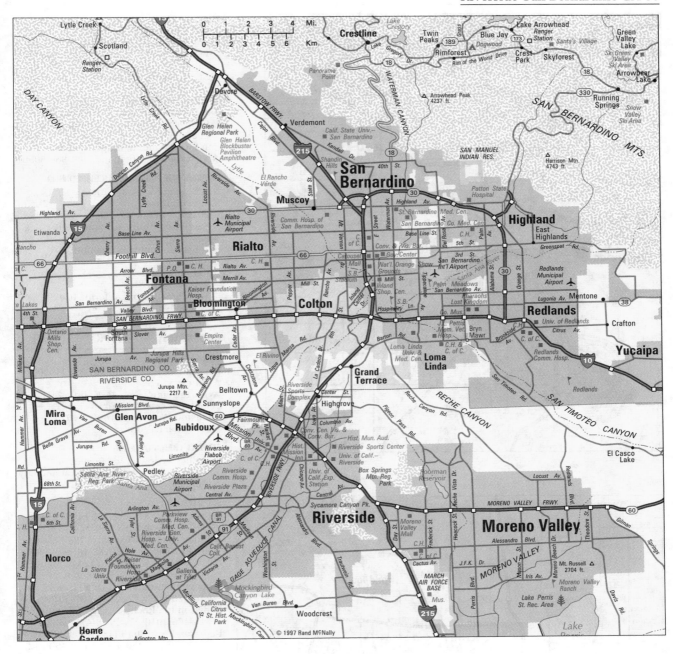

© 1997 Rand McNally

Castle Amusement Park (family recreational park), 3500 Polk St., 909/785-4140

Glen Ivy Hot Springs Spa, 25000 Glen Ivy Rd., Corona, 909/277-3529

March Field Museum (aircraft), at March Air Force Base, off I-215 and Van Buren in Moreno Valley, 909/655-3725

Riverside Art Museum, 3425 Mission Inn Ave., 909/684-7111

Riverside Municipal Museum, 3720 Orange St., 909/782-5273

INFORMATION SOURCES: RIVERSIDE

Riverside Visitors & Convention Bureau
3443 Orange St.
Riverside, California 92501
909/222-4700

Greater Riverside Chamber of Commerce
3685 Main St., Suite 350
Riverside, California 92501
909/683-7100

SELECTED HOTELS: SAN BERNARDINO

Best Western Sands, 606 North H St., 909/889-8391; FAX 909/889-8394

La Quinta Inn, 205 E. Hospitality Ln., 909/888-7571; FAX 909/884-3864

Radisson Hotel & Conference Center, 295 North E St., 909/381-6181; FAX 909/381-5288

Ramada Inn, 2000 Ostrems Way, 909/887-3001; FAX 909/880-3792

San Bernardino Hilton, 285 E. Hospitality Lane, 909/889-0133; FAX 909/381-4299

SELECTED RESTAURANTS: SAN BERNARDINO

La Potiniere, in the San Bernardino Hilton, 909/889-0133

Marie Callender's, 800 E. Highland, 909/882-1754

Red Lobster, 195 E. Hospitality Ln., 909/888-2288

Spencer's, in the Radisson Hotel & Convention Center, 909/381-6181

Stuart Anderson's Black Angus, 290 E. Hospitality Ln., 909/885-7551

TGI Friday's, 390 E. Hospitality Ln., 909/888-9934

SELECTED ATTRACTIONS: SAN BERNARDINO

Asistencia Mission, 26930 Barton Rd., Redlands, 909/793-5402

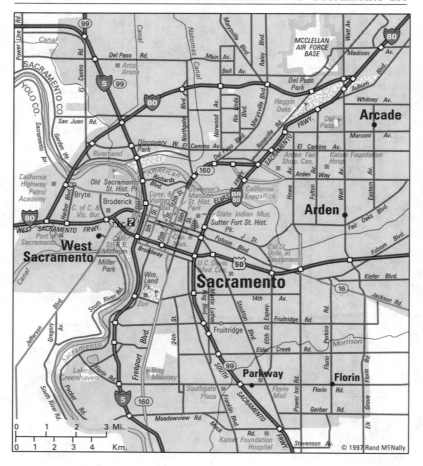

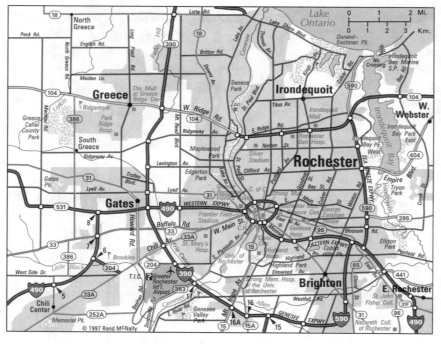

Heritage House, corner of 8th & D sts., 909/384-5114

Historical Glass Museum (open weekends; weekdays for groups by appointment, call 2 weeks in advance), 1157 Orange St., Redlands, 909/798-0868

San Bernardino Civic Light Opera, 562 W. 4th, 909/386-7353

San Bernardino County Museum, 2024 Orange Tree Lane, Redlands, 909/798-8570

San Manuel Indian Bingo, 5797 N. Victoria Ave., Highland, 909/864-5050

INFORMATION SOURCES: SAN BERNARDINO

San Bernardino Convention & Visitors Bureau
201 N. E St., Suite 103
San Bernardino, California 92401
909/889-3980; 800/TO-RTE-66

San Bernardino Area Chamber of Commerce
P.O. Box 658
546 W. Sixth St.
San Bernardino, California 92402
909/885-7515

Rochester, New York

City map: left
Population: (*838,000) 231,636 (1990C)
Altitude: 515 feet
Average Temp.: Jan., 24°F.; July, 71°F.
Telephone Area Code: 716
Time and Weather: 716/974-1616
Time Zone: Eastern

AIRPORT TRANSPORTATION:

Six miles to downtown Rochester.
Taxicab, major hotel courtesy car and city bus service.

SELECTED HOTELS:

➔Holiday Inn Airport, 911 Brooks Ave., 716/328-6000; FAX 716/328-1012

Holiday Inn Genesee Plaza, 120 E. Main St., 716/546-6400; FAX 716/546-3908

Hyatt Regency Rochester, 125 E. Main St., 716/546-1234; FAX 716/546-6777

➔Marriott Fairfield Inn, 1200 Brooks Ave., 716/529-5000; FAX 716/529-5011

Radisson Inn Rochester, 175 Jefferson Rd., 716/475-1910; FAX 716/475-9633

Radisson Rochester Plaza Hotel, 70 State St., 716/546-3450; FAX 716/546-8712

➔Ramada Inn Airport, 1273 Chili Ave., 716/464-8800; FAX 716/464-0395

Rochester Airport Marriott, 1890 W. Ridge Rd., 716/225-6880; FAX 716/225-8188

Rochester Marriott Thruway Hotel, 5257 W. Henrietta Rd., 716/359-1800; FAX 716/359-1349

Strathallan Hotel, 550 East Ave., 716/461-5010; FAX 716/461-3387

SELECTED RESTAURANTS:

Daisy Flour Mill, 1880 Blossom Rd., 716/381-1880

Depot Restaurant, 41 N. Main St., Pittsford, 716/381-9991

Edward's, 13 S. Fitzhugh, 716/423-0140

Lloyd's, 289 Alexander St., 716/546-2211

Maplewood Inn, 3500 East Ave., 716/381-7700

Richardson's Canal House, 1474 Marsh Rd., Pittsford, 716/248-5000

Sabrina's, in the Strathallan Hotel,
716/461-5010
Spring House, 3001 Monroe Ave.,
716/586-2300

SELECTED ATTRACTIONS:
Casa Larga Vineyards (tours), 2287 Turk
Hill Rd., Fairport, 716/223-4210
Genesee Country Village, Flint Hill Rd.,
Mumford, 716/538-6822
High Falls (museum & historic district),
Platt St. & Brown's Race, 716/325-2030
High Falls of the Genesee, Pont de Rennes
bridge over the Genesee River
International Museum of Photography &
George Eastman House, 900 East Ave.,
716/271-3361
Memorial Art Gallery of the University of
Rochester, 500 University Ave.,
716/473-7720
Rochester Museum & Science Center, 657
East Ave., 716/271-4320
Rochester Philharmonic Orchestra, Gibbs
& Main, 716/454-2620
Seabreeze Amusement Park, 4600 Culver
Rd., 716/323-1900
The Strong Museum, 1 Manhattan Square,
corner of Chestnut & Woodbury,
716/263-2700

INFORMATION SOURCES:
Greater Rochester Visitors Association
126 Andrews St.
Rochester, New York 14604-1102
716/546-3070; 800/677-7282
Greater Rochester Metro Chamber of
Commerce
55 Saint Paul St.
Rochester, New York 14604
716/454-2220

Sacramento, California

City map: page 90
Population: (*1,168,100) 369,365 (1990C)
Altitude: 25 feet
Average Temp.: Jan., 45°F.; July, 75°F.
Telephone Area Code: 916
Time: 916/646-2000 **Weather:**
916/646-2000
Time Zone: Pacific

AIRPORT TRANSPORTATION:
Twelve miles from Sacramento
Metropolitan to downtown Sacramento.
Taxicab, airporter limousine and hotel
limousine service.

SELECTED HOTELS:
Best Western Sandman, 236 Jibboom St.,
916/443-6515; FAX 916/43-8346
Beverly Garland Hotel, 1780 Tribute Rd.,
916/929-7900; FAX 916/921-9147
Canterbury Inn, 1900 Canterbury Rd.,
916/927-0927; FAX 916/641-8594
Clarion Hotel, 700 16th St., 916/444-8000;
FAX 916/442-8129
Holiday Inn—Capitol Plaza, 300 J St.,
916/446-0100; FAX 916/446-0117
✈Host Airport Hotel, 6945 Airport Blvd.,
916/922-8071; FAX 916/929-8636
Hyatt Regency Sacramento, 1209 L St.,
916/443-1234; FAX 916/321-6699
Radisson Hotel Sacramento, 500 Leisure
Lane, 916/922-2020; FAX 916/649-9463

Red Lion Hotel, 2001 Point West Way,
916/929-8855; FAX 916/564-7706
Red Lion's Sacramento Inn, 1401 Arden
Way, 916/922-8041; FAX 916/922-0386
Sacramento Hilton Inn, 2200 Harvard,
916/922-4700; 916/922-8418
Sheraton Rancho Cordova, 11211 Point
East Dr., Rancho Cordova,
916/638-1100; FAX 916/638-5803

SELECTED RESTAURANTS:
Aldo's Restaurant, in the Town & Country
Village Shopping Center, Fulton &
Marconi, 916/483-5031
Biba, 2801 Capitol Ave., 916/455-2422
California Fat's, 1015 Front St.,
916/441-7966
The Firehouse, 1112 2nd St.,
916/442-4772
Frank Fat's, 806 L St., 916/442-7092
Il Fornaio, 400 Capitol Mall,
916/446-4100
Pheasant Club, 2525 Jefferson Blvd.,
West Sacramento, 916/371-9530

Shot of Class, 1020 11th St., 916/447-5340
Terrace Grill, 544 Pavillion Ln.,
916/920-3800

SELECTED ATTRACTIONS:
California State Railroad Museum, 2nd & I
St., 916/448-4466
Crocker Art Museum, 3rd & O St.,
916/264-5423
Discovery Museum, 101 I St., Old
Sacramento, 916/264-7057
Discovery Museum Learning Center,
3615 Auburn Blvd., 916/277-6180
Historic Governor's Mansion, 16th & H
St., 916/323-3047
Sacramento Zoo, in William Land Park,
corner of Sutterville Rd. & Land Park
Dr., 916/264-5885
State Capitol, 10th St. & Capitol Mall,
916/324-0333
State Indian Museum, 26th and K sts.,
916/324-0971
Sutter's Fort, 27th & L sts., 916/445-4422
Waterworld USA, 1600 Exposition Blvd.,
916/924-0556

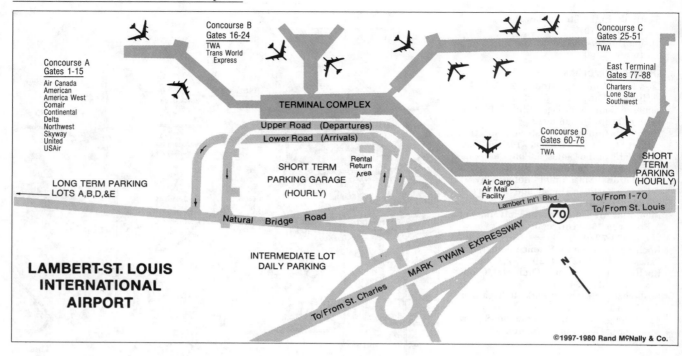

Concourse B
Gates 16-24
TWA
Trans World
Express

Concourse C
Gates 25-51
TWA

Concourse A
Gates 1-15

Air Canada
American
America West
Comair
Continental
Delta
Northwest
Skyway
United
USAir

East Terminal
Gates 77-88

Charters
Lone Star
Southwest

TERMINAL COMPLEX

Upper Road   (Departures)
Lower Road   (Arrivals)

Concourse D
Gates 60-76
TWA

SHORT TERM
PARKING GARAGE
(HOURLY)

Rental
Return
Area

SHORT
TERM
PARKING
(HOURLY)

Air Cargo
Air Mail
Facility

LONG TERM PARKING
LOTS A,B,D,&E

Lambert Int'l. Blvd.

To/From I-70
To/From St. Louis

70

Natural   Bridge   Road

INTERMEDIATE LOT
DAILY PARKING

MARK TWAIN EXPRESSWAY

To/From St. Charles

N

**LAMBERT-ST. LOUIS
INTERNATIONAL
AIRPORT**

©1997-1980 Rand McNally & Co.

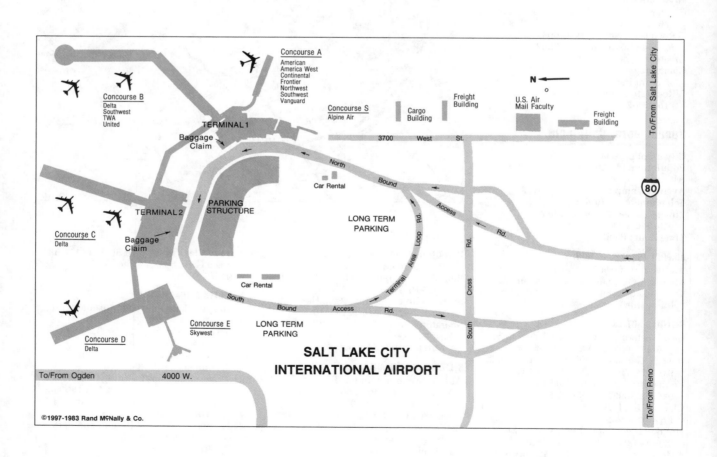

Concourse A

American
America West
Continental
Frontier
Northwest
Southwest
Vanguard

Concourse B

Delta
Southwest
TWA
United

Concourse S
Alpine Air

Cargo
Building

Freight
Building

U.S. Air
Mail Faculty

Freight
Building

N

TERMINAL 1

Baggage
Claim

3700   West   St.

North
Bound

Car Rental

TERMINAL 2

PARKING
STRUCTURE

Access

Rd.

80

Baggage
Claim

LONG TERM
PARKING

Terminal Area Loop Rd.

Cross

Concourse C
Delta

Car Rental

South   Bound   Access   Rd.

South

Concourse E
Skywest

LONG TERM
PARKING

**SALT LAKE CITY
INTERNATIONAL AIRPORT**

Concourse D
Delta

To/From Ogden   4000 W.

To/From Reno

To/From Salt Lake City

©1997-1983 Rand McNally & Co.

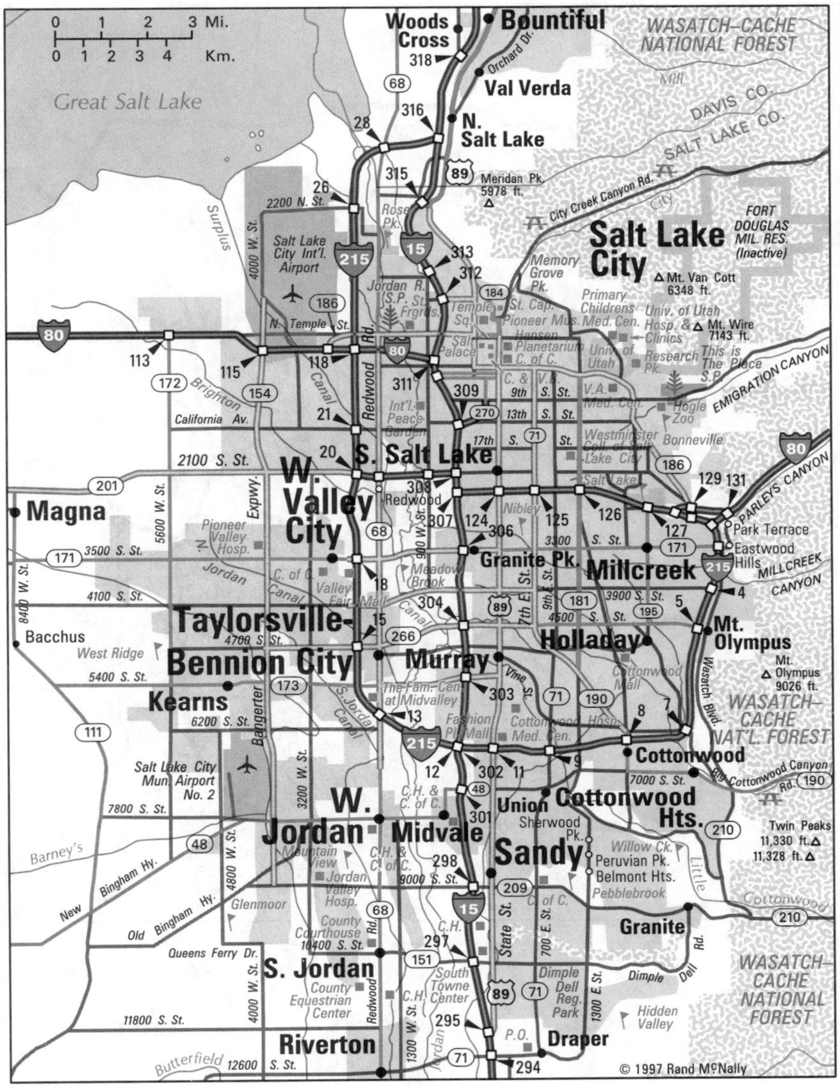

INFORMATION SOURCES:

Sacramento Convention & Visitors Bureau
 1421 K St.
 Sacramento, California 95814
 916/264-7777
Visitor Information Center
 1104 Front St.
 Old Sacramento, California 95814
 916/442-7644 (7 days a week)
Sacramento Metropolitan Chamber of
Commerce
 917 7th St.
 Sacramento, California 95814
 916/552-6800

St. Louis, Missouri

City map: page 91
Population: (*2,238,700) 396,685 (1990C)
Altitude: 470 feet
Average Temp.: Jan., 32°F.; July, 79°F.
Telephone Area Code: 314
Time: 314/321-2522 **Weather:**
 314/321-2222
Time Zone: Central

AIRPORT TRANSPORTATION:

See map on page 92.
Fifteen miles to downtown St. Louis.
Taxicab and limousine bus service.

SELECTED HOTELS:

Adam's Mark, 4th & Chestnut,
 314/241-7400; FAX 314/241-6618
Cheshire Inn & Lodge, 6300 Clayton Rd.,
 314/647-7300; FAX 314/647-0442
Frontenac Hilton Hotel, 1335 S.
 Lindbergh Blvd., 314/993-1100;
 FAX 314/993-8546
Hotel Majestic, 1019 Pine St.,
 314/436-2355; FAX 314/436-0223
Hyatt Regency St. Louis, 1 St. Louis
 Union Station, 314/231-1234;
 FAX 314/923-3970
Regal Riverfront Hotel, 200 S. 4th St.,
 314/241-9500; FAX 314/241-9601
✈Renaissance Hotel, 9801 Natural Bridge
 Rd., 314/429-1100; FAX 314/429-3625
The Ritz-Carlton St. Louis, 100 Carondelet
 Plaza, 314/863-6300; FAX 314/863-3525
✈St. Louis Airport Hilton, 10330 Natural
 Bridge Rd., 314/426-5500;
 FAX 314/426-3429
✈St. Louis Airport Marriott, I-70 at
 Lambert Int'l Airport, 314/423-9700;
 FAX 314/423-0213
St. Louis Marriott Pavilion, 1 S.
 Broadway, 314/421-1776;
 FAX 314/331-9029
Seven Gables Inn, 26 N. Meramec St.,
 Clayton, 314/863-8400;
 FAX 314/863-8846

SELECTED RESTAURANTS:

Dierdorf & Hart's, at St. Louis Union
 Station, 314/421-1772
Dominic's, 5101 Wilson Ave.,
 314/771-1632
Giovanni's on the Hill, 5201 Shaw,
 314/772-5958
Hannegan's, 719 N. 2nd St., 314/241-8877
Henry VIII, in the Henry VIII Hotel, 4690
 N. Lindbergh Blvd., Bridgeton,
 314/731-3040

Lynch Street Bistro, 1031 Lynch St.,
 314/772-5777
Kemoll's Restaurant, 211 N. Broadway,
 314/421-0555
Tony's, 410 Market St., 314/231-7007

SELECTED ATTRACTIONS:

Anheuser-Busch Brewery, 12th & Lynch,
 314/577-2626
Gateway Arch, 314/425-4465
Gateway Riverboat Cruises, 314/621-4040
Grant's Farm, 10501 Gravois,
 314/843-1700
Missouri Botanical Garden, 4344 Shaw,
 314/577-5100
St. Louis Art Museum, One Fine Arts Dr.,
 Forest Park, 314/721-0067
St. Louis Science Center, 5050 Oakland
 Ave., 314/289-4400
St. Louis Union Station, Market St.
 between 18th & 20th, 314/421-6655
St. Louis Zoo, US 40 & Hampton Ave.,
 Forest Park, 314/781-0900
Six Flags Over Mid-America, Eureka,
 314/938-5300

INFORMATION SOURCES:

St. Louis Convention & Visitors
Commission
 10 S. Broadway, Suite 1000
 St. Louis, Missouri 63102
 314/421-1023
 Business Info. 800/325-7962;
 Visitor Info. 800/888-3861
St. Louis Regional Commerce & Growth
Association
 100 S. 4th St., Suite 500
 St. Louis, Missouri 63102
 314/231-5555

Salt Lake City, Utah

City map: above
Population: (*801,000) 159,936 (1990C)
Altitude: 4,260 feet
Average Temp.: Jan., 27°F.; July, 77°F.
Telephone Area Code: 801
Time: 801/975-1212 **Weather:**
 801/575-7669
Time Zone: Mountain

© 1997 Rand McNally

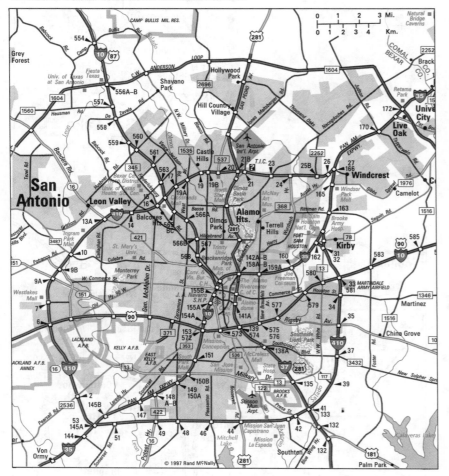

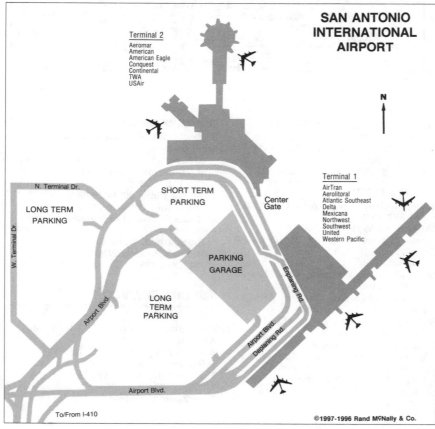

AIRPORT TRANSPORTATION:
See map on page 92.
Six miles to downtown Salt Lake City.
Taxicab, bus, and limousine bus service.

SELECTED HOTELS:
Doubletree Hotel, 215 W. South Temple, 801/531-7500; FAX 801/328-1289
Holiday Inn Downtown, 999 S. Main St., 801/359-8600; FAX 801/359-7186
Little America Hotel & Towers, 500 S. Main St., 801/363-6781; FAX 801/596-5911
Red Lion—Salt Lake City, 255 S. West Temple, 801/328-2000; FAX 801/532-1953
✈Salt Lake Airport Hilton, 5151 Wiley Post Way, 801/539-1515; FAX 801/539-1113
Salt Lake City Marriott, 75 S. West Temple, 801/531-0800; FAX 801/532-4127
Salt Lake Hilton, 150 W. 500 South, 801/532-3344; FAX 801/531-0705

SELECTED RESTAURANTS:
Benihana of Tokyo, 165 S. West Temple St., 801/322-2421
Cafe Pierpont, 122 W. Pierpont Ave., 801/364-1222
Cowboy Grub, 2350½ Foothill Blvd., 801/466-8334
La Caille at Quail Run, 9565 Wasatch Blvd., 801/942-1751
Market Street Grill, 54 Market St., 801/322-4668
Mikado Japanese Restaurant, 67 W. 100 South St., 801/328-0929
Ristorante Della Fontana, 336 S. 4th East, 801/328-4243

SELECTED ATTRACTIONS:
Beehive House, State St. & South Temple, 801/240-2672
Family History Library, 35 N. West Temple, 801/240-2331
Hansen Planetarium, 15 S. State St., 801/538-2098
Hogle Zoo, 2600 E. Sunnyside Ave., 801/582-1631
Lagoon Amusement Park & Pioneer Village, 17 mi. north on I-15, 801/451-8000
Museum of Church History & Art, 45 N. West Temple, 801/240-3310
Temple Square, 50 W. North Temple, 801/240-2534
This Is The Place State Park, 2601 E. Sunnyside Ave., 801/584-8392
Utah Museum of Fine Arts, south of the Marriott Library, Univ. of Utah campus, 801/581-7049
Utah State Capitol, 350 N. Main, 801/538-3000
Violin Making School of America (tours Sept. to May by appointment), 308 East 200 South, 801/364-3651

INFORMATION SOURCES:
Salt Lake Convention and Visitors Bureau
180 S. West Temple St.
Salt Lake City, Utah 84101
801/521-2822
Salt Lake Area Chamber of Commerce
175 E. 400 S., Suite 600
Salt Lake City, Utah 84111
801/364-3631

San Antonio, Texas

City map: page 94
Population: (*1,158,000) 935,933 (1990C)
Altitude: 505 to 1,000 feet
Average Temp.: Jan., 51°F.; July, 84°F.
Telephone Area Code: 210
Time: 210/226-3232 **Weather:**
210/606-3617
Time Zone: Central

AIRPORT TRANSPORTATION:

See map on page 94.
Eight miles to downtown San Antonio.
Taxicab and limousine bus service.

SELECTED HOTELS:

Best Western Continental Inn, 9735 I-35
N., 210/655-3510; FAX 210/655-0778
Embassy Suites Northwest, 7750 Briaridge
St., 210/340-5421; FAX 210/340-1843
Hilton Palacio del Rio, 200 S. Alamo St.,
210/222-1400; FAX 210/270-0761
Hotel St. Anthony, 300 E. Travis St.,
210/227-4392; FAX 210/227-0915
Hyatt Regency San Antonio, 123 Losoya,
210/222-1234; FAX 210/227-4925
La Mansion del Rio, 112 College St.,
210/225-2581; FAX 210/226-0389
Plaza San Antonio Hotel, 555 S. Alamo
St., 210/229-1000; FAX 210/229-1418
San Antonio Marriott Riverwalk, 711 E.
Riverwalk, 210/224-4555;
FAX 210/224-2754
✈The Sheraton Fiesta Hotel, 37 NE. Loop
410, 210/366-2424; FAX 210/341-0410

SELECTED RESTAURANTS:

The Bayous Riverside, 517 N. Presa,
210/223-6403
Beladi Ranch., 1039 NE. Loop 410,
210/826-2371
Boudro's, 421 E. Commerce, 210/224-8484
Chez Ardid Restaurant Gastronomique,
1919 San Pedro, 210/732-3203
Fig Tree, 515 Paseo la Villita,
210/224-1976
Grey Moss Inn, 19010 Scenic Loop Rd.,
210/695-8301
Las Canarias, in La Mansion del Rio, 12
College St., 210/225-2581
Paesano's, 1715 McCullough Ave.,
210/226-9541
Restaurant Biga, 206 E. Locust,
210/225-0722

SELECTED ATTRACTIONS:

The Alamo, Alamo Plaza, 210/225-1391
Brackenridge Park, 3500 block of N. St.
Mary's St., 210/207-8480
La Villita Historical District, on the River
Walk between S. Alamo & E. Nueva sts.,
210/207-8610
Market Square (El Mercado), 514 W.
Commerce St., 210/207-8600
The River Walk, downtown San Antonio
San Antonio Missions National Historical
Park, 2202 Roosevelt Ave.,
210/229-5701
San Antonio Zoo & Aquarium, 3903 N. St.
Mary's St., 210/734-7183
Texas Adventure, Alamo Plaza, across
from the Alamo, 210/227-8224
Tower of the Americas, in HemisFair Park,
210/207-8615

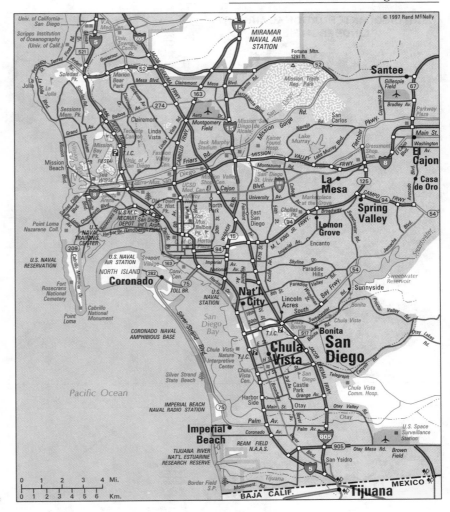
© 1997 Rand M9Nally

University of Texas Institute of Texan
Cultures at San Antonio, 801 S. Bowie
St., 210/558-2300
Witte Museum, 3801 Broadway St., Brack-
enridge Park, 210/820-2111

INFORMATION SOURCES:

San Antonio Convention and Visitors
Bureau
121 Alamo Plaza
P.O. Box 2277
San Antonio, Texas 78298
210/270-8700; 800/447-3372
Visitor Information Center
317 Alamo Plaza
San Antonio, Texas 78205
210/207-8748; 800/447-3372
Chamber of Commerce of Greater San
Antonio
602 E. Commerce St.
San Antonio, Texas 78205
210/229-2100

San Diego, California

City map: above
Population: (*2,158,900) 1,110,549
(1990C)
Altitude: Sea level to 823 feet

Average Temp.: Jan., 57°F.; July, 71°F.
Telephone Area Code: 619
Time: 619/853-1212 **Weather:**
619/289-1212
Time Zone: Pacific

AIRPORT TRANSPORTATION:

See map on page 96.
Three miles to downtown San Diego.
Taxicab and bus service.

SELECTED HOTELS:

Best Western Hanalei Hotel, 2270 Hotel
Circle N., 619/297-1101;
FAX 619/297-6049
✈Best Western Posada Inn, 5005 N.
Harbor Dr., 619/224-3254;
FAX 619/224-2186
Best Western Shelter Island Marina Inn,
2051 Shelter Island Dr., 619/222-0561;
FAX 619-222-9760
Bristol Court, 1055 First Ave.,
619/232-6141; FAX 619/232-0118
Embassy Suites San Diego Bay Down-
town, 601 Pacific Hwy.,
619/239-2400; FAX 619/239-1520
Glorietta Bay Inn, 1630 Glorietta Blvd.,
619/435-3101; FAX 619/435-6182
✈Holiday Inn on the Bay, 1355 N. Harbor
Dr., 619/232-3861; FAX 619/232-4924

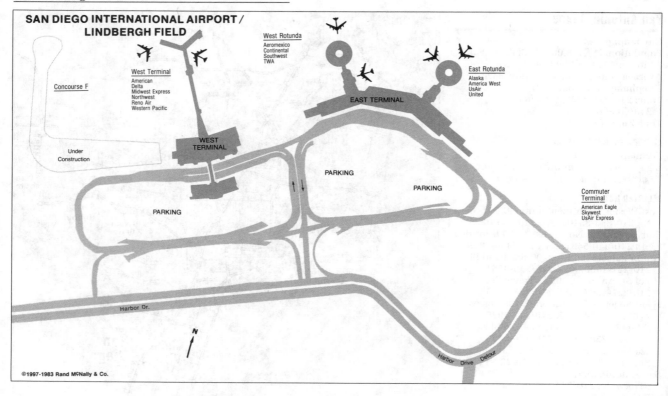

SAN DIEGO INTERNATIONAL AIRPORT / LINDBERGH FIELD

Concourse F

Under Construction

West Terminal
American
Delta
Midwest Express
Northwest
Reno Air
Western Pacific

WEST TERMINAL

West Rotunda
Aeromexico
Continental
Southwest
TWA

EAST TERMINAL

East Rotunda
Alaska
America West
UsAir
United

Commuter Terminal
American Eagle
Skywest
UsAir Express

PARKING
PARKING
PARKING

Harbor Dr.

Harbor Drive Detour

N

©1997-1983 Rand McNally & Co.

North Terminal
American
American Eagle
United
United Express
United Shuttle

Boarding Area D

Boarding Area E

Boarding Area F

International Terminal
Aeroflot
Air China
Air France
Asiana Airlines
British Airways
Canadian Int'l
China Airlines
EVA
Finnair

Japan
KLM Royal Dutch
Korean Air
LACSA
Lufthansa
Mexicana
Northwest
Philippine
Qantas

Singapore
TACA
Tower Air
United
Virgin Atlantic

Boarding Area C

PARKING GARAGE

Lower Road
Upper Road

Boarding Area B

Car Rental
Car Rental
Car Rental
Car Rental
Car Rental
Car Rental

Road 18
Road 16

ALL RENTAL CAR RETURNS

Boarding Area A

South Terminal
Air Canada
Alaska
American Trans Air
America West
Continental
Delta
Hawaiian
Midwest Express
Northwest
Rich Int'l
Southwest
TWA
USAir
USAir Express

Hilton Hotel

Road 2

101

N

SAN FRANCISCO INTERNATIONAL AIRPORT

©1997-1984 Rand McNally & Co.

Hotel del Coronado, 1500 Orange Ave., Coronado, 619/522-8000; FAX 619/522-8238

Hyatt Islandia, 1441 Quivira Rd., 619/224-1234; FAX 619/224-0348

Hyatt Regency San Diego, 1 Market Pl., 619/232-1234; FAX 619/233-6464

Quality Resort, 875 Hotel Circle S., 619/298-8281; FAX 619/295-5610

Rancho Bernardo Inn, 17550 Bernardo Oaks Dr., 619/487-1611; FAX 619/673-0311

San Diego Hilton Beach & Tennis Resort, 1775 E. Mission Bay Dr., 619/276-4010; FAX 619/275-7991

San Diego Marriott Hotel & Marina, 333 W. Harbor Dr., 619/234-1500; FAX 619/234-8678

✈Sheraton San Diego Hotel & Marina, 1380 Harbor Island Dr., 619/291-2900; FAX 619/692-2337

Town & Country Hotel, 500 Hotel Circle N., 619/291-7131; FAX 619/291-3584

Westgate Hotel, 1055 2nd Ave., 619/238-1818; FAX 619/557-3737

Wyndham Hotel at Emerald Bay, 400 W. Broadway, 619/239-4500; FAX 619/239-3274

SELECTED RESTAURANTS:

Anthony's Star of the Sea Room, Harbor Dr. & Ash, 619/232-7408

El Bizcocho, in the Rancho Bernardo Inn, 619/487-1611

Gourmet Room, in the Town & Country Hotel, 619/291-7131

Grant Grill, in the U. S. Grant Hotel, 326 Broadway, 619/239-6806

The Marine Room, 2000 Spindrift Dr., La Jolla, 619/459-7222

Mister A's, 2550 5th Ave., Financial Center, 619/239-1377

Old Trieste, 2335 Morena Blvd., 619/276-1841

Thee Bungalow, 4996 W. Point Loma Blvd., 619/224-2884

Tom Ham's Lighthouse, 2150 Harbor Island Dr., 619/291-9110

Top O' the Cove, 1216 Prospect, La Jolla, 619/454-7779

Trattoria Acqua, 1298 Prospect St., 619/454-0709

SELECTED ATTRACTIONS:

Balboa Park (museums, theaters, gardens, galleries), center of city

Cabrillo National Monument, on the tip of Point Loma, 619/557-5450

Gaslamp Quarter National Historic District, (Victorian-era buildings, shops, restaurants, theaters), Downtown, 619/233-4682

Horton Plaza (shopping, dining, entertainment), Downtown, 619/238-1596

Museum of Contemporary Art, 1001 Kettner Blvd. at Broadway & 700 Prospect St., La Jolla, 619/454-3541

Old Town State Historic Park, (Visitor Center) 4002 Wallace St., 619/220-5422

San Diego Zoo, off Park Blvd. in Balboa Park, 619/234-3153

Seaport Village, (shopping, dining, entertainment), 849 W. Harbor Dr., 619/235-4013

Sea World of California, on Sea World Dr., 619/226-3901

Stephen Birch Aquarium-Museum, Scripps Institution of Oceanography, 2300 Expedition Way, La Jolla, 619/534-FISH

Wild Animal Park, 15500 San Pasqual Valley Rd., Escondido, 619/234-6541

INFORMATION SOURCES:

San Diego Convention and Visitors Bureau
401 B St., Suite 1400
San Diego, California 92101-4237
619/232-3101

International Visitor Information Center
11 Horton Plaza
1st Ave. & F St.
San Diego, California 92101
619/236-1212

Greater San Diego Chamber of Commerce
402 W. Broadway, Suite 1000
San Diego, California 92101
619/232-0124

San Francisco-Oakland, California

City map: page 98
Population: San Francisco, Oakland-San Jose (*5,390,900) San Francisco, 723,959; Oakland 372,242 (1990C)
Altitude: Sea level to 934 feet
Average Temp.: San Francisco Jan., 50°F.; July, 59°F. Oakland Jan., 48°F.; July, 63°F.
Telephone Area Codes: San Francisco 415; Oakland 510
Time: 415/767-8900 **Weather:** 415/936-1212
Time Zone: Pacific

AIRPORT TRANSPORTATION:

See maps on pages 96 and 99.

Fifteen miles to downtown San Francisco from San Francisco International; 25 miles to downtown Oakland from San Francisco International Airport. Eight miles to downtown Oakland from Oakland International.

Taxicab, bus, and limousine bus service to downtown San Francisco. Taxicab, limousine, bus, and BART service to downtown Oakland.

SELECTED HOTELS: SAN FRANCISCO

✈Clarion Hotel—San Francisco Airport, 401 E. Millbrae Ave., Millbrae, 415/692-6363; FAX 415/697-8735

Clift Hotel, 495 Geary St., 415/775-4700; FAX 415/441-4621

The Donatello, 501 Post St., 415/441-7100; FAX 415/885-8842

Fairmont Hotel & Tower, 950 Mason St., on Nob Hill, 415/772-5000; FAX 415/837-0587

Grand Hyatt on Union Square, 345 Stockton St., 415/398-1234; FAX 415/391-1780

Harbor Court Hotel, 165 Steuart St., 415/882-1300; FAX 415-882-1313

Holiday Inn—San Francisco Airport North, 275 S. Airport Blvd., South San Francisco, 415/837-3550; FAX 415/873-4524

Holiday Inn Union Square, 480 Sutter St., 415/398-8900; FAX 415/989-8823

Huntington Hotel—Nob Hill, 1075 California St., 415/474-5400; FAX 415/474-6227

Hyatt Regency San Francisco, 5 Embarcadero Center, 415/788-1234; FAX 415/398-2567

Mark Hopkins Inter-Continental, Number One Nob Hill, 415/392-3434; FAX 415/421-3302

Miyako Hotel, 1625 Post St., 415/922-3200; FAX 415/921-0417

Park Plaza San Francisco Airport, 1177 Airport Blvd., Burlingame, 415/342-9200; FAX 415/342-1655

The Phoenix, 601 Eddy St., 415/776-1380; FAX 415/885-3109

The Queen Anne, 1590 Sutter St., 415/441-2828; FAX 415/775-5212

The Renaissance Stanford Court Hotel, 905 California St., 415/989-3500; FAX 415/391-0513

San Francisco Airport Hilton, San Francisco International Airport, 415/589-0770; FAX 415/589-4696

San Francisco Hilton & Towers, 333 O'Farrell St., 415/771-1400; FAX 415/771-6807

San Francisco Marriott, 55 Fourth St., 415/896-1600; FAX 415/896-6176 & 415/777-2799

The Westin St. Francis, 335 Powell St., 415/397-7000; FAX 415/774-0124

SELECTED RESTAURANTS: SAN FRANCISCO

Fleur de Lys, 777 Sutter St., 415/673-7779

Fournou's Ovens, in The Renaissance Stanford Court Hotel, 415/989-1910

Harbor Village, 4 Embarcadero Center, 415/781-8833

Harry Denton's, 161 Steuart St., 415/882-1333

McCormick & Kuleto's, 900 North Point, in Ghiradelli Square, 415/929-1730

One Market Restaurant, One Market St., 415/777-5577

Palio D'Asti, 640 Sacramento St., 415/395-9800

Tadich Grill, 240 California St., 415/391-1849

Tommy Toy's Haute Cuisine Chinoise, 655 Montgomery St., 415/397-4888

Vanessi's, 1177 California St., 415/771-2422

Washington Square Bar & Grill, 1707 Powell St., 415/982-8123

The Waterfront Restaurant, Pier 7, The Embarcadero, 415/391-2696

SELECTED ATTRACTIONS: SAN FRANCISCO

Alcatraz Island, San Francisco Bay, ferry leaves from Pier 41, Fisherman's Wharf, 415/546-2700

Ansel Adams Center, 250 Fourth St., 415/495-7000

California Palace of the Legion of Honor (European art museum), Lincoln Park, 34th Ave. & Clement St., 415/863-3330.

Chinatown, Grant Ave. & Stockton St. (begins at Grant & Bush)

Coit Tower/Telegraph Hill, northeast San Francisco, reached via Lombard St.

Exploratorium, 3601 Lyon St., 415/561-0360

Fisherman's Wharf, on Jefferson St. between Hyde & Powell sts.

Golden Gate Bridge, spans the entrance to San Francisco Bay

Golden Gate Park, (museums, arboretum, Japanese garden), from Stanyan St. to the Pacific Ocean, between Fulton St. & Lincoln Blvd.

North Beach (night-life area), northeast sector of San Francisco, Columbus Ave. is the main artery

San Francisco Maritime National Historic Park, Fisherman's Wharf, Hyde & Jefferson sts., 415/929-0202

San Francisco Museum of Modern Art, 151 3rd St., 415/357-4000

San Francisco Zoo, Sloat Blvd. & 45th Ave., 415/753-7080

Underwater World, Fisherman's Wharf, Pier 39, 888/SEADIVE

Union Street, from the 1600 to the 2200 block

INFORMATION SOURCES: SAN FRANCISCO

San Francisco Convention & Visitors Bureau
Convention Plaza
201 Third St., Suite 900
San Francisco, California 94103
415/974-6900

San Francisco Visitor Information Center
Powell & Market sts., by the cable car turnaround.
Lower Level, Hallidie Plaza
San Francisco, California 94102
415/391-2000

San Francisco Chamber of Commerce
465 California St., 9th Floor
San Francisco, California 94104
415/392-4520

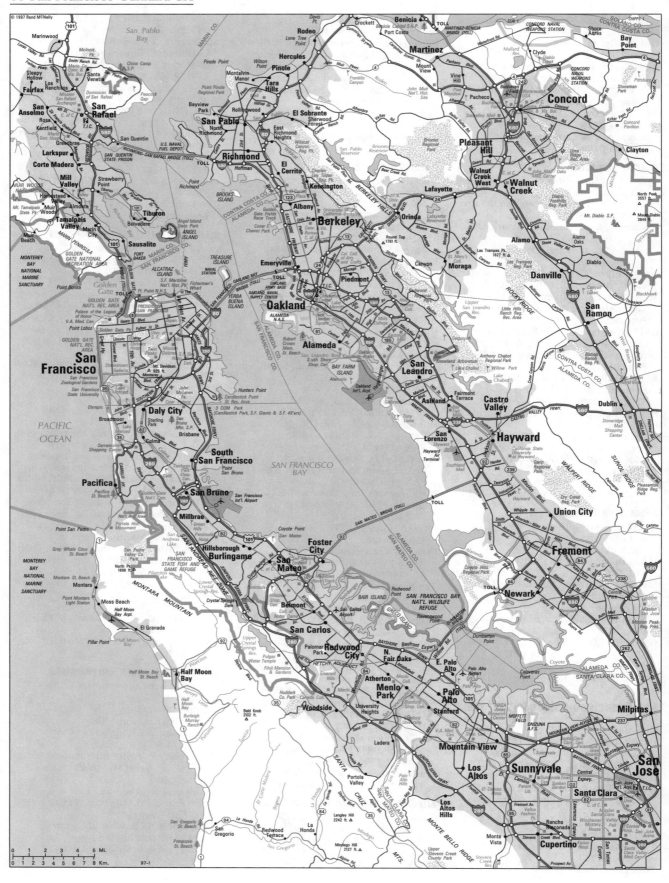

SELECTED HOTELS: OAKLAND

✈Best Western Park Plaza, 150
Hegenberger Rd., 510/635-5300;
FAX 510/635-9661

Claremont Resort & Spa, Domingo &
Ashby aves., 510/843-3000;
FAX 510/848-6208

Clarion Suites Lake Merritt, 1800 Madison
St., 510/832-2300; FAX 510/832-7150

Executive Inn—Hayward Airport, 20777
Hesperian Blvd., Hayward,
510/732-6300; FAX 510/783-2265

✈Hampton Inn, 8465 Enterprise Way,
510/632-8900; FAX 510/632-4713

Holiday Inn—Bay Bridge, 1800 Powell St.,
Emeryville, 510/658-9300;
FAX 510/547-8166

✈Holiday Inn—Oakland Airport, 500
Hegenberger Rd., 510/562-5311;
FAX 510/636-1539

✈Oakland Airport Hilton, 1 Hegenberger
Rd., 510/635-5000; FAX 510/729-0491

Oakland Marriott City Center, 1001 Broadway, 510/451-4000; FAX 510/835-3466

Waterfront Plaza Hotel, 10 Washington
St., 510/836-3800; FAX 510/832-5695

SELECTED RESTAURANTS: OAKLAND

Bay Wolf Restaurant, 3853 Piedmont Ave.,
510/655-6004

Crogan's Seafood House & Bar, 6101 La
Salle Ave., 510/339-2098

Hong Kong East Ocean Seafood, 3199
Powell St., Emeryville, 510/655-3388

La Brasserie, 542 Grand Ave.,
510/893-6206

Oliveto, 5655 College Ave., 510/547-5356

P.J.'s Gingerbread House, 741 5th St.,
510/444-7373

Scott's Seafood Grill & Bar, 2 Broadway,
510/444-3456

Trader Vic's, 9 Anchor Dr., Emeryville
510/653-3400

SELECTED ATTRACTIONS: OAKLAND

Camron-Stanford House (1876; tours),
1418 Lakeside Dr., 510/836-1976

Children's Fairyland, in Lakeside Park at
Grand & Bellevue aves., 510/452-2259

Jack London Village, (museums, shops,
restaurants), 30 Jack London Square,
510/893-7956

Lakeside Park/Lake Merritt, 510/238-3208

Marine World Africa U.S.A., Marine
World Pkwy., Vallejo, 707/643-ORCA

Oakland Museum, 10th & Oak St.,
510/238-3401

Rotary Nature Center, in Lakeside Park at
Bellevue & Perkins aves., 510/238-3739

Takara Sake Company (slide show and
tasting room, open daily), 708
Addison St., Berkeley, 510/540-8250

Trial & Show Gardens, in Lakeside Park,
510/238-3208

INFORMATION SOURCES: OAKLAND

Oakland Convention and Visitors Bureau
550 10th St., Suite 214
Oakland, California 94607
510/839-9000; 800/262-5526

Oakland Chamber of Commerce
475 14th St.
Oakland, California 94612-1928
510/874-4800

Terminal 1
Alaska
American
America West
Delta
Horizon Air
Sierra Expressway
Southwest

N

International
Terminal
Corsair
Martinair
Taesa
United

From Airport Dr. & I-880

PARKING

Car Rental
Return Area

Car
Rental

To
Airport Dr.
& I-880

Terminal 2
Southwest

Car
Rental

OAKLAND
INTERNATIONAL
AIRPORT

©1997-1996 Rand McNally & Co.

San Jose, California

City map: page 100
Population: San Francisco-San Jose-Oak-
land(*5,390,900) 782,248 (1990C)
Altitude: 87 feet
Average Temp.: Jan., 51°F.; July, 65°F.
Telephone Area Code: 408
Time: 415/767-8900 **Weather:**
415/936-1212
Time Zone: Pacific

AIRPORT TRANSPORTATION:

Five miles to downtown San Jose.
Taxicab and bus service.

SELECTED HOTELS:

The Beverly Heritage Hotel, 1820 Barber
Lane, Milpitas, 408/943-9080;
FAX 408/432-8617

Clarion President's Inn, 3200 Monterey
Rd., 408/972-2200; FAX 408/972-2632

The Fairmont Hotel, 170 S. Market St.,
408/998-1900; FAX 408/287-1648

Holiday Inn—Park Center Plaza,
Almaden Blvd., 408/998-0400;
FAX 408/289-9081

✈Hospitality Inn, 1755 N. First St.,
408/453-3133; FAX 408/452-1849

Hyatt Sainte Claire, 302 S. Market St.,
408/885-1234; FAX 408/977-0403

✈Hyatt San Jose Airport, 1740 N. First St.,
408/993-1234; FAX 408/453-0259

✈Le Baron Hotel, 1350 North 1st St.,
408/453-6200; FAX 408/437-9693

✈Red Lion Hotel, 2050 Gateway Pl.,
408/453-4000; FAX 408/437-2898

San Jose Hilton & Towers, 300 Almaden
Blvd., 408/287-2100; FAX 408/947-4489

SELECTED RESTAURANTS:

Emile's, 545 S. 2nd St., 408/289-1960
Eulipia, 374 S. 1st St., 408/280-6161
Lou's Village, 1465 W. San Carlos St.,
408/293-4570

Ninth Floor, in the Le Baron Hotel,
408/453-6200

Paolo's Continental Restaurant, 333
W. San Carlos, first floor of the
Riverfront Tower, 408/294-2558

SELECTED ATTRACTIONS:

American Museum of Quilts and Textiles,
60 S. Market St., 408/971-0323

Children's Discovery Museum of San Jose,
180 Woz Way, 408/298-5437

Fallon House, 175 W. St. John,
408/993-8182

Japanese Friendship Garden, 1500 Senter
Rd. in Kelley Park, 408/277-4192

Monterey Bay Aquarium, 886 Cannery
Row, Monterey, 408/648-4800

Paramount's Great America, between US
101 & CA 237, Santa Clara,
408/988-1776

Raging Waters, 2333 S. White Rd.,
408/270-8000

Roaring Camp & Big Trees Narrow Gauge
Railroad, Felton, 408/335-4484

Rosicrucian Egyptian Museum, Park,
Planetarium & Art Gallery, Park &
Naglee aves., 408/947-3636

San Jose Historical Museum (25 acres of
original and replica 1890s buildings),
1600 Senter Rd. in Kelley Park,
408/287-2290

San Jose Museum of Art, 110 S. Market
St., 408/294-2787

Tech Museum of Innovation, 145 W. San
Carlos St., 408/279-7150

Winchester Mystery House, 525 S.
Winchester Blvd., 408/247-2000

INFORMATION SOURCES:

San Jose Convention & Visitors Bureau
333 W. San Carlos, Suite 1000
San Jose, California 95110
408/295-9600; FYI Events
Line 408/295-2265

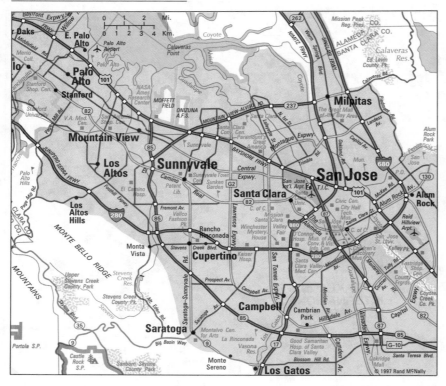

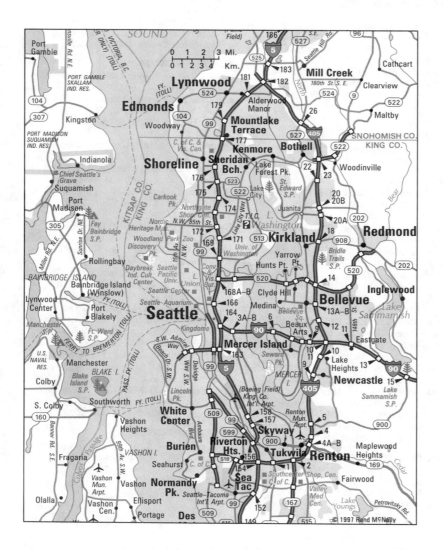

Visitor & Business Center
   San Jose McEnery Convention Center
   150 W. San Carlos
   San Jose, California 95113
   408/283-8833
San Jose Metropolitan Chamber of
Commerce
   180 S. Market St.
   San Jose, California 95113
   408/291-5250

Seattle, Washington

City map: lower left
Population: (*2,565,600) 516,259 (1990C)
Altitude: Sea level to 520 feet
Average Temp.: Jan., 41°F.; July, 66°F.
Telephone Area Code: 206
Time: 206/361-8463 **Weather:**
   206/526-6087
Time Zone: Pacific

AIRPORT TRANSPORTATION:
See map on page 101.
Fourteen miles to downtown Seattle.
Taxicab, limousine bus, Metro Transit,
   and Airporter service.

SELECTED HOTELS:
Crowne Plaza, 1113 6th Ave.,
   206/464-1980; FAX 206/340-1617
→Doubletree Inn—Southcenter, 205
   Strander Blvd., 206/246-8220;
   FAX 206/575-4743
Four Seasons Olympic Hotel, 411
   University St., 206/621-1700;
   FAX 206/682-9633
→Holiday Inn Sea-Tac Airport, 17338
   Pacific Hwy. S., 206/248-1000;
   FAX 206/242-7089
Hyatt Regency Bellevue, 900 Bellevue
   Way NE, Bellevue, 206/462-1234;
   FAX 206/646-7567
The Madison Renaissance Hotel, 515
   Madison St., 206/583-0300;
   FAX 206/622-8635
→Radisson Hotel Seattle Airport, 17001
   Pacific Hwy. S., 206/244-6000;
   FAX 206/246-6835
→Red Lion Hotel/Sea-Tac, 18740
   Pacific Hwy. S., 206/246-8600;
   FAX 206/242-9727
Seattle Hilton—Downtown, 1301 6th Ave.,
   206/624-0500; FAX 206/682-9029
→Seattle Marriott Sea-Tac Airport, 3201 S.
   176th St., 206/241-2000;
   FAX 206/248-0789
Sheraton Seattle Hotel & Towers, 1400 6th
   Ave., 206/621-9000; FAX 206/621-8441
The Westin Hotel, 1900 5th Ave.,
   206/728-1000; FAX 206/728-2259

SELECTED RESTAURANTS:
Carvery, Seattle-Tacoma International
   Airport, ticket level—main terminal,
   206/433-5622
Fuller's, in the Sheraton Seattle Hotel &
   Towers, 206/621-9000
The Hunt Club, in the Sorrento Hotel, 900
   Madison, 206/622-6400
Jonah's, in the Best Western Bellevue Inn,
   11211 Main St., Bellevue, 206/455-5240
Maximilien in the Market, 81A Pike St.,
   206/682-7270
Nikko, in The Westin Hotel, 206/728-1000

The Painted Table, in the Alexis Hotel,
   1007 1st Ave. at Madison, 206/624-4844
Ray's Boathouse, 6049 Seaview NW,
   206/789-3770
Reiner's, 1106 8th Ave., 206/624-2222

SELECTED ATTRACTIONS:
Hiram M. Chittenden Locks, 3015 NW
   54th St., Ballard, 206/783-7059
Museum of Flight, 9404 East Marginal
   Way S., 206/764-5700
Pacific Science Center, 200 Second Ave.
   N. in Seattle Center, 206/443-2001
Pike Place Market, First & Pike sts.,
   206/682-7453
Seattle Aquarium, Pier 59 in Waterfront
   Park, 206/386-4320
Seattle Art Museum, 100 University St.,
   206/654-3100
Seattle Underground Tour, 206/682-1511
Space Needle, corner of 5th & Broad in
   Seattle Center, 206/443-2100
Tillicum (Indian) Village Tour, Blake
   Island State Park (tour starts from Pier
   56 on the Seattle Waterfront),
   206/443-1244
Woodland Park Zoo, 50th & Fremont Ave.
   N., 206/684-4800

INFORMATION SOURCES:
Seattle-King County Convention &
Visitors Bureau/Convention Sales
   520 Pike St., Suite 1300
   Seattle, Washington 98101
   206/461-5800
Seattle-King County Convention &
Visitors Bureau/Visitor Information
   Level 1, Galleria
Washington State Convention & Trade
Center
   800 Convention Pl.
   Seattle, Washington 98101
   206/461-5840
Greater Seattle Chamber of Commerce
   1301 5th Ave., Suite 2400
   Seattle, Washington 98101-2603
   206/389-7200

Shreveport, Louisiana

City map: right
Population: (*296,300) 198,525 (1990C)
Altitude: 204 feet
Average Temp.: Jan., 48°F.; July, 83°F.
Telephone Area Code: 318
Time and Weather: 318/425-0211
Time Zone: Central

AIRPORT TRANSPORTATION:
Eight miles to downtown Shreveport.
Taxicab, limousine and bus service.

SELECTED HOTELS:
Best Western Chateau Suite Hotel, 201
   Lake St., 318/222-7620;
   FAX 318/424-2014
Comfort Inn Bossier, 1100 Delhi, Bossier
   City, 318/221-2400; FAX 318/221-2909
Fairfield Inn by Marriott, 6245 S. Westport
   Ave., 318/686-0102; FAX 318/686-8791
Hampton Inn Bossier, 1005 Gould Dr.,
   Bossier City, 318/752-1112;
   FAX 318/752-1405
Holiday Inn Downtown, 102 Lake St.,
   318/222-7717; FAX 318/221-5951

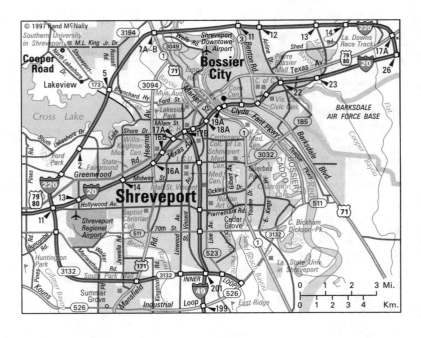

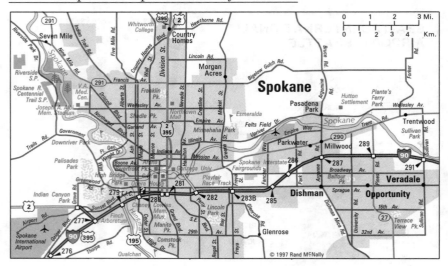

➤Holiday Inn Express-Airport, 5101
  Westwood Park Dr., 318/631-2000;
  FAX 318/631-2800
➤Holiday Inn Financial Plaza, 5555
  Financial Plaza, 318/688-3000;
  FAX 318/687-4462
Isle of Capri Hotel, 3033 Hilton Dr.,
  Bossier City, 318/747-2400;
  FAX 318/747-6822
La Quinta Motor Inn, 309 Preston Blvd.,
  Bossier City, 318/747-4400;
  FAX 318/747-1516
Ramada Inn, 750 Isle of Capri Blvd.,
  Bossier City, 318/746-8410;
  FAX 318/742-4269
➤Ramada Inn Shreveport, 5116
  Monkhouse Dr., 318/635-7531;
  FAX 318/635-1600
The Remington Suite Hotel, 220 Travis
  St., 318/425-5000; FAX (same)
Sheraton Shreveport, 1419 E. 70th St.,
  318/797-9900; FAX 318/798-2923

SELECTED RESTAURANTS:

Chadwick's, in the Holiday Inn
  Downtown, 318/222-7717
Chianti, 6535 Line Ave., 318/868-8866
Dudley & Gerald's South Louisiana
  Kitchen, 2421 E. 70th, 318/797-3010
Monsieur Patou, 855 Pierremont Rd.,
  Suite 135, 318/868-9822
Rennick's, in the Sheraton Shreveport
  Hotel, 318/797-9900
Shogun of Japan, 1409 E. 70th St.,
  318/798-1001
T.S. Station, 750 Shreveport-Barksdale
  Hwy., 318/865-3594

SELECTED ATTRACTIONS:

American Rose Center, 8877
  Jefferson-Page Rd., off I-20,
  318/938-5402
Eighth Air Force Museum, Barksdale Air
  Force Base, Bossier City, 318/456-3067
Louisiana State Exhibit Museum, 3015
  Greenwood Rd., 318/632-2020
Pioneer Heritage Center (authentic
  pioneer buildings), NE corner of
  Louisiana State University—Shreveport
  campus, 318/797-5332

Sports Museum of Champions, 700 Clyde
  Fant Pkwy., 318/221-0712
Touchstone Wildlife and Art Museum, US
  80 East, about 2 miles east of the
  Bossier City city limits, 318/949-2323

INFORMATION SOURCES:

Shreveport-Bossier Convention and
Tourist Bureau
  629 Spring St.
  Shreveport, Louisiana 71101
  318/222-9391; 800/551-8682
Shreveport Chamber of Commerce
  400 Edwards
  Shreveport, Louisiana 71101
  318/677-2500

Spokane, Washington

City map: above
Population: (*317,500) 177,196 (1990C)
Altitude: 1,898 feet
Average Temp.: Jan., 26°F.; July, 70°F.
Telephone Area Code: 509
Time: 976-1616 **Weather:** 509/624-8905
Time Zone: Pacific

AIRPORT TRANSPORTATION:

Five miles to downtown Spokane.
Taxicab, airporter limousine and
  limousine service.

SELECTED HOTELS:

Best Western Trade Winds Downtown, W.
  907 3rd Ave., 509/838-2091;
  FAX 509/838-2094
Best Western Trade Winds North, N. 3033
  Division St., 509/326-5500;
  FAX 509/328-1357
Cavanaugh's Inn at the Park, W. 303 N.
  River Dr., 509/326-8000;
  FAX 509/325-7329
Cavanaugh's River Inn, N. 700 Division
  St., 509/326-5577; FAX 509/326-1120
Courtyard by Marriott, N. 401 Riverpoint
  Blvd., 509/456-7600; FAX 509/456-0969
Quality Inn Oakwood, N. 7919 Division
  St., 509/467-4900; FAX 509/467-4933
Quality Inn Valley Suites, E. 8923 Mission
  Ave., 509/928-5218;
  FAX 509/928-5218 ext. 597

➤Ramada Inn, at Spokane International
  Airport, 509/838-5211;
  FAX 509/838-1074
Red Lion City Center, N. 322 Spokane
  Falls Ct., 509/455-9600;
  FAX 509/455-6285
Red Lion Spokane Valley, N. 1100 Sulli-
  van Rd., 509/924-9000;
  FAX 509/922-4965
Shilo Inn, E. 923 3rd Ave., 509/535-9000;
  FAX 509/535-5740
WestCoast Ridpath Hotel, W. 515 Sprague
  Ave., 509/838-2711; FAX 509/747-6970

SELECTED RESTAURANTS:

Ankeny's, in the WestCoast Ridpath Hotel,
  509/838-6311
Chapter Eleven, E. 105 Mission Ave.,
  509/326-0466
Clinkerdaggers, 621 W. Mallon,
  509/328-5965
1881, in the Red Lion City Center Hotel,
  509/455-9600
The Mustard Seed, W. 245 Spokane Falls
  Blvd., 509/747-2689
The Onion Bar and Grill, W. 302
  Riverside, 509/747-3852
Patsy Clark's Mansion, W. 2208 2nd Ave.,
  509/838-8300
Spokane House, in the Friendship Inn,
  4301 W. Sunset Hwy., 509/838-1471
Stockyards Inn, 3827 E. Boone Ave.,
  509/534-1212
Two Moon Cafe, in the Mars Hotel, 300 W.
  Sprague, 509/747-6277

SELECTED ATTRACTIONS:

Antique 1909 Looff Carousel, on Spokane
  Falls Blvd. between Washington &
  Howard, in Riverfront Park,
  509/625-6600
Centennial Trail, follows the Spokane
  River from downtown to the
  Washington/Idaho state line
Cheney Cowles Memorial Museum
  (Eastern Washington State Historical
  Society), W. 2316 First Ave.,
  509/456-3931
Downtown Skywalk Shopping System
Manito Park/Japanese Gardens, 21st &
  Bernard, 509/625-6622
Riverfront Park, N. 507 Howard,
  509/625-6600

INFORMATION SOURCES:

Spokane Regional Convention and
Visitors Bureau
  W. 926 Sprague, Suite 180
  Spokane, Washington 99204
  Business Info. 509/624-1341;
  Visitor Info. 509/747-3230;
  800/248-3230
Spokane Area Chamber of Commerce
  W. 1020 Riverside
  Spokane, Washington 99201
  509/624-1393

Syracuse, New York

City map: page 103
Population: (*529,500) 163,860 (1990C)
Altitude: 406 feet
Average Temp.: Jan., 24°F.; July, 72°F.
Telephone Area Code: 315
Time and Weather: 315/474-8481
Time Zone: Eastern

AIRPORT TRANSPORTATION:
Ten miles to downtown Syracuse.
Taxicab and hotel shuttle service.

SELECTED HOTELS:
✈Best Western Airport Inn, at Hancock
International Airport, North Syracuse,
315/455-7362; FAX 315/455-6840
Courtyard by Marriott, 6415 Yorktown
Circle, East Syracuse, 315/432-0300;
FAX 315/432-9950
Four Points by Sheraton, 441 Electronics
Pkwy., Liverpool, 315/457-1122;
FAX 315/451-1269
Hampton Inn, 6605 Old Collamer Rd.,
East Syracuse, 315/463-6443;
FAX 315/432-1080
Holiday Inn Airport Area, 6701 Buckley
Rd., North Syracuse, 315/457-4000;
FAX 315/453-7877
Holiday Inn East, 6501 College Dr., East
Syracuse, 315/437-2761;
FAX 315/463-0028
Hotel Syracuse at Radisson Plaza, 500 S.
Warren St., 315/422-5121;
FAX 315/422-3440
Quality Inn North, 1308 Buckley Rd., N.
Syracuse, 315/451-1212;
FAX 315/453-8050
Sheraton University, 801 University Ave.,
315/475-3000; FAX 315/475-3311
Syracuse Marriott, 6302 Carrier Pkwy.,
East Syracuse, 315/432-0200;
FAX 315/433-1210
Syracuse Sheraton Inn, Electronics Pkwy.,
Liverpool, 315/457-1122;
FAX 315/451-1269

SELECTED RESTAURANTS:
Barbagallo's Tavern, 6772 Old Collamer
Rd., East Syracuse, 315/437-7715
Casa Di Copani, 3414 Burnet Ave.,
315/463-1031
Grimaldi's Chop House, 6400 Yorktown
Circle, East Syracuse, 315/437-1461
Tower Restaurant, 701 E. Genessee St.,
315/474-7251
Pastabilities, 311 S. Franklin St.,
315/474-1153

SELECTED ATTRACTIONS:
Burnet Park Zoo, 1 Conservation Pl.,
315/435-8516 or -8511
The Erie Canal Museum & Urban Cultural
Park Visitor Center, 318 Erie Blvd. E. at
Montgomery St., 315/471-0593
The Museum of Science & Technology,
Jefferson St. Armory at Franklin St.,
315/425-0747
The Octagon House, 5420 W. Genessee St.,
Camillus, 315/488-7800
Onondaga Historical Museum, 321 Mont-
gomery St., 315/428-1864
Onondaga Park, Roberts Ave. & Crossett
St., 315/473-4330
Sainte Marie among the Iroquois (fort), 1
Onondaga Lake Parkway, Liverpool,
315/453-6767 or 451-PARK
The Salt Museum, in Onondaga Lake
Park, Liverpool, 315/453-6715 or
451-PARK

INFORMATION SOURCES:
Syracuse Convention & Visitors Bureau
572 S. Salina St.
Syracuse, New York 13202-3320
315/470-1900 or -1910; 800/234-4797

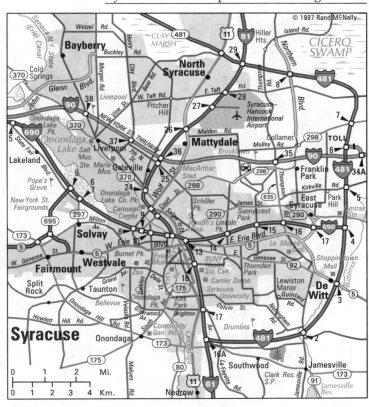

Greater Syracuse Chamber of Commerce
572 S. Salina St.
Syracuse, New York 13202
315/470-1800

Tampa-St. Petersburg, Florida

City map: page 104
Population: (*1,812,000 Tampa-St. Peters-
burg-Clearwater Metro Area) Tampa
280,150; St. Petersburg 238,629 (1990C)
Altitude: Tampa 57 feet; St. Petersburg 44
feet
Average Temp.: Jan., 61°F.; July, 82°F.
Telephone Area Code: 813
Time and Weather: 813/888-9700
Time Zone: Eastern

AIRPORT TRANSPORTATION:
See map on page 105.
Five miles from Tampa International to
downtown Tampa; 25 miles to
downtown St. Petersburg. Ten miles
from St. Petersburg/Clearwater Int'l.
Airport to St. Petersburg.
Taxicab and limousine service to Tampa
and St. Petersburg; also bus service to
Tampa.

SELECTED HOTELS: TAMPA
Best Western, 820 E. Busch Blvd.,
813/933-4011; FAX 813/932-1784
✈Crowne Plaza, 700 N. Westshore Blvd.,
813/289-8200; FAX 813/289-9166
Doubletree Guest Suites—Tampa Bay,
3050 N. Rocky Point Dr. W.,
813/888-8800; FAX 813/888-8743
Holiday Inn Downtown, 111 W. Fortune
St., 813/223-1351; FAX 813/221-2000

Howard Johnson Main Gate, 4139 E.
Busch Blvd., 813/988-9191;
FAX 813/989-3544
Hyatt Regency Tampa, 211 N. Tampa
St., 813/225-1234; FAX 813/273-0234
✈Hyatt Regency Westshore, 6200
Courtney Campbell Causeway,
813/874-1234; FAX 813/281-9168
✈Radisson Bay Harbor Inn, 7700
Courtney Campbell Causeway,
813/281-8900; FAX 813/281-0189
Ramada Inn USF, 400 E. Bearss Ave.,
813/961-1000; FAX 813/961-5704
Sheraton Grand Hotel Westshore, 4860 W.
Kennedy Blvd., 813/286-4400;
FAX 813/286-4053
✈Tampa Airport Marriott, Tampa Int'l
Airport, 813/879-5151;
FAX 813/873-0945
✈Tampa Marriott Westshore, 1001 N.
Westshore Blvd., 813/287-2555;
FAX 813/289-5464
Western Comfort Inn, 9331 Adamo Dr.,
813/621-5511; FAX 813/626-6032
✈Westshore Airport Hotel, 4500 W.
Cypress St., 813/879-4800;
FAX 813/873-1832

SELECTED RESTAURANTS: TAMPA
Armani's, in the Hyatt Regency
Westshore, 813/874-1234
Bern's Steak House, 1208 S. Howard Ave.,
813/251-2421
C.K.'s Revolving Rooftop Restaurant, in
the Tampa Airport Marriott,
813/879-5151
The Colonnade, 3401 Bayshore Blvd.,
813/839-7558

The Columbia, 2117 E. 7th Ave.,
813/248-4961

Cypress Room, in the Saddlebrook Resort,
5700 Saddlebrook Way, Wesley Chapel
(25 miles north of Tampa on I-75),
813/973-1111

Don Shula's Steakhouse, in the Sheraton
Grand Hotel Westshore, 813/286-4400

Old Spaghetti Warehouse, 1911 N. 13th
St., in Ybor Square, 813/248-1720

Oyster Catchers, in the Hyatt Regency
Westshore, 813/874-1234

SELECTED ATTRACTIONS: TAMPA

Adventure Island, 10001 McKinley,
813/987-5660

Busch Gardens, Busch Blvd. & 40th St.,
813/987-5082

Children's Museum of Tampa, 7550 North
Blvd., 813/935-8441

The Florida Aquarium, 701 Channelside
Dr., 813/273-4000

Henry B. Plant Museum, 401 W. Kennedy
Blvd., 813/254-1891

Lowry Park Zoo, 7530 North Blvd.,
813/935-8552

Museum of Science & Industry, 4801 E.
Fowler Ave., 813/987-6300

Tampa Museum of Art, 600 N. Ashley,
813/274-8130

Ybor City State Museum, 1818 Ninth Ave.,
   813/247-6323
Ybor Square, 8th Ave. & 13th St.,
   813/247-4497

INFORMATION SOURCES: TAMPA

Tampa/Hillsborough Convention &
Visitors Association
   111 Madison St., Suite 1010
   Tampa, Florida 33602-4706
   813/223-1111; 800/44-TAMPA
Greater Tampa Chamber of Commerce
   401 E. Jackson, Suite 2100
   P.O. Box 420
   Tampa, Florida 33601
   813/228-7777

SELECTED HOTELS: ST. PETERSBURG

Days Inn, 2595 54th Ave. N.,
   813/522-3191; FAX 813/527-6120
Days Inn Marina Beach Resort, 6800 Sun-
   shine Skyway Ln., 813/867-1151;
   FAX 813/864-4494
Don CeSar Beach Resort & Spa, 3400 Gulf
   Blvd., St. Pete Beach, 813/360-1881;
   FAX 813/367-7597
✈Holiday Inn Airport, 3535 Ulmerton
   Rd., Clearwater, 813/577-9100;
   FAX 813/573-5022
Holiday Inn South, 4601 34th St. S.,
   813/867-3131; FAX 813/867-2025
La Quinta, 4999 34th St. N., (US 19),
   813/527-8421; FAX 813/527-8851
St. Petersburg Hilton, 333 First St. S.,
   813/894-5000; FAX 813/894-7655
Tradewinds Resort, 5500 Gulf Blvd., St.
   Pete Beach, 813/367-6461;
   FAX 813/562-1214

SELECTED RESTAURANTS: ST. PETERSBURG

Alessi's at The Pier, 800 2nd Ave. NE,
   813/894-1133
Billy's Original Stone Crab & Steak House,
   1 Colony Rd., 813/866-2115
The Columbia, at The Pier, 800 2nd Ave.
   NE, 813/822-8000
The Lobster Pot, 17814 Gulf Blvd.,
   Reddington Shores, 813/391-8592
Parker's Landing, in the Days Inn Marina
   Beach Resort, 813/867-1151

SELECTED ATTRACTIONS: ST. PETERSBURG

Great Explorations (hands-on museum),
   1120 4th St. S., 813/821-8992
Museum of Fine Arts, 255 Beach Dr. NE,
   813/896-2667
P. Buckley Moss Gallery, 190 Fourth Ave.
   NE, 813/894-2899
The Pier, on the waterfront at the end of
   2nd Ave. NE
St. Petersburg Museum of History, 335
   Second Ave. NE, 813/894-1052
Salvador Dali Museum, 1000 Third St. S.,
   813/823-3767
Sunken Gardens, 1825 Fourth St. N.,
   813/896-3186

INFORMATION SOURCES: ST. PETERSBURG

St. Petersburg/Clearwater Area
Convention & Visitors Bureau
   St. Petersburg ThunderDome
   1 Stadium Dr., Suite A
   St. Petersburg, Florida 33705
   813/582-7892; visitor information:
   800/345-6710

Suncoast Welcome Center
   2001 Ulmerton Rd.
   Clearwater, Florida 34622
   813/573-1449
St. Petersburg Area Chamber of Commerce
   100 2nd Ave. N.
   P.O. Box 1371
   St. Petersburg, Florida 33731
   Business Info. 813/821-4069
   Visitor Info. 813/821-4715

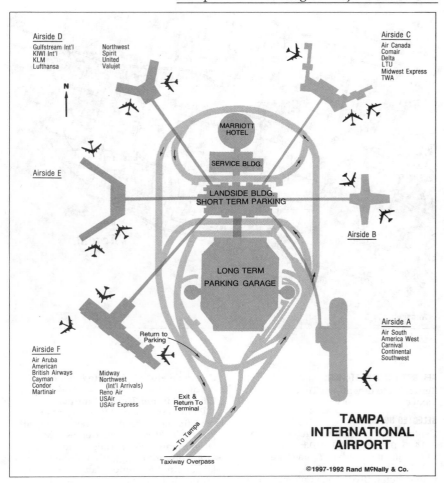

TAMPA
INTERNATIONAL
AIRPORT

©1997-1992 Rand McNally & Co.

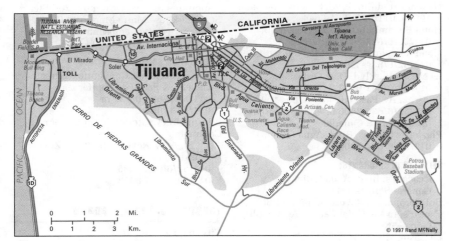

© 1997 Rand McNally

Tijuana, Baja California, Mexico

City map: above
Population: (*2,893,900 San Diego-
   Tijuana Metro Area) 698,752 (1990C)
Altitude: 499 feet
Average Temp.: Jan., 55°F.; July, 70°F.;
Telephone Code: 011/52/66
Time: None **Weather:** None
Time Zone: Pacific

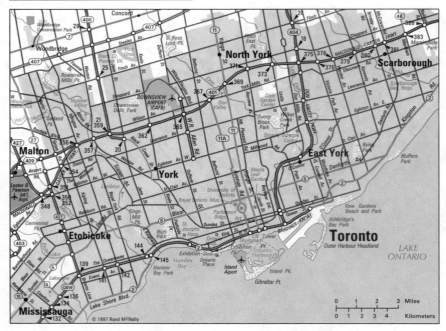

AIRPORT TRANSPORTATION:
Ten miles to downtown Tijuana.
Taxicab and bus service.

SELECTED HOTELS:
Centenario Plaza, Blvd. Agua Caliente
   1426, 011/52/6/681-8103
El Conquistador, Blvd. Agua Caliente
   1777, 011/52/6/681-7955
Grand Hotel, Blvd. Agua Caliente 4500,
   011/52/6/681-7000 or 800/546-4030 (in
   the U.S.)
Hacienda del Río, Blvd. Sanchez Taboada
   10606, 011/52/6/684-8644
Hotel Bugambilias, Av. Tijuana 1600,
   011/52/6/623-8411 thru 16
Hotel Real del Río, Jose Ma. Velasco 1409,
   011/52/6/634-3100
La Mesa Inn, Blvd. Diaz Ordaz 50,
   011/52/6/681-6522
Lucerna, Av. Paseo de los Heroes 10902,
   011/52/6/634-2000 or 800/LUCERNA
   (in the U.S. & Canada)
Plaza Las Glorias, Blvd. Agua Caliente
   011/52/6/681-7200

SELECTED RESTAURANTS:
Boccaccio's, Blvd. Agua Caliente &
   General Salinas 11250
Bol Corona, Av. Revolución & 2nd St.
Caesar's, in the Hotel Caesar, Av. Revolu-
   ción & 5th St.
La Costa, 7th St. 8131
La Escondida, Santa Monica 1
La Placita, Av. Revolución 961
Tia Juana Tilly's, in the Fronton Palacio
   Jai Alai, Av. Revolución 701

SELECTED ATTRACTIONS:
Avenida Revolución (shopping)
Bullfights, held in El Toreo de Tijuana,
   Blvd. Agua Caliente 100, and the Plaza
   Monumental, Paseo Monumental in the
   Playas District

Cañon de vinos L.A. Cetto (winery),
   Cañon Johnson 2108, Col. Hidalgo
Centro Cultural Tijuana (museum,
   Omnimax theater, Mexican arts and
   crafts shopping arcade, performing arts
   theater), Paseo de los Heroes & Mina
Hipodromo Caliente (horse and
   greyhound racing), Blvd. Agua Caliente
Jai alai, in the Fronton Palacio, Av. Rev-
   olución & 7th St.
Mexitlan (scale models of more than 200
   of Mexico's historical and architectural
   monuments), Av. Ocampo & 2nd St.
State Park José María Morelos y Pavón
   (creative center, aquarium, theater),
   Blvd. Insurgentes 16000

INFORMATION SOURCES:
Tijuana Tourism & Convention Bureau
   Cina St. & Paseo de los Heroes
   011/52/6/684-05/37 or
   011/52/6/684-0538
Information Center of the Chamber of
Commerce
   1st St. & Av. Revolución 8206, Zona
   Centro
   011/52/6/688-1685 or
   011/52/6/685-8472

Toronto, Ontario, Canada

City map: above
Population: (*3,893,046) 636,395 (1991C)
Altitude: 275 ft.
Average Temp.: Jan., 23°F.; July, 69°F.
Telephone Area Code: 416
Time: (none) **Weather:** 416/739-4507
Time Zone: Eastern

AIRPORT TRANSPORTATION:
See map on page 107.
Eighteen miles to downtown Toronto.
Taxicab and bus service.

SELECTED HOTELS:
Four Seasons Hotel, 21 Avenue Rd. at
   Yorkville, 416/964-0411;
   FAX 416/964-2301
Howard Johnson Downtown Plaza, the
   Westbury, 475 Yonge St., 416/924-0611;
   FAX 416/924-5061
Inn on the Park, 1100 Eglinton Ave. E.,
   Don Mills, 416/444-2561;
   FAX 416/446-3308
The King Edward Hotel, 37 King St. E.,
   416/863-9700; FAX 416/367-5515
Park Plaza, 4 Avenue Rd., 416/924-5471;
   FAX 416/924-4933
Royal York, 100 Front St. W.,
   416/368-2511; FAX 416/368-9040
Sheraton Centre Hotel & Towers, 123
   Queen St. W., 416/361-1000;
   FAX 416/947-4854
✈Sheraton Gateway, at the Lester B.
   Pearson International Airport,
   905/672-7000; FAX 905/672-7100
The Sutton Place Hotel, 955 Bay St.,
   416/924-9221; FAX 416/924-1778
Toronto Colony Hotel, 89 Chestnut St.,
   416/977-0707; FAX 416/977-1136
Toronto Hilton, 145 Richmond St. W.,
   416/869-3456; FAX 416/869-3187

SELECTED RESTAURANTS:
The Acadian Room, in the Royal York
   Hotel, 416/368-2511
Chopstix and Rice, 1 Adelaide St. E.,
   416/363-7423
Fisherman's Wharf, 145 Adelaide St. W.,
   416/364-1346
Hy's Steakhouse, 73 Richmond St. W.,
   416/364-1792
Lighthouse, in the Westin Harbour Castle
   Hotel, 1 Harbour Sq., 416/869-1600
The Old Mill, 21 Old Mill Rd.,
   416/236-2641
Old Spaghetti Factory, 54 The Esplanade,
   416/864-9761
Splendido, 88 Harbord St., 416/929-7788

SELECTED ATTRACTIONS:
Art Gallery of Ontario, 317 Dundas St. W.,
   416/977-0414
Black Creek Pioneer Village, 1000 Murray
   Ross Pkwy., Downsview, 416/736-1733
Casa Loma, 1 Austin Terrace,
   416/923-1171
CN Tower, 301 Front St. W., 416/360-8500
Harbourfront Centre, 235 Queen's Quay
   W., 416/973-3000
Metro Toronto Zoo, 361A Old Finch Ave.,
   Scarborough, 416/392-5900
National Hockey League Hall of Fame,
   10 Front St. W. (Yonge & Front sts.),
   416/360-7765
Ontario Place, 955 Lakeshore Blvd. W.,
   416/314-9900
Ontario Science Centre, 770 Don Mills
   Rd., 416/429-4100
Royal Ontario Museum, 100 Queen's Park
   Rd., 416/586-5549
SkyDome, 1 Blue Jays Way, 416/341-3663

INFORMATION SOURCES:
Metropolitan Toronto Convention &
Visitors Association
   Queen's Quay Terminal at Harbourfront
   Centre
   Box 126
   207 Queens Quay W., Suite 590
   Toronto, Ontario M5J 1A7
   416/203-2600; 800/363-1990

Canadian Consulate General
   1251 Avenue of the Americas
   New York, New York 10020-1175
   212/596-1600

Tucson, Arizona

City map: lower right
Population: (*608,200) 405,390 (1990C)
Altitude: 2,386 feet
Average Temp.: Jan., 50°F.; July, 86°F.
Telephone Area Code: 520
Time: 676-1676 **Weather:** 520/294-2522
Time Zone: Mountain Standard

AIRPORT TRANSPORTATION:

Ten miles to downtown Tucson.
Taxicab, limousine, van and bus service.

SELECTED HOTELS:

Arizona Inn, 2200 E. Elm St.,
   520/325-1541; FAX 520/881-5830
✦Best Western Inn at the Airport, 7060 S.
   Tucson Blvd., 520/746-0271;
   FAX 520/889-7391
Best Western Tucson InnSuites Hotel,
   6201 N. Oracle Rd., 520/297-8111;
   FAX 520/297-2935
Country Suites by Carlson, 7411 N. Oracle
   Rd., 520/575-9255; FAX 520/575-8671
Doubletree Hotel, 445 S. Alvernon Way,
   520/881-4200; FAX 520/323-5225
Embassy Suites Hotel, 5335 E. Broadway,
   520/745-2700; FAX 520/790-9232
✦Embassy Suites Hotel & Conference
   Center, 7051 S. Tucson Blvd.,
   520/573-0700; FAX 520/741-9645
Holiday Inn City Center, 181 W.
   Broadway, 520/624-8711;
   FAX 520/623-8121
Holiday Inn—Palo Verde, 4550 S. Palo
   Verde Blvd., 520/746-1161;
   FAX 520/741-1170
InnSuites, 102 N. Alvernon Way,
   520/795-0330; FAX 520/326-2111
Loews Ventana Canyon Resort, 7000 N.
   Resort Dr., 520/299-2020;
   FAX 520/299-6832
Pueblo Inn, 350 S. Freeway,
   520/622-6611; FAX 520/622-8143
Quality Hotel & Suites, 475 N. Granada,
   520/622-3000; FAX 520/623-8922
Quality Inn University, 1601 N. Oracle
   Rd., 520/623-6666; FAX 520/884-7422
Radisson Suite Hotel, 9555 E. Speedway
   Blvd., 520/721-7100; FAX 520/721-1991
Viscount Suite Hotel, 4855 E. Broadway
   Blvd., 520/745-6500; FAX 520/790-5114
Wayward Winds Lodge, 707 W. Miracle
   Mile, 520/791-7526; FAX 520/791-9502

SELECTED RESTAURANTS:

Charles, 6400 E. El Dorado Circle,
   520/296-7173
Daniel's, in the St. Philip's Plaza, 4340 N.
   Campbell Ave., 520/742-3200
Encore Med, 2959 N. Swan, 520/881-6611
Gold Room, at the Westward Look Resort,
   245 E. Ina Rd., 520/297-1151
Janos, 150 N. Main, 520/884-9426
Le Rendez-Vous, 3844 E. Fort Lowell,
   520/323-7373
Saguaro Corners, 3750 S. Old Spanish
   Trail, 520/886-5424
Scordato's Restaurant, 4405 W. Speedway,
   520/792-3055

The Tack Room, 2800 N. Sabino Canyon
   Rd., 520/722-2800

SELECTED ATTRACTIONS:

Arizona-Sonora Desert Museum, 2021 N.
   Kinney Rd., 520/883-1380
Colossal Cave, Old Spanish Trail, 17 miles
   southeast of Tucson, 520/647-7275
Grace H. Flandrau Planetarium and
   Science Center, at the University of
   Arizona, Cherry Ave. & University
   Blvd., 520/621-4515

International Wildlife Museum, 4800 W.
   Gates Pass Rd., 520/617-1439
Old Tucson Studios (famous movie loca-
   tion and "Old West" town), 201 S. Kin-
   ney Rd., 520/883-0100
Pima Air & Space Museum, 6000 E.
   Valencia Rd., 520/574-9658
Sabino Canyon Tours, 520/749-2861
Tucson Botanical Gardens, 2150 N.
   Alvernon Way, 520/326-9255

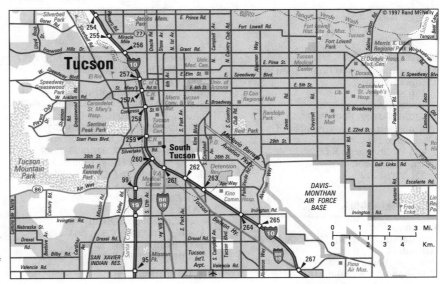

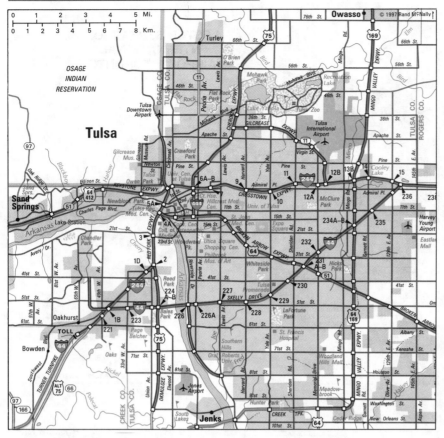

Rosie's Rib Joint, 8125 E. 49th St.,
918/663-2610

SELECTED ATTRACTIONS:
Allen Ranch, 196th & S. Memorial,
918/366-3010
Bell's Amusement Park, 3901 E. 21st,
918/744-1991
Creek Nation Bingo, 81st St. & Riverside,
918/299-0100
Discoveryland, W. 41st St., 5 mi. west of
OK Hwy. 97, 918/245-6552
Gilcrease Museum, 1400 Gilcrease Rd.,
918/596-2700
Oral Roberts University campus, 7777 S.
Lewis, 918/495-6807
Perryman Wrangler Ranch, 11524 S.
Elwood, 918/299-2997
Philbrook Museum of Art, 2727 S.
Rockford Rd., 918/749-7941
Tulsa Rose Garden/Woodward Park, 21st
& Peoria, 918/746-5155
Tulsa Zoo & Living Museum, in Mohawk
Park, 5701 E. 36th St. N., 918/669-6200

INFORMATION SOURCE:
Convention & Visitors Bureau,
Metropolitan Tulsa Chamber of Commerce
616 S. Boston Ave., Suite 100
Tulsa, Oklahoma 74119-1298
918/585-1201

Vancouver, British Columbia, Canada

City map: page 109
Population: (*1,602,502) 471,844 (1991C)
Altitude: Sea level to 40 ft.
Average Temp.: Jan., 36.5°F.; July, 72°F.
Telephone Area Code: 604
Time: (none) **Weather:** 604/664-9010
Time Zone: Pacific

AIRPORT TRANSPORTATION:

See map on page 109.
Eleven miles to downtown Vancouver.
Taxicab and bus service.

SELECTED HOTELS:

The Coast Plaza at Stanley Park, 1733
Comox St., 604/688-7711;
FAX 604/688-5934
✈Delta Vancouver Airport Hotel &
Marina, 3500 Cessna Dr., Richmond,
604/278-1241; FAX 604/276-1975
Hotel Georgia, 801 W. Georgia St.,
604/682-5566; FAX 604/682-8192
Hotel Vancouver, 900 W. Georgia St.,
604/684-3131; FAX 604/662-1929
Hyatt Regency, 655 Burrard St.,
604/683-1234; FAX 604/689-3707
Pan Pacific Hotel, 999 Canada Pl.,
604/662-8111; FAX 604/685-8690
Wall Centre Garden Hotel, 1088 Burrard
St., 604/331-1000; FAX: 604/893-7200
Waterfront Centre Hotel, 900 Canada
Place Way, 604/691-1991;
FAX 604/691-1999
Westin Bayshore, 1601 W. Georgia St.,
604/682-3377; FAX 604/687-3102

SELECTED RESTAURANTS:

The Cannery, 2205 Commissioner St.,
604/254-9606

INFORMATION SOURCES:
Metropolitan Tucson Convention and
Visitors Bureau
130 S. Scott
Tucson, Arizona 85701
520/624-1817; 800/638-8350
Tucson Metropolitan Chamber of
Commerce
465 W. St. Mary's Rd.
Tucson, Arizona 85702
520/792-1212

Tulsa, Oklahoma

City map: above
Population: (*615,600) 367,302 (1990C)
Altitude: 711 feet
Average Temp.: Jan., 39°F.; July, 83°F.
Telephone Area Code: 918
Time: 918/477-1000 **Weather:**
918/743-3311
Time Zone: Central

AIRPORT TRANSPORTATION:

Eight miles to downtown Tulsa.
Taxicab and limousine service.

SELECTED HOTELS:

Adam's Mark Tulsa, 100 E. 2nd St.,
918/582-9000; FAX 918/560-2261
Best Western Trade Winds Central Inn,
3141 E. Skelly Dr., 918/749-5561;
FAX 918/520/749-6312

Best Western Trade Winds East Inn, 3337
E. Skelly Dr., 918/743-7931;
FAX 918/743-4308
Doubletree Hotel Downtown, 616 W. 7th
St., 918/587-8000; FAX 520/587-1642
Econo Lodge, 11620 E. Skelly Dr.,
918/437-9200; FAX 918/520/437-2935
Holiday Inn Central, 8181 E. Skelly Dr.,
918/663-4541; FAX 918/665-7109
Marriott Southern Hills, 1902 E. 71st St.
S., 918/493-7000; FAX 918/481-7147
✈Radisson Inn Tulsa Airport, 2201 N.
77th East Ave., 918/835-9911;
FAX 918/838-2452
Ramada Inn, 5000 E. Skelly Dr.,
918/622-7000; FAX 918/664-9353
Tulsa Sheraton, 10918 E. 41st,
918/627-5000; FAX 918/627-4003

SELECTED RESTAURANTS:

Bravo! Ristorante, in the Adam's Mark
Tulsa Hotel, 918/560-2254
Charlie Mitchells, 81st St. & Lewis,
918/299-2100
Fountains Restaurant, 6540 S. Lewis Ave.,
918/749-9915
Grady's American Grill, 7007 S. Memorial
Dr., 918/254-7733
Interurban Restaurant, 717 S. Houston,
918/585-3134
The Olive Garden, 7019 S. Memorial Dr.,
918/254-0082
The Polo Grill, 2038 Utica Sq.,
918/744-4280

Captain's Palace, 309 Belleville St.,
604/388-9191
Cavalier Grill, in the Hotel Georgia,
604/682-5566
Hy's Encore, 637 Hornby St.,
604/683-7671
Monk McQueen's Fresh Seafood & Oyster
Bar, 601 Stamps Landing, 604/877-1351
Mulvaney's Restaurant, 1535 Johnston St.,
on Granville Island, 604/685-6571
1066 Restaurant, 1066 W. Hastings St.,
604/689-1066
Umberto al Porto, 321 Water St.,
604/683-8376

SELECTED ATTRACTIONS:

Chinatown (includes the Dr. Sun Yat-Sen
Classical Chinese Garden), bounded by
Hastings, Georgia, Carrall & Princess sts.
Gastown (1880s district; includes the
Gastown Steam Clock), bounded by
Water, Seymour, Cordova, & Columbia
sts.
Granville Island, underneath the south
end of Granville St. bridge,
604/666-5784
Grouse Mountain (skiing, all-year
recreation), 6400 Nancy Greene Way,
North Vancouver, 604/984-0661
Museum of Anthropology, 6393 NW
Marine Dr., University of British
Columbia, 604/822-3825
Pacific Space Centre/H. R. MacMillan
Planetarium, 1100 Chestnut St.,
604/738-7827
Science World, Quebec St. &
Terminal Ave., 604/268-6363
Vancouver Art Gallery, 750 Hornby St.,
604/682-5621
Vancouver Maritime Museum/St. Roch
National Historic Site, 1905 Ogden
Ave., 604/257-8300
Vancouver Public Aquarium, located in
Stanley Park (which includes numerous
other major attractions), 604/682-1118

INFORMATION SOURCES:

Greater Vancouver Convention & Visitors
Bureau
Suite 210, Waterfront Centre
200 Burrard St.
Vancouver, British Columbia V6C 3L6
604/682-2222
Vancouver Tourist Info Centre
Plaza Level, Waterfront Centre
200 Burrard St.
Vancouver, British Columbia V6C 3L6
604/683-2000
Canadian Consulate General
1251 Avenue of the Americas
New York, New York 10020-1175
212/596-1600

Washington, D.C.

City map: page 110
Population: (*3,808,700) 606,900 (1990C)
Altitude: 1 to 410 feet
Average Temp.: Jan., 36°F.; July, 79°F.
Telephone Area Code: 202
Time: 202/844-2525 **Weather:**
202/936-1212
Time Zone: Eastern

AIRPORT TRANSPORTATION:

See map on page 111.

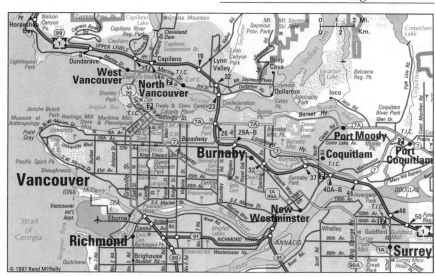

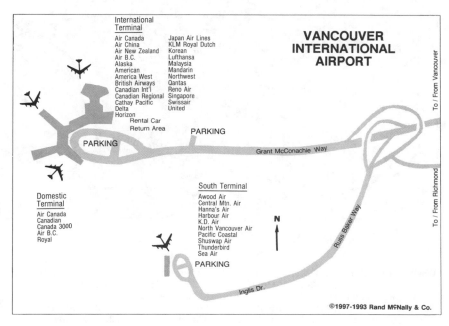

Three miles from Washington National
Airport to downtown Washington; 26
miles from Dulles International Airport
to downtown Washington; 37 miles
from Baltimore-Washington
International Airport to downtown
Washington.
Taxicab, bus, and rapid service between
National Airport and downtown
Washington; taxicab and bus service
to Dulles International Airport;
taxicab, bus, and train service to
Baltimore-Washington International
Airport.

SELECTED HOTELS:

The Capital Hilton, 1001 16th St. at K St.
NW, 202/393-1000; FAX 202/639-5784
Four Seasons Hotel, 2800 Pennsylvania
Ave. NW, 202/342-0444;
FAX 202/944-2076

Georgetown Inn, 1310 Wisconsin Ave.
NW, 202/333-8900; FAX 202/625-1744
Grand Hyatt, 1000 H St. NW,
202/582-1234; FAX 202/637-4781
The Hay-Adams Hotel, 800 16th St. NW,
202/638-6600; FAX 202/638-2716
Loews L'Enfant Plaza Hotel, 480 L'Enfant
Plaza SW, 202/484-1000;
FAX 202/646-4456
Madison Hotel, 1177 15th St. NW,
202/862-1600; FAX 202/785-1255
One Washington Circle Hotel, 1
Washington Circle NW, 202/872-1680;
FAX 202/887-4989
The Ritz-Carlton, 2100 Massachusetts
Ave. NW, 202/293-2100;
FAX 202/293-0641
The Sheraton-Carlton Hotel, 923 16th St.
NW, at K St., 202/638-2626;
FAX 202/638-4231

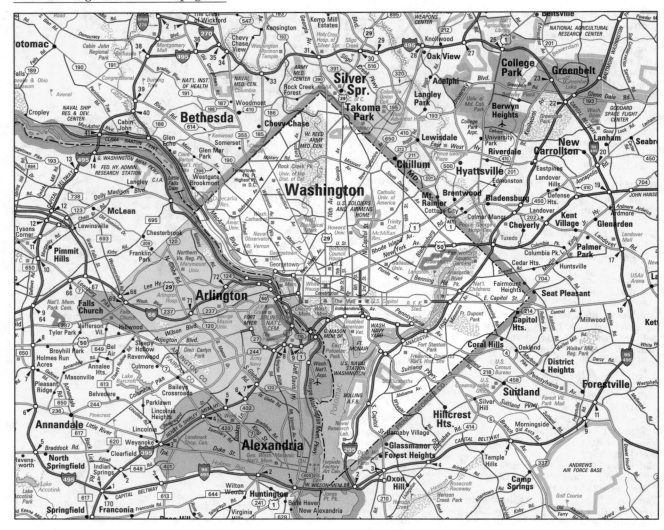

Washington Hilton and Towers, 1919
    Connecticut Ave. NW, 202/483-3000;
    FAX 202/232-0438
The Watergate Hotel, 2650 Virginia Ave.
    NW, 202/965-2300; FAX 202/337-7915

SELECTED RESTAURANTS:

Cantina Romana Ristorante, 3251 Prospect
    St. NW, 202/337-5130
Fran O'Brien's Steak House, in the Capitol
    Hilton Hotel, 202/393-1000
Jockey Club Restaurant, in The
    Ritz-Carlton Hotel, 202/293-2100
Le Lion D'or, 1150 Connecticut Ave. NW,
    18th St. entrance, 202/296-7972
Maison Blanche Restaurant, 1725 F St.
    NW, 202/842-0070
Montpelier, in the Madison Hotel,
    202/862-1600
Seasons, in the Four Seasons Hotel,
    202/342-0444
1789 Restaurant, 1226 36th St. NW,
    202/965-1789

SELECTED ATTRACTIONS:

The Jefferson Memorial, Tidal Basin Dr.
    (South Bank), East Potomac Park,
    202/426-6841

The Korean War Veterans' Memorial, 23rd
    St. SW & Independence Ave.,
    202/426-6841
The Lincoln Memorial, 23rd St. NW &
    Constitution Ave., 202/426-6841
National Air & Space Museum, 7th St. &
    Indepedence Ave. SW, 202/357-2700
National Gallery of Art, 6th St. &
    Constitution Ave. NW, 202/737-4215
National Museum of American History,
    14th St. & Constitution Ave. NW,
    202/357-2700
National Museum of Natural History, 10th
    St. & Constitution Ave. NW,
    202/357-2700
United States Capitol, National Mall (East
    End), 202/225-6827
Vietnam Veterans' Memorial, Constitution
    Ave., Henry Bacon Dr. & 22nd St. NW,
    202/426-6841
The Washington Monument, National
    Mall at 15th St. NW & Constitution
    Ave., 202/426-6841
The White House, 1600 Pennsylvania Ave.
    NW, 202/456-7041

INFORMATION SOURCE:

Washington, D.C. Convention and Visitors
Association
    1212 New York Ave. NW, Suite 600
    Washington, D.C. 20005-3992
    202/789-7000

Winnipeg, Manitoba, Canada

City map: page 111
Population: (*652,354) 616,790 (1991C)
Altitude: 915 feet
Average Temp.: Jan., 3°F.; July, 67°F.
Telephone Area Code: 204
Time: 204/783-2119 **Weather:**
    204/983-2050
Time Zone: Central

AIRPORT TRANSPORTATION:

Eight miles to downtown Winnipeg.
Taxicab, bus, airport limousine and hotel
    shuttle service.

SELECTED HOTELS:

✈Best Western International Inn,
    1808 Wellington Ave., 204/786-4801;
    FAX 204/786-1329

Charter House Hotel, 330 York Ave.,
204/942-0101; FAX 204/956-0665
Crowne Plaza, 350 St. Mary Ave.,
204/942-0551; FAX 204/943-8702
The Delta Winnipeg, 288 Portage Ave.,
204/956-0410; FAX 204/947-1129
Holiday Inn South, 1330 Pembina Hwy.,
204/452-4747; FAX 204/284-2751
Hotel Fort Garry, 222 Broadway,
204/942-8251; FAX 204/956-2351
Marlborough Ramada, 331 Smith St.,
204/942-6411; FAX 204/942-2017
Place Louis Riel All-Suite Hotel, 190
Smith St., 204/947-6961;
FAX 204/947-3029
✈Radisson Suite Hotel, 1800 Wellington
Ave., 204/783-1700; FAX 204/786-6588
Sheraton Winnipeg, 161 Donald St.,
204/942-5300; FAX 204/943-7975
Travelodge Downtown, 360 Colony St.,
204/786-7011; FAX 204/772-1443
The Westin Hotel, 2 Lombard Pl.,
204/957-1350; FAX 204/956-1791

SELECTED RESTAURANTS:

Alycia's, 559 Cathedral Ave.,
204/582-8789
Café Jardin, 340 Provencher Blvd., in the
Cultural Center, 204/233-9515
Fork & Cork Bistro, 218 Sherbrook,
204/783-5754
Hy's Steak Loft, 216 Kennedy St.,
204/942-1000
The Olive Garden, 1544 Portage Ave.,
204/774-9725
The Round Table, 800 Pembina Hwy.,
204/453-3631
La Vieille Gare, 630 Des Meurons,
204/237-5015

SELECTED ATTRACTIONS:

Assiniboine Park & Zoo, Corydon Ave. &
Shaftsbury Rd., 204/986-6921
The Forks Market, downtown Winnipeg,
behind the Via Rail Station,
204/942-6302; The Forks Info. Line
204/942-6309
IMAX Theatre, 3rd Floor, Portage Place,
393 Portage Ave., 204/956-4629
Lower Fort Garry National Historic Site,
20 miles north of Winnipeg on MB
Hwy. 9, 204/785-6050
Manitoba Children's Museum, in the
Kinsmen Building, 45 Forks Market Rd.,
204/956-KIDS or 204/956-1888
Manitoba Museum of Man & Nature (mu-
seum, science center, planetarium), 190
Rupert Ave., 204/956-2830
Paddlewheel/River Rouge Tours, Water
Ave. at Gilroy St., 204/947-6843
Royal Canadian Mint (tours May 1–Aug.
31), 520 Lagimodiere Blvd.,
204/257-3359
Winnipeg Art Gallery, 300 Memorial
Blvd., 204/786-6641

INFORMATION SOURCES:

Tourism Winnipeg
320-25 Forks Market Rd.
Winnipeg, Manitoba, Canada R3C 4S8
204/943-1970; 800/665-0204
Canadian Consulate General
1251 Avenue of the Americas
New York, New York 10020-1175
212/596-1600

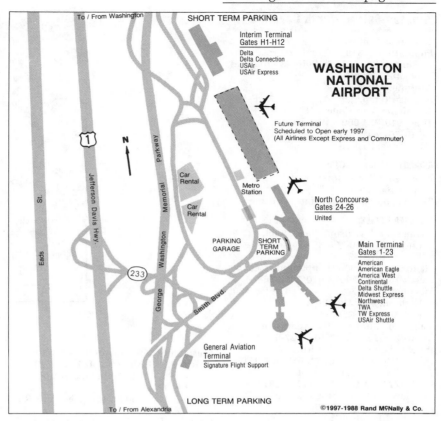

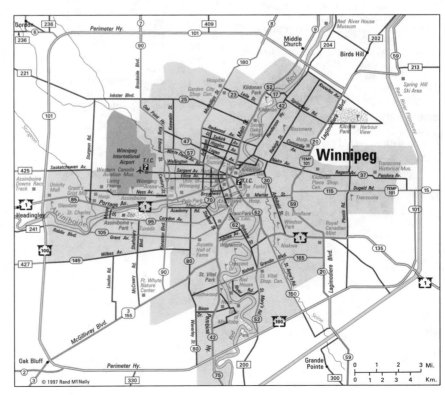

Winston-Salem, North Carolina

City map: right
Population: (*319,500 Greensboro-
Winston Salem-High Point Metro Area)
143,485 (1990C)
Altitude: 912 feet
Average Temp.: Jan., 41°F.; July, 78°F.
Telephone Area Code: 910
Time: 910/773-0000 **Weather:**
910/761-8411
Time Zone: Eastern

AIRPORT TRANSPORTATION:

Nineteen miles to downtown
Winston-Salem.
Taxicab, bus and limousine service.

SELECTED HOTELS:

Adam's Mark Winston Plaza Hotel, 425 N.
Cherry St., 910/725-3500;
FAX 910/721-2230
Hampton Inn, 1990 Hampton Inn Ct.,
910/760-1660; FAX 910/768-9168
Hawthorne Inn & Conference Center, 420
High St., 910/777-3000;
FAX 910/777-3282
Radisson Marque, 460 N. Cherry St.,
910/725-1234; FAX 910/722-9182
✈Ramada Inn North—Airport, 531 Akron
Dr., 910/767-8240; FAX 910/661-9513
Salem Inn, 127 S. Cherry St.,
910/725-8561; FAX 910/725-2318
Tanglewood Resort, 4060 Clemmons Rd.,
Clemmons, 910/766-0591;
FAX 910/766-1571

SELECTED RESTAURANTS:

The Dirtwater Fox, in the Radisson
Marque Hotel, 910/725-1234
Old Salem Tavern, 736 S. Main St.,
910/748-8585
Ryan's, 719 Coliseum Dr., 910/724-6132
The Vineyards, 120 Reynolda Village,
910/748-0269
Winston Bar & Grill, in the Adam's Mark
Winston Plaza Hotel, 910/725-3500

SELECTED ATTRACTIONS:

Historic Bethabara Park, 2147 Bethabara
Rd., 910/924-8191

Museum of Early Southern Decorative
Arts, 924 S. Main St., 910/721-7360
Old Salem, 600 S. Main St. & Academy,
910/721-7300
Piedmont Craftsmen, 1204 Reynolda Rd.,
910/725-1516
Reynolda House Museum of American
Art, 2250 Reynolda Rd., 910/725-5325
R.J. Reynolds Tobacco Company,
Whitaker Park/Reynolds Blvd.,
910/741-5718
SciWorks, 400 W. Hanes Mill Rd.,
910/767-6730
Southeastern Center for Contemporary
Art, 750 Marguerite Dr., 910/725-1904
Tanglewood Park, intersection Hwy. 158 &
Louisville Clemmons Rd., West
Clemmons, 910/766-0591

INFORMATION SOURCES:

Winston-Salem Convention and Visitors
Bureau
601 W. 4th St.
P.O. Box 1408
Winston-Salem, North Carolina 27102
910/777-3787; 800/331-7018
Winston-Salem Visitor Center
601 N. Cherry St., Suite 100
Winston-Salem, North Carolina 27101
910/777-3796; 800/331-7018
Greater Winston-Salem Chamber of
Commerce
601 W. 4th
P.O. Box 1408
Winston-Salem, North Carolina 27102
910/777-3787

© 1997 Rand McNally

Maps: United States, Canada, and Mexico

Introduction

One of the most important parts of any driving trip is knowing the best way to get to your destination. Using the detailed, accurate maps found in this atlas, you can easily plan your trip to avoid the all-too-common frustrations of wrong turns and misjudged mileage.

The maps in this section include a United States map; maps of the 50 states; a Canada map; and maps of Alberta, Atlantic provinces, British Columbia, Manitoba, Ontario, Québec, and Saskatchewan, and Mexico.

Among the many features to be found on the maps, the following are of special use in trip planning:

Detailed Transportation Routes. The atlas differentiates between toll roads, freeways, routes under construction, principal highways and various secondary roads.

Place Indexes. An index to cities and towns is conveniently located with each state and province map, as well as the map of Mexico. Capitals are

noted at the head of each index; land area and total population are also provided.

The United States map includes indexes to National Parks and National Monuments.

Distance Guides. Mileage can be computed by using either the map scale included with each map, or by referring to the accumulated mileage numbers that appear between the red pointers located along major highways.

Trip Planning

A key element to a successful trip is determining the exact location of your destination and the most direct way to get there.

Locating the Destination. To locate your destination, look in the alphabetical listing of cities and towns accompanying the appropriate map. Each town or city has a map reference key, composed of a letter and a number. To find a town on the map with a reference

key of B-5, for example, look down the side of the map for the letter B, and draw an imaginary line across the map until it intersects with an imaginary line drawn up or down from the number 5. Your destination will be within an inch-and-a-quarter square surrounding this point.

Marking the Route. Once you have located your destination, determine the most direct route by considering both distance and type of road. A secondary road may seem to provide a shortcut, while in actuality it takes more time because of lower speed limits, unimproved surface conditions, etc.

If time is a consideration, toll roads and freeways most often provide the quickest ride and should be used wherever possible.

To ease your map reading while driving, mark your chosen route with a see-through, felt-tip marker in a color that won't conflict with the lines, names, or symbols shown on the map.

Legend

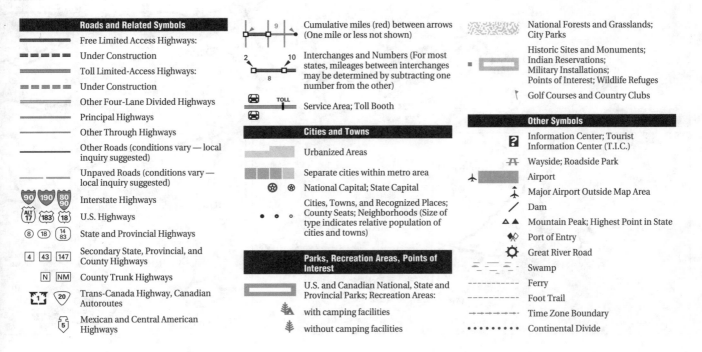

Roads and Related Symbols	
	Free Limited Access Highways:
	Under Construction
	Toll Limited-Access Highways:
	Under Construction
	Other Four-Lane Divided Highways
	Principal Highways
	Other Through Highways
	Other Roads (conditions vary — local inquiry suggested)
	Unpaved Roads (conditions vary — local inquiry suggested)
90 190 80/90	Interstate Highways
ALT 17 183 18	U.S. Highways
8 18 14/83	State and Provincial Highways
4 43 147	Secondary State, Provincial, and County Highways
N NM	County Trunk Highways
1 20	Trans-Canada Highway, Canadian Autoroutes
5	Mexican and Central American Highways

9	Cumulative miles (red) between arrows (One mile or less not shown)
2 10 8	Interchanges and Numbers (For most states, mileages between interchanges may be determined by subtracting one number from the other)
TOLL	Service Area; Toll Booth

Cities and Towns	
	Urbanized Areas
	Separate cities within metro area
⊛ ⊛	National Capital; State Capital
• • ○	Cities, Towns, and Recognized Places; County Seats; Neighborhoods (Size of type indicates relative population of cities and towns)

Parks, Recreation Areas, Points of Interest	
	U.S. and Canadian National, State and Provincial Parks; Recreation Areas:
🌲	with camping facilities
🌿	without camping facilities

	National Forests and Grasslands; City Parks
	Historic Sites and Monuments; Indian Reservations; Military Installations; Points of Interest; Wildlife Refuges
⌐	Golf Courses and Country Clubs

Other Symbols	
?	Information Center; Tourist Information Center (T.I.C.)
禾	Wayside; Roadside Park
✈	Airport
✈	Major Airport Outside Map Area
/	Dam
▲ ▲	Mountain Peak; Highest Point in State
✹	Port of Entry
✿	Great River Road
— —	Swamp
----------	Ferry
----------	Foot Trail
->->->->	Time Zone Boundary
••••••••	Continental Divide

National Parks

Nat'l Monuments and Memorials

97–1

Alabama

Population: 4,062,608
(1990 Census)
Land Area: 50,750 sq. mi.
Capital: Montgomery

Cities and Towns

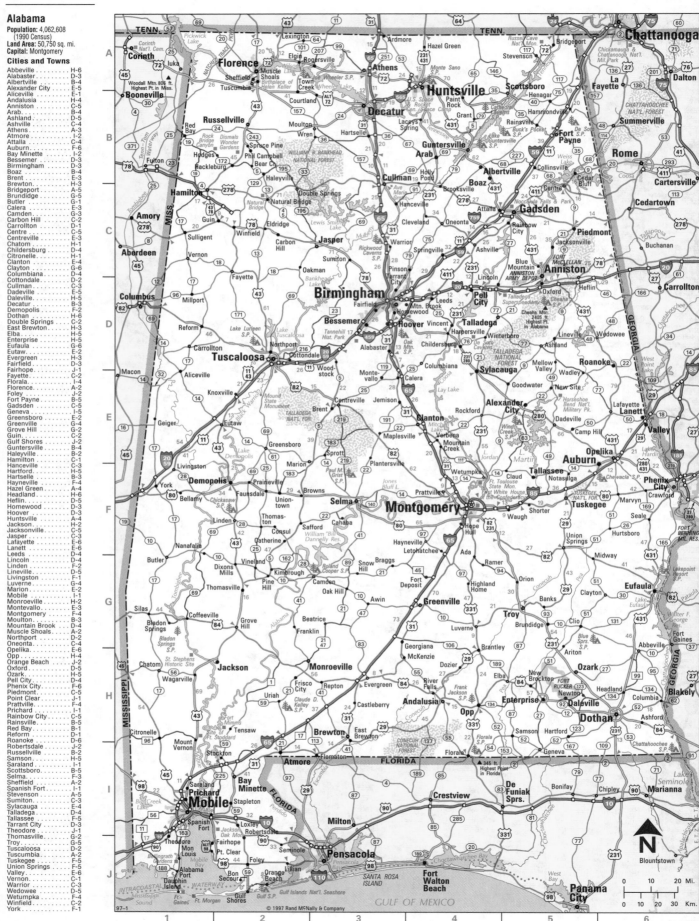

© 1997 Rand McNally & Company

97–1

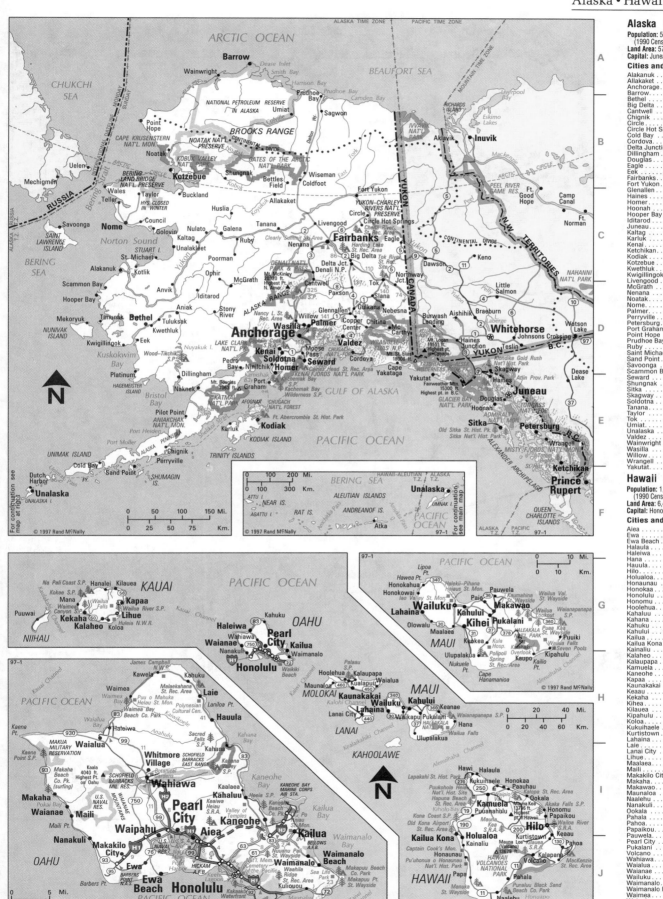

Alaska

Population: 551,947 (1990 Census)
Land Area: 570,374 sq. mi.
Capital: Juneau

Cities and Towns

Hawaii

Population: 1,115,274 (1990 Census)
Land Area: 6,423 sq. mi.
Capital: Honolulu

Cities and Towns

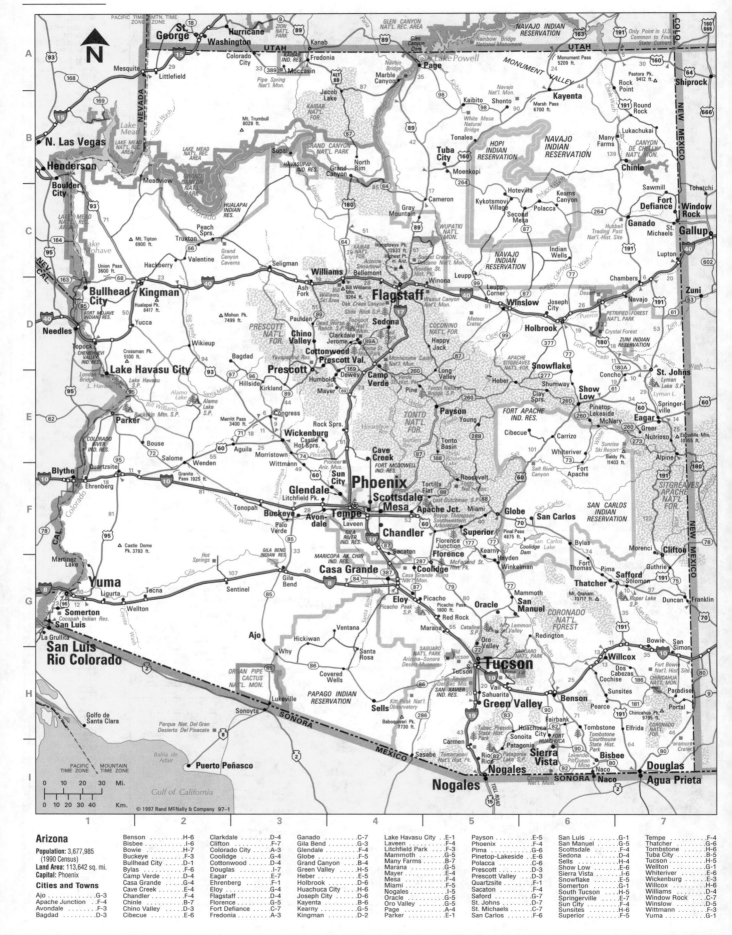

Arizona

Population: 3,677,985
(1990 Census)
Land Area: 113,642 sq. mi.
Capital: Phoenix

Cities and Towns

Ajo	G-3
Apache Junction	F-4
Avondale	F-3
Bagdad	D-3
Benson	H-6
Bisbee	I-6
Bowie	H-7
Buckeye	F-3
Bullhead City	D-1
Bylas	F-6
Camp Verde	D-4
Casa Grande	G-4
Cave Creek	E-4
Chandler	F-4
Chinle	B-7
Chino Valley	D-3
Cibecue	E-6
Clarkdale	D-4
Clifton	F-7
Colorado City	A-3
Coolidge	G-4
Cottonwood	D-4
Douglas	I-7
Eagar	E-7
Ehrenberg	F-1
Eloy	G-4
Flagstaff	D-4
Florence	G-5
Fort Defiance	C-7
Fredonia	A-3
Ganado	C-7
Gila Bend	G-3
Glendale	F-4
Globe	F-5
Grand Canyon	B-4
Green Valley	H-5
Heber	E-5
Holbrook	D-6
Huachuca City	H-6
Joseph City	D-6
Kayenta	B-6
Kearny	G-5
Kingman	D-2
Lake Havasu City	E-1
Laveen	F-4
Litchfield Park	F-3
Mammoth	G-5
Many Farms	B-7
Marana	G-5
Mayer	E-4
Mesa	F-4
Miami	F-5
Nogales	I-5
Oracle	G-5
Oro Valley	G-5
Page	A-4
Parker	E-1
Payson	E-5
Phoenix	F-4
Pima	G-6
Pinetop-Lakeside	E-6
Polacca	C-6
Prescott	D-3
Prescott Valley	D-3
Quartzsite	F-1
Sacaton	F-4
Saford	G-7
St. Johns	D-7
St. Michaels	C-7
San Carlos	F-6
San Luis	G-1
San Manuel	G-5
Scottsdale	F-4
Sedona	D-4
Sells	H-4
Show Low	E-6
Sierra Vista	I-6
Snowflake	E-5
Somerton	G-1
South Tucson	H-5
Springerville	E-7
Sun City	F-4
Sunsites	H-6
Superior	F-5
Tempe	F-4
Thatcher	G-6
Tombstone	H-6
Tuba City	B-5
Tucson	H-5
Wellton	G-1
Whiteriver	E-6
Wickenburg	E-3
Willcox	H-6
Williams	D-4
Window Rock	C-7
Winslow	D-5
Wittmann	F-3
Yuma	G-1

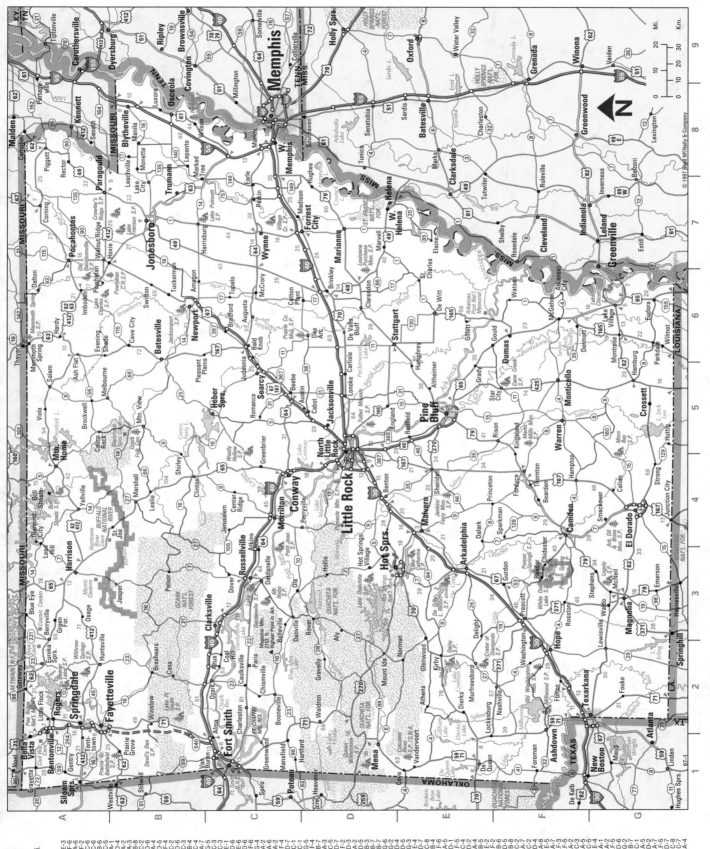

Arkansas

Population: 2,362,239
(1990 Census)
Land Area: 52,075 sq. mi.
Capital: Little Rock

Cities and Towns

Arkadelphia ... E-3
Arkansas City ... A-6
Ash Flat ... F-2
Ashdown ... C-6
Augusta ... C-6
Bald Knob ... B-6
Batesville ... D-5
Bella Vista ... A-2
Benton ... D-1
Bentonville ... A-2
Berryville ... A-2
Blytheville ... B-8
Booneville ... C-2
Brinkley ... D-4
Bull Shoals ... F-4
Cabot ... C-5
Camden ... F-4
Charleston ... C-2
Clarendon ... C-3
Clarksville ... B-4
Clinton ... B-4
Conway ... C-4
Corning ... F-3
Crossett ... G-3
Danville ... C-3
Dardanelle ... C-3
De Queen ... C-6
De Valls Bluff ... D-6
Des Arc ... D-6
De Witt ... D-6
Dumas ... F-6
El Dorado ... G-4
Eureka Springs ... A-2
Evening Shade ... A-6
Fayetteville ... A-2
Fordyce ... F-4
Forrest City ... D-7
Fort Smith ... C-1
Greenwood ... C-1
Hamburg ... G-4
Hampton ... F-4
Harrison ... A-3
Helena ... D-7
Hope ... E-2
Hot Springs ... D-3
Huntsville ... A-3
Jacksonville ... C-5
Jasper ... A-3
Jonesboro ... B-7
Lake City ... B-7
Lake Village ... G-6
Lewisville ... F-2
Little Rock ... D-4
Lonoke ... D-5
Magnolia ... G-3
Malvern ... E-4
Marianna ... D-7
Marshall ... B-4
McGehee ... F-6
Melbourne ... F-5
Mena ... D-2
Monticello ... F-5
Morrilton ... C-4
Mount Ida ... D-3
Mountain Home ... A-5
Mountain View ... B-5
Murfreesboro ... D-2
Nashville ... D-2
Newport ... C-6
North Little Rock ... D-4
Osceola ... B-8
Ozark ... C-2
Paragould ... A-7
Paris ... C-2
Perryville ... C-4
Piggott ... A-8
Pine Bluff ... E-5
Pocahontas ... A-6
Prescott ... E-2
Rison ... F-5
Rogers ... A-2
Russellville ... C-3
Salem ... A-5
Searcy ... C-5
Siloam Springs ... A-1
Springdale ... A-2
Star City ... F-5
Stuttgart ... D-6
Texarkana ... F-1
Trumann ... B-7
Van Buren ... C-1
Viola ... A-5
Waldron ... D-2
Walnut Ridge ... A-7
Warren ... F-5
West Helena ... D-7
West Memphis ... C-8
Wynne ... C-7
Yellville ... A-4

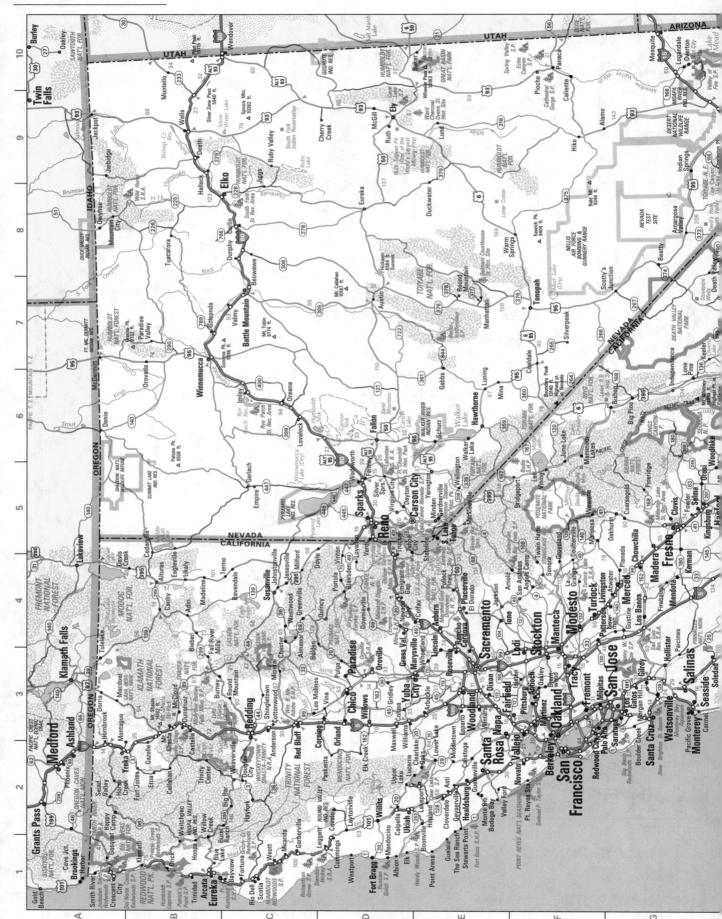

© 1997 Rand McNally & Company

97-1

PACIFIC OCEAN

California

Population: 29,839,250 (1990 Census)
Land Area: 155,973 sq. mi.
Capital: Sacramento

Cities and Towns

Adelanto	I-7	Delano	J-10
Alpine	K-8	Desert Hot Springs	E-2
Alturas	B-4	Dixon	K-9
Anderson	C-3	Downieville	G-3
Antioch	F-3	Earlimart	F-5
Apple Valley	I-7	El Centro	I-4
Arcata	B-1	Encinitas	B-3
Arroyo Grande	H-4	Escondido	B-1
Atascadero	H-5	Eureka	I-7
Atwater	F-4	Exeter	K-9
Auburn	E-4	Fairfield	E-2
Avalon	K-6	Fillmore	H-4
Avenal	H-5	Firebaugh	K-7
Arvin	I-6	Fort Bragg	D-3
Bakersfield	H-5	Fortuna	J-5
Barstow	I-7	Frazier Park	D-3
Beaumont	J-8	Fremont	I-4
Berkeley	F-3	Fresno	G-4
Bishop	G-6	Gilroy	L-7
Blythe	J-10	Glendale	E-2
Bodega Bay	K-8	Grass Valley	E-4
Boulder Creek	B-4	Greenfield	G-4
Brawley	C-3	Gridley	D-3
Brentwood	F-3	Grover Beach	D-3
Bridgeport	F-5	Guadalupe	J-7
Buellton	I-4	Gustine	G-4
Burney	B-3	Hanford	H-5
California City	I-7	Healdsburg	G-8
Calipatria	K-8		
Calistoga	E-3	Hemet	H-5
Cambria	H-4	Hesperia	I-8
Carlsbad	K-7	Hollister	G-3
Carmel	G-3	Holtville	D-4
Carpinteria	I-5	Huron	H-5
Chico	D-3	Imperial	K-9
Chowchilla	F-4	Independence	K-7
Chula Vista	L-7	Indio	J-8
Cloverdale	E-2	Ione	E-4
Clovis	G-4	Jackson	E-4
Coalinga	H-5	Joshua Tree	K-9
Colusa	D-3	Julian	K-8
Corcoran	H-5	Kerman	G-4
Corning	D-3	King City	G-4
Corona	J-7	Kingsburg	H-5
Crescent City	A-1	Lake Elsinore	J-7
Death Valley	G-6	Lake Isabella	H-6
		Lakeport	E-3
Los Gatos	J-8	Lancaster	I-6
Madera	J-7	Lemoore	H-5
Mammoth Lakes	K-9	Lincoln	E-4
Manteca	H-5	Livingston	F-4
Markleeville	G-6	Lodi	E-4
Marysville	E-4	Lompoc	I-4
Mendota	E-4	Long Beach	J-6
Merced	F-4	Los Angeles	I-6
Milpitas	K-8	Los Banos	G-4
Modesto	F-4		
Mojave	H-4	Orland	G-5
Montebello	I-6	Oroville	G-5
Monterey	G-3	Oxnard	I-5
Morgan Hill	J-7	Pacific Grove	F-4
Morro Bay	H-4	Palm Desert	E-5
Mount Shasta	B-3	Palm Springs	F-3
Napa	E-3	Palmdale	I-6
Needles	I-10	Palo Alto	F-3
Nevada City	E-4	Paradise	H-4
Newman	F-4	Paso Robles	B-3
Newport Beach	J-6	Patterson	F-4
Novato	E-3	Perris	I-6
Oakdale	F-4	Pittsburg	I-9
Oakland	F-3	Placerville	E-3
Oildale	H-5	Pollock Pines	I-3
Ontario	J-7	Pomona	H-4
		Porterville	H-4
Roseville	E-3	Quincy	E-3
Sacramento	D-3	Ramona	K-8
Salinas	J-5	Rancho Cordova	E-4
San Andreas	F-4	Red Bluff	C-3
San Bernardino	J-8	Redding	C-3
San Clemente	J-6	Redlands	J-7
San Diego	K-7	Redwood City	F-3
San Francisco	E-3	Ridgecrest	K-7
San Jacinto	J-8	Rio Dell	B-1
San Jose	G-3	Riverside	H-6
San Juan Capistrano	J-7	Rosamond	E-2
San Luis Obispo	H-4		
San Simeon	F-3	South Lake Tahoe	E-5
Santa Ana	J-7	Stockton	E-3
Santa Barbara	I-5	Susanville	C-4
Santa Clarita	I-6	Taft	I-6
Santa Cruz	F-3	Tehachapi	J-7
Santa Maria	I-4	Temecula	K-7
Santa Paula	I-5	Thousand Oaks	I-5
Santa Rosa	E-3	Tracy	F-3
Saratoga	F-3	Truckee	F-2
Seaside	C-3	Tulare	G-3
Selma	F-3	Turlock	K-7
Shafter	H-5	Ukiah	J-7
Simi Valley	H-7	Vallejo	I-4
Solvang	G-1	Vacaville	E-3
Sonora	J-6	Victorville	I-5
		Visalia	I-7
		Vista	J-6
		Wasco	H-5
		Watsonville	H-6
		Weaverville	I-4
		Willows	D-4
		Winters	E-3
		Woodlake	G-5
		Woodland	J-6
		Wrightwood	K-8
		Yreka	A-3
		Yuba City	H-9
		Yucca Valley	F-4

Nevada

Population: 1,206,152 (1990 Census)
Land Area: 109,806 sq. mi.
Capital: Carson City

Cities and Towns

Alamo	F-9	Fallon	D-6
Amargosa Valley	G-8	Fernley	D-5
Austin	D-7	Gabbs	E-7
Battle Mountain	C-8	Gardnerville	E-5
Beatty	F-7	Genoa	B-7
Beowawe	C-8	Golconda	B-7
Boulder City	G-10	Goldfield	E-6
Caliente	F-10	Halleck	E-6
Carlin	C-8	Hawthorne	G-10
Carson City	D-5	Henderson	F-9
Coaldale	F-7	Hiko	A-9
Dayton	D-5	Imlay	A-9
Deeth	B-9	Indian Springs	H-9
Denio	A-7	Jackpot	E-7
Duckwater	E-8	Jarbidge	F-10
Dunphy	C-8	Jiggs	C-8
Elko	C-9	Las Vegas	G-10
Ely	E-9	Laughlin	H-10
Empire	C-5	Logandale	F-10
Eureka	D-8	Lovelock	C-6
		Lund	D-9
Oreana	D-6	Lyon (Manhattan)	E-7
Orovada	D-5	McDermitt	A-7
Overton	F-10	McGill	E-9
Owyhee	B-8	Mesquite	F-10
Pahrump	B-7	Mina	E-6
Panaca	F-10	Minden	E-5
Pioche	E-6	Montello	B-9
Reno	E-5	Mountain City	A-9
Round Mountain	E-7	Nelson	H-9
Ruby Valley	C-9		
Schurz	D-5		
Scotty's Junction	E-7		
Searchlight	H-9		
Silver Springs	D-5		
Silverpeak	C-8		
Stateline	E-5		
Tonopah	E-7		
Tuscarora	G-7		
Valmy	E-7		
Virginia City	D-5		
Wadsworth	D-5		
Walker Lake	E-6		
Warm Springs	F-8		
Wellington	E-6		
Wells	B-9		
Winnemucca	B-7		
Yerington	E-5		

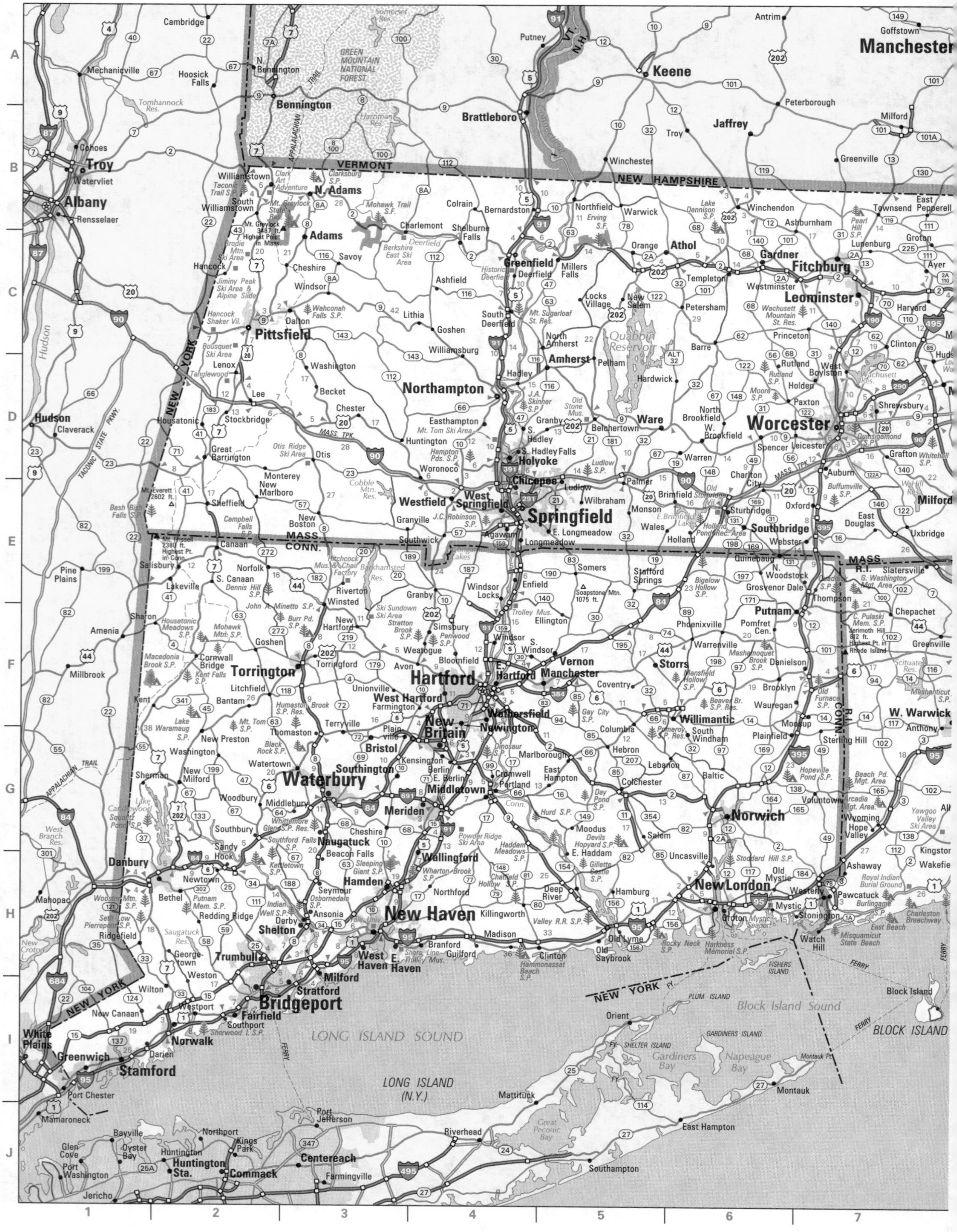

A
B
C
D
E
F
G
H
I
J
1
2
3
4
5
6
7
Manchester
Keene
Brattleboro
Bennington
N. Bennington
Troy
Albany
Cohoes
Watervliet
Rensselaer
Mechanicville
Hoosick Falls
Cambridge
Putney
Antrim
Goffstown
Peterborough
Milford
Jaffrey
Winchester
Greenville
GREEN MOUNTAIN NATIONAL FOREST
APPALACHIAN TRAIL
VERMONT
NEW HAMPSHIRE
Williamstown
N. Adams
Adams
Pittsfield
Dalton
Lenox
Lee
Stockbridge
Great Barrington
Sheffield
Housatonic
Hudson
Claverack
Colrain
Charlemont
Shelburne Falls
Bernardston
Northfield
Warwick
Winchendon
Ashburnham
Townsend
East Pepperell
Greenfield
Deerfield
Millers Falls
Orange
Athol
Gardner
Fitchburg
Leominster
Templeton
Westminster
Petersham
Locks Village
New Salem
Ashfield
Lithia
Goshen
Williamsburg
Northampton
South Deerfield
North Amherst
Amherst
Pelham
Quabbin Reservoir
Hadley
Barre
Hardwick
Princeton
Rutland
Holden
West Boylston
Clinton
Harvard
Ayer
Groton
Lunenburg
Worcester
Shrewsbury
Paxton
Spencer
Leicester
Grafton
Auburn
Milford
Ware
Belchertown
Granby
North Brookfield
W. Brookfield
Warren
Charlton City
Easthampton
Huntington
Holyoke
S. Hadley Falls
Chicopee
Ludlow
Wilbraham
Palmer
Brimfield
Sturbridge
Southbridge
Oxford
East Douglas
Uxbridge
Westfield
West Springfield
Springfield
E. Longmeadow
Longmeadow
Agawam
Granville
Southwick
Monson
Wales
Holland
Webster
Otis
Monterey
New Marlboro
New Boston
Woronoco
Chester
Becket
Washington
MASS. TPK.
TACONIC STATE PKWY.
NEW YORK
MASS.
CONN.
R.I.
Canaan
Salisbury
Lakeville
Sharon
Norfolk
S. Canaan
Winsted
Riverton
Granby
Enfield
Somers
Stafford Springs
Windsor Locks
Ellington
Thompson
Putnam
Pomfret Cen.
Quinebaug
N. Woodstock
Grosvenor Dale
Slatersville
Chepachet
Greenville
Goshen
New Hartford
Torrington
Torringford
Simsbury
Weatogue
Avon
Bloomfield
Windsor
S. Windsor
Vernon
Manchester
Hartford
E. Hartford
West Hartford
Farmington
Unionville
Litchfield
Bantam
Cornwall Bridge
Kent
Coventry
Storrs
Willimantic
Phoenixville
Warrenville
Danielson
Brooklyn
Wauregan
Moosup
Plainfield
Sterling Hill
W. Warwick
Anthony
Wethersfield
Newington
New Britain
Plainville
Bristol
Terryville
Thomaston
New Preston
Washington
Sherman
New Milford
Watertown
Waterbury
Southington
Kensington
Berlin
E. Berlin
Middletown
Cromwell
Portland
Marlborough
East Hampton
Hebron
Columbia
South Windham
Lebanon
Baltic
Colchester
Norwich
Voluntown
Wyoming
Hope Valley
Kingston
Wakefield
Woodbury
Middlebury
Meriden
Southbury
Cheshire
Naugatuck
Beacon Falls
Wallingford
Moodus
E. Haddam
Salem
Uncasville
New London
Groton
Mystic
Old Mystic
Westerly
Pawcatuck
Stonington
Watch Hill
Ashaway
Danbury
Newtown
Sandy Hook
Bethel
Redding Ridge
Ridgefield
Seymour
Hamden
Northford
Ansonia
Derby
Shelton
New Haven
Killingworth
Deep River
Hamburg
Old Lyme
Old Saybrook
Madison
Clinton
Guilford
Branford
West Haven
E. Haven
Milford
Stratford
Trumbull
Bridgeport
Fairfield
Southport
Westport
Weston
Wilton
George-town
New Canaan
Norwalk
Darien
Stamford
Greenwich
Port Chester
Mamaroneck
White Plains
Mahopac
Amenia
Millbrook
Pine Plains
LONG ISLAND SOUND
LONG ISLAND (N.Y.)
Block Island Sound
BLOCK ISLAND
Block Island
Orient
PLUM ISLAND
FISHERS ISLAND
GARDINERS ISLAND
SHELTER ISLAND
Gardiners Bay
Napeague Bay
Montauk Pt.
Montauk
Mattituck
Riverhead
East Hampton
Southampton
Great Peconic Bay
Port Jefferson
Northport
Kings Park
Bayville
Glen Cove
Oyster Bay
Huntington
Huntington Sta.
Commack
Centereach
Farmingville
Port Washington
Jericho
FERRY

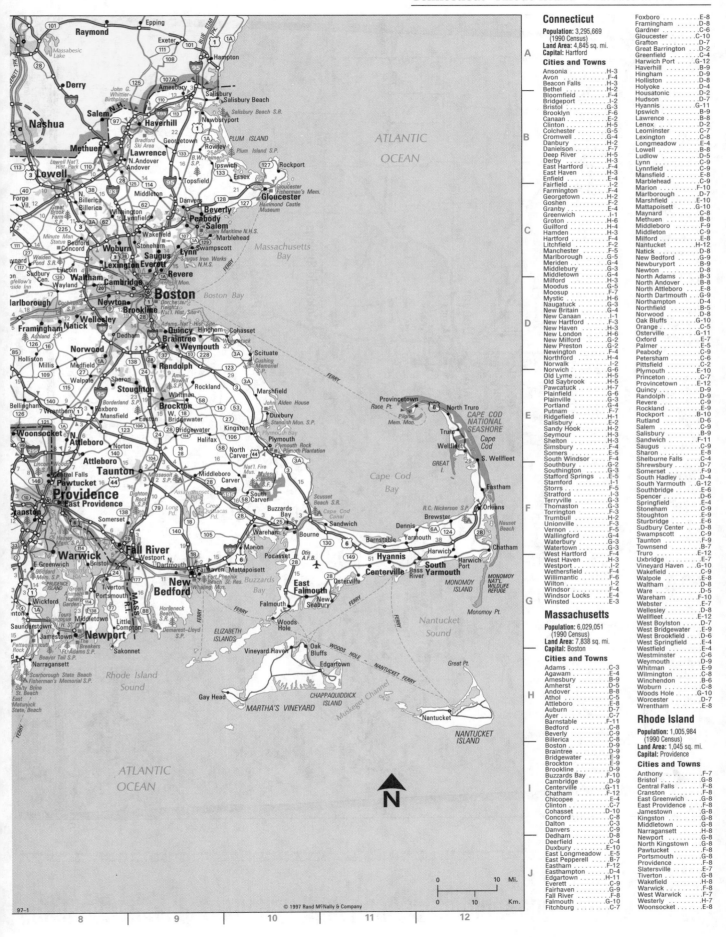

Connecticut

Population: 3,295,669 (1990 Census)
Land Area: 4,845 sq. mi.
Capital: Hartford

Cities and Towns

Ansonia H-3
Avon F-4
Beacon Falls H-3
Bethel H-2
Bloomfield F-4
Bridgeport I-2
Bristol G-3
Brooklyn F-6
Canaan E-2
Clinton H-5
Colchester G-5
Cromwell G-4
Danbury H-2
Danielson F-7
Deep River H-5
Derby H-3
East Hartford F-4
East Haven H-3
Enfield E-4
Fairfield I-2
Farmington F-4
Georgetown H-2
Goshen F-2
Granby E-4
Greenwich I-1
Groton H-6
Guilford H-4
Hamden H-3
Hartford F-4
Litchfield F-2
Manchester F-5
Marlborough G-5
Meriden G-4
Middlebury G-3
Middletown G-4
Milford H-3
Moodus G-5
Moosup F-7
Mystic H-6
Naugatuck G-3
New Britain G-4
New Canaan I-1
New Hartford F-3
New Haven H-3
New London H-6
New Milford G-2
New Preston G-2
Newington F-4
Northford H-4
Norwalk I-2
Norwich G-6
Old Lyme H-5
Old Saybrook H-5
Pawcatuck H-7
Plainfield G-6
Plainville G-4
Portland G-4
Putnam F-7
Ridgefield H-2
Salisbury E-2
Sandy Hook H-2
Seymour H-3
Shelton H-3
Simsbury F-4
Somers E-5
South Windsor F-4
Southbury G-2
Southington G-3
Stafford Springs E-5
Stamford I-1
Storrs F-5
Stratford I-3
Terryville G-3
Thomaston G-3
Torrington F-3
Trumbull H-2
Unionville F-4
Vernon F-5
Wallingford G-4
Waterbury G-3
Watertown G-3
West Hartford F-4
West Haven H-3
Westport I-2
Wethersfield F-4
Willimantic F-6
Wilton I-2
Windsor F-4
Windsor Locks F-4
Winsted E-3

Massachusetts

Population: 6,029,051 (1990 Census)
Land Area: 7,838 sq. mi.
Capital: Boston

Cities and Towns

Adams C-3
Agawam E-4
Amesbury B-9
Amherst D-5
Andover B-8
Athol C-5
Attleboro D-7
Auburn D-7
Ayer C-7
Barnstable F-11
Bedford C-8
Beverly C-9
Billerica C-8
Boston D-9
Braintree E-9
Bridgewater E-9
Brockton E-9
Brookline D-9
Buzzards Bay F-10
Cambridge D-9
Centerville G-11
Chatham G-12
Chicopee E-4
Clinton C-7
Cohasset D-10
Concord C-8
Dalton C-3
Danvers C-9
Dedham D-8
Deerfield C-4
Duxbury E-10
East Longmeadow . . .E-5
East Pepperell B-7
Eastham F-12
Easthampton D-4
Edgartown H-11
Everett C-9
Fairhaven G-9
Fall River F-8
Falmouth G-10
Fitchburg C-7
Foxboro E-8
Framingham D-8
Gardner C-6
Gloucester C-10
Grafton D-7
Great Barrington D-2
Greenfield C-4
Harwich Port G-12
Haverhill B-9
Hingham D-9
Holliston D-8
Holyoke D-4
Housatonic D-2
Hudson D-7
Hyannis G-11
Ipswich B-9
Lawrence B-8
Lenox D-2
Leominster C-7
Lexington C-8
Longmeadow E-4
Lowell B-8
Ludlow D-5
Lynn C-9
Lynnfield C-9
Mansfield E-8
Marblehead C-9
Marion F-10
Marlborough D-7
Marshfield E-10
Mattapoisett G-10
Maynard C-8
Methuen B-8
Middleboro F-9
Middleton C-9
Milford E-8
Nantucket H-12
Natick D-8
New Bedford G-9
Newburyport B-9
Newton D-8
North Adams B-3
North Andover B-8
North Attleboro E-8
North Dartmouth G-9
Northampton D-4
Northfield B-5
Norwood D-8
Oak Bluffs G-10
Orange C-5
Osterville G-11
Oxford E-7
Palmer E-5
Peabody C-9
Petersham C-6
Pittsfield C-2
Plymouth E-10
Princeton C-7
Provincetown E-12
Quincy D-9
Randolph D-9
Revere C-9
Rockland E-9
Rockport B-10
Rutland D-6
Salem C-9
Salisbury B-9
Sandwich F-11
Saugus C-9
Sharon E-8
Shelburne Falls C-4
Shrewsbury D-7
Somerset F-8
South Hadley D-4
South Yarmouth G-12
Southbridge E-6
Spencer D-6
Springfield E-4
Stoneham C-9
Stoughton E-9
Sturbridge E-6
Sudbury Center D-8
Swampscott C-9
Taunton F-9
Townsend B-7
Truro E-12
Uxbridge E-7
Vineyard Haven G-10
Wakefield C-9
Walpole E-8
Waltham D-8
Wareham F-10
Webster E-7
Wellesley D-8
Wellfleet E-12
West Boylston D-7
West Bridgewater E-9
West Brookfield D-6
West Springfield E-4
Westfield E-4
Westminster C-6
Weymouth D-9
Whitman E-9
Wilmington C-8
Winchendon B-6
Woburn C-8
Woods Hole G-10
Worcester D-7
Wrentham E-8

Rhode Island

Population: 1,005,984 (1990 Census)
Land Area: 1,045 sq. mi.
Capital: Providence

Cities and Towns

Anthony F-7
Bristol G-8
Central Falls F-8
Cranston F-8
East Greenwich G-8
East Providence F-8
Jamestown G-8
Kingston G-8
Middletown G-8
Narragansett H-8
Newport G-8
North Kingstown G-8
Pawtucket F-8
Portsmouth G-8
Providence F-8
Slatersville E-7
Tiverton G-8
Wakefield H-8
Warwick F-7
West Warwick F-7
Westerly H-7
Woonsocket E-8

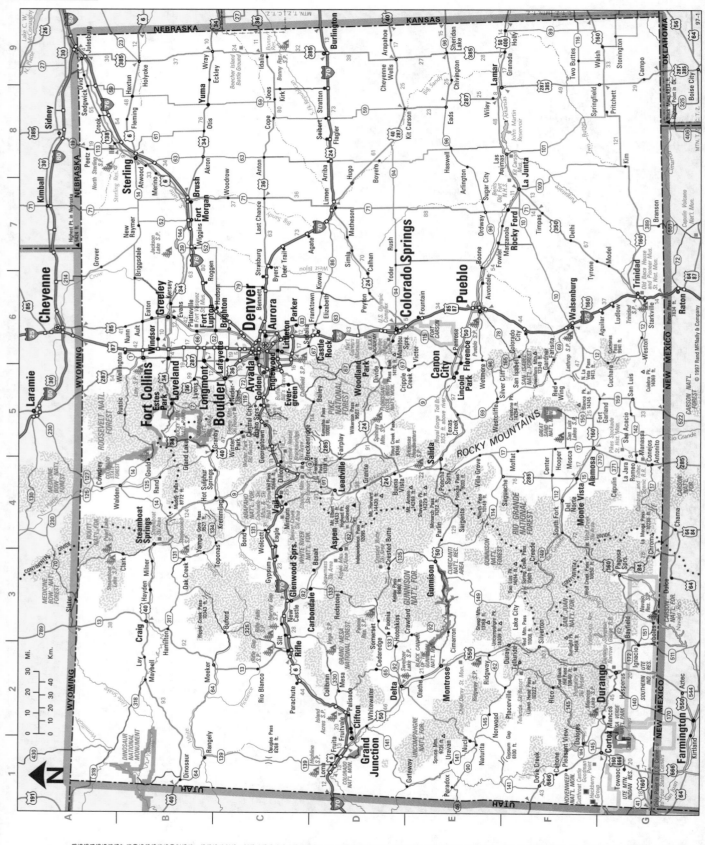

Colorado
Population: 3,307,912
(1990 Census)
Land Area: 103,730 sq. mi.
Capital: Denver

Cities and Towns

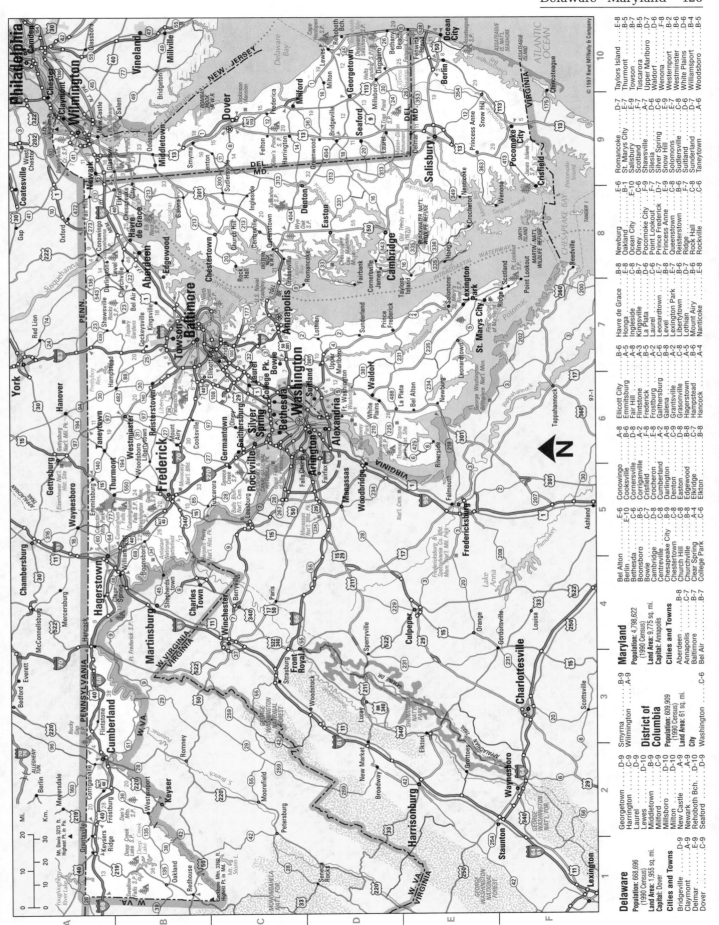

Florida

Population: 13,003,362
(1990 Census)
Land Area: 53,997 sq. mi.
Capital: Tallahassee

Cities and Towns

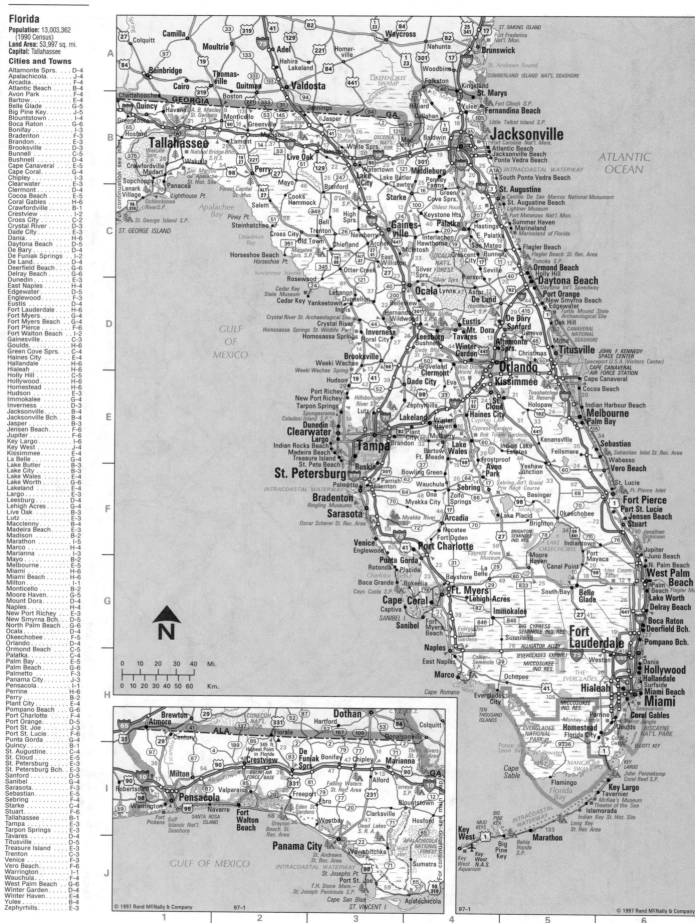

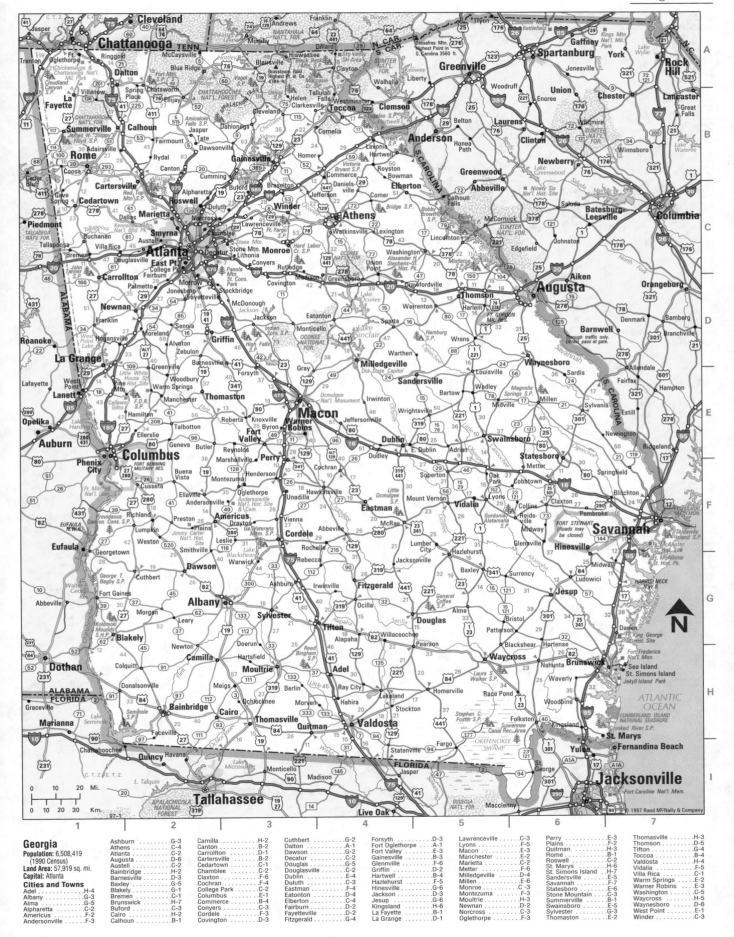

Idaho

Population: 1,011,986
(1990 Census)
Land Area: 82,751 sq. mi.
Capital: Boise

Cities and Towns

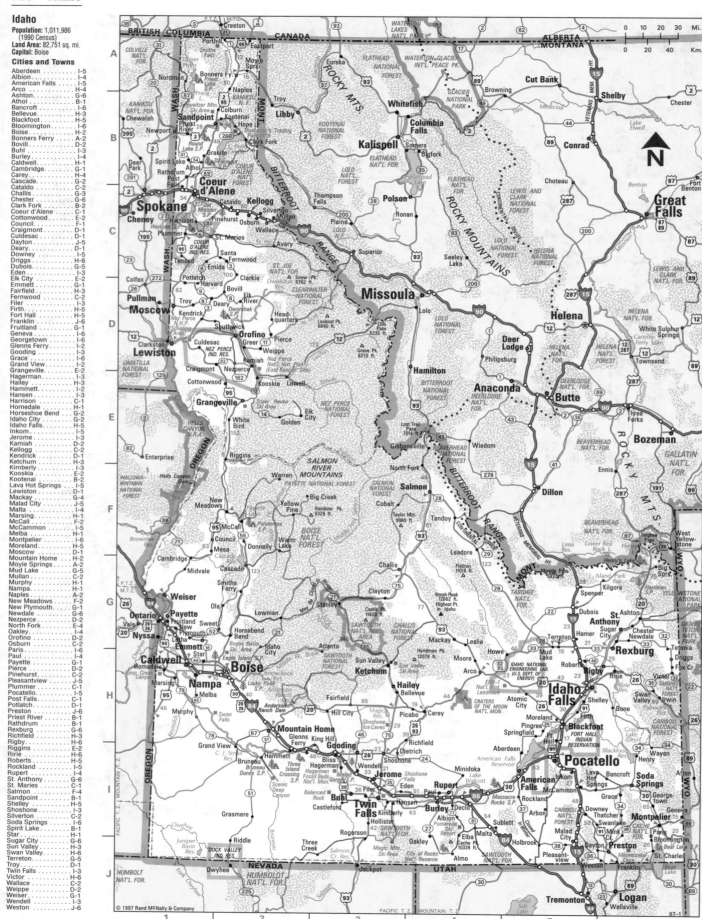

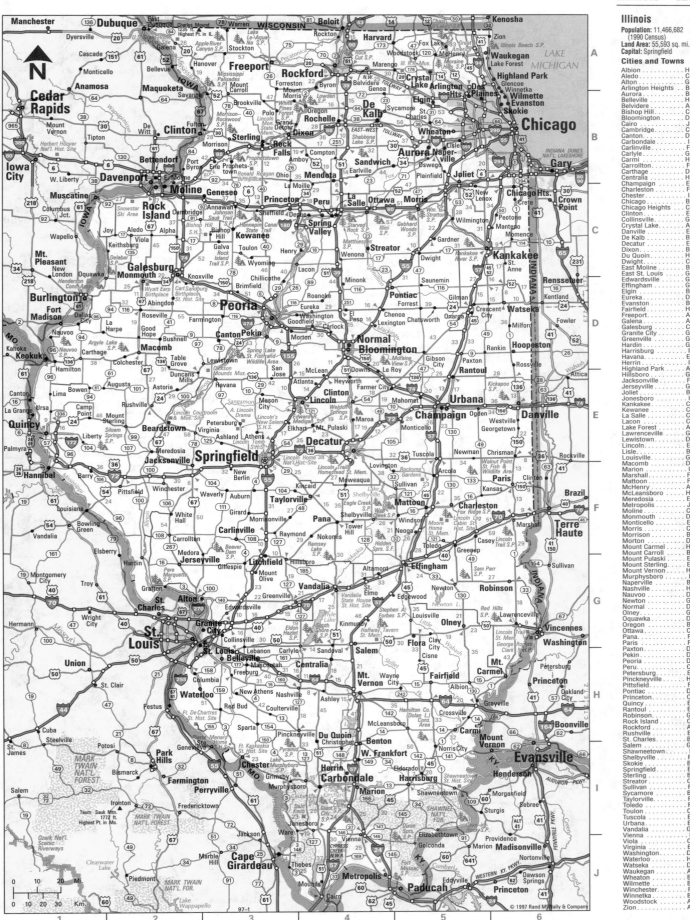

Illinois

Population: 11,466,682
(1990 Census)
Land Area: 55,593 sq. mi.
Capital: Springfield

Cities and Towns

Albion	H-5
Aledo	C-2
Alton	G-3
Arlington Heights	B-5
Aurora	B-5
Belleville	H-3
Belvidere	A-4
Bishop Hill	C-3
Bloomington	D-4
Cairo	J-4
Cambridge	C-2
Canton	D-3
Carbondale	I-4
Carlinville	F-3
Carlyle	G-4
Carmi	H-5
Carrollton	F-2
Carthage	D-1
Centralia	H-4
Champaign	E-5
Charleston	F-5
Chester	I-3
Chicago	B-6
Chicago Heights	C-6
Clinton	E-3
Collinsville	G-3
Crystal Lake	A-5
Danville	E-6
De Kalb	B-4
Decatur	E-4
Dixon	B-3
Du Quoin	H-4
Dwight	D-5
East Moline	B-2
East St. Louis	G-3
Edwardsville	G-3
Effingham	G-5
Elgin	B-5
Eureka	D-4
Evanston	B-6
Fairfield	H-5
Freeport	A-3
Galena	A-2
Galesburg	C-2
Granite City	G-3
Greenville	G-3
Hardin	G-2
Harrisburg	I-5
Havana	D-3
Herrin	I-4
Highland Park	A-6
Hillsboro	F-3
Jacksonville	F-2
Jerseyville	G-2
Joliet	B-5
Jonesboro	I-4
Kankakee	C-5
Kewanee	C-3
La Salle	C-4
Lacon	C-3
Lake Forest	A-6
Lawrenceville	G-6
Lewistown	D-3
Lincoln	E-4
Lisle	B-5
Louisville	G-5
Macomb	D-2
Marion	I-4
Marshall	F-6
Mattoon	F-5
McHenry	A-5
McLeansboro	H-5
Meredosia	E-2
Metropolis	J-4
Moline	C-2
Monmouth	D-2
Monticello	E-5
Morris	C-5
Morrison	B-3
Morton	D-3
Mount Carmel	H-6
Mount Carroll	B-3
Mount Pulaski	E-4
Mount Sterling	E-2
Mount Vernon	H-4
Murphysboro	I-4
Naperville	B-5
Nashville	H-4
Nauvoo	D-1
Newton	G-5
Normal	D-4
Olney	G-5
Oquawka	D-2
Oregon	B-4
Ottawa	C-4
Pana	F-4
Paris	F-6
Paxton	D-5
Pekin	D-3
Peoria	D-3
Peru	C-4
Petersburg	E-3
Pinckneyville	H-4
Pittsfield	F-2
Pontiac	D-4
Princeton	C-4
Quincy	E-1
Rantoul	E-5
Robinson	G-6
Rock Island	C-2
Rockford	A-4
Rushville	E-2
St. Charles	B-5
Salem	G-4
Shawneetown	I-5
Shelbyville	F-4
Skokie	B-6
Springfield	E-3
Sterling	B-3
Streator	C-4
Sullivan	F-5
Sycamore	B-4
Taylorville	F-4
Toledo	F-5
Toulon	C-3
Tuscola	E-5
Urbana	E-5
Vandalia	I-4
Vienna	I-4
Viola	C-2
Virginia	E-2
Washington	D-3
Waterloo	H-2
Watseka	D-6
Waukegan	A-6
Wheaton	B-5
Wilmette	B-6
Winchester	F-2
Winnetka	B-6
Woodstock	A-5
Zion	A-6

Indiana
Population: 5,564,228
(1990 Census)
Land Area: 35,870 sq. mi.
Capital: Indianapolis

Cities and Towns

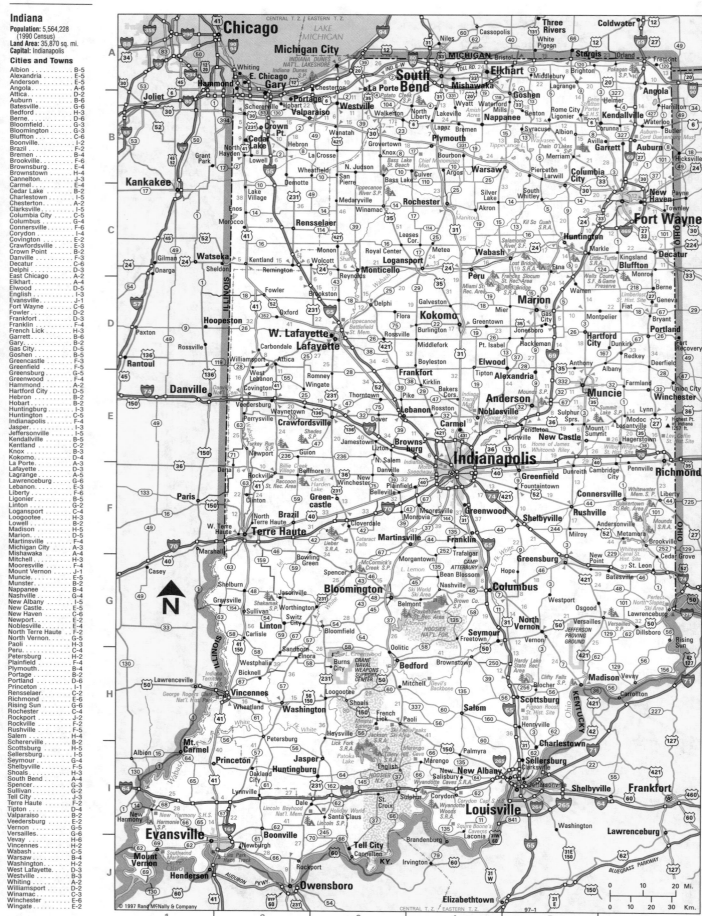

N

© 1997 Rand McNally & Company

97-1

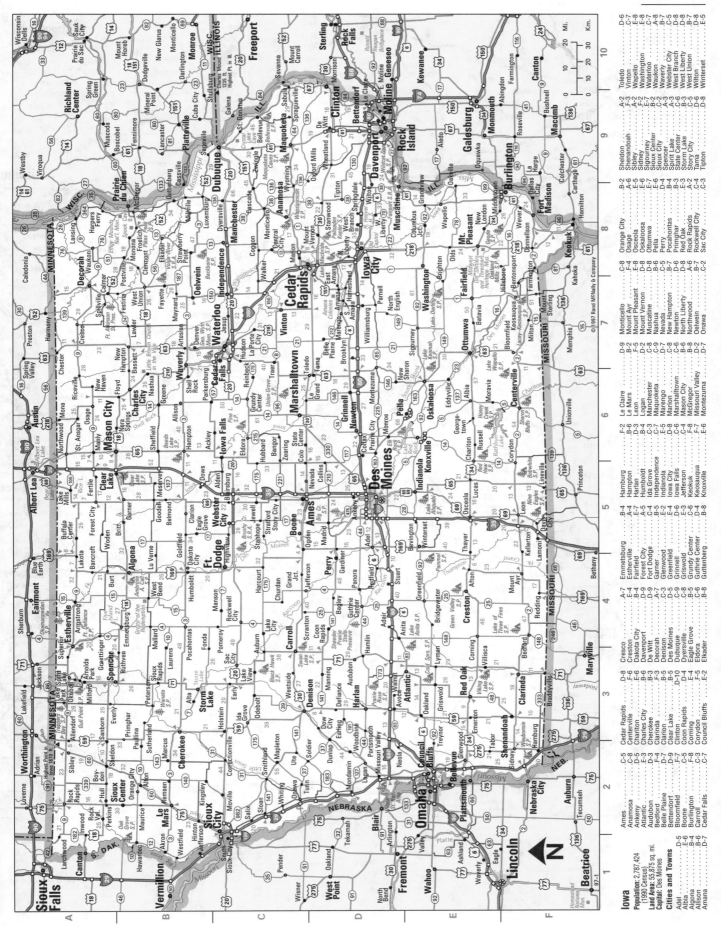

Iowa
Population: 2,787,424
(1990 Census)
Land Area: 55,875 sq. mi.
Capital: Des Moines

Cities and Towns

Adel	D-5
Albia	E-6
Algona	B-4
Allison	C-7
Amana	D-7
Ames	C-5
Anamosa	C-8
Ankeny	D-5
Atlantic	D-3
Audubon	D-3
Bedford	E-4
Belle Plaine	D-7
Bettendorf	C-9
Bloomfield	E-7
Boone	C-5
Burlington	D-9
Carroll	C-4
Cedar Falls	C-7
Cedar Rapids	C-8
Centerville	E-6
Charles City	B-6
Cherokee	B-3
Clarinda	E-3
Clarion	C-5
Clear Lake	B-5
Clinton	C-9
Corning	E-4
Corydon	E-6
Council Bluffs	D-2
Cresco	A-7
Creston	D-4
Dakota City	B-4
Davenport	C-9
De Witt	C-9
Decorah	A-7
Denison	C-3
Des Moines	D-5
Dubuque	B-8
Dyersville	B-8
Eagle Grove	C-5
Eldora	C-6
Elkader	B-8
Emmetsburg	B-4
Estherville	A-4
Fairfield	D-7
Forest City	B-5
Fort Dodge	C-4
Garner	B-5
Glenwood	D-2
Greenfield	D-4
Grinnell	D-6
Griswold	D-3
Grundy Center	C-6
Guthrie Center	D-4
Guttenberg	B-8
Hamburg	E-2
Hampton	B-6
Harlan	D-3
Humboldt	B-4
Ida Grove	C-3
Independence	C-8
Indianola	D-5
Iowa Falls	C-6
Jefferson	C-4
Keokuk	E-8
Keosauqua	E-7
Knoxville	D-6
Le Claire	C-9
Le Mars	B-2
Leon	E-5
Logan	D-2
Manchester	C-8
Maquoketa	C-9
Marengo	D-7
Marion	C-8
Marshalltown	C-6
Mason City	B-6
McGregor	B-8
Missouri Valley	D-2
Montezuma	D-6
Monticello	C-8
Mount Ayr	E-4
Mount Pleasant	D-8
Mount Vernon	C-8
Muscatine	D-8
Nashua	B-7
Nevada	C-5
New Hampton	B-7
Newton	D-6
North Liberty	C-8
Northwood	A-6
Oelwein	C-7
Onawa	C-2
Orange City	B-2
Osage	B-6
Osceola	D-5
Oskaloosa	D-6
Ottumwa	D-6
Pella	D-6
Perry	D-4
Pocahontas	B-4
Primghar	B-3
Red Oak	D-3
Rock Rapids	A-2
Rockwell City	C-4
Sac City	C-3
Sheldon	B-2
Shenandoah	E-3
Sibley	A-2
Sidney	E-2
Sigourney	D-7
Sioux Center	B-2
Sioux City	C-2
Spencer	B-3
Spirit Lake	A-3
State Center	C-6
Storm Lake	B-3
Story City	C-5
Tama	C-7
Tipton	C-8
Toledo	C-7
Vinton	C-7
Wapello	D-8
Washington	D-7
Waterloo	C-7
Waukon	A-8
Waverly	C-7
Webster City	C-5
West Branch	C-8
West Liberty	C-8
West Union	B-7
Wilton	C-8
Winterset	D-5

Kentucky

Population: 3,698,969
(1990 Census)
Land Area: 39,732 sq. mi.
Capital: Frankfort

Cities and Towns

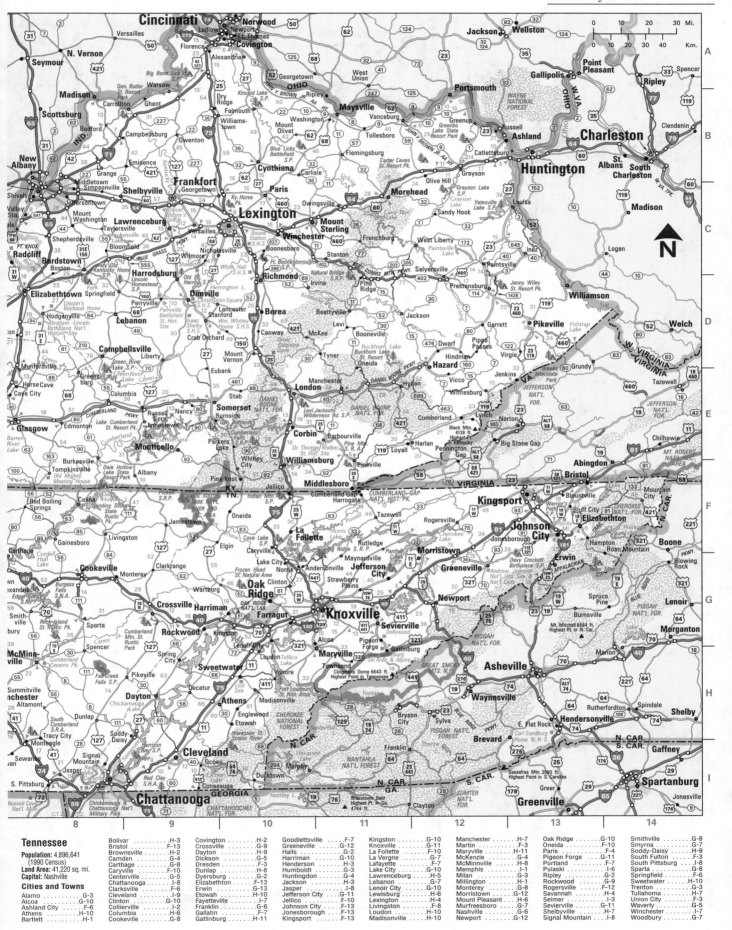

Tennessee

Population: 4,896,641 (1990 Census)
Land Area: 41,220 sq. mi.
Capital: Nashville

Cities and Towns

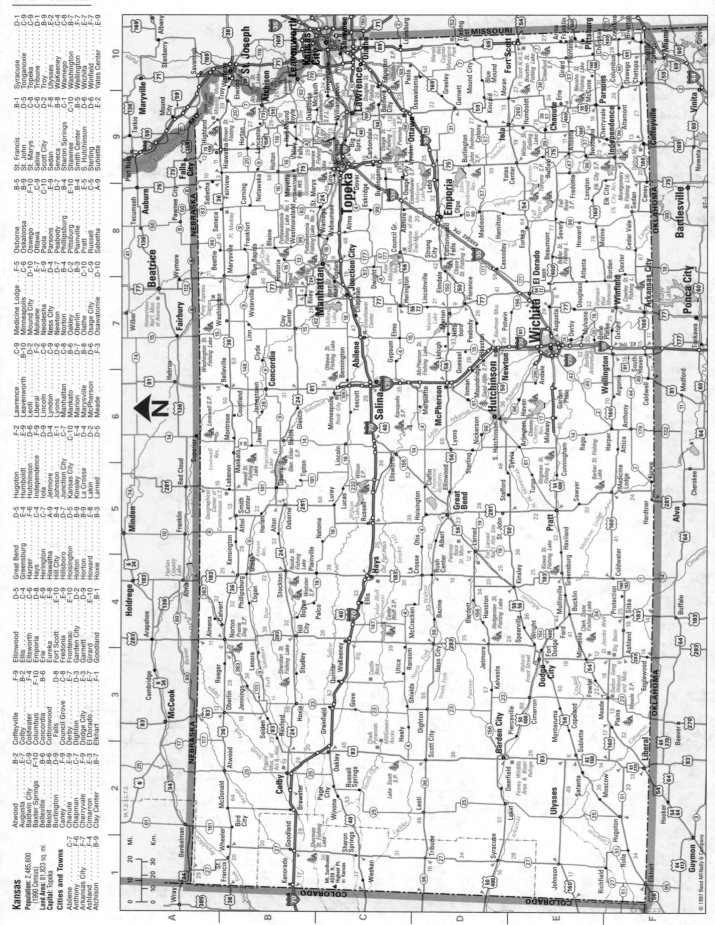

Kansas

Population: 2,485,600
(1990 Census)
Land Area: 81,823 sq. mi.
Capital: Topeka

Cities and Towns

© 1997 Rand McNally & Company

GULF OF MEXICO

Louisiana

Population: 4,238,216
(1990 Census)
Land Area: 43,566 sq. mi.
Capital: Baton Rouge

Cities and Towns

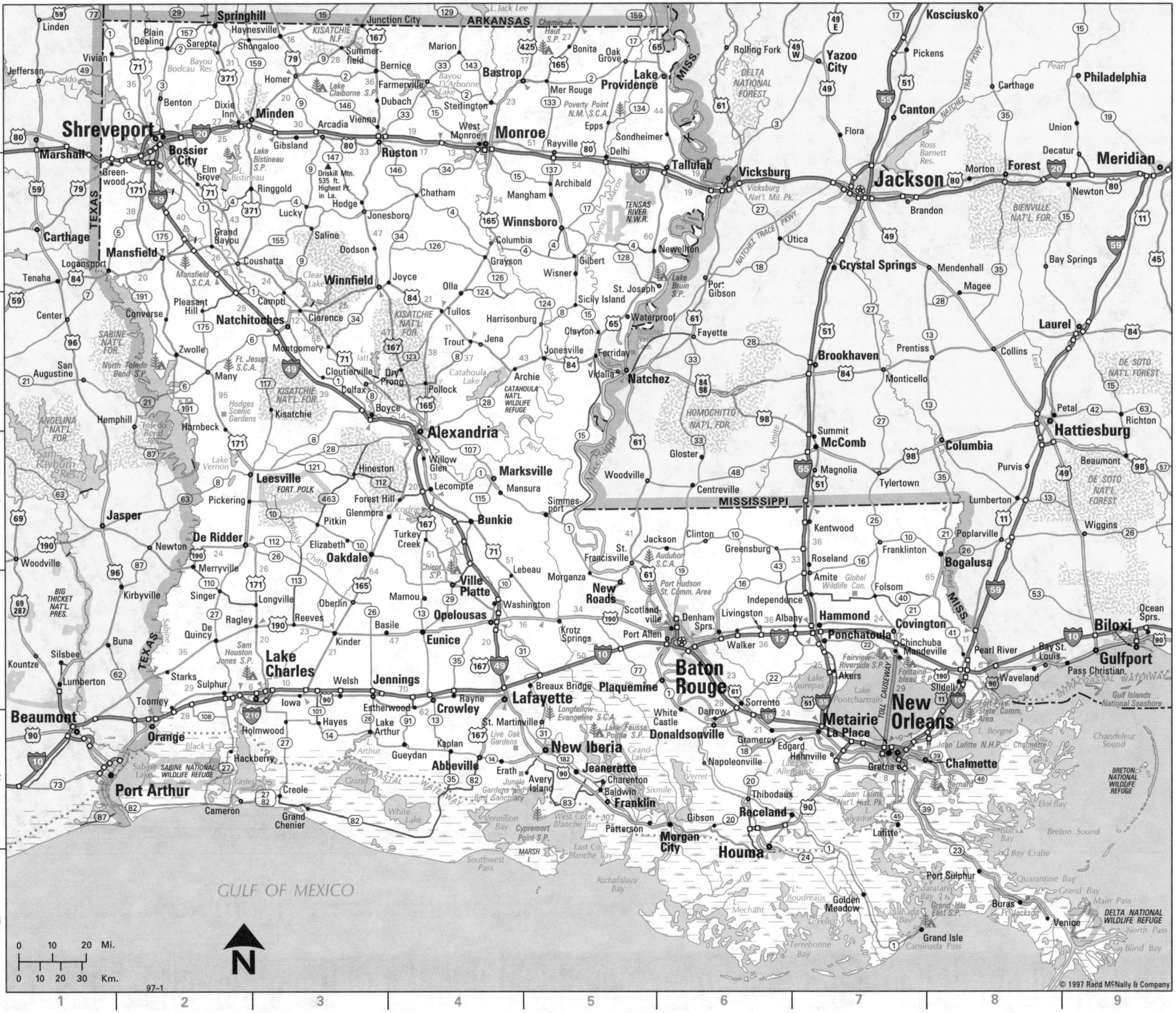

Maine

Population: 1,233,223
(1990 Census)
Land Area: 30,865 sq. mi.
Capital: Augusta

Cities and Towns

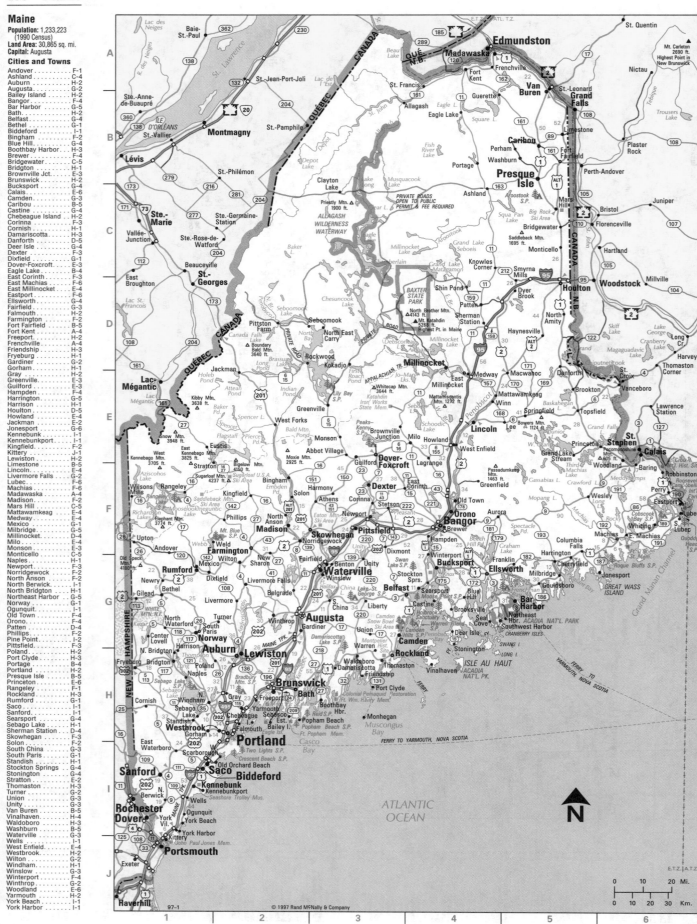

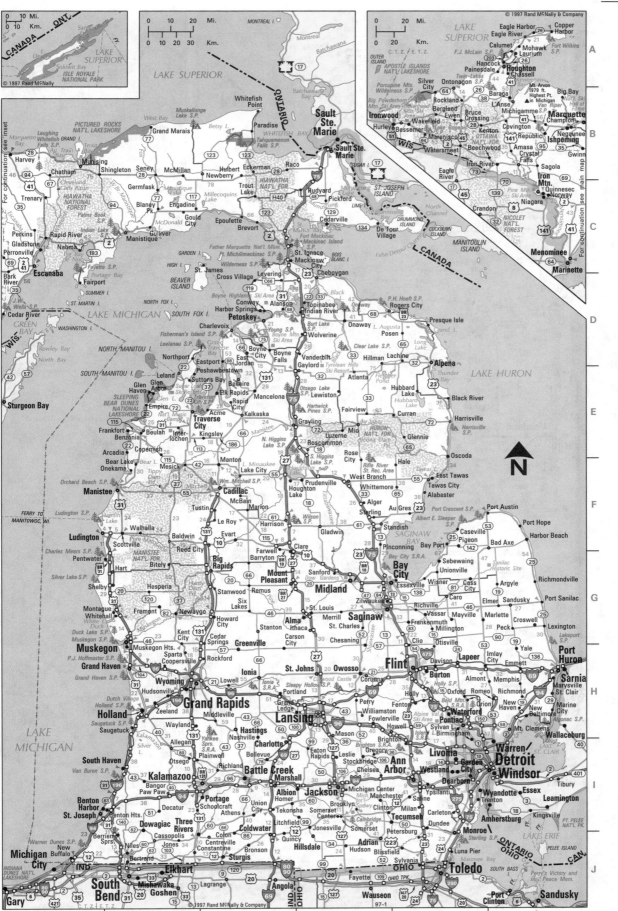

Michigan

Population: 9,328,784 (1990 Census)
Land Area: 56,809 sq. mi.
Capital: Lansing

Cities and Towns

Adrian	J-4
Albion	I-4
Allegan	I-2
Alma	G-4
Alpena	D-5
Ann Arbor	I-5
Bad Axe	F-6
Baldwin	F-2
Battle Creek	I-3
Bay City	G-4
Bellaire	E-3
Benton Harbor	I-1
Benton Heights	I-1
Berrien Springs	J-2
Bessemer	B-5
Big Rapids	G-3
Birmingham	I-5
Boyne City	D-3
Brighton	I-5
Burton	H-5
Cadillac	F-3
Caro	G-5
Cass City	G-5
Cassopolis	J-2
Cedar Springs	G-3
Centreville	J-3
Charlevoix	D-3
Charlotte	I-3
Cheboygan	D-4
Chelsea	I-4
Clare	F-3
Clio	H-5
Coldwater	J-3
Corunna	H-4
Croswell	G-6
Crystal Falls	B-6
Davison	H-5
Dearborn	I-5
Detroit	I-5
Dowagiac	I-2
East Tawas	F-5
Escanaba	C-1
Evart	F-3
Fenton	H-5
Flint	H-5
Frankenmuth	G-5
Frankfort	E-2
Fremont	G-2
Garden City	I-5
Gaylord	D-4
Gladstone	C-1
Gladwin	F-4
Grand Haven	H-2
Grand Ledge	H-4
Grand Rapids	H-3
Grayling	E-3
Greenville	H-3
Hancock	A-6
Harbor Beach	F-6
Harbor Springs	D-3
Harrison	F-4
Hart	H-2
Hastings	H-3
Hillsdale	J-4
Holland	I-2
Holly	H-5
Houghton	A-6
Howell	H-4
Hudson	J-4
Hudsonville	H-2
Imlay City	H-5
Ionia	H-3
Iron Mountain	C-6
Iron River	B-6
Ironwood	B-5
Ishpeming	B-6
Ithaca	G-4
Jackson	I-4
Jonesville	I-4
Kalamazoo	I-3
Kalkaska	E-3
L'Anse	B-6
Lake City	F-3
Lansing	H-4
Lapeer	H-5
Livonia	I-5
Ludington	F-1
Mackinaw City	C-3
Manistee	F-2
Manistique	C-1
Marlette	G-5
Marquette	B-6
Marshall	I-3
Marysville	H-6
Mason	H-4
Menominee	C-6
Midland	G-4
Monroe	J-5
Mount Clemens	H-6
Mount Pleasant	G-3
Munising	B-6
Muskegon	G-2
Muskegon Heights	G-2
Negaunee	B-6
New Buffalo	J-1
Newberry	B-3
Niles	J-2
Norway	C-6
Ontonagon	B-5
Owosso	H-4
Paw Paw	I-2
Petoskey	D-3
Plainwell	H-3
Pontiac	H-5
Port Huron	H-6
Portage	I-3
Reed City	H-3
Rockford	H-3
Rogers City	D-4
St. Clair	H-6
Saginaw	G-4
St. Ignace	C-3
St. Johns	H-4
St. Joseph	I-1
Saline	I-5
Sandusky	G-6
Sault Ste. Marie	B-4
South Haven	I-2
Sparta	H-2
Standish	F-4
Sturgis	J-3
Tawas City	F-5
Tecumseh	J-4
Three Rivers	J-2
Traverse City	E-2
Trenton	I-5
Vassar	G-5
Wakefield	B-5
Warren	I-6
West Branch	F-4
Westland	I-5
Wyandotte	I-5
Wyoming	H-2
Ypsilanti	I-5
Zeeland	H-2

Minnesota

Population: 4,387,029
(1990 Census)
Land Area: 79,617 sq. mi.
Capital: St. Paul

Cities and Towns

Ada E-1
Aitkin F-4
Albert Lea J-4
Alexandria G-2
Anoka H-4
Aurora D-5
Austin J-5
Bagley D-2
Barnesville F-1
Baudette C-3
Belle Plaine H-4
Bemidji D-3
Benson G-2
Big Lake G-4
Biwabik D-5
Blooming Prairie . J-5
Blue Earth J-4
Brainerd F-3
Breckenridge . . . F-1
Buffalo H-4
Caledonia J-6
Cambridge H-4
Cannon Falls . . . I-5
Chaska H-4
Chatfield J-5
Chisholm D-5
Cloquet E-5
Cokato H-3
Crookston D-1
Crosby F-4
Delano H-4
Detroit Lakes . . . E-2
Duluth E-5
East Grand Forks . D-1
Elbow Lake G-2
Elk River H-4
Ely D-6
Eveleth D-5
Fairmont J-3
Faribault I-4
Farmington H-4
Fergus Falls F-2
Foley G-4
Forest Lake H-5
Gaylord I-3
Glencoe H-3
Glenwood G-2
Grand Marais . . . B-6
Grand Rapids . . . E-4
Granite Falls H-2
Hallock C-1
Hastings H-5
Hawley E-1
Hutchinson H-3
International Falls . C-4
Ivanhoe I-1
Jackson J-3
Jordan H-4
Kasson I-5
La Crescent J-6
Lake City I-5
Lake Crystal I-3
Lakeland H-5
Le Sueur I-4
Litchfield H-3
Little Falls G-3
Long Prairie G-3
Luverne J-1
Madelia I-3
Madison H-1
Mahnomen E-2
Mankato I-4
Marshall I-2
Milaca G-4
Minneapolis H-4
Montevideo H-2
Montgomery I-4
Monticello G-4
Moorhead E-1
Moose Lake F-5
Mora G-4
Nashwauk E-4
New Prague I-4
New Ulm I-3
Northfield I-4
Olivia H-3
Ortonville G-1
Owatonna I-4
Park Rapids E-3
Paynesville G-3
Perham F-2
Pine City G-5
Pine Island I-5
Pipestone I-1
Plainview I-6
Preston J-5
Princeton G-4
Red Lake Falls . . D-1
Red Wing I-5
Redwood Falls . . I-2
Rochester I-5
Roseau B-2
St. Cloud G-3
St. James I-3
St. Joseph G-3
St. Paul H-5
St. Peter I-4
Sandstone F-5
Sauk Centre G-3
Sauk Rapids G-3
Savage H-4
Shakopee H-4
Silver Bay E-6
Slayton I-2
Sleepy Eye I-3
Spring Valley . . . J-5
Springfield I-3
Staples F-3
Stewartville J-5
Stillwater H-5
Thief River Falls . D-2
Tracy I-2
Two Harbors E-6
Tyler I-1
Virginia D-5
Wabasha I-6
Wadena F-2
Walker E-3
Warren C-1
Waseca I-4
Wells J-4
Wheaton G-1
White Bear Lake . H-5
Willmar H-3
Windom J-2
Winona I-6
Worthington J-2
Zimmerman G-4

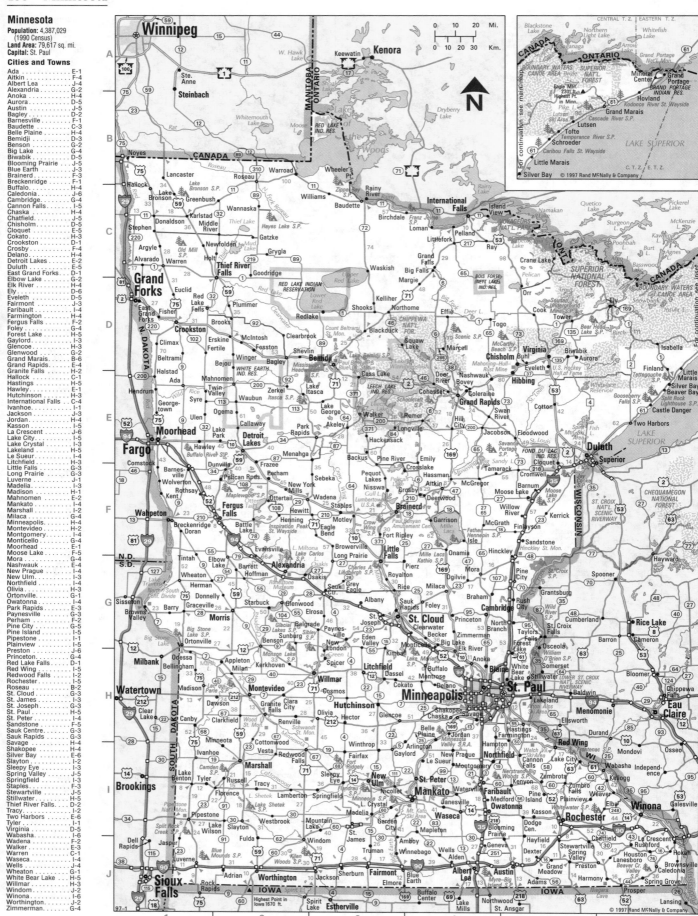

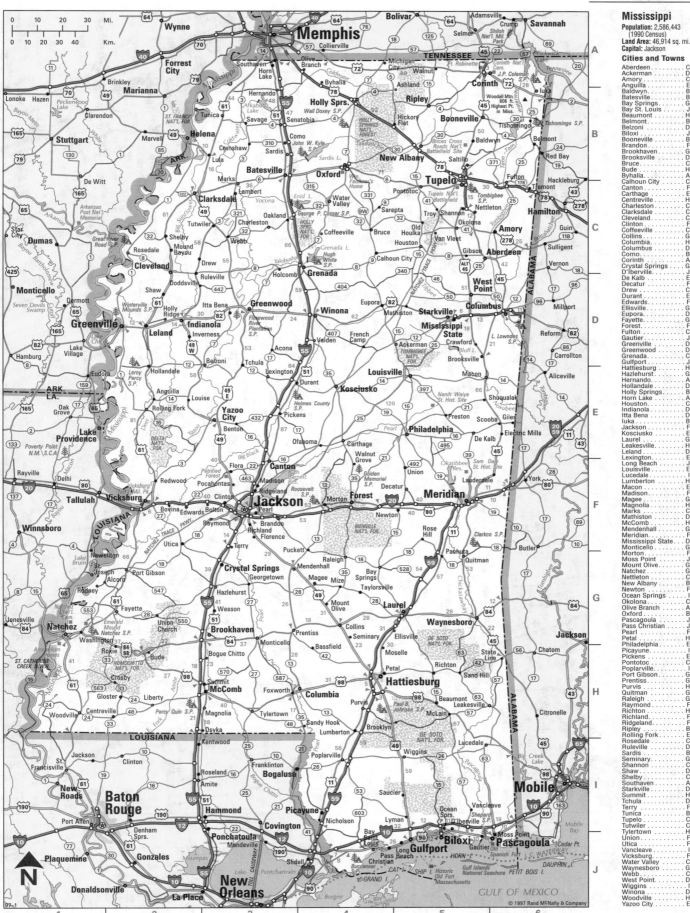

© 1997 Rand McNally & Company

97-1

Missouri
Population: 5,137,804
(1990 Census)
Land Area: 68,898 sq. mi.
Capital: Jefferson City

Cities and Towns

Arnold	D-7
Aurora	F-3
Ava	F-4
Belton	C-2
Bethany	C-3
Blue Springs	C-2
Bolivar	E-4
Bonne Terre	D-7
Boonville	C-4
Bowling Green	C-6
Branson	F-4
Brookfield	B-4
Butler	D-2
California	D-4
Cameron	C-3
Cape Girardeau	E-8
Carthage	F-2
Caruthersville	G-8
Centralia	C-5
Charleston	E-9
Chillicothe	B-3
Clinton	D-3
Columbia	C-5
Crystal City	D-7
De Soto	D-7
Dexter	E-8
El Dorado Springs	E-3
Eureka	D-7
Eveningshade	E-5
Excelsior Springs	C-3
Farmington	D-7
Festus	D-7
Fredericktown	E-7
Fulton	C-5
Grandview	C-2
Hannibal	B-6
Harrisonville	D-2
Hayti	G-8
Independence	C-2
Jackson	E-8
Jefferson City	D-5
Joplin	F-2
Kansas City	C-2
Kennett	G-8
Kirksville	B-5
Lamar	E-2
Lebanon	E-4
Lexington	C-3
Liberty	C-2
Louisiana	C-6
Macon	B-5
Malden	F-8
Marshall	C-4
Marshfield	E-4
Maryville	B-2
Mexico	C-5
Moberly	C-5
Monett	F-3
Mountain Grove	E-5
Mountain View	F-6
Neosho	F-2
Nevada	E-2
New Madrid	F-8
Nixa	F-4
Odessa	C-3
Osage Beach	D-5
Ozark	F-4
Pacific	D-6
Palmyra	B-6
Perryville	E-7
Platte City	C-2
Pleasant Hill	D-2
Poplar Bluff	F-7
Potosi	D-6
Republic	F-3
Richmond	C-3
Rolla	D-6
St. Charles	D-7
St. Clair	D-6
St. James	D-6
St. Joseph	C-2
St. Louis	D-7
Ste. Genevieve	D-7
Salem	D-6
Savannah	B-2
Sedalia	D-4
Sikeston	E-8
Springfield	F-4
Sullivan	D-6
Trenton	B-3
Troy	C-6
Union	D-6
Warrensburg	D-3
Washington	D-6
Waynesville	E-5
Webb City	F-2
Wentzville	D-6
West Plains	F-5

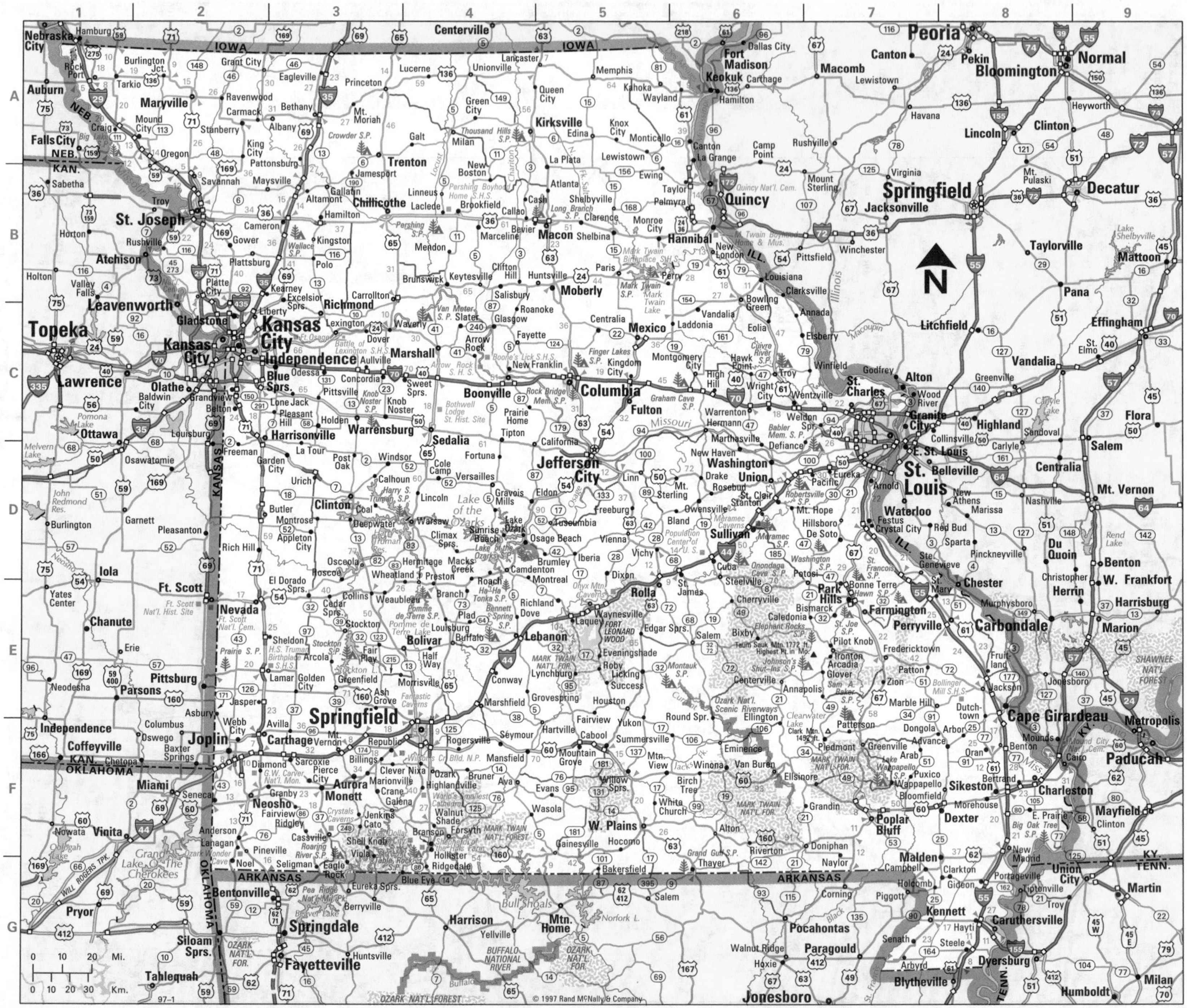

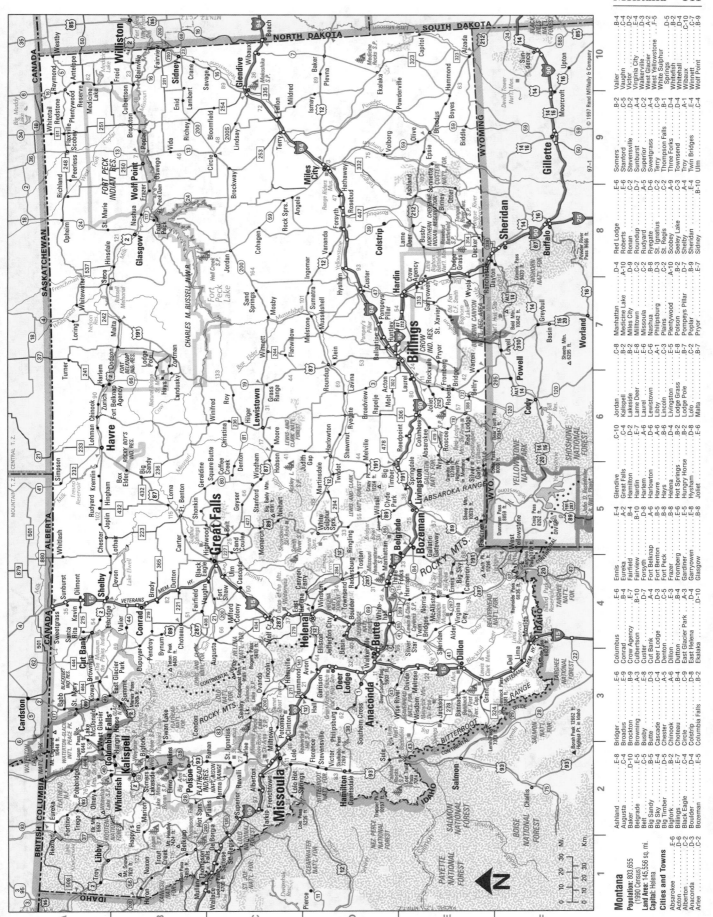

Montana

Population: 803,655
(1990 Census)
Land Area: 145,556 sq. mi.
Capital: Helena

Cities and Towns

Absarokee	E-6
Acton	D-6
Alberton	C-2
Anaconda	C-3
Arlee	C-2
Ashland	E-9
Augusta	B-4
Baker	D-10
Belgrade	D-4
Belt	B-5
Big Sandy	B-5
Big Sky	D-4
Big Timber	D-5
Bigfork	B-2
Billings	D-6
Black Eagle	B-4
Boulder	C-3
Bozeman	D-4
Bridger	E-6
Broadus	D-9
Brockton	B-10
Browning	A-3
Busby	E-8
Butte	C-3
Cascade	B-4
Chester	A-5
Chinook	A-6
Choteau	B-4
Circle	C-9
Colstrip	D-8
Columbia Falls	B-2
Columbus	E-6
Conrad	B-4
Crow Agency	E-7
Culbertson	B-10
Custer	D-7
Cut Bank	A-4
Deer Lodge	C-3
Denton	B-5
Dillon	D-3
Dutton	B-4
East Glacier Park	A-3
East Helena	C-4
Ekalaka	D-10
Ennis	E-6
Eureka	A-2
Fairfield	B-4
Fairview	B-10
Forsyth	D-8
Fort Belknap	A-6
Fort Benton	B-5
Fort Peck	B-8
Frazer	B-9
Fromberg	E-6
Gardiner	E-5
Garryowen	E-8
Glasgow	B-8
Glendive	C-10
Great Falls	B-4
Hamilton	C-2
Hardin	D-7
Harlem	A-6
Harlowton	C-5
Havre	A-5
Hays	B-6
Helena	B-4
Hot Springs	B-2
Hungry Horse	B-2
Hysham	D-8
Joliet	E-6
Jordan	C-8
Kalispell	B-2
Lakeside	B-2
Lame Deer	E-8
Laurel	D-6
Lewistown	C-6
Libby	A-1
Lincoln	B-3
Livingston	D-4
Lodge Grass	E-7
Lodge Pole	B-7
Lolo	C-2
Malta	A-6
Manhattan	D-4
Medicine Lake	B-10
Miles City	D-8
Milltown	C-2
Missoula	C-2
Nashua	B-9
Philipsburg	C-3
Plains	B-2
Plentywood	A-10
Polson	B-2
Pompeys Pillar	D-7
Poplar	B-9
Pryor	E-7
Red Lodge	E-6
Roberts	E-6
Ronan	B-2
Roundup	C-7
Rudyard	A-5
Ryegate	C-6
St. Ignatius	B-2
St. Regis	B-1
Scobey	A-9
Seeley Lake	B-3
Shelby	A-4
Sheridan	E-4
Sidney	B-10
Somers	B-2
Stanford	C-5
Stevensville	C-2
Sunburst	A-4
Superior	B-1
Sweetgrass	A-4
Terry	C-9
Thompson Falls	B-1
Three Forks	D-4
Townsend	C-4
Troy	A-1
Twin Bridges	D-3
Ulm	B-4
Valier	B-2
Vaughn	C-5
Victor	C-2
Virginia City	D-4
Walkerville	C-3
West Glacier	A-2
West Yellowstone	F-5
White Sulphur	
Springs	C-5
Whitefish	B-2
Whitehall	C-3
Wibaux	C-10
Winnett	C-7
Wolf Point	B-9

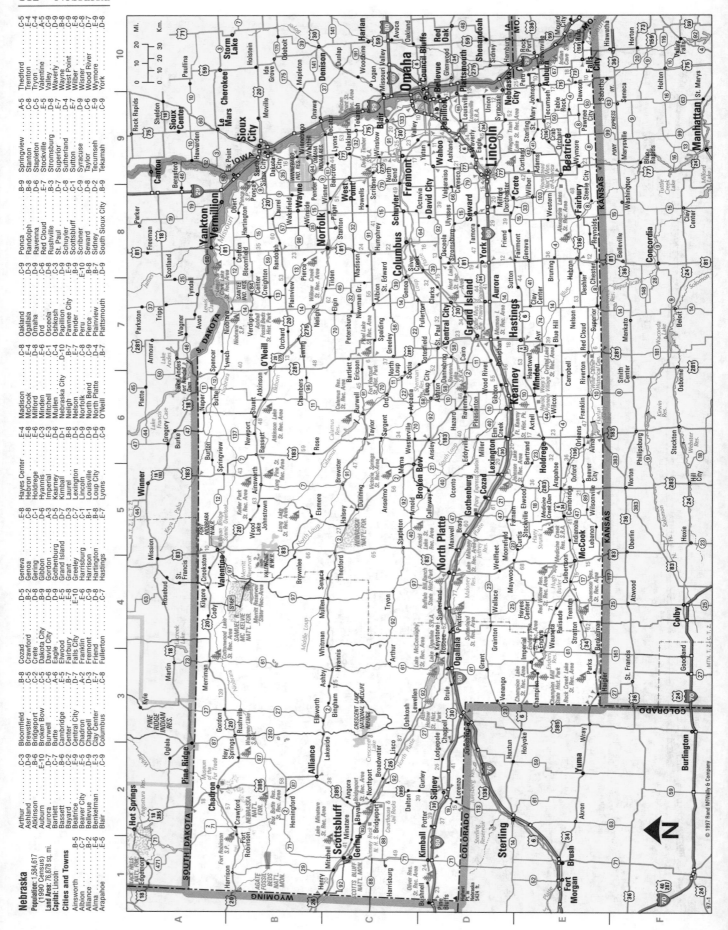

Nebraska

Population: 1,584,617
(1990 Census)
Land Area: 76,878 sq. mi.
Capital: Lincoln

Cities and Towns

Ainsworth ... B-5
Albion ... C-7
Alliance ... A-6
Alma ... E-6
Arapahoe ... E-5

Arthur ... C-5
Ashland ... D-9
Auburn ... D-9
Aurora ... D-8
Bassett ... B-6
Bayard ... D-7
Beatrice ... E-9
Beaver City ... E-6
Bellevue ... C-9
Blair ... C-9

Bloomfield ... B-8
Brewster ... C-6
Bridgeport ... D-7
Broken Bow ... C-6
Burwell ... C-7
Butte ... B-7
Cambridge ... E-6
Center ... B-8
Central City ... C-8
Chadron ... A-2
Chappell ... D-6
Clay Center ... D-8
Columbus ... C-8

Cozad ... D-6
Crawford ... A-2
Crete ... D-9
Dakota City ... B-9
David City ... C-8
Eagle ... D-9
Elwood ... E-6
Fairbury ... E-8
Falls City ... E-10
Franklin ... E-7
Friend ... D-8
Fullerton ... C-8

Geneva ... D-8
Genoa ... C-8
Gering ... D-7
Gibbon ... D-7
Gordon ... A-4
Gothenburg ... D-6
Grant ... D-5
Greeley ... C-7
Harrisburg ... D-7
Harrison ... A-2
Hartington ... B-8
Hastings ... D-7

Hayes Center ... E-4
Hebron ... E-8
Holdrege ... E-6
Imperial ... D-3
Hyannis ... C-3
Kearney ... D-7
Kimball ... D-6
Laurel ... B-8
Lexington ... D-6
Lincoln ... D-9
Louisville ... D-9
Loup City ... C-7
Lyons ... C-9

Madison ... C-8
McCook ... E-5
Milford ... D-8
Mitchell ... D-6
Minden ... D-7
Mullen ... C-4
Nebraska City ... D-9
Neligh ... C-7
Nelson ... E-8
Norfolk ... C-8
North Bend ... C-9
North Platte ... D-6
O'Neill ... B-7

Oakland ... C-9
Ogallala ... D-5
Omaha ... C-9
Ord ... C-7
Osceola ... C-8
Oshkosh ... D-5
Papillion ... C-9
Pawnee City ... E-9
Pender ... B-9
Peru ... D-9
Pierce ... C-8
Plattsmouth ... C-9

Ponca ... B-9
Randolph ... B-8
Ravenna ... D-7
Red Cloud ... E-7
Rushville ... A-3
St. Paul ... C-7
Schuyler ... C-8
Scottsbluff ... D-6
Scribner ... C-9
Seward ... D-8
Sidney ... D-6
Plainview ... B-8
South Sioux City ... B-9

Springview ... B-6
Stanton ... C-8
Stapleton ... C-6
Stockville ... D-6
Stromsburg ... C-8
Superior ... E-7
Sutherland ... D-5
Sutton ... D-8
Syracuse ... D-9
Taylor ... C-6
Tecumseh ... D-9
Tekamah ... C-9

Thedford ... C-5
Trenton ... E-4
Tryon ... C-5
Valentine ... A-5
Waverly ... D-9
Wayne ... B-8
West Point ... C-9
Wilber ... D-9
Wisner ... C-8
Wood River ... D-7
Wymore ... E-9
York ... D-8

© 1997 Rand McNally & Company

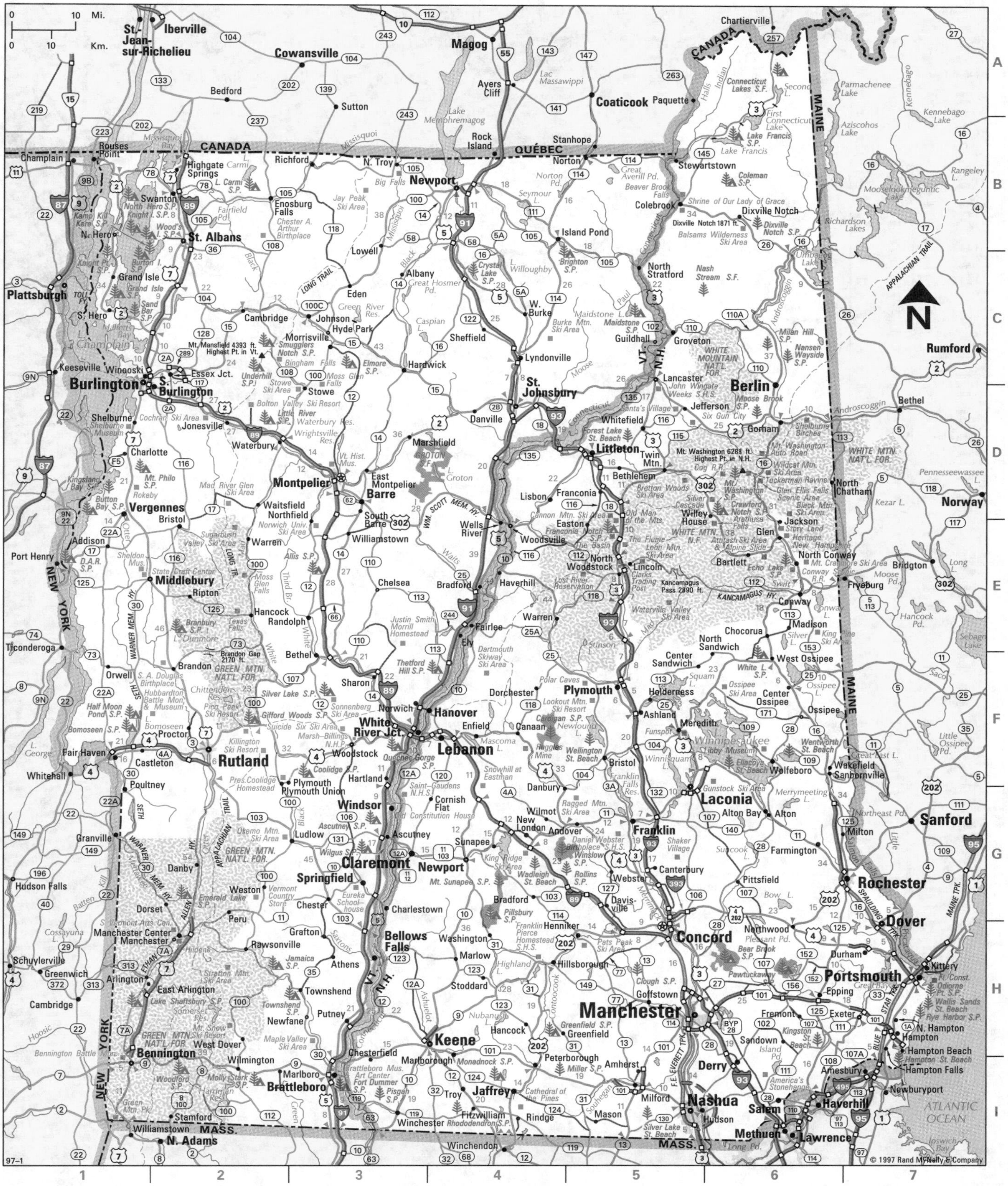

New Hampshire

Population: 1,113,915 (1990 Census)
Land Area: 8,969 sq. mi.
Capital: Concord

Cities and Towns

Ashland F-5
Berlin D-6
Bristol F-5
Charlestown G-3
Claremont G-3
Concord H-5
Conway E-6
Derry I-6
Dover H-7
Durham H-7
Enfield F-4
Epping H-6
Exeter H-7
Farmington G-6
Franklin G-5
Goffstown H-5
Gorham D-6
Groveton C-5
Hampton H-7
Hampton Beach . . .H-7
Hanover F-4
Henniker H-5
Hillsborough H-4
Hudson I-6
Jaffrey I-4
Keene H-4
Laconia F-5
Lancaster C-5
Lebanon F-4
Lisbon D-4
Littleton D-5
Manchester H-5
Marlborough H-4
Meredith F-5
Milford I-5
Nashua I-5
New London G-4
Newport G-4
North Conway E-6
Ossipee F-6
Peterborough I-4
Pittsfield G-6
Plymouth F-5
Portsmouth H-7
Rochester G-7
Salem I-6
Troy I-4
Whitefield D-5
Winchester I-3
Wolfeboro F-6
Woodsville E-4

Vermont

Population: 564,964 (1990 Census)
Land Area: 9,249 sq. mi.
Capital: Montpelier

Cities and Towns

Barre D-3
Bellows Falls H-3
Bennington I-1
Brandon F-2
Brattleboro I-3
Bristol E-2
Burlington C-1
Chelsea E-3
Enosburg Falls B-2
Essex Junction C-2
Fair Haven F-1
Guildhall C-5
Hardwick C-3
Hyde Park C-3
Island Pond B-4
Johnson C-3
Ludlow G-3
Lyndonville C-4
Manchester H-2
Manchester Cen. . . .H-2
Middlebury E-2
Montpelier D-3
Newfane H-3
Newport B-4
North Hero B-1
Northfield E-3
Poultney G-1
Proctor F-2
Putney H-3
Richford B-3
Rutland F-2
St. Albans B-2
St. Johnsbury D-4
South Barre D-3
South Burlington . . .D-2
Springfield G-3
Swanton B-2
Vergennes D-1
Waterbury D-2
White River Jct. F-3
Windsor G-3
Winooski C-1
Woodstock F-3

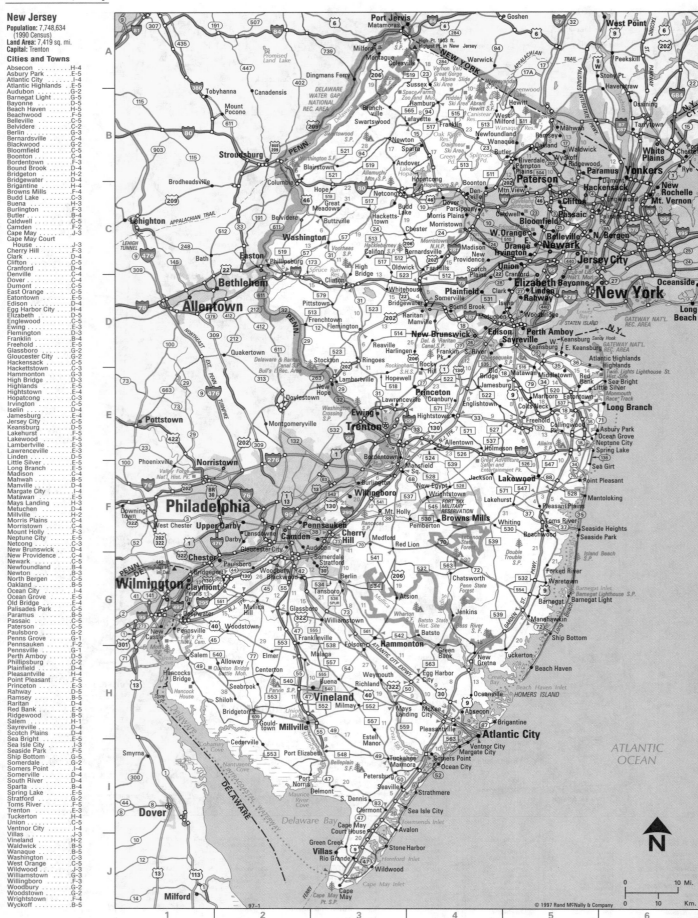

© 1997 Rand McNally & Company

© 1997 Rand McNally & Company

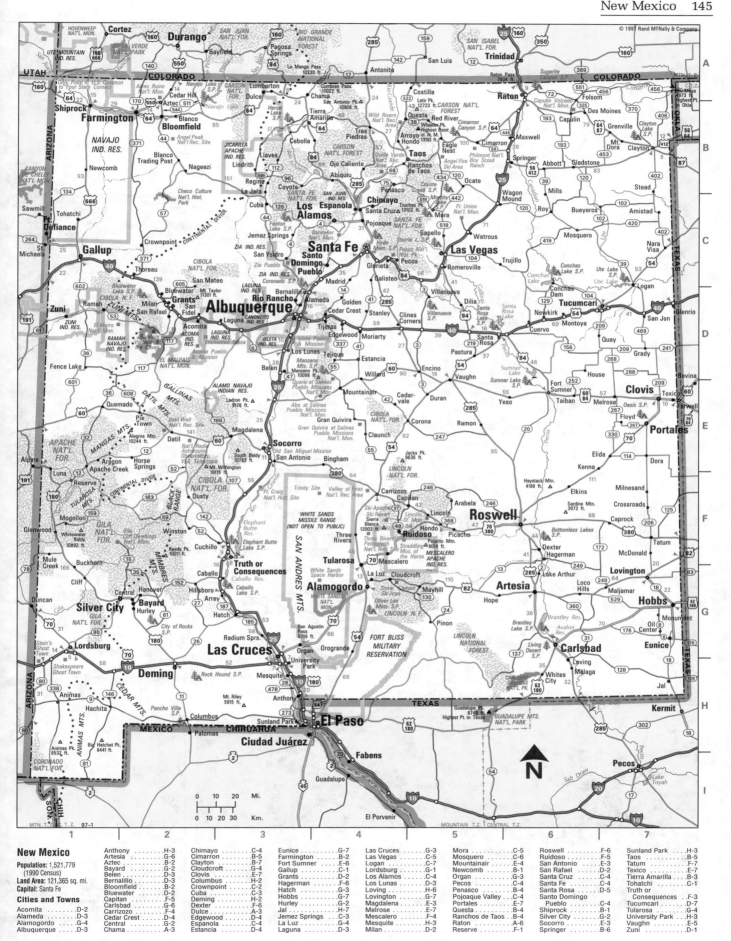

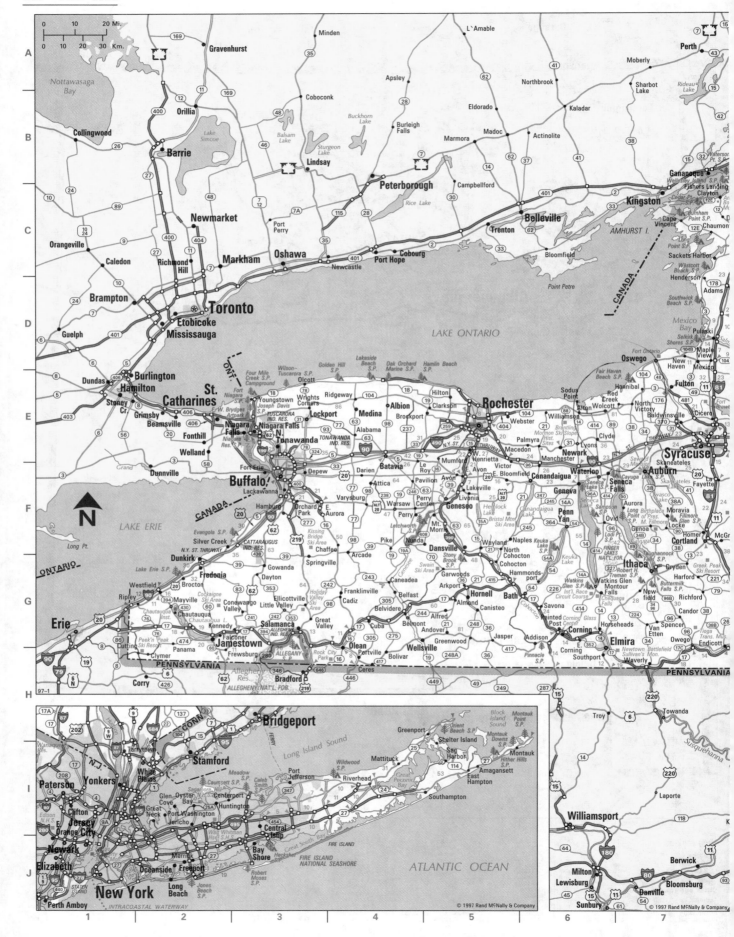

© 1997 Rand McNally & Company

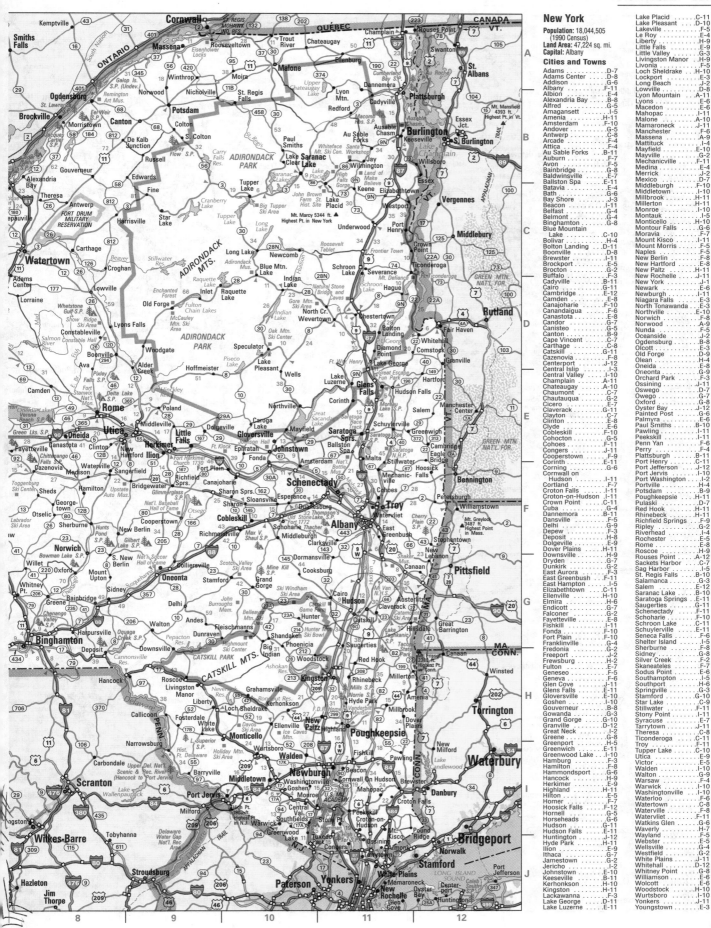

New York

Population: 18,044,505
(1990 Census)
Land Area: 47,224 sq. mi.
Capital: Albany

Cities and Towns

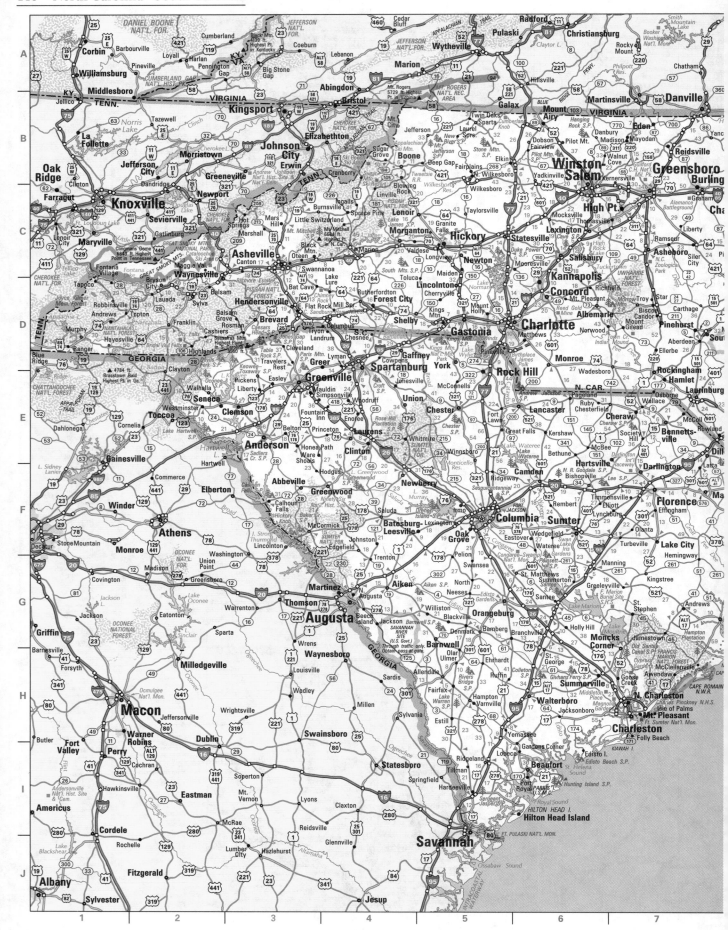

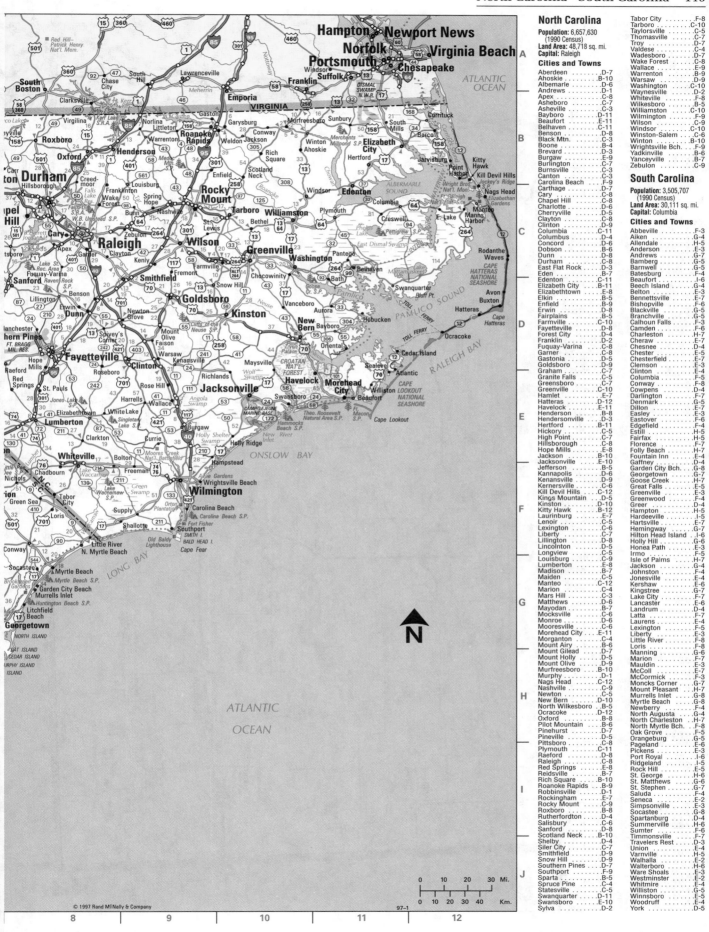

North Carolina
Population: 6,657,630
(1990 Census)
Land Area: 48,718 sq. mi.
Capital: Raleigh

Cities and Towns

Aberdeen	D-7
Ahoskie	B-10
Albemarle	D-6
Andrews	D-1
Apex	C-8
Asheboro	C-7
Asheville	C-3
Bayboro	D-11
Beaufort	E-11
Belhaven	C-11
Benson	D-8
Black Mtn.	C-3
Boone	B-3
Brevard	D-3
Burgaw	E-9
Burlington	C-7
Burnsville	C-3
Canton	C-2
Carolina Beach	F-9
Carthage	D-7
Cary	C-8
Chapel Hill	C-8
Charlotte	D-6
Cherryville	D-5
Clayton	C-8
Clinton	D-9
Columbia	C-11
Columbus	D-4
Concord	D-6
Dobson	B-6
Dunn	D-8
Durham	C-8
East Flat Rock	D-3
Eden	B-7
Edenton	C-11
Elizabeth City	B-11
Elizabethtown	E-8
Elkin	B-5
Enfield	B-9
Erwin	D-8
Fairplains	B-5
Farmville	C-10
Fayetteville	D-8
Forest City	D-4
Franklin	D-2
Fuquay-Varina	C-8
Garner	C-8
Gastonia	D-5
Goldsboro	D-9
Graham	C-7
Granite Falls	C-5
Greensboro	C-7
Greenville	C-10
Hamlet	E-7
Hatteras	D-12
Havelock	E-11
Henderson	B-8
Hendersonville	D-3
Hertford	B-11
Hickory	C-5
High Point	C-7
Hillsborough	C-8
Hope Mills	E-8
Jackson	B-10
Jacksonville	E-10
Jefferson	B-5
Kannapolis	D-6
Kenansville	D-9
Kernersville	C-6
Kill Devil Hills	C-12
Kings Mountain	D-5
Kinston	D-10
Kitty Hawk	B-12
Laurinburg	E-7
Lenoir	C-5
Lexington	C-6
Liberty	C-7
Lillington	D-8
Lincolnton	D-5
Longview	C-5
Louisburg	C-9
Lumberton	E-8
Madison	B-7
Maiden	C-5
Manteo	C-12
Marion	C-4
Mars Hill	C-3
Matthews	D-6
Mayodan	B-7
Mocksville	C-6
Monroe	D-6
Mooresville	C-6
Morehead City	E-11
Morganton	C-4
Mount Airy	B-6
Mount Gilead	D-7
Mount Holly	D-5
Mount Olive	D-9
Murfreesboro	B-10
Murphy	D-1
Nags Head	C-12
Nashville	C-9
Newton	C-5
New Bern	D-10
North Wilkesboro	B-5
Ocracoke	D-12
Oxford	B-8
Pilot Mountain	B-6
Pinehurst	D-7
Pineville	D-6
Pittsboro	C-8
Plymouth	C-11
Raeford	D-8
Raleigh	C-8
Red Springs	E-8
Reidsville	B-7
Rich Square	B-10
Roanoke Rapids	B-9
Robbinsville	D-1
Rockingham	E-7
Rocky Mount	C-9
Roxboro	B-8
Rutherfordton	D-4
Salisbury	C-6
Sanford	D-8
Scotland Neck	B-10
Shelby	D-4
Siler City	C-7
Smithfield	C-8
Snow Hill	D-9
Southern Pines	D-7
Southport	F-9
Sparta	B-5
Spruce Pine	C-4
Statesville	C-5
Swanquarter	D-11
Swansboro	E-10
Sylva	D-2
Tabor City	F-8
Tarboro	C-10
Taylorsville	C-5
Thomasville	C-7
Troy	D-7
Valdese	C-4
Wadesboro	D-7
Wake Forest	C-8
Wallace	E-9
Warrenton	B-9
Warsaw	D-9
Washington	C-10
Waynesville	D-2
Whiteville	F-8
Wilkesboro	B-5
Williamston	C-10
Wilmington	F-9
Wilson	C-9
Windsor	C-10
Winston-Salem	C-6
Winton	B-10
Wrightsville Bch.	F-9
Yadkinville	B-6
Yanceyville	B-7
Zebulon	C-9

South Carolina
Population: 3,505,707
(1990 Census)
Land Area: 30,111 sq. mi.
Capital: Columbia

Cities and Towns

Abbeville	F-3
Aiken	G-4
Allendale	H-5
Anderson	E-3
Andrews	G-7
Bamberg	G-5
Barnwell	G-5
Batesburg	F-4
Beaufort	I-6
Beech Island	G-4
Belton	E-3
Bennettsville	E-7
Bishopville	F-6
Blackville	G-5
Branchville	G-5
Calhoun Falls	F-3
Camden	F-5
Charleston	H-7
Cheraw	E-7
Chesnee	D-4
Chester	E-5
Chesterfield	E-6
Clemson	E-3
Clinton	E-4
Columbia	F-5
Conway	F-8
Cowpens	D-4
Darlington	F-7
Denmark	G-5
Dillon	E-7
Easley	E-3
Eastover	F-6
Edgefield	F-4
Estill	H-5
Fairfax	H-5
Florence	F-7
Folly Beach	H-7
Fountain Inn	E-4
Gaffney	D-4
Garden City Bch.	G-8
Georgetown	G-7
Goose Creek	H-7
Great Falls	E-5
Greenville	E-3
Greenwood	E-3
Greer	D-4
Hampton	H-5
Hardeeville	I-5
Hartsville	E-7
Hemingway	G-7
Hilton Head Island	I-6
Holly Hill	G-6
Honea Path	E-3
Irmo	F-5
Isle of Palms	H-7
Jackson	G-4
Johnston	F-4
Jonesville	E-4
Kershaw	E-6
Kingstree	F-7
Lake City	F-7
Lancaster	E-6
Landrum	D-4
Latta	F-7
Laurens	E-4
Lexington	F-5
Liberty	E-3
Little River	F-8
Loris	F-8
Manning	G-6
Marion	F-7
Mauldin	E-3
McColl	E-7
McCormick	F-3
Moncks Corner	G-7
Mount Pleasant	H-7
Murrells Inlet	G-8
Myrtle Beach	G-8
Newberry	F-4
North Augusta	G-4
North Charleston	H-7
North Myrtle Bch.	F-8
Oak Grove	F-5
Orangeburg	G-5
Pageland	E-6
Pickens	E-3
Port Royal	I-6
Ridgeland	I-5
Rock Hill	E-5
St. George	H-6
St. Matthews	G-6
St. Stephen	G-7
Saluda	F-4
Seneca	E-2
Simpsonville	E-4
Socastee	G-8
Spartanburg	D-4
Summerville	H-6
Sumter	F-6
Timmonsville	F-7
Travelers Rest	D-3
Union	E-4
Varnville	H-5
Walhalla	E-2
Walterboro	H-6
Ware Shoals	E-3
Westminster	E-2
Whitmire	E-4
Williston	G-5
Winnsboro	E-5
Woodruff	E-4
York	D-5

North Dakota

Population: 641,364
(1990 Census)
Land Area: 68,994 sq. mi.
Capital: Bismarck

Cities and Towns

Abercrombie E-10
Anamoose C-6
Aneta D-9
Arthur D-9
Ashley F-7
Beach D-1
Belfield D-2
Berthold B-4
Beulah D-4
Bisbee B-6
Bismarck E-5
Bottineau B-4
Bowbells A-3
Bowman F-2
Burlington C-6
Cando B-7
Cannon Ball F-5
Carrington C-7

Carson E-4
Casselton D-9
Cavalier A-9
Center D-4
Cooperstown C-8
Crosby A-2
Devils Lake B-7
Dickinson D-3
Drake C-6
Drayton A-9
Dunseith B-7
Edgeley E-7
Edinburg C-7

Edmore B-8
Elgin E-4
Ellendale F-8
Enderlin D-9
Fairmount F-10
Fessenden C-6
Finley C-9
Flasher E-4
Forman E-9
Fort Totten B-7
Fort Yates F-5
Gackle E-7

Garrison C-4
Glen Ullin E-4
Glenburn B-4
Grafton B-9
Grand Forks C-9
Gwinner D-9
Halliday D-3
Hankinson F-10
Harvey C-6
Hatton C-9
Hazen D-4
Hebron E-7

Hettinger F-3
Hillsboro C-9
Hunter C-9
Jamestown D-7
Kenmare B-4
Killdeer D-3
Kindred D-9
Kulm E-7
Lakota B-8
Lamoure E-8
Langdon A-8
Lansford B-4
Larimore C-9

Leeds B-7
Leonard D-9
Lidgerwood E-9
Linton E-6
Lisbon D-9
Maddock C-6
Mandan E-5
Manning D-3
Manvel B-9
Max C-5
Mayville C-9
Mcclusky C-5

Medina D-7
Medora D-2
Michigan B-8
Milnor E-9
Minnewaukan B-6
Minot B-5
Minto B-9
Mohall A-4
Mott E-3
Munich A-7
Napoleon E-6
Neche A-9
New England E-3

New Leipzig E-4
New Rockford C-7
New Salem E-4
New Town C-3
Northwood C-9
Oakes E-8
Park River B-9
Parshall C-4
Powers Lake A-3
Ray A-7
Richardton E-3
Rolette A-6
Rolla A-6

Rugby B-6
St. Thomas B-9
Scranton F-2
Sherwood B-3
Stanley B-3
Stanton D-4
Steele D-6
Strasburg F-6
Thompson C-9
Tioga B-2
Towner B-5
Turtle Lake C-5
Underwood D-5

Valley City D-8
Velva B-5
Wahpeton E-10
Wahalla A-8
Washburn D-5
Watford City C-2
West Fargo D-10
Westhope B-5
Williston B-2
Willow City B-5
Wilton D-5
Wishek E-6
Wyndmere E-9

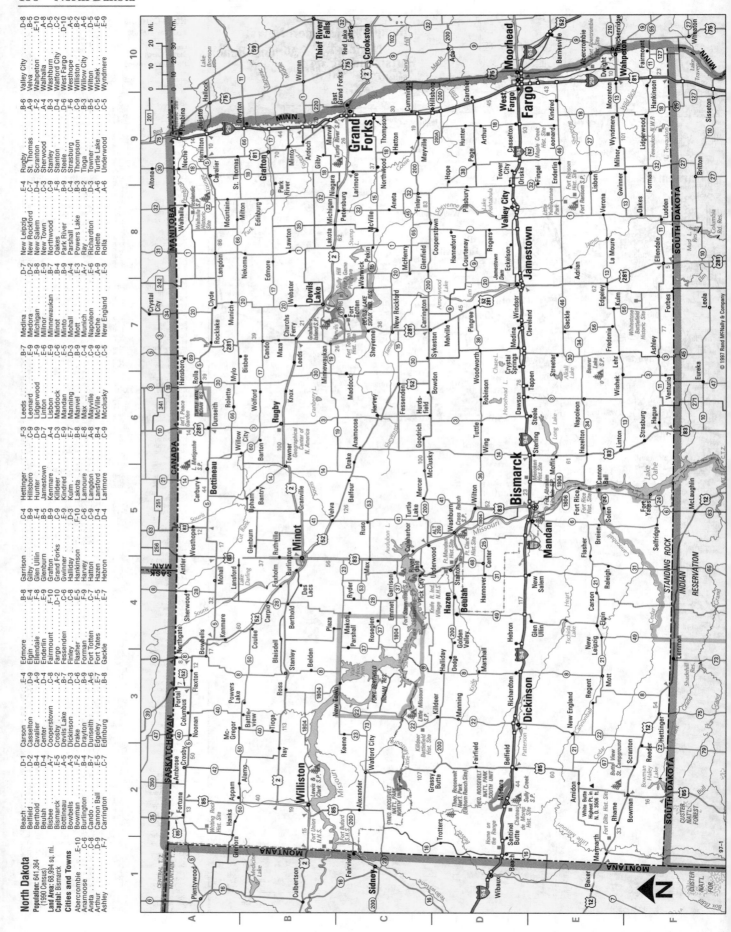

© 1997 Rand McNally & Company

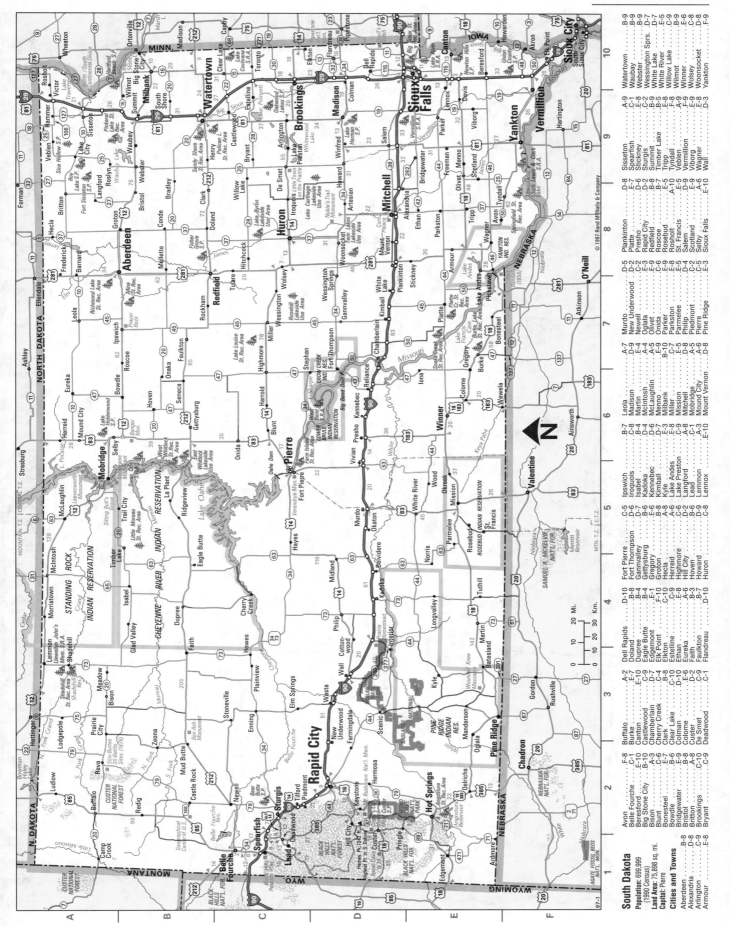

South Dakota
Population: 699,999
(1990 Census)
Land Area: 75,898 sq. mi.
Capital: Pierre

© 1997 Rand McNally & Company

97-1

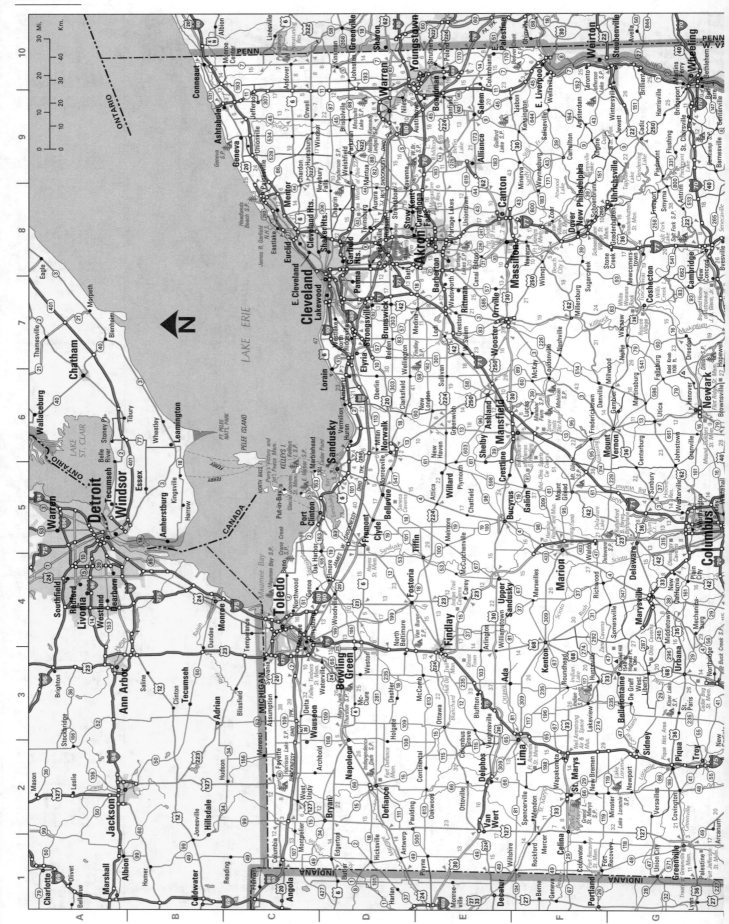

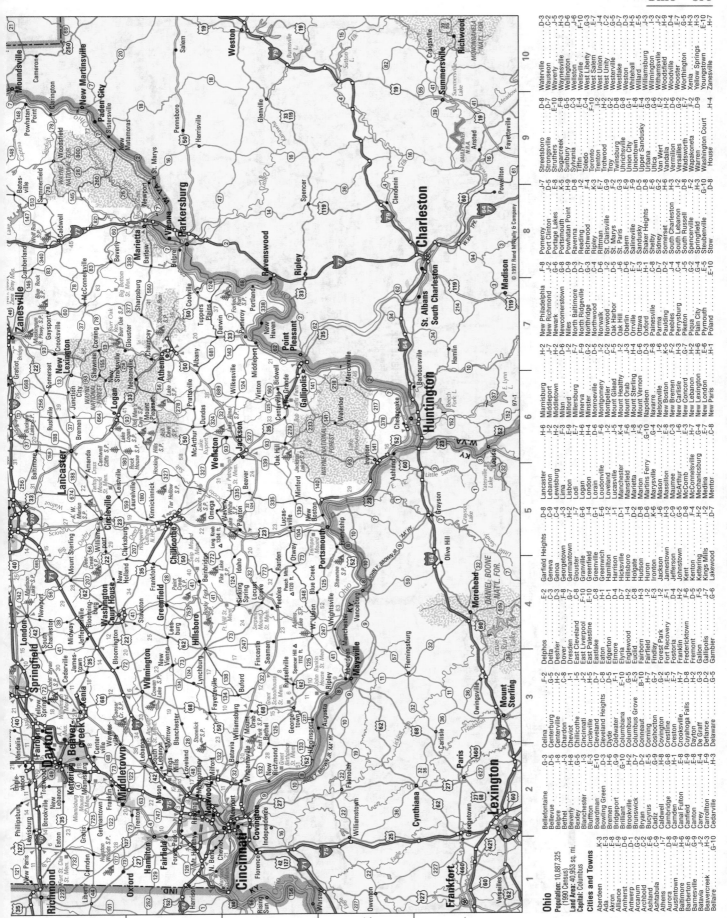

Ohio

Population: 10,887,325
(1990 Census)
Land Area: 40,953 sq. mi.
Capital: Columbus

Cities and Towns

Aberdeen	K-3
Ada	E-3
Akron	E-8
Alliance	E-9
Amherst	D-6
Antwerp	D-1
Arcanum	G-1
Archbold	C-2
Ashland	E-6
Ashtabula	C-9
Athens	J-7
Austintown	D-8
Aurora	D-8
Barberton	E-8
Barnesville	H-6
Batavia	J-2
Beavercreek	H-2
Bellaire	H-7

Bellefontaine	G-3
Bellevue	D-5
Belpre	J-8
Bethel	J-3
Bexley	H-4
Beverly	J-7
Blanchester	I-2
Bluffton	E-3
Boardman	E-10
Bowling Green	D-3
Bremen	H-6
Brookville	G-1
Brooklyn	D-7
Brunswick	D-7
Bryan	C-1
Bucyrus	E-5
Cadiz	G-8
Caldwell	H-6
Cambridge	G-7
Camden	H-1
Canal Fulton	E-8
Canfield	E-9
Canton	E-8
Carey	E-4
Carrollton	F-8
Cedarville	H-2

Celina	G-2
Centerburg	G-5
Centerville	H-1
Chardon	D-8
Cheviot	I-1
Chillicothe	H-5
Cincinnati	J-1
Circleville	H-5
Cleveland	D-7
Cleveland Heights	D-8
Clyde	D-5
Columbiana	E-9
Columbus	G-4
Columbus Grove	E-2
Conneaut	C-10
Corning	H-6
Coshocton	F-7
Covington	G-2
Crestline	E-5
Creston	E-7
Crooksville	H-6
Cuyahoga Falls	E-8
Dayton	H-2
De Graff	G-3
Defiance	D-2
Delaware	G-4

Delphos	F-2
Delta	D-3
Deshler	D-3
Dover	F-8
Dresden	G-6
East Cleveland	D-8
East Liverpool	F-10
East Palestine	E-10
Eastlake	D-8
Eaton	H-1
Elmore	D-4
Elyria	D-7
Englewood	H-1
Euclid	D-8
Fairborn	H-2
Fairfield	I-1
Findlay	E-3
Forest Park	I-1
Fort Recovery	G-1
Fostoria	E-4
Franklin	H-2
Fredericktown	F-5
Fremont	D-4
Gahanna	G-5
Galion	E-5
Gallipolis	J-7
Gambier	G-6

Garfield Heights	D-8
Geneva	C-9
Georgetown	J-3
Glouster	H-6
Greenfield	I-4
Greenville	G-1
Hamilton	I-1
Harrison	I-1
Hicksville	D-1
Hillsboro	I-3
Holgate	D-2
Hudson	E-8
Huron	D-6
Ironton	K-6
Jackson	J-6
Jamestown	H-2
Jefferson	C-9
Johnstown	G-5
Kenton	F-3
Kettering	H-2
Kings Mills	I-2
Lakewood	D-7

Lancaster	D-8
Lebanon	C-9
Lima	C-4
Lisbon	J-3
Lodi	I-7
Logan	G-4
London	I-4
Loudonville	I-2
Loveland	I-2
Lucasville	K-4
Manchester	I-3
Mansfield	I-4
Marietta	D-2
Marion	D-2
Martins Ferry	G-4
Mason	I-6
Massillon	D-5
Maumee	I-3
Mechanicsburg	I-3
Medina	D-7
Mentor	D-7

Miamisburg	H-6
Middleport	I-2
Middletown	F-3
Milan	E-7
Milford	I-9
Millersburg	F-7
Minerva	E-6
Monroe	G-5
Montgomery	I-2
Montpelier	I-2
Mount Gilead	F-5
Mount Healthy	I-2
Mount Orab	J-3
Mount Sterling	H-4
Mount Vernon	G-6
Napoleon	G-10
Navarre	I-2
Nelsonville	F-8
New Boston	K-5
New Carlisle	H-3
New Concord	I-2
New Lebanon	G-7
New Lexington	H-6
New London	E-6
New Paris	C-8

New Philadelphia	H-2
New Richmond	J-7
Newark	H-2
Newcomerstown	J-2
Niles	D-6
North Baltimore	E-7
North Ridgeville	F-7
Northridge	D-5
Northwood	C-4
Norwalk	D-6
Norwood	E-7
Oak Harbor	E-7
Oak Hill	D-6
Oberlin	J-3
Orville	H-4
Ottawa	H-1
Oxford	D-7
Painesville	I-6
Parma	D-7
Peebles	K-5
Pemberville	G-7
Perrysburg	C-4
Piketon	I-5
Piqua	G-2
Plain City	H-2
Plymouth	E-6
Poland	H-1

Pomeroy	F-8
Port Clinton	J-2
Portsmouth	G-8
Powhatan Point	D-3
Ravenna	C-4
Reading	I-1
Richwood	F-4
Ripley	D-6
Rittman	E-7
St. Clairsville	G-9
St. Marys	F-2
St. Paris	G-3
Salem	D-6
Salineville	E-3
Sandusky	E-7
Shaker Heights	H-1
Shelby	C-8
Sidney	D-7
South Charleston	C-4
South Lebanon	J-4
South Russell	J-5
Spencerville	D-8
Springfield	H-3
Steubenville	H-3
Stow	G-10

Streetsboro	J-7
Strongsville	D-5
Struthers	E-8
Sugarcreek	K-5
Swanton	H-9
Sylvania	C-3
Tiffin	E-4
Toledo	F-4
Toronto	E-7
Trenton	G-9
Trotwood	H-2
Troy	F-2
Twinsburg	G-9
Union City	E-7
Uniontown	H-5
Upper Sandusky	E-8
Urbana	E-4
Utica	G-3
Van Wert	E-2
Vandalia	H-2
Vermilion	G-7
Versailles	I-2
Wadsworth	D-8
Wapakoneta	E-7
Warren	H-3
Washington Court House	G-10
	D-8

Waterville	D-3
Wauseon	E-7
Waverly	F-8
Waynesville	C-3
Wellington	F-8
Wellston	E-4
Wellsville	C-4
West Liberty	F-10
West Salem	E-7
West Union	G-2
West Unity	G-9
Westerville	D-7
Westlake	H-5
Whitehall	E-8
Williamsburg	G-3
Willoughby	J-2
Willard	E-2
Wooster	E-7
Worthington	G-5
Xenia	E-7
Yellow Springs	H-3
Youngstown	D-9
Zanesville	H-7

© 1997 Rand McNally & Company

Oklahoma

Population: 3,157,604
(1990 Census)

Land Area: 68,679 sq. mi.

Capital: Oklahoma City

Cities and Towns

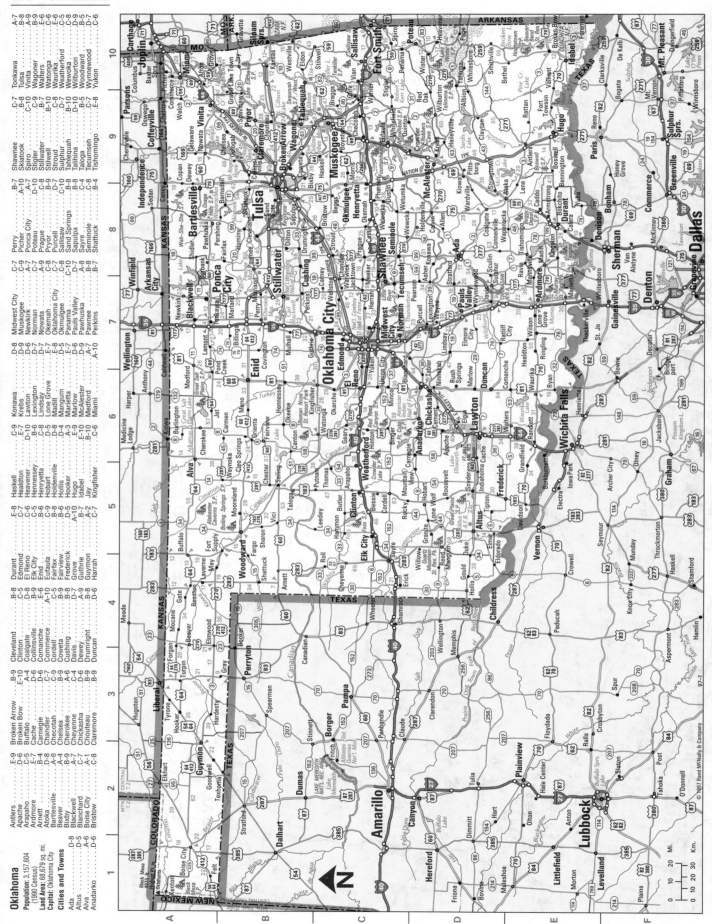

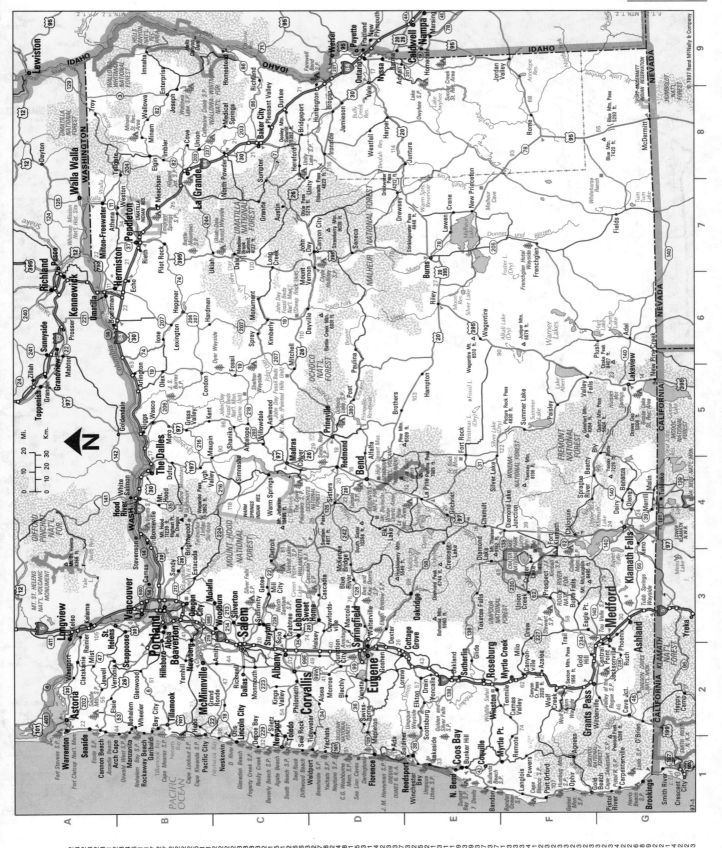

Oregon

Population: 2,853,733
(1990 Census)
Land Area: 96,003 sq. mi.
Capital: Salem

Cities and Towns

Albany	C-2
Aloha	B-3
Amity	C-2
Ashland	G-3
Astoria	A-2
Baker City	C-8
Bandon	E-1
Bay City	B-2
Beaverton	B-3
Bend	D-4
Boardman	B-6
Brookings	G-1
Bunker Hill	E-1
Burns	D-7
Cannon Beach	A-2
Canyon City	D-7
Canyonville	F-2
Cave Junction	G-2
Central Point	G-2
Clatskanie	B-5
Coos Bay	E-1
Coquille	E-1
Corvallis	C-2
Cottage Grove	D-2
Dallas	C-2
Drain	D-2
Eagle Point	G-2
Elgin	B-8
Enterprise	B-8
Eugene	D-2
Florence	D-1
Fossil	C-5
Gold Beach	F-1
Grants Pass	G-2
Heppner	C-6
Hermiston	B-6
Hillsboro	B-3
Hood River	B-4
Jacksonville	G-2
John Day	D-7
Joseph	B-8
Junction City	D-2
Klamath Falls	G-4
La Grande	B-8
Lakeside	E-1
Lakeview	G-5
Lebanon	C-3
Lincoln City	C-1
Madras	C-4
McMinnville	C-2
Medford	G-2
Mill City	C-3
Milton-Freewater	A-7
Molalla	C-3
Monmouth	C-2
Myrtle Creek	F-2
Myrtle Point	E-1
Newberg	C-3
Newport	C-1
North Bend	E-1
Nyssa	D-9
Oakridge	D-3
Ontario	D-9
Oregon City	B-3
Pendleton	B-7
Phoenix	G-2
Pilot Rock	B-7
Port Orford	F-1
Portland	B-3
Prospect	F-3
Rainier	A-3
Redmond	D-4
Reedsport	E-1
Roseburg	E-2
St. Helens	B-3
Salem	C-2
Sandy	B-3
Scappoose	B-3
Seaside	A-2
Silverton	C-3
Springfield	D-2
Stayton	C-3
Sublimity	C-3
Sutherlin	E-2
Sweet Home	C-3
The Dalles	B-4
Tillamook	B-2
Toledo	C-1
Umatilla	A-6
Union	B-8
Vale	C-9
Veneta	D-2
Vernonia	B-2
Waldport	C-1
Warm Springs	C-3
Warrenton	A-2
Weston	B-7
Woodburn	C-3

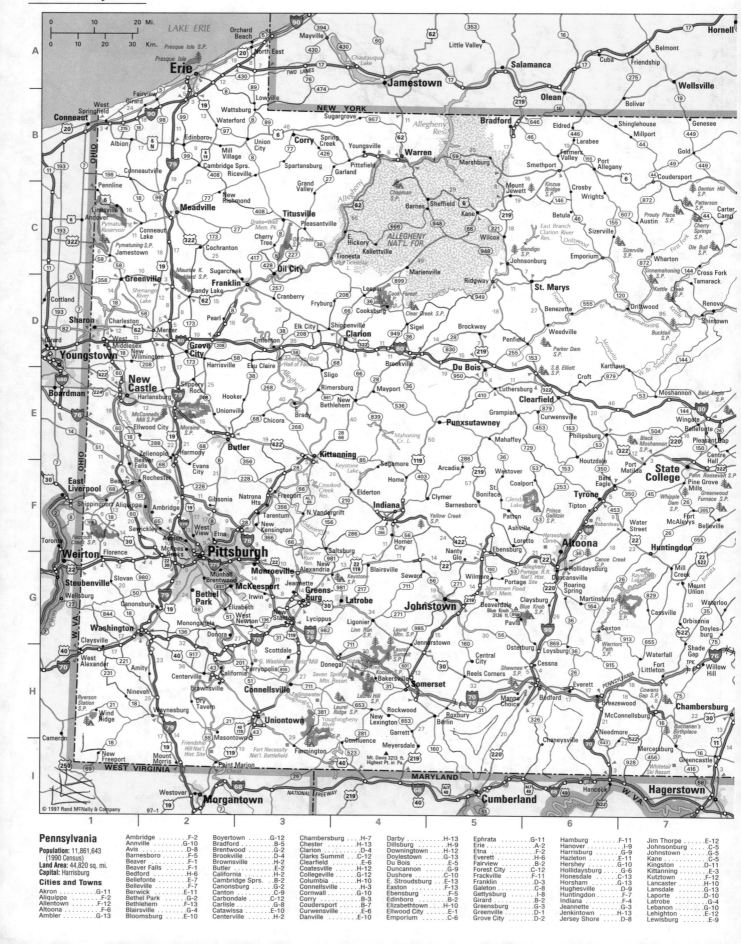

© 1997 Rand McNally & Company   97-1

Pennsylvania

Population: 11,861,643 (1990 Census)
Land Area: 44,820 sq. mi.
Capital: Harrisburg

Cities and Towns

Akron	G-11
Aliquippa	F-2
Allentown	F-12
Altoona	F-6
Ambler	G-13
Ambridge	F-2
Annville	G-10
Avis	D-8
Barnesboro	F-5
Beaver	F-2
Beaver Falls	F-1
Bedford	H-6
Bellefonte	E-7
Belleville	F-7
Berwick	E-11
Bethel Park	G-2
Bethlehem	F-13
Blairsville	G-4
Bloomsburg	E-10
Boyertown	G-12
Bradford	B-5
Brentwood	G-2
Brookville	D-4
Brownsville	H-2
Butler	E-2
California	H-2
Cambridge Sprs.	B-2
Canonsburg	G-2
Canton	C-9
Carbondale	C-12
Carlisle	G-8
Catawissa	E-10
Centerville	H-2
Chambersburg	H-7
Chester	H-13
Clarion	D-4
Clarks Summit	C-12
Clearfield	E-6
Coatesville	H-12
Collegeville	G-12
Columbia	H-10
Connellsville	H-3
Cornwall	G-10
Corry	B-3
Coudersport	B-7
Curwensville	E-6
Danville	E-10
Darby	H-13
Dillsburg	H-9
Downingtown	H-12
Doylestown	G-13
Du Bois	E-5
Duncannon	G-9
Dushore	C-10
E. Stroudsburg	E-13
Easton	F-13
Ebensburg	F-5
Edinboro	B-2
Elizabethtown	H-10
Ellwood City	E-1
Emporium	C-6
Ephrata	G-11
Erie	A-2
Etna	F-2
Everett	H-6
Fairview	B-2
Forest City	C-12
Frackville	F-11
Franklin	D-3
Galeton	C-8
Gettysburg	I-8
Girard	B-2
Greensburg	G-3
Greenville	D-1
Grove City	D-2
Hamburg	F-11
Hanover	I-9
Harrisburg	H-9
Hazleton	E-11
Hershey	G-10
Hollidaysburg	G-6
Honesdale	C-13
Horsham	G-13
Hughesville	D-9
Huntingdon	F-7
Indiana	F-4
Jeannette	G-3
Jenkintown	H-13
Jersey Shore	D-8
Jim Thorpe	E-12
Johnsonburg	C-5
Johnstown	G-5
Kane	C-5
Kingston	D-11
Kittanning	E-3
Kutztown	F-12
Lancaster	H-10
Lansdale	G-13
Laporte	D-10
Latrobe	G-4
Lebanon	G-10
Lehighton	E-12
Lewisburg	E-9

390 to 15 to 83 to YORK to 4
Wmsport Harrisburg

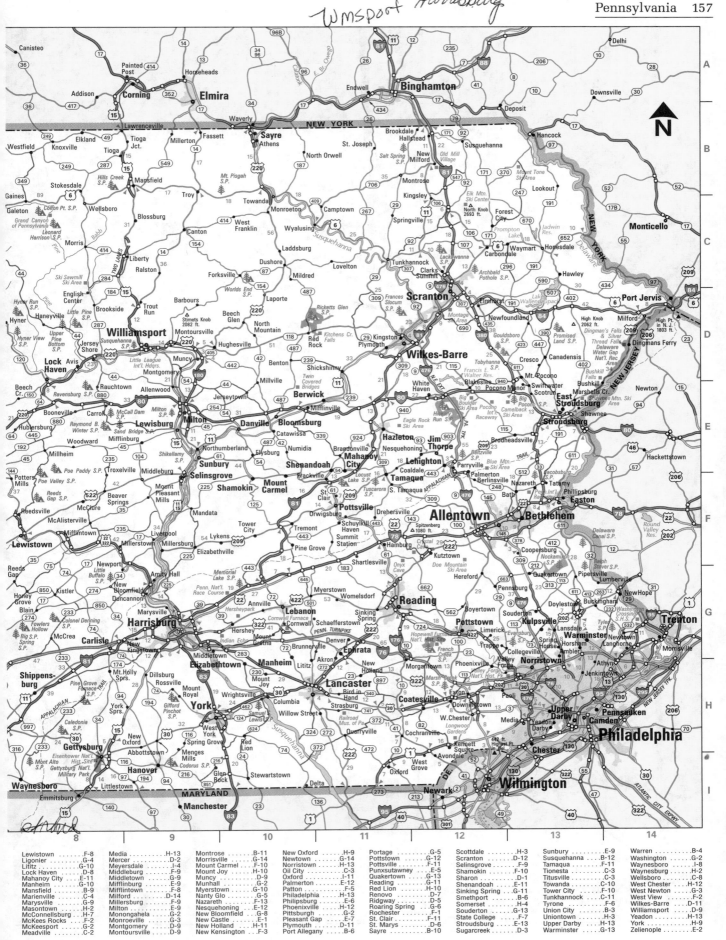

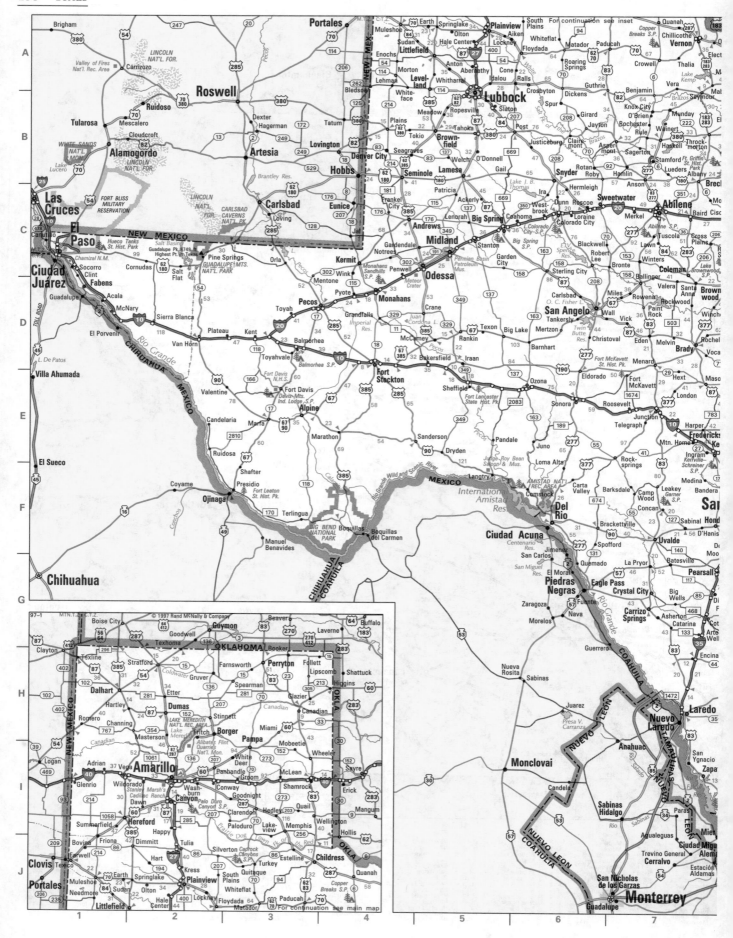

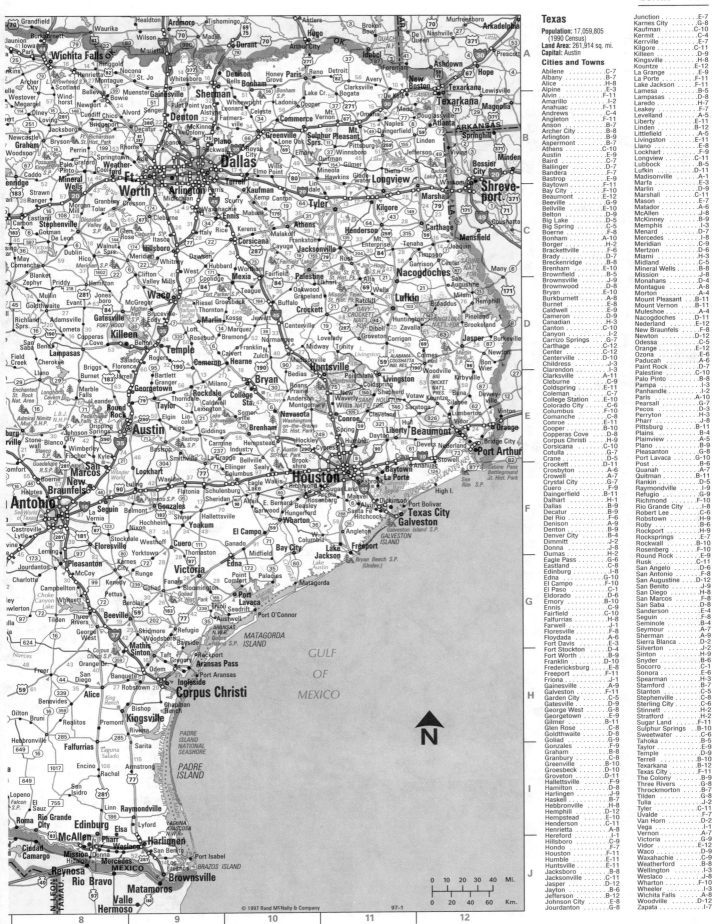

Texas

Population: 17,059,805
(1990 Census)
Land Area: 261,914 sq. mi.
Capital: Austin

Cities and Towns

97-1

0 10 20 30 40 Mi.

0 20 40 60 Km.

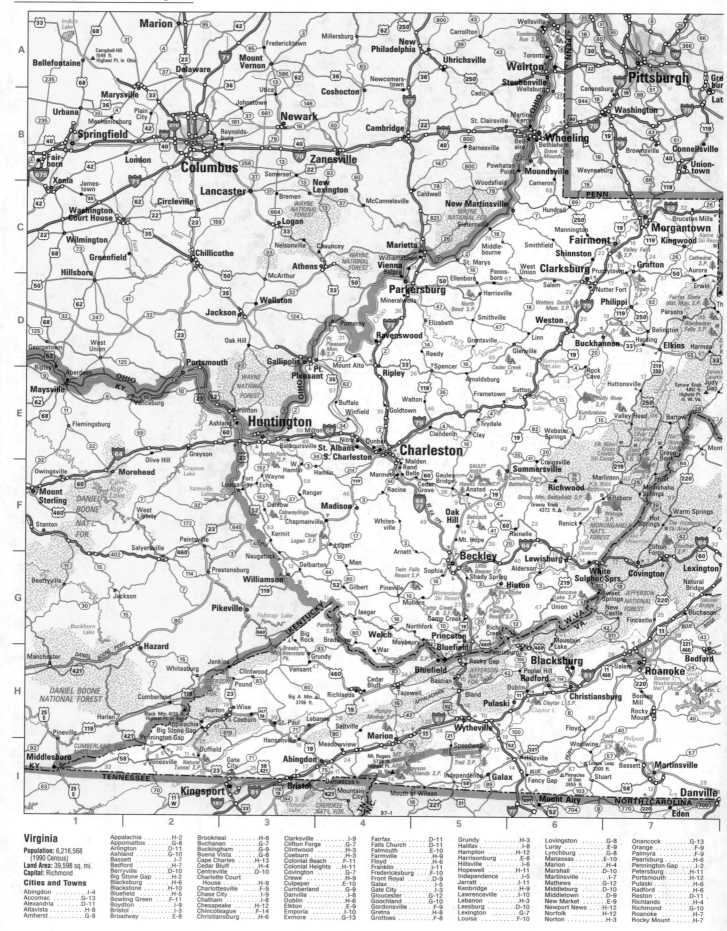

Virginia

Population: 6,216,568
(1990 Census)
Land Area: 39,598 sq. mi.
Capital: Richmond

Cities and Towns

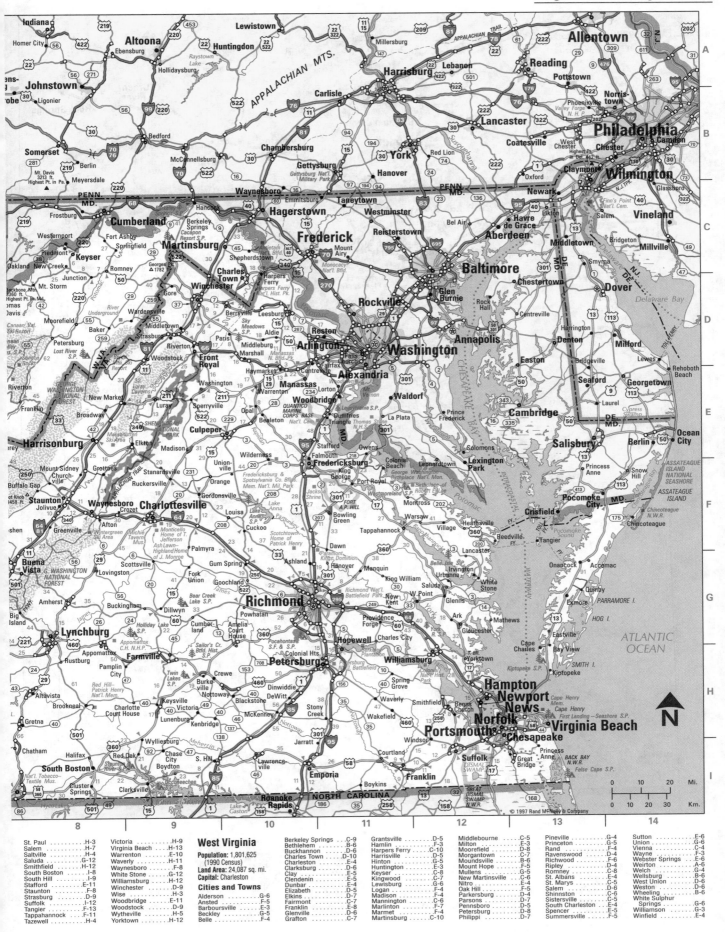

Utah

Population: 1,727,784 (1990 Census)
Land Area: 82,168 sq. mi.
Capital: Salt Lake City

Cities and Towns

© 1997 Rand McNally & Company

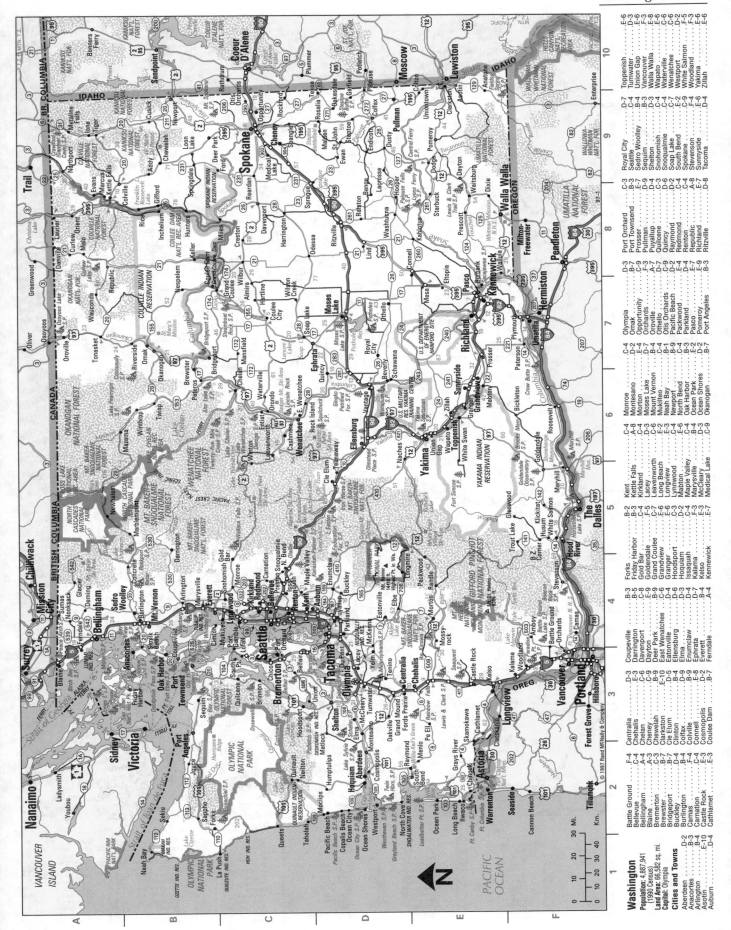

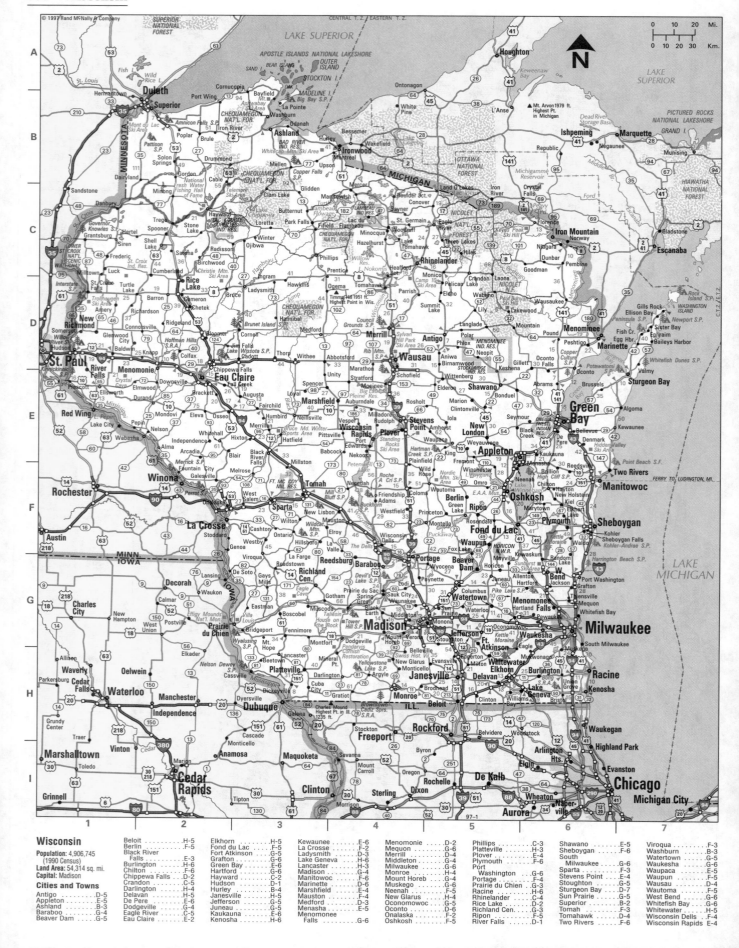

© 1997 Rand McNally & Company

Wisconsin

Population: 4,906,745 (1990 Census)
Land Area: 54,314 sq. mi.
Capital: Madison

Cities and Towns

Antigo	D-5
Appleton	E-5
Ashland	B-3
Baraboo	G-4
Beaver Dam	G-5

Beloit	H-5
Berlin	F-5
Black River Falls	E-3
Burlington	H-6
Chilton	F-6
Chippewa Falls	D-2
Crandon	C-5
Darlington	H-4
Delavan	H-5
Dodgeville	G-4
Eagle River	C-5
Eau Claire	E-2

Elkhorn	H-5
Fond du Lac	F-5
Fort Atkinson	G-5
Green Bay	E-6
Hartford	G-6
Hayward	C-2
Hudson	D-1
Janesville	H-5
Jefferson	G-5
Juneau	G-5
Kaukauna	E-6
Kenosha	H-6

Kewaunee	E-6
La Crosse	F-2
Ladysmith	D-3
Lake Geneva	H-6
Lancaster	H-3
Madison	G-4
Manitowoc	F-6
Marinette	D-6
Marshfield	E-4
Mauston	F-4
Medford	D-3
Menasha	E-5
Menomonee Falls	G-6

Menomonie	D-2
Mequon	G-6
Merrill	D-4
Middleton	G-4
Milwaukee	G-6
Monroe	H-4
Mount Horeb	G-4
Muskego	G-6
Neenah	F-5
New Glarus	H-4
Oconomowoc	G-5
Oconto	D-6
Onalaska	F-2
Oshkosh	F-5

Phillips	C-3
Platteville	H-3
Plover	E-4
Plymouth	F-6
Port Washington	G-6
Portage	G-4
Prairie du Chien	G-3
Racine	H-6
Rhinelander	C-4
Rice Lake	D-2
Richland Cen.	G-3
Ripon	F-5
River Falls	D-1

Shawano	E-5
Sheboygan	F-6
South Milwaukee	G-6
Sparta	F-3
Stevens Point	E-4
Stoughton	G-5
Sturgeon Bay	D-7
Sun Prairie	G-5
Superior	B-2
Tomah	F-3
Tomahawk	D-4
Two Rivers	F-6

Viroqua	F-3
Washburn	B-3
Watertown	G-5
Waukesha	G-6
Waupaca	E-5
Waupun	F-5
Wausau	D-4
Wautoma	E-5
West Bend	G-6
Whitefish Bay	G-6
Whitewater	H-5
Wisconsin Dells	F-4
Wisconsin Rapids	E-4

Wyoming

Population: 455,975 (1990 Census)
Land Area: 97,105 sq. mi.
Capital: Cheyenne

Cities and Towns

Afton D-1
Albin F-9
Alpine C-1
Alva G-5
Baggs D-6
Bairoil D-6
Basin B-4
Bar Nunn C-6
Big Horn A-6
Big Piney D-2
Bondurant C-2
Buffalo B-6
Burlington B-4
Burns F-9
Carpenter F-9
Casper C-6
Centennial E-7
Cheyenne F-8
Chugwater E-8
Clearmont A-6
Cody A-4
Cokeville D-1
Daniel C-2
Dayton A-5
Deaver A-4
Devils Tower A-8
Diamondville D-1
Douglas D-7
Dubois C-2
Eden D-3
Edgerton C-6
Elk Mountain E-6
Emblem B-4
Evanston E-1
Farson D-3
Fort Bridger E-2
Fort Laramie E-8
Fort Washakie C-3
Freedom C-1
Gillette A-7
Glendo D-8
Glenrock D-7
Granger E-2
Green River E-3
Greybull B-4
Guernsey D-8
Hanna D-6
Horse Creek E-8
Hudson C-4
Hulett A-8
Hyattville B-5
Jackson C-1
Jeffrey City D-5
Kaycee C-6
Kemmerer D-1
Kinnear C-3
La Barge D-2
Lagrange F-9
Lance Creek D-8
Lander D-4
Laramie E-7
Linch C-6
Lingle E-9
Lovell A-4
Lusk D-9
Lyman E-2
Manville D-8
Marbleton D-2
Medicine Bow E-6
Meeteetse B-4
Midwest C-6
Moorcroft A-8
Moose C-1
Mountain View E-2
Newcastle B-8
Opal D-2
Osage B-8
Pavillion C-3
Pine Bluffs F-9
Pinedale C-2
Powell A-4
Ranchester A-5
Rawlins D-6
Riverton C-4
Rock River E-7
Rock Springs D-3
Saratoga E-6
Sheridan A-6
Shoshoni C-4
Sinclair D-6
Smoot D-1
Superior D-4
Thayne C-1
Thermopolis B-4
Torrington E-9
Teton Village C-1
Wamsutter D-5
Wheatland E-8
Worland B-5
Wright B-6
Yellowstone National
  Park A-2

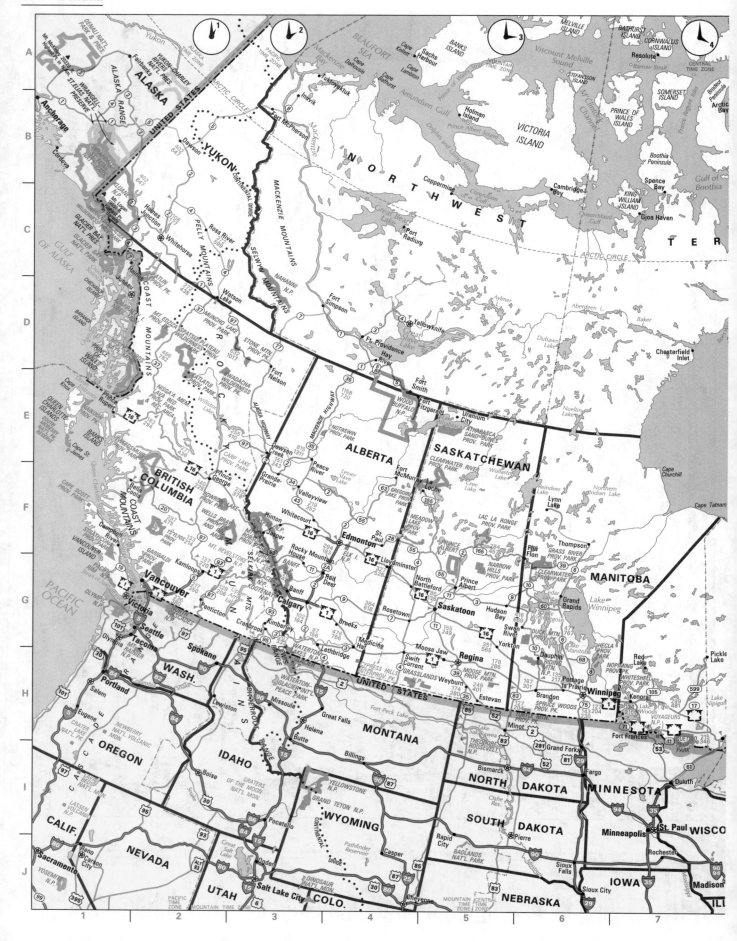

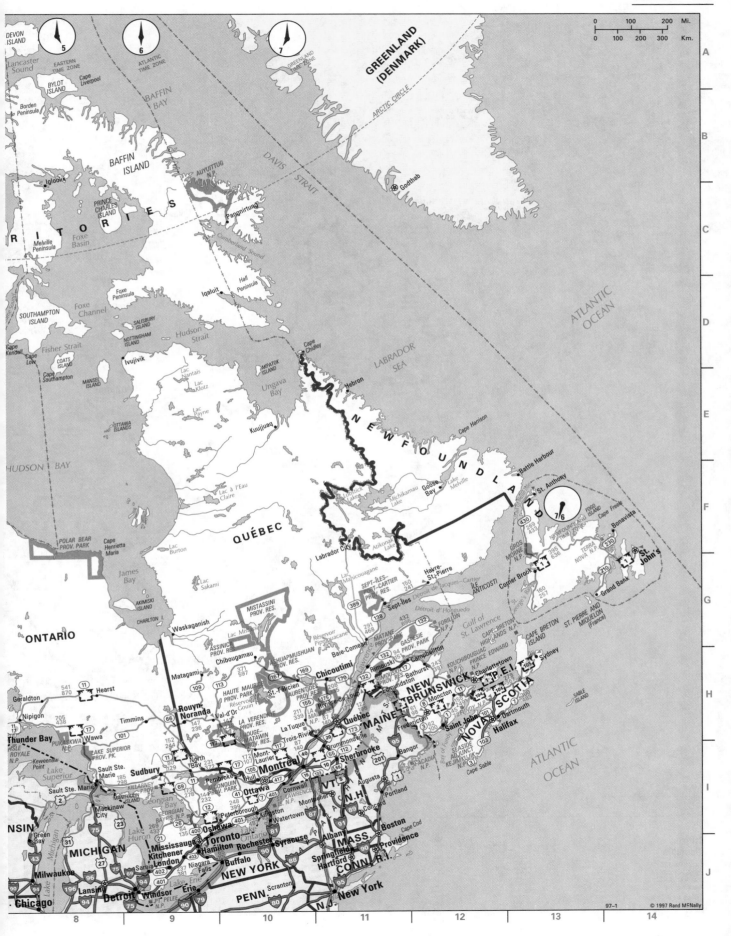

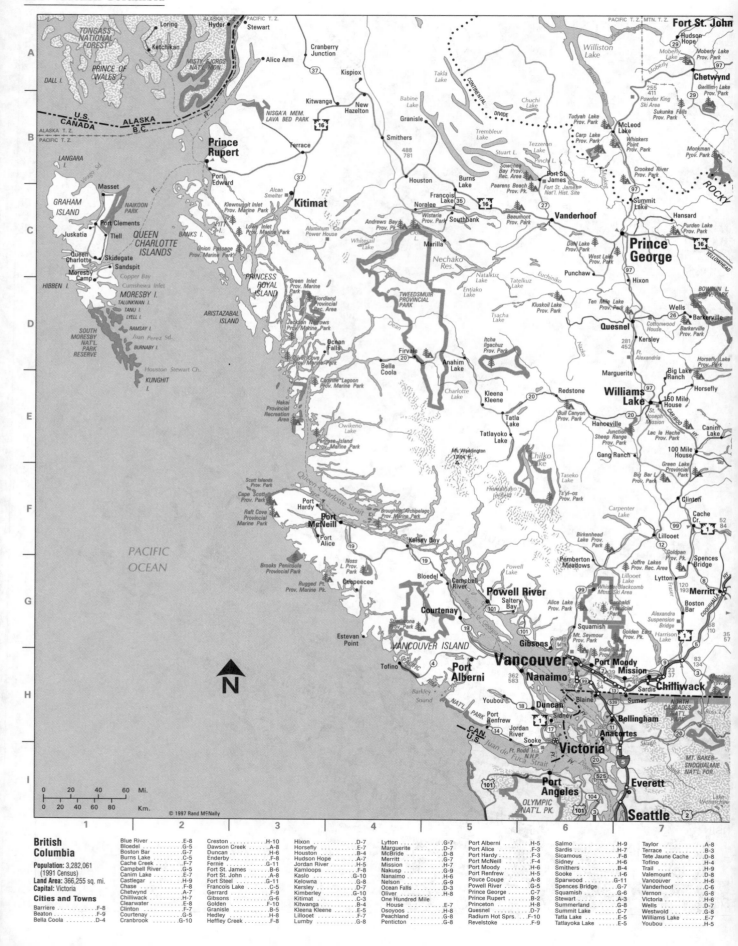

N

British Columbia

Population: 3,282,061 (1991 Census)
Land Area: 366,255 sq. mi.
Capital: Victoria

Cities and Towns

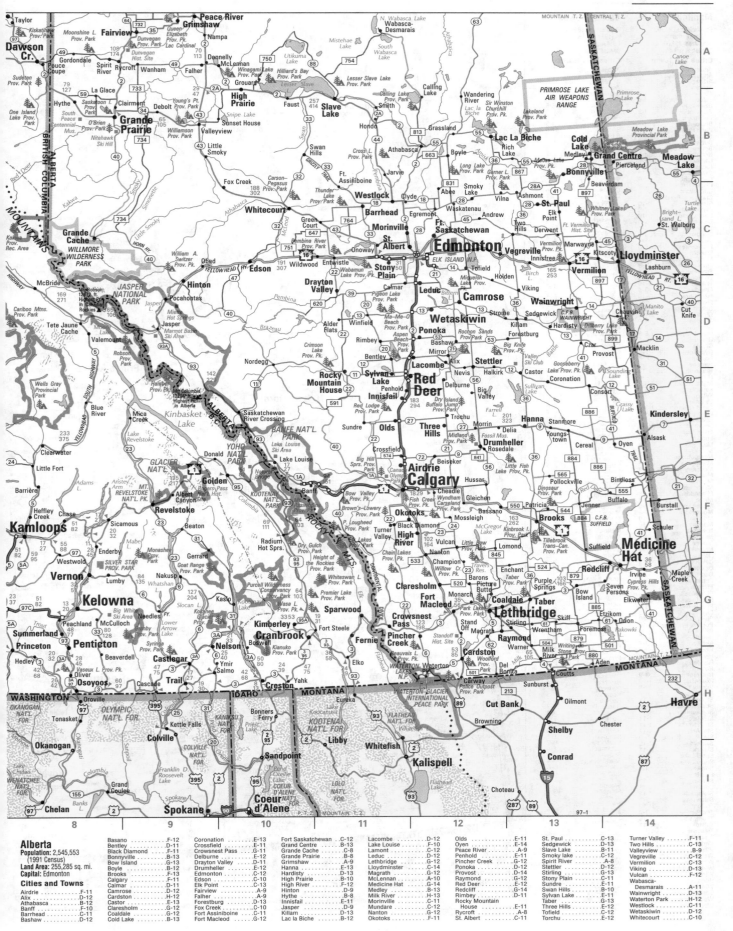

Manitoba

Population: 1,091,942
(1991 Census)
Land Area: 251,000 sq. mi.
Capital: Winnipeg

Cities and Towns

Saskatchewan

Population: 988,928
(1991 Census)
Land Area: 251,700 sq. mi.
Capital: Regina

Cities and Towns

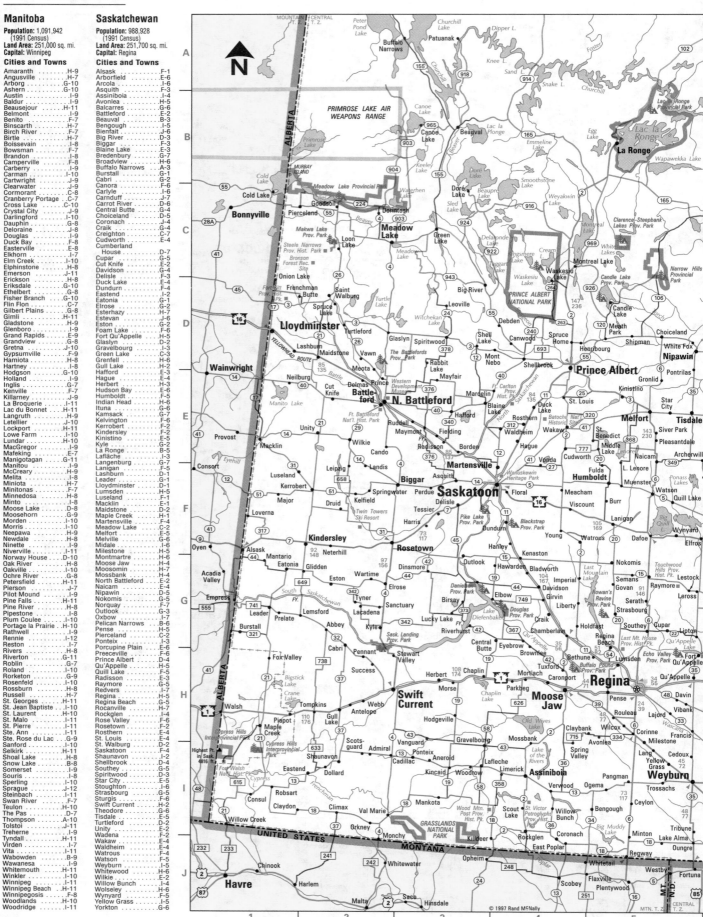

© 1997 Rand McNally

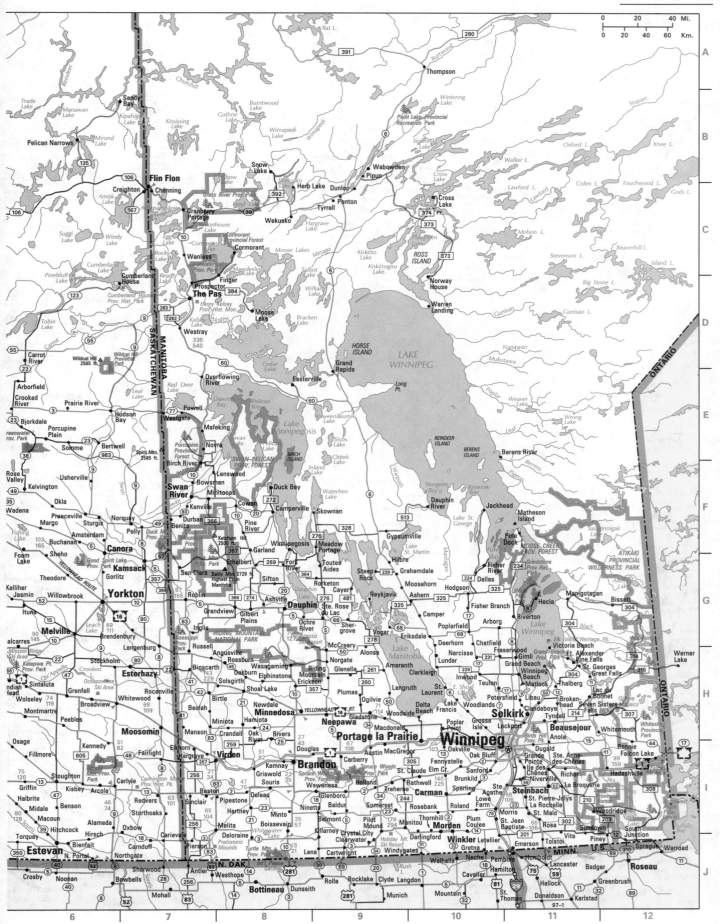

For continuation see map at lower right

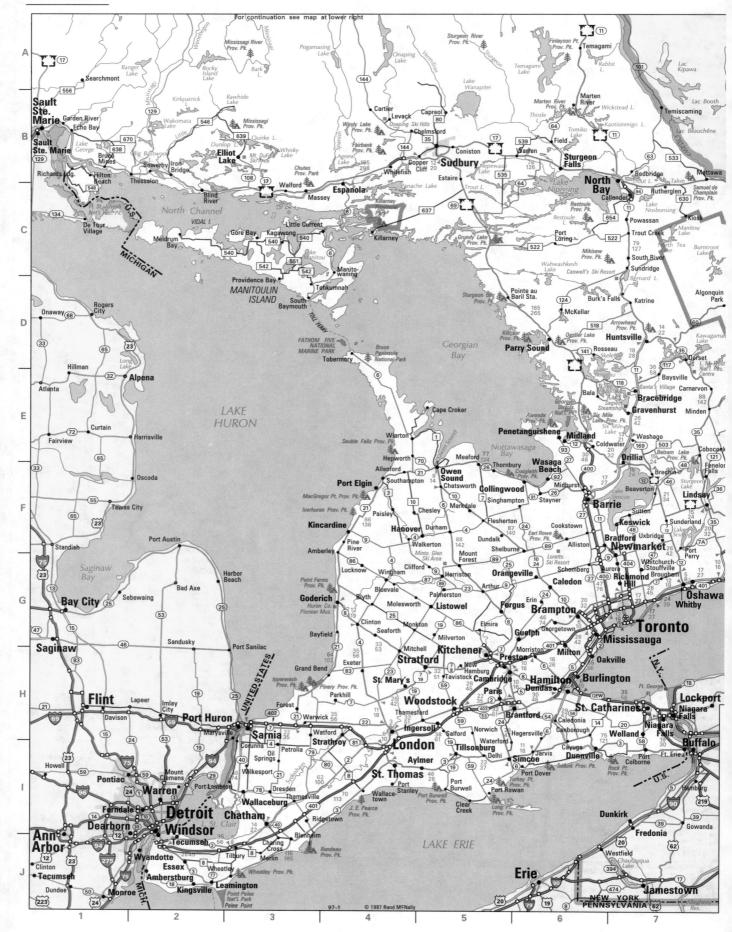

97-1   © 1997 Rand McNally

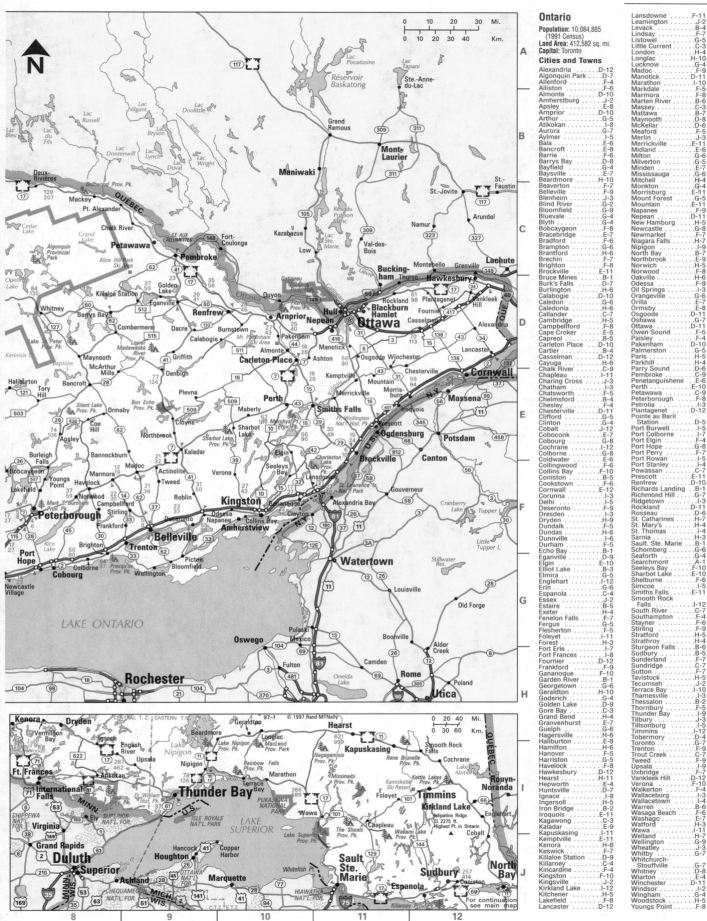

Ontario

Population: 10,084,885
(1991 Census)
Land Area: 412,582 sq. mi.
Capital: Toronto

Cities and Towns

Québec

Population: 6,895,963
(1991 Census)
Land Area: 594,860 sq. mi.
Capital: Québec

Cities and Towns

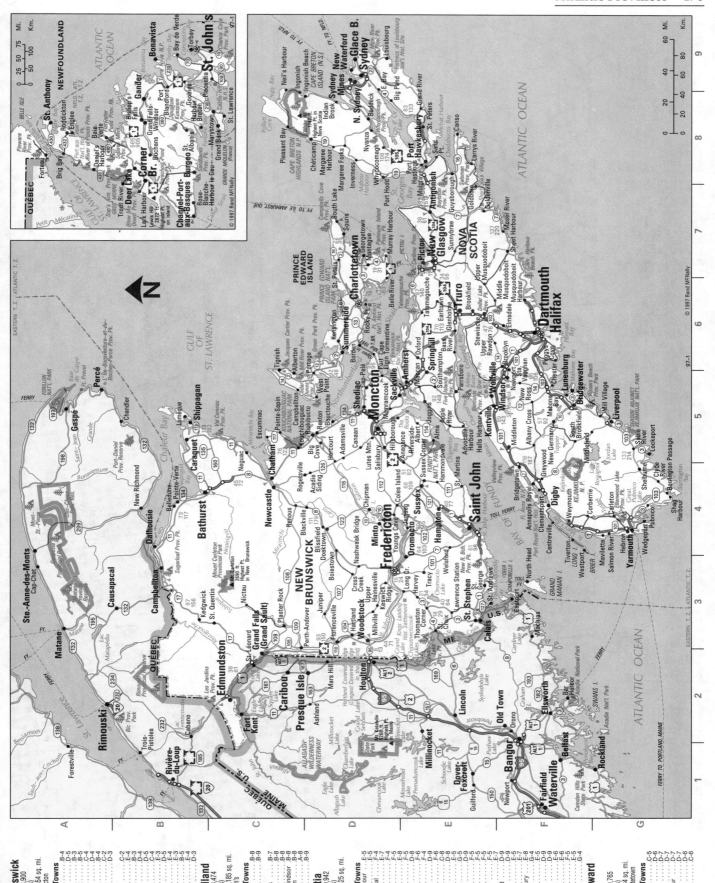

Mexico

Population: 67,395,826
Land Area: 761,605 sq. mi.
Capital: Mexico City

Cities and Towns

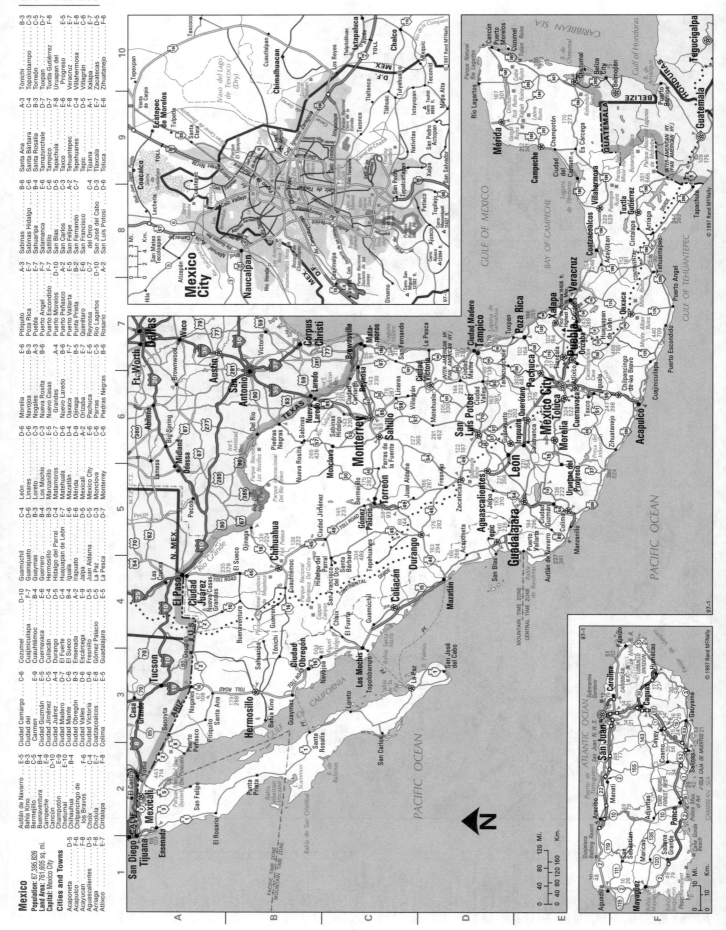

Doing Business in Canada

The provisions of the North American Free Trade Agreement (NAFTA) make commerce across the U.S./Canada border less restrictive than even before. The 1995 signing of the "open skies" agreement between the two countries spurred the creation of new air routes and more direct flights between destinations on both sides of the border.

In general, Canada is probably more user-friendly to Americans doing business there than any other "foreign" country. In many ways, Canada is hardly "foreign" at all. The language is the same for the most part (English is widely spoken in French-speaking Quebec) and the American traveler finds hotel, restaurant and car rental chains with familiar names. Even the time zones generally correspond to those south of the border.

Americans doing business in Canada should be aware that there are real, though subtle, differences between the two countries. In many cases, they relate to distinctions in attitude, philosophy, lifestyle and mores.

Canadians can be fiercely nationalistic, ready to protect their identity and wary of being culturally assimilated by their powerful next-door neighbor. Canadians have a high regard for public services. They take pride in their educational system, are respectful of police and generally are intolerant of public littering and vandalism.

A knowledge of basic Canadian geography will stand a visitor in good stead, as will the recognition of prominent Canadian politicians and an understanding of important current issues.

Canadians may be less inclined than Americans to conduct business in a social setting, particularly with the escalation in recent years (due in part to an increase in taxes) of the cost of dining out. (One exception might be a business-related visit to a sporting event; Canadians tend to be enthusiastic sports fans, particularly of professional hockey and baseball.)

Airlines: The two major Canadian carriers are Air Canada 800/776-3000 and Canadian Airlines 800/426-7000 which operate to major U.S. cities and between cities within Canada. American, Delta, Northwest, United and USAir all operate between the U.S. and Canada.

Rail: VIA Rail Canada 800/561-3949 is Canada's passenger-train network. Popular with business travelers are the express trains between Toronto and Montreal (four hours).

Hotels: Major hotel chains such as Hilton, Sheraton, Westin, Inter-Continental and Holiday Inn operate hotels in all major cities in Canada. Three major Canadian chains are: Canadian Pacific Hotels, 800/441-1414; Four Seasons Hotels, 800/332-3442; and Delta Hotels, 800/877-1133.

Toronto, Montreal and Vancouver are major convention cities and frequently "book up." Be sure to make reservations well in advance.

Entry Requirements: Neither passports nor visas are required for Americans crossing into Canada. Travelers need only carry an acceptable form of identification, such as a birth certificate or voter's registration card, in combination with a photo ID such as a driver's license. It is necessary to declare business materials that are carried into Canada but most people have no trouble bringing in non-commercial quantities of such items as product literature, technical manuals, service booklets, etc., providing they have no commercial value and are not subject to tax or duty.

Currency: Banks are the best choice for exchanging U.S. money; ATMs are readily available.

Credit Cards: Major U.S. credit cards are accepted throughout Canada. Telephone calling cards are also widely accepted.

Sales Tax: Taxes can escalate the cost of a business trip. Federal tax on goods and services is 7%. In addition, most provinces levy an additional tax which can run as high as 12%.

GST Refunds: The federal goods and services tax (GST) is rebatable to visitors including the GST portion of hotel bills. Applications are available from Summerside Tax Center Vistor Rebate Program, 275 Pope Road, Summerside, P.E.I. C1N 6C6, Canada 902/432-5608. Original receipts must accompany the claim. (Note: The GST paid on car rentals and restaurant meals is not rebatable.)

Business/Banking Hours: Hours in Canada are similar to those in the United States with some regional differences.

Car Rentals: Avis, Budget and Hertz all do business in Canada. Tilden Interrent is the largest Canadian car rental firm and reservations from the U.S. can be made through their National Rental affiliate at 800/227-7368.

Driving: Canada uses the metric system. Speed limits are posted in kilometers and gasoline is sold in liters. A U.S. driver's license is valid. Seat belts are mandatory.

Language Differences: Essentially, a knowledge of the French language is not necessary in Canada, even when doing business in French-speaking Québec. However, translation services may be necessary for drafting business documents such as contracts and sales and distribution agreements.

Doing Business In Mexico

The North American Free Trade Agreement (NAFTA) is bringing new business travelers to Mexico in significant numbers. While doing business in Mexico may seem similar — on the surface — to operating in the United States, it is, in truth, quite different.

In Mexico, all decisions are made by the top executive of the company. If he or she is not available, there will be no decision. Cultivate relationships with any and all subordinates who can get you access to the decision-maker but do not expect anything more from them than information and access.

Business protocol in Mexico is formal. Because titles are important in Mexico, businesspeople should address everyone formally, as a sign of respect, until the individual asks to be referred to by his or her first name. A common business title is *Licenciado* (meaning college graduate). Business dress for both men and women should be tailored and conservative.

In Mexico, a great deal of importance is placed on the development of a business relationship. There may be several business meetings held before the Mexicans decide if they want to do business with a particular person. Aggressive sales tactics, the "hard sell" approach, usually fail.

The most successful meetings are held over long luncheon or dinner gatherings. Always suggest meal-time appointments and be prepared to spend the afternoon or the evening. There will be little talk of business or politics; the Mexicans prefer to relax and talk of family and friends. Do not be discouraged; there is time for the discussion of business details, after lunch and after they have "taken your measure" and decided if they want to do business with you. "Power breakfasts" are beginning to catch on in Mexico City but are not universally popular.

The family is the centerpiece of life in Mexico and it is an honor to be invited into the home of your host, especially on Sunday or for a family celebration. It's customary to bring a gift for the hostess; good liquor or wine is always acceptable. Do not take offense when the host does not open a gift right away; this is considered rude in Mexico where gifts are regarded as a personal matter and not for public display.

The Mexican concentration on family and friends is at the root of the "manana" syndrome with drives many American businesspeople to distraction. It is important to understand the Mexicans have different priorities than their American counterparts. Business gets done but in a more leisurely fashion. Be prepared to adapt your methods and build all deadlines with "manana" in mind.

Airlines: The two major Mexican carriers are Aeromexico (800/237-6639) and Mexicana Airlines 800/531-7921, which operate to some U.S. cities and between cities within Mexico. American, Continental, Delta and USAir fly U.S.-Mexico routes.

Hotels: Major U.S. hotel chains including Sheraton, Hyatt, Westin and Radisson are represented in larger cities. Business-travel oriented Mexico chains include Fiesta Americana 800/343-7821, Camino Real 800/722-6466 and Continental Plaza Hotels 800/882-6684.

Car Rentals: Hertz, Avis and Budget all do business in Mexico.

Driving: A U.S. driver's license is valid but U.S. insurance is not. You must purchase special Mexican insurance coverage. A new system of four-lane toll roads helps cut driving time between major cities but these roads are expensive by U.S. standards.

Ground Travel: In the major business centers of Mexico City, Guadalajara and Monterrey, traffic can be horrendous at most times of the day. Plenty of time should be allowed for travel to meetings. In Mexico City, a centrally-located hotel is a must.

Entry Requirements: Since signing NAFTA, Mexico has done away with the more complicated business visas formerly required. Business travelers only need a tourist card and proof of U.S. citizenship.

Business/Banking Hours: Most Mexican businesses operate from 10 a.m. to 1 or 2 p.m. with two hours off for lunch; businesses re-open from 4 p.m. to 7 p.m. Banks are generally open from 9 a.m. - 1:30 p.m.

Currency: Exchange booths give the best rates when exchanging U.S. dollars for Mexican pesos; the peso can be subject of volatile fluctuations. ATMs are located in major cities.

Credit Cards: Major U.S. credit cards are accepted in many hotels and restaurants and generally yield the most favorable exchange rates. Using telephone calling cards is usually cheaper than paying telephone surcharges for calls made from hotel rooms. Telephone service can be slow and/or spotty.

Sales Tax: The Value Added Tax (VAT) is 15%. In addition, there's an airport departure tax for $12 for international flights; domestic flights are assessed a local tax.

Language Differences: Spanish is the official language of Mexico and while many Mexicans have some understanding of English, it is best to use an interpreter for business negotiations.

Doing Business In Europe

The concept of the "global village" is taking shape more rapidly in Europe than anywhere else in the business world. The borders between European countries are evaporating as the nations continue the momentum caused by the end of the Cold War and the re-unification of Germany. Essentially, a "United States of Europe" is forming.

Known originally as the European Community (EC), one of the primary goals of today's European Union, or EU, is to establish a single marketplace, where goods and services can be freely exchanged, and where business is not encumbered by government intervention.

Because it's competing with centuries-old traditions, the concept still has many wrinkles to iron out but, essentially, it's working. Membership in the EU is continuing to expand and a number of EU countries have already dismantled border controls, enabling travelers to enter without showing their passports. One of the most controversial issues facing unification is money. It is hoped that by the year 2000, a standardized single currency, known as "ecu" (European Currency Unit), and a regional central bank debut.

Much of the "buzz" in the European business community centers on the trans-national standardization movement which has impacted the manufacturing and government procurement side as well. Today, companies wishing to sell and market their products will first have to certify them according to "ISO-9000" standards, the European-wide system of quality assurance.

Europeans are far more conservative and formal in their business dealings than their North American counterparts. To make a good impression, dress conservatively, speak properly and "tone down" your gestures and attitudes.

Meetings should be scheduled and reconfirmed from three to four weeks in advance. Arrive promptly and shake hands with everyone, including secretaries, but acknowledge senior officers first. Pay close attention to titles; Europeans follow a strict chain-of-command in business. Never use someone's first name until you're invited to do so.

Prepare for some generic small talk before getting to the meeting's agenda. Take careful notes, as Europeans tend to favor precision in their business dealings. Following the meeting, send a letter re-stating your discussion and points of agreement.

Business hours vary in many countries, but a safe bet is to schedule meetings between 8 a.m. and noon, or 2 and 5 p.m. As a rule, meetings are conducted more slowly than in North America.

Travel in Europe is generally a high quality experience because hospitality and service standards meet and frequently exceed those experienced in North America.

Airlines: All the major U.S. airlines, including American, Delta, and United, have greatly expanded service between the U.S. and Europe in recent years. There are also major European carriers which offer service between the U.S. and Europe and between European cities, including: Air France 800/237-2747; British Airways 800/247-9297; KLM Royal Dutch Airlines 800/374-7747; Lufthansa German Airlines 800/645-3880; Scandinavian Airlines 800/221-2350; and Swissair 800/221-4750.

Ground Transportation: Rail service is much more extensive and frequent in Europe than in the United States and is an excellent alternative for travel between cities within Europe.

Taxis are readily available, although expensive by U.S. standards. Most major European cities, including London and Paris, have excellent subway systems, often with connecting service to airports.

Hotels: European countries offer a wide range of quality hotels in a number of price categories. Major U.S. hotel companies, including Hilton Hotels, Holiday Inns, Hyatt Hotels, Marriott Hotels and Sheraton Hotels, have properties throughout Europe. Note: Hotel rooms are generally small by U.S. standards and if you book a "single" room, expect a twin-sized bed.

Entry Requirements: A U.S. passport is required for entry to all European countries.

Currency: Banks are the most convenient place for exchanging money.

Credit Cards: All major U.S. credit cards are widely accepted in most European countries.

Car Rentals: The major U.S. chains all have affiliates in Europe. The major cities of Europe suffer the same traffic congestion as American cities and "demon" speeds prevail on superhighways such as the autobahn. If you rent a car, you will need an International Driver's License.

Taxes/Tipping: Value Added Taxes are widely assessed throughout Europe and can push travel costs up by as much as 18 percent. Refund policies vary from country to country.

Languages: English is becoming the universal language of business but a working knowledge of French, Spanish or German can be a big help. If possible, carry business cards with both English and the language of the country where you are doing business. Most major hotels can provide translation services for business proposals and correspondence.

Doing Business in Asia

It is easier to do business in Asia today than it was a decade ago but most Americans will still find it a challenging process. Each of the more than 20 countries comprising Asia holds dear its own customs which, if breached, can easily blow a business deal or relationship, regardless of its importance or longevity.

The differing levels of economic development throughout Asia can be confusing for Americans who are used to a McDonalds on every corner and a dial tone at the other end of every telephone. For example, Vietnam is building its first five-star hotels while Hong Kong is tearing down its revered Hilton to make way for commercial buildings. Manila lacks the resources to guarantee electricity 24 hours a day while everything runs around the clock in Tokyo.

However, there are a couple of pointers that work in every country. First, be patient. Bring your common sense and leave your expectations at home. Asians, particularly the Thais, the Indonesians and the Chinese, have a different concept of time than Americans; things get done when they get done and in some countries, promptness is considered rude. Form is more important than substance; protocol can make or break a deal, so acquaint yourself with a country's customs before departing. Expect to spend more time socializing than in the United States.

Familiarize yourself with cultural differences. A cultural faux pas, such as wearing the wrong color to a meeting or displaying the soles of your shoes, could strangle business prospects.

Asians are, for the most part, devoutly religious. Islam, Buddhism, Hinduism and Catholicism are the dominate religions and holy days account for considerable time off from business. Asians also are deeply respectful of their political leaders. Criticize them and you may be escorted back to your hotel or even to the airport.

Political volatility is a fact of life in many Asian countries which necessitates security measures Americans are unaccustomed to and often offended by. You may be searched multiple times before boarding an aircraft or have your belongings scanned before allowed entry to a hotel.

Airlines: Relaxed trade restrictions between the United States and Asian countries have spawned new transpacific flights. United Airlines 800/241-6522 offers the most extensive schedule. Asian carriers fly from a number of U.S. cities and their on-board service can give you some insight into Asian manners. The major Asian carriers include Japan Air Lines 800/525-3663; Singapore Airlines 800/742-3333; Thai Airways International 800/426-5204; and Cathay Pacific 800/233-ASIA.

Ground Transportation: Getting around once you're on the ground in Asia can be frustrating. With the exception of Singapore, traffic in Asia is nightmarish. It literally can take hours to go just a few miles. Bangkok is the most congested but other cities are not far behind. Buses and trains are extremely crowded. When taking cabs, expect to negotiate prices. Unless the cab is metered, expect to haggle over the price; refusing to bargain is considered rude.

Hotels: Book well in advance and be prepared to pay high rates, especially in major convention cities such as Bangkok, Singapore, Hong Kong and Taiwan. Most U.S. chains have a presence in major Asian cities; Holiday Inn (800/465-4329) has the most extensive network. Four Seasons 800/332-3442, Inter-Continental 800/327-0200, Shangri-la 800/942-5050, Mandarin Oriental 800/526-6566, Peninsula 800/262-9467 and Leading Hotels 800/223-6800 are overseas chains well represented in Asia.

Entry Requirements Most Asian countries do not require visas for American citizens. Bringing in commercial and business materials is fraught with hassles in most places; check with the appropriate embassy for details before leaving. Ship bulk materials well in advance and expect them to be scrutinized. Many countries are wary of allowing anything in that could be viewed as controversial or threatening to the sitting government.

Currency: Banks are the most convenient choice for exchanging money.

Credit Cards: Visa and MasterCard are not accepted everywhere but American Express is widely recognized throughout Asia. Telephone calling cards are not widely used and International Direct Dialing is not available in all countries. Travelers checks are widely accepted in major cities.

Taxes/Tipping: Most countries tack on a service charge to hotel bills, restaurant checks and the like. Do not leave an additional tip. Tipping is not as prevalent in Asia as it is in the United States; in some countries, such as China, it is officially prohibited. Porters should be tipped as should cab drivers who have been especially helpful or patient.

Language Differences: Many business hotels provide translators and translation services. Not everyone speaks English and those who do are not necessarily fluent. Learn at least a few words, buy a phrase book and always carry a written copy of the name of your hotel and address in the local language.

International Travel Information

This section of the atlas is designed to present an overview of the continents and nations of the world. Included are accurate and up-to-date maps of the world, North America, South America, Africa, the Eastern Mediterranean Lands, Europe and Western Asia, Asia, Australia and New Zealand, and Antarctica. Each map provides information about the geographical interrelationships between nations and locates major cities.

The maps are accompanied by a country directory and other features to give the

businessperson a concise world overview both in the home office and "on the road" in a foreign land. Hints for interfacing successfully with foreign business enterprises are found on pages 177–180.

Businesspersons can plan daily business activities using the World Time Zone Map and Quick Travel Data directory. Information for each country in the directory includes telephone codes, holidays, entry requirements, climate, clothing, and foreign consulate telephone number in the United States. The Air Distances chart provides mileages between

major world cities; busy travelers can plan to use time during long flights to complete preparations for work at their intended destinations.

The Passport and Foreign Travel Information feature summarizes current information about the U.S. passport and foreign laws that can affect international travel. A quick review of both the maps and other material in this section can provide the tips needed to ensure a worry-free business trip that achieves its goal.

Legend: World Maps

INHABITED LOCATIONS

The size of type indicates the relative economic and political importance of the locality.

□ Research Station

• Luxor

◉ Boise

▣ **Auckland**

⚓ **PARIS**

Alternate Names

**Copenhagen
(København)**

**SAINT PETERSBURG
(LENINGRAD)**

English, second official language, historical, or alternate names are shown in parentheses.

Capitals of Political Units

BUDAPEST — National

Cardiff — State

POLITICAL BOUNDARIES

International

━━━━ Demarcated and Undemarcated

━━ - - ━━ Disputed de jure

Internal

──────── State, Province, etc. (Second order political unit)

SOUTH SANDWICH ISLANDS (U.K.) — Administering Country

TRANSPORTATION

──────── Primary Road

HYDROGRAPHIC FEATURES

Shoreline

River, Stream

Intermittent Stream

Lake, Reservoir

Salt Lake

Intermittent Lake, Reservoir

Ice Shelf

Reefs

TOPOGRAPHIC FEATURES

Nev. Sajama △ 21,463 — Elevation Above Sea Level

Elevations are given in feet.

ARCTIC OCEAN

GREENLAND
(Den.)

JAN MAYEN
(Norway)

Baffin Bay

Arctic

ALASKA
(U.S.)

Dawson

Reykjavík

ICELAND

FAEROE IS.
(Den.)

Anchorage

NORTH

Hudson
Bay

Juneau

CANADA

UNITED
KINGDOM

Edmonton

IRELAND

London

ALEUTIAN IS.

Vancouver

Winnipeg

Seattle

Montréal

NEWFOUNDLAND

St. John's

AMERICA

Ottawa

Chicago

Detroit

UNITED STATES

New York

San Francisco

Washington

AZORES
(Port.)

PORTUGAL

Madrid

SPAIN

Atlanta

GIBRALTAR
(U.K.)

Los Angeles

MIDWAY IS.
(U.S.)

Tropic of Cancer

Houston

New Orleans

MEXICO

Gulf of Mexico

CANARY ISLANDS
(Sp.)

W. SAHARA

MOROCCO

ALG

ATLANTIC

BAHAMAS

HAWAIIAN ISLANDS
(U.S.)

Havana

Mexico City

Veracruz

CUBA

HAITI

DOM. REP.

PUERTO RICO (U.S.)

MAURITANIA

MAL

BELIZE

JAMAICA

GUADELOUPE (Fr.)

CAPE VERDE

PACIFIC

HOND.

Caribbean
Sea

MARTINIQUE (Fr.)

SENEGAL

Dakar

GUAT.

BARBADOS

GAMBIA

EL SAL.

NIC.

TRINIDAD AND TOBAGO

GUINEA-BISSAU

GUINEA

BURKINA
FASO

COSTA
RICA

Caracas

GUYANA

SIERRA LEONE

COTE
D'IVOIRE

GHANA

PANAMA

VENEZUELA

Georgetown

SURINAME

FRENCH GUIANA

LIBERIA

PALMYRA
(U.S.)

Bogotá

COLOMBIA

Equator

KIRIBATI

GALAPAGOS ISLANDS
(Ecua.)

Quito

ECUADOR

Belém

Manaus

Fortaleza

SOUTH

MARQUESAS IS.
(Fr.)

BRAZIL

Recife

OCEAN

PERU

AMERICA

WESTERN
SAMOA

Lima

Salvador

OCEAN

AMERICAN
SAMOA

La Paz

Brasília

ST. HELENA
(U.K.)

TAHITI

TONGA

COOK
ISLANDS
(N.Z.)

FRENCH POLYNESIA

BOLIVIA

Sucre

Tropic of Capricorn

EASTER ISLAND
(Chile)

Rio de Janeiro

PARAGUAY

São Paulo

Antofagasta

ARGENTINA

URUGUAY

Valparaíso

Santiago

Montevideo

ARCH. DE JUAN
FERNÁNDEZ
(Chile)

Buenos
Aires

CHATHAM IS.
(N.Z.)

FALKLAND IS.
(U.K.)

SOUTH GEORGIA
(U.K.)

Punta Arenas

TIERRA DEL FUEGO

SOUTH SANDWICH IS.
(U.K.)

SOUTH ORKNEY IS.
(U.K.)

SOUTH SHETLAND IS.
(U.K.)

Antarctic Circle

Weddell
Sea

Scale 1:107,000,000; one inch to 1697 miles
Robinson Projection

0   400   800   1200   1600   2000 Miles

0   600   1200   1800   2400   3000 Kilometers

ARCTIC OCEAN

SVALBARD
(Norway)

ZEMLYA FRANTSA-
IOSIFA

NOVAYA
ZEMLYA

Circle

R U S S I A   Okhotsk   60°

NORWAY   FINLAND   BERING
Oslo   St. Petersburg   Sea of Okhotsk   SEA
SWEDEN   SAKHALIN
orth Sea DEN.   Moscow   Novosibirsk
NETH. Berlin EST.
GERMANY Warsaw LAT.   Irkutsk   45°
POLAND BELARUS   HOKKAIDO
Paris   Kiev   Vladivostok
FRANCE AUS. HUNG. UKRAINE   KAZAKHSTAN   Ulan Bator   NORTH   Sea of Japan HONSHŪ
SWITZ. ROM. MOLD.   MONGOLIA   KOREA
ITALY BOSN.   Beijing   SOUTH   JAPAN
Rome   BUL.   Black Sea   GEO.   A S I A   KOREA Tōkyō
ALB. GREECE Ankara ARM. AZER.   Seoul   KYŪSHŪ
Athens   TURKEY TURKMENISTAN KYRG.   CHINA
CYPRUS LEB. SYRIA   TAJIK.   Shanghai   30°
ISRAEL IRAQ Tehrān   Kābol   PACIFIC
Algiers TUNISIA JORDAN Baghdad AFGHANISTAN   Tropic of Cancer
Tripoli Cairo KUWAIT I R A N   New Delhi NEPAL   15°
ERIA   LIBYA EGYPT SAUDI QATAR PAKISTAN   BHU.   Guangzhou TAIWAN
Riyadh ARABIA U.A.E.   Karachi   HONG KONG NORTHERN MARIANA WAKE
NIGER   Mecca OMAN   I N D I A Ha Noi MACAU (U.K.) ISLANDS (U.S.) (U.S.)
CHAD SUDAN   YEMEN Red Sea   Bombay   MYANMAR LAOS HAINAN South China GUAM 15°
A F R I C A   Aden DJIBOUTI ARABIAN SOCOTRA   (BURMA) Yangon THAILAND Sea (U.S.)
NIGERIA   Addis SEA (Yem.)   Madras Bay of Bangkok VIETNAM Manila PHILIPPINES
Lagos CENTRAL AFRICAN Abāba LAKSHADWEEP Bengal CAMBODIA Thanh Pho Ho MARSHALL
CAMEROON REPUBLIC ETHIOPIA (INDIA)   SRI LANKA Chi Minh FED. STATES OF ISLANDS
EQUATORIAL   SOMALIA   Colombo MALDIVES BRUNEI MICRONESIA
GUINEA GABON UGANDA KENYA   Mogadishu MALAYSIA PALAU
SAO TOME ZAIRE RWANDA   SEYCHELLES   SINGAPORE BORNEO   Equator 0°
AND PRINCIPE BURUNDI   Nairobi   NEW GUINEA
Brazzaville Kinshasa TANZANIA Dar es Salaam   SUMATRA Jakarta PAPUA SOLOMON
Luanda   I N D I A N   JAVA I N D O N E S I A NEW GUINEA ISLANDS
ANGOLA ZAMBIA   COMOROS   COCOS
ZIMBABWE   MADAGASCAR   ISLANDS Darwin   CORAL SEA VANUATU 15°
NAMIBIA BOTSWANA MOZAMBIQUE Antananarivo MAURITIUS O C E A N (Austl.) NEW FIJI
Pretoria SWAZILAND Maputo REUNION   A U S T R A L I A CALEDONIA Tropic of Capricorn
SOUTH LESOTHO Durban (Fr.)   Brisbane (Fr.)
AFRICA   Perth   Sydney   30°
Cape Town   Melbourne Canberra Auckland
                                                              NORTH I.
                                                   TASMANIA NEW ZEALAND Wellington
                            ÎLES KERGUÉLEN   Hobart SOUTH I. 45°
                            (Fr.)

                                                                                      60°

                                                   Antarctic Circle

A N T A R C T I C A   Copyright by Rand McNally & Co.   75°
                             Made in U.S.A.
                             DM-510000-2A-QR1-   B

15° 30° 45° 60° 75° 90° 105° 120° 135° 150° 165° 180°

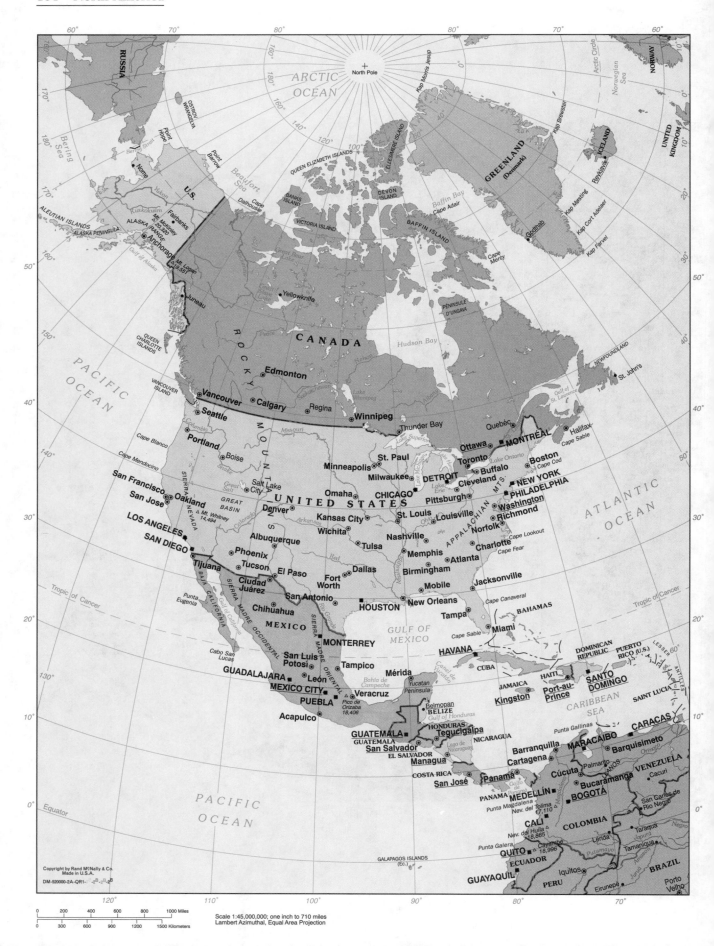

Scale 1:45,000,000; one inch to 710 miles
Lambert Azimuthal, Equal Area Projection

GULF OF MEXICO

Cape Sable Miami

BAHAMAS

Tropic of Cancer

HAVANA

CUBA

Mérida

YUCATAN PENINSULA

MEXICO

GUAT.

Belmopan
BELIZE

Gulf of Honduras

HONDURAS

Tegucigalpa

San Salvador

EL SALVADOR

Managua

NICARAGUA

Lago de Nicaragua

San José

COSTA RICA

Panamá

PANAMA

Canal de Yucatán

JAMAICA

Kingston

HAITI

Port-au-Prince

DOMINICAN REPUBLIC

SANTO DOMINGO

PUERTO RICO (U.S.)

LESSER ANTILLES

GUADELOUPE (Fr.)

SAINT LUCIA

CARIBBEAN SEA

Punta Gallinas

Barranquilla

MARACAIBO

CARACAS

Barquisimeto

TRINIDAD AND TOBAGO

Cartagena

Golfo de Panamá

Cúcuta

Palmarito

Boca Grande

Orinoco

MEDELLÍN

Bucaramanga

LLANOS

VENEZUELA

GUYANA

Georgetown

Paramaribo

Cayenne

SURINAME

FRENCH GUIANA

Cabo Caciporé

Nev. del Tolima 17,110

Punta Magdalena

BOGOTÁ

COLOMBIA

Cacuri

PAKARIMA MTS.

San Carlos de Río Negro

Boa Vista

Cabo Norte

CALI

Nev. del Huila 18,865

Punta Galera

QUITO

Lérida

Taraquá

Macapá

Ilha de Marajó

Baía de Marajó

Belém

São Luis

Equator

GALÁPAGOS ISLANDS (Ec.)

Cayambe 18,996

ECUADOR

GUAYAQUIL

Punta Pariñas

Iquitos

Putumayo

Japurá

Tamaniquá

MANAUS

Santarém

Amazon

Imperatriz

Fortaleza

ILHA FERNANDO DE NORONHA

Equator

Eirunepé

Juruá

B R A Z I L

Teresina

Cabo de São Roque

Chiclayo

P E R U

Purus

Madeira

Porto Velho

Conceição

Alta Floresta

Conceição do Araguaia

Represa de Sobradinho

Natal

RECIFE

Nev. Huascarán 22,133

A N D E S

Ji-Parana

PLANALTO DO MATO GROSSO

São Francisco

Feira de Santana

Aracaju

Callao

Lima

Cusco

Puerto Heath

Nev. Illampu 21,066

Trinidad

Cuiabá

BRASÍLIA

SERRA DO ESPINHAÇO

SALVADOR

Itabuna

Punta Carreta

LA PAZ

Lago Titicaca

BOLIVIA

Goiânia

Ponta da Baleia

Arequipa

Oruro

Santa Cruz de la Sierra

Sucre

Uberlândia

Represa de Três Marias

Nev. Sajama 21,463

Iquique

Nev. Ojos del Salado 22,615

GRAN CHACO

Pilcomayo

PARAGUAY

Anambaí

Londrina

BELO HORIZONTE

Cabo de São Tomé

Antofagasta

Punta Ballenita

San Miguel de Tucumán

Asunción

SÃO PAULO

RIO DE JANEIRO

Santo André

Punta Cachos

Santiago del Estero

Goya

Florianópolis

Santa Maria

ISLA SAN AMBROSIO (Chile)

Tropic of Capricorn

Tropic of Capricorn

ISLA SAN FÉLIX (Chile)

PACIFIC OCEAN

Santa María

PORTO ALEGRE

ARCHIPIÉLAGO JUAN FERNÁNDEZ (Chile)

CÓRDOBA

Cerro Aconcagua 22,831

Valparaíso

Santiago

ROSARIO

Santa Fe

URUGUAY

Ponta do Bojuru

Lagoa dos Patos

MONTEVIDEO

BUENOS AIRES

La Plata

Punta del Este

Río de la Plata

Lagoa Mirim

Concepción

Punta Morguilla

Bahía Blanca

Mar del Plata

C H I L E

Valdivia

Neuquén

A R G E N T I N A

Cabo Quedal

Golfo San Matías

Península Valdés

ISLA GRANDE DE CHILOÉ

ARCHIPIÉLAGO DE LOS CHONOS

PATAGONIA

A N D E S

Península de Taitao

Cabo dos Bahías

Golfo San Jorge

Comodoro Rivadavia

Punta Medanoso

ISLA WELLINGTON

Bahía Grande

FALKLAND ISLANDS (U.K.)

WEST FALKLAND

Stanley

EAST FALKLAND

ATLANTIC OCEAN

Cabo Deseado

Punta Arenas

ISLA SANTA INÉS

TIERRA DEL FUEGO

Strait of Magellan

Cape Horn (Cabo de Hornos)

SOUTH GEORGIA (U.K.)

Drake Passage

SOUTH SHETLAND ISLANDS (U.K.)

SOUTH ORKNEY ISLANDS (U.K.)

SOUTH SANDWICH ISLANDS (U.K.)

BOUVET (Nor.)

Antarctic Circle

ALEXANDER ISLAND

Antarctic Peninsula

Scale 1:45,000,000; one inch to 710 miles
Lambert Azimuthal, Equal Area Projection

0 200 400 600 800 1000 Miles

0 300 600 900 1200 1500 Kilometers

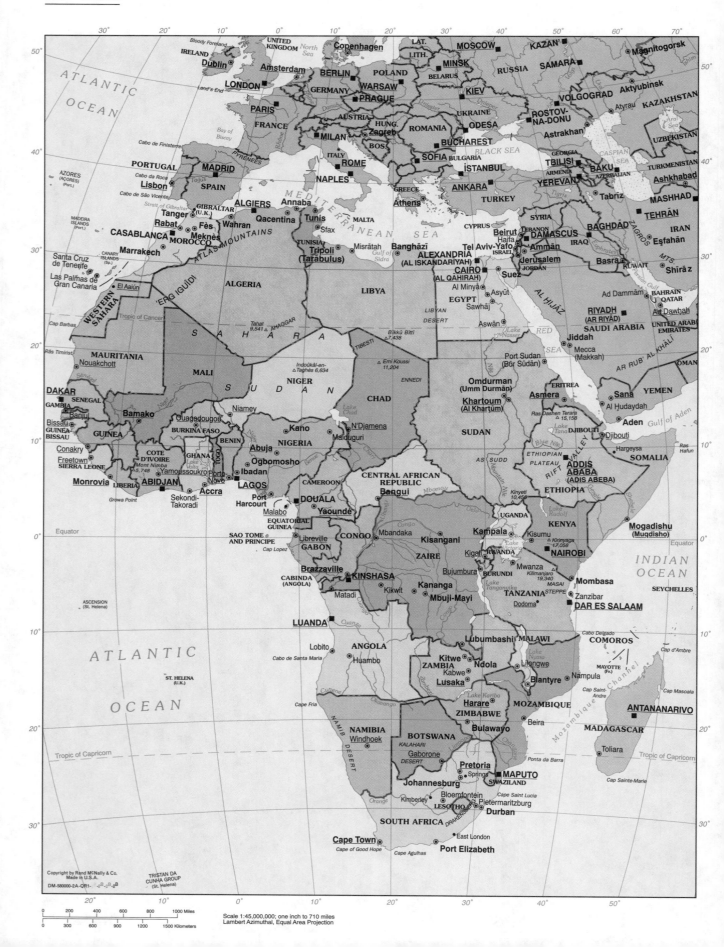

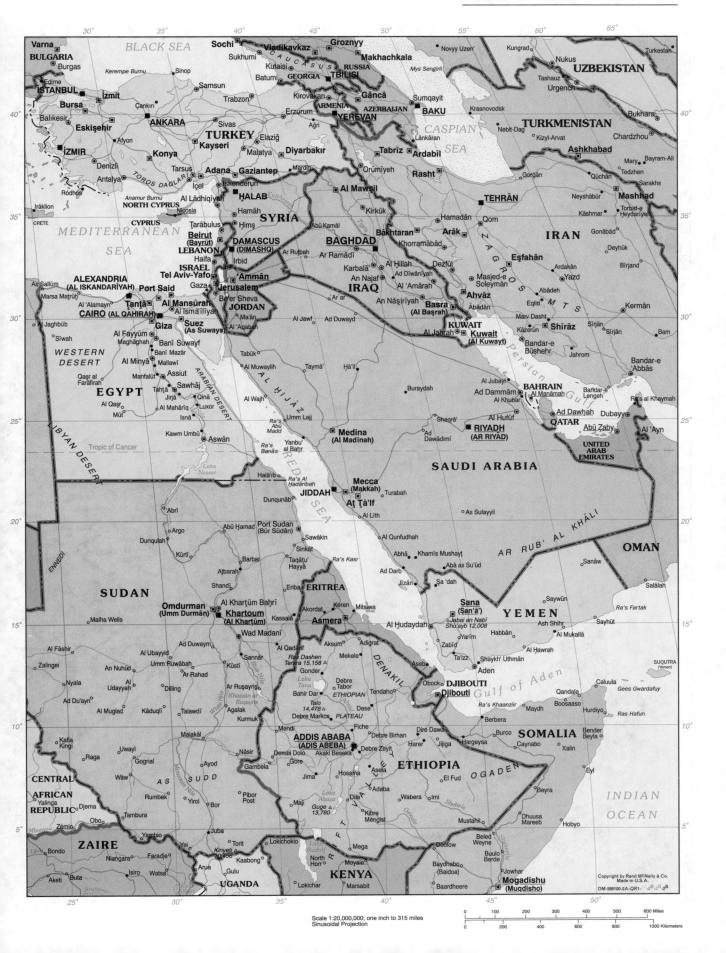

Scale 1:20,000,000; one inch to 315 miles
Sinusoidal Projection

| | 100 | 200 | 300 | 400 | 500 | 600 Miles |
| 0 | 200 | 400 | 600 | 800 | 1000 Kilometers |

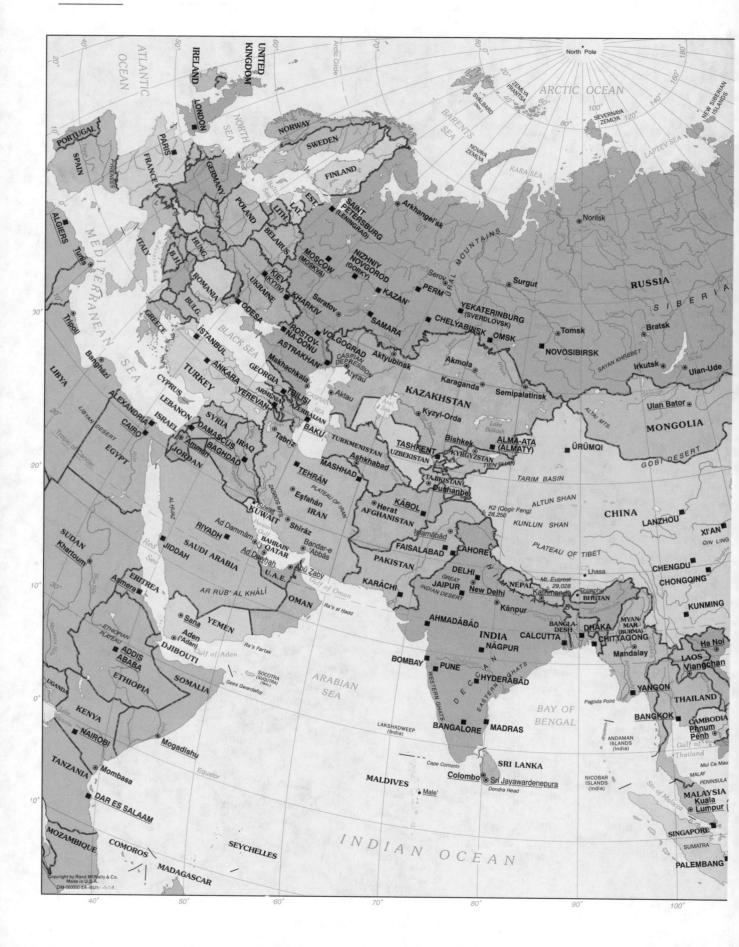

North Pole

ATLANTIC OCEAN

ARCTIC OCEAN

IRELAND
UNITED KINGDOM
LONDON
PORTUGAL
SPAIN
PARIS
FRANCE
NORWAY
SWEDEN
FINLAND
ZEMLYA FRANTSA
SVALBARD (Nor.)
SEVERNAYA ZEMLYA
NEW SIBERIAN ISLANDS
NORTH SEA
BARENTS SEA
KARA SEA
LAPTEV SEA
NOVAYA ZEMLYA
Arctic Circle

ALGIERS
Tunis
MEDITERRANEAN SEA
ITALY
GERMANY
POLAND
BELARUS
EST.
LAT.
LITH.
SAINT PETERSBURG (LENINGRAD)
Arkhangel'sk
Norilsk
RUSSIA
SIBERIA

HUNG.
B. H.
ROMANIA
BULG.
UKRAINE
KIEV (KYYIV)
MOSCOW (MOSKVA)
NIZHNIY NOVGOROD (GORKY)
Serov
Surgut
URAL MOUNTAINS
Tomsk
Bratsk

PORTUGAL
GREECE
ODESA
KHARKIV
Saratov
KAZAN'
PERM'
YEKATERINBURG (SVERDLOVSK)
CHELYABINSK
OMSK
NOVOSIBIRSK
Irkutsk
Ulan-Ude

Tripoli
İSTANBUL
BLACK SEA
ROSTOV-NA-DONU
VOLGOGRAD
SAMARA
Aktyubinsk
Akmola
SAYAN KHREBET
Ulan Bator

Bağhāzī
TURKEY
ANKARA
GEORGIA
ASTRAKHAN'
Makhachkala
CASPIAN DEPRESSION
Atyrau
Karaganda
Semipalatinsk
ALTAI MTS.
MONGOLIA

LIBYA
CYPRUS
LEBANON
SYRIA
ARMENIA
YEREVAN
TBILISI
AZERBAIJAN
CASPIAN SEA
Aktau
KAZAKHSTAN
Kyzyl-Orda
Lake Balkhash
ÜRÜMQI
GOBI DESERT

ALEXANDRIA
ISRAEL
DAMASCUS
BAKÜ
Tabrīz
Aral Sea
TASHKENT
Bishkek
ALMA-ATA (ALMATY)
CAIRO
JORDAN
IRAQ
BAGHDAD
TURKMENISTAN
UZBEKISTAN
KYRGYZSTAN
TIEN SHAN
TARIM BASIN
ALTUN SHAN
CHINA
LANZHOU

EGYPT
Tropic of Cancer
LIBYAN DESERT
AMman
MASHHAD
Ashkhabad
TAJIKISTAN
Dushanbe
KÂBOL
KUNLUN SHAN
XI'AN
QIN LING

AL ḤIJĀZ
ZAGROS MTS.
TEHRÂN
Eşfahān
IRAN
Herat
AFGHANISTAN
K2 (Qogir Feng) 28,250
PLATEAU OF TIBET
CHENGDU
CHONGQING

SUDAN
Khartoum
Red Sea
JIDDAH
SAUDI ARABIA
KUWAIT
Kuwait
Ad Dammâm
BAHRAIN
QATAR
Ad Dawḥah
Shîrâz
Bandar-e 'Abbās
Islamâbâd
Lhasa
KUNMING

RIYADH
Abū Ẓaby
U.A.E.
FAISALABAD
LAHORE
PAKISTAN
DELHI
New Delhi
NEPAL
Mt. Everest 29,028
Kathmandu
Thimphu
BHUTAN
Mandalay

ERITREA
Asmera
PLATEAU OF IRAN
Gulf of Oman
KARÂCHÎ
JAIPUR
GREAT INDIAN DESERT
Kânpur
BANGLA-DESH
DHAKA
CHITTAGONG
MYANMAR (BURMA)
Ha Noi

ETHIOPIAN PLATEAU
ADDIS ABABA
DJIBOUTI
OMAN
Ra's al Ḥadd
AR RUB' AL KHÂLÎ
AHMADÂBÂD
INDIA
NÂGPUR
CALCUTTA
LAOS
Viangchan

ETHIOPIA
Sana
Aden ('Adan)
YEMEN
Gulf of Aden
Ra's Fartak
BOMBAY
PUNE
HYDERÂBÂD
WESTERN GHATS
EASTERN GHATS
DECCAN
YANGON
THAILAND

UGANDA
KENYA
SOMALIA
SOCOTRA (SUQUTRA) (Yem.)
Gees Gwardafuy
ARABIAN SEA
BANGALORE
MADRAS
BAY OF BENGAL
Pagoda Point
BANGKOK
CAMBODIA
Phnum Pénh

NAIROBI
Mogadishu
LAKSHADWEEP (India)
ANDAMAN ISLANDS (India)
Gulf of Thailand

TANZANIA
Mombasa
Equator
Cape Comorin
SRI LANKA
Colombo
Sri Jayawardenepura
Dondra Head
NICOBAR ISLANDS (India)
Mui Ca Mau

DAR ES SALAAM
MALDIVES
Male'
MALAY PENINSULA
Str. of Malacca

MOZAMBIQUE
COMOROS
MADAGASCAR
SEYCHELLES
INDIAN OCEAN
MALAYSIA
Kuala Lumpur
SUMATRA
SINGAPORE
PALEMBANG

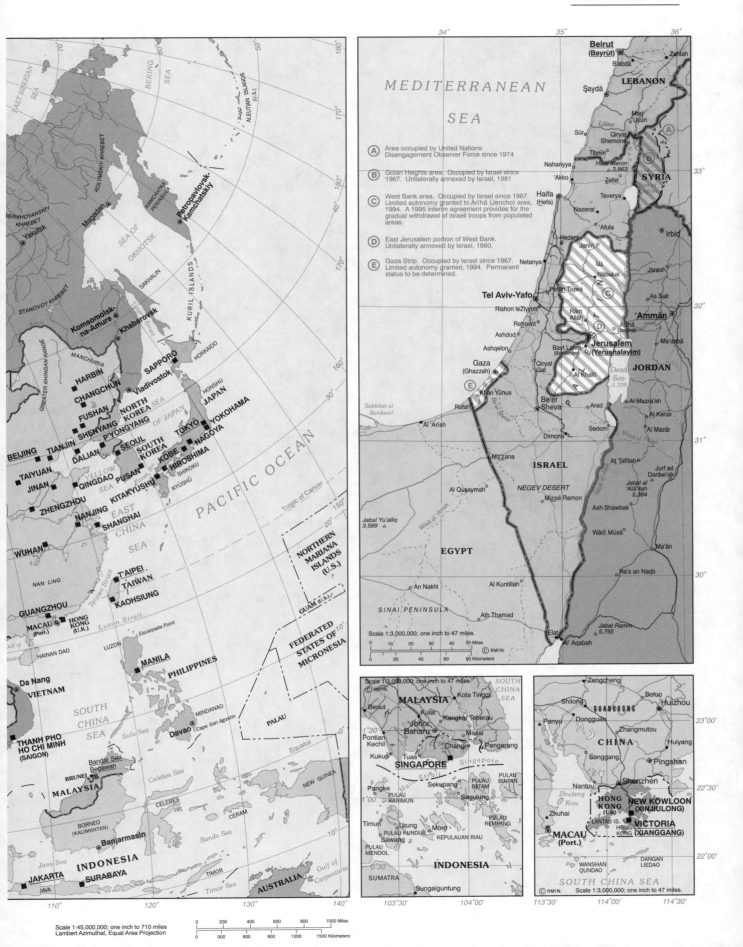

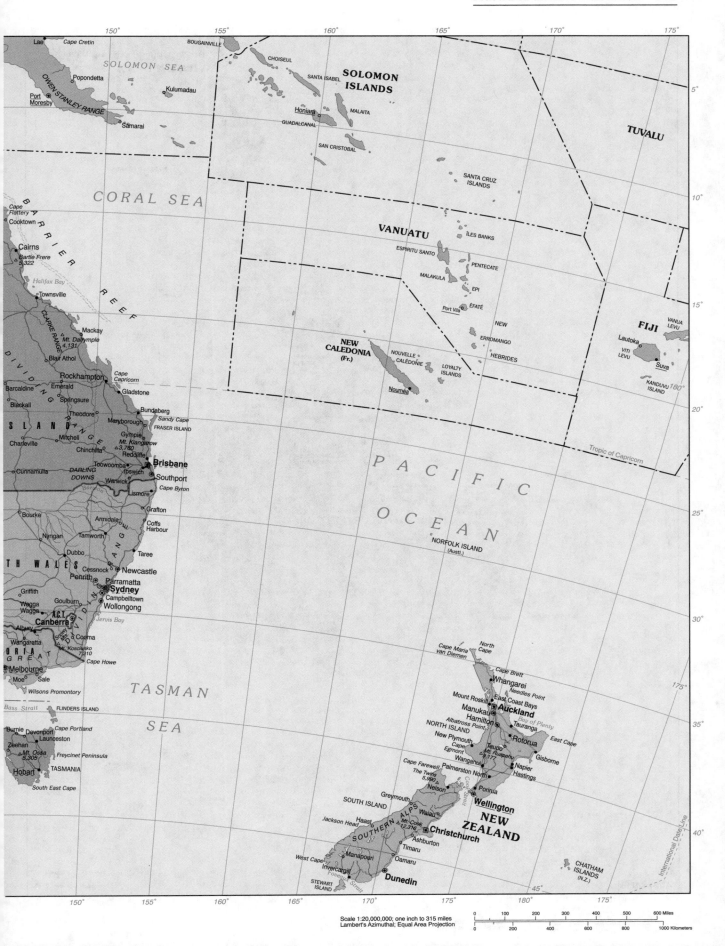

SOLOMON SEA

OWEN STANLEY RANGE

Lae
Cape Cretin
Popondetta
Port Moresby
Kulumadau
Samarai

BOUGAINVILLE
CHOISEUL
SANTA ISABEL
SOLOMON ISLANDS
Honiara
MALAITA
GUADALCANAL
SAN CRISTOBAL

SANTA CRUZ ISLANDS

CORAL SEA

Cape Flattery
Cooktown

VANUATU

ÎLES BANKS

ESPIRITU SANTO
PENTECATE
MALAKULA
EPI
Port Vila
ÉFATÉ

TUVALU

Cairns
Bartle Frere 5,322

Halifax Bay
Townsville

BARRIER REEF

CLARKE RANGE
Mackay
Mt. Dalrymple 4,131
Blair Athol

NEW ERROMANGO
HEBRIDES

FIJI
VANUA LEVU
Lautoka
VITI LEVU
Suva

Rockhampton
Cape Capricorn

DIVIDING RANGE

Barcaldine
Emerald
Springsure
Blackall
Theodore
Mitchell
Charleville

Gladstone
Bundaberg
Sandy Cape
FRASER ISLAND
Maryborough
Gympie
Mt. Kiangarow 3,760
Chinchilla
Toowoomba

NEW CALEDONIA (Fr.)
NOUVELLE CALÉDONIE
LOYALTY ISLANDS
Nouméa

KANDUVU ISLAND

S L A N D

Cunnamulla
DARLING DOWNS
Warwick
Lismore

Redcliffe
Brisbane
Ipswich
Southport
Cape Byron

Tropic of Capricorn

P A C I F I C

Bourke

Grafton
Coffs Harbour

Armidale

O C E A N

T H   W A L E S
Nyngan
Tamworth
Dubbo
Taree

DIVIDING RANGE

Cessnock
Newcastle
Penrith
Parramatta
Sydney
Campbelltown
Wollongong

NORFOLK ISLAND (Austl.)

Griffith
Goulburn
Wagga Wagga
A.C.T. Canberra
Cooma
Albury
Wangaratta
Mt. Kosciusko 7,310
Cape Howe

Jervis Bay

Cape Maria van Diemen
North Cape

O R I A
G R E A T

Melbourne
Moe
Sale
Wilsons Promontory

T A S M A N

Cape Brett
Whangarei
Needles Point
East Coast Bays
Mount Roskill
Auckland
Manukau
Hamilton
Bay of Plenty
Tauranga
East Cape

Bass Strait
FLINDERS ISLAND

S E A

Albatross Point
NORTH ISLAND
New Plymouth
Cape Egmont
Mt. Egmont
Taupo
Mt. Ruapehu 9,177
Rotorua
Gisborne

Burnie
Devonport
Cape Portland
Zeehan
Launceston
Mt. Ossa 5,305
Freycinet Peninsula

Wanganui
Palmerston North
Napier
Hastings

Hobart
TASMANIA
South East Cape

Cape Farewell
The Twins 5,990
Nelson
Porirua
Wellington

Greymouth
NEW ZEALAND
Cook Strait
SOUTH ISLAND
Waiau

Jackson Head
Haast
Mt. Cook 12,316
SOUTHERN ALPS
Christchurch
Ashburton
Timaru

West Cape
Manapouri
Oamaru
Invercargill
STEWART ISLAND
Foveaux Strait
Dunedin

CHATHAM ISLANDS (N.Z.)

International Date Line

Scale 1:20,000,000; one inch to 315 miles
Lambert's Azimuthal; Equal Area Projection

0 100 200 300 400 500 600 Miles
0 200 400 600 800 1000 Kilometers

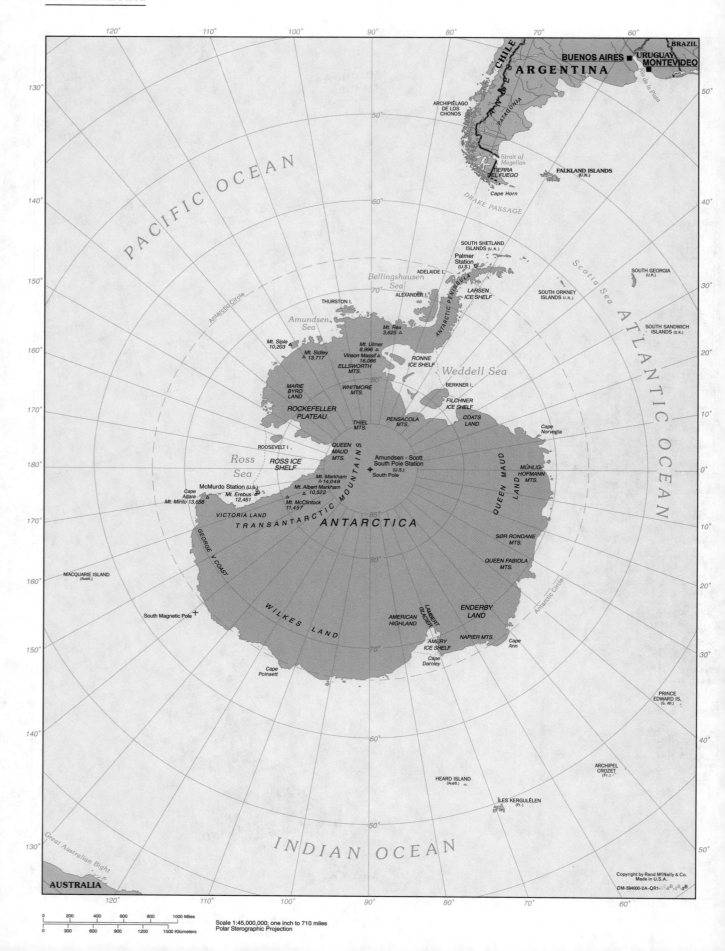

BRAZIL

BUENOS AIRES ■   ■ URUGUAY
MONTEVIDEO ■

ARGENTINA

CHILE

Río de la Plata

ARCHIPIÉLAGO
DE LOS
CHONOS

PATAGONIA

Strait of
Magellan

TIERRA
DEL FUEGO

Cape Horn

FALKLAND ISLANDS
(U.K.)

DRAKE PASSAGE

PACIFIC OCEAN

SOUTH SHETLAND
ISLANDS (U.K.)

Palmer
Station
(U.S.)

ADELAIDE I.

ALEXANDER I.

Bellingshausen
Sea

Antarctic Circle

THURSTON I.

Amundsen
Sea

Mt. Rex
3,625 △

LARSEN
ICE SHELF

Scotia Sea

SOUTH GEORGIA
(U.K.)

SOUTH ORKNEY
ISLANDS U.K.)

SOUTH SANDWICH
ISLANDS (U.K.)

ANTARCTIC PENINSULA

Mt. Siple
10,203 △

Mt. Sidley
△ 13,717

Mt. Ulmer
8,996 △
Vinson Massif △
16,066
ELLSWORTH
MTS.

RONNE
ICE SHELF

MARIE
BYRD
LAND

WHITMORE
MTS.

Weddell Sea

BERKNER I.

FILCHNER
ICE SHELF

ATLANTIC OCEAN

ROCKEFELLER
PLATEAU

THIEL
MTS.

PENSACOLA
MTS.

COATS
LAND

Cape
Norvegia

ROOSEVELT I.

QUEEN
MAUD
MTS.

Amundsen - Scott
South Pole Station
(U.S.)
✛ South Pole

MÜHLIG-
HOFMANN
MTS.

Ross
Sea

ROSS ICE
SHELF

QUEEN MAUD LAND

McMurdo Station (U.S.)

Mt. Markham
△ 14,049
Mt. Albert Markham
△ 10,552

Mt. Erebus
12,451

Cape
Adare
Mt. Minto 13,658

Mt. McClintock
11,457

TRANSANTARCTIC MOUNTAINS

ANTARCTICA

SØR RONDANE
MTS.

VICTORIA LAND

QUEEN FABIOLA
MTS.

MACQUARIE ISLAND
(Austl.)

GEORGE V COAST

South Magnetic Pole ✛

WILKES LAND

AMERICAN
HIGHLAND

LAMBERT GLACIER

ENDERBY
LAND

NAPIER MTS.

Cape
Ann

Antarctic Circle

AMERY
ICE SHELF

Cape
Darnley

Cape
Poinsett

PRINCE
EDWARD IS.
(S. Afr.)

Great Australian Bight

ARCHIPEL
CROZET
(Fr.)

HEARD ISLAND
(Austl.)

ÎLES KERGUÉLEN
(Fr.)

INDIAN OCEAN

AUSTRALIA

0   200   400   600   800   1000 Miles
0   300   600   900   1200   1500 Kilometers

Scale 1:45,000,000; one inch to 710 miles
Polar Sterographic Projection

World Time Zone Map

The earth's surface is divided into 24 time zones. Each zone represents 15° of longitude or one hour of time. The zero time zone centers on the Greenwich meridian, 0° longitude. Since the earth rotates to the east, time zones to the west of Greenwich are earlier; to the east, later.

Local standard time can be determined for any area in the world by adding one hour for each time zone counted in an easterly direction from one's own zone, or by subtracting one hour for each zone counted in a westerly direction. The International Date Line (I.D.L. at 180° longitude) separates one day from the next: when it is Sunday east of the line, it is Monday west of the line.

h   hour
m   minute

Air Distances Between Cities

	Apia, Western Samoa	Azores Islands	Beijing, China	Berlin, Germany	Bombay, India	Buenos Aires, Argentina	Calcutta, India	Cape Town, South Africa	Cape Verde Islands	Chicago, U.S.A.	Darwin, Australia	Denver, U. S. A.	Gibraltar	Hong Kong	Honolulu, Hawaii, U.S.A.	Istanbul, Turkey	Juneau, Alaska, U.S.A.	London, United Kingdom	Los Angeles, U.S.A	Manila, Philippines	Melbourne, Australia	Mexico City, Mexico
Apia		9644	5903	9743	8154	6931	7183	9064	10246	6557	3843	5653	10676	5591	2604	10175	5415	9789	4828	4993	3113	5449
Azores Islands	9644		6565	2185	5967	5417	6549	5854	1499	3093	10209	3991	1249	7572	7180	2975	4526	1527	4794	8250	12101	4385
Beijing	5903	6565		4567	2964	11974	2024	8045	7763	6592	3728	6348	6009	1226	5067	4379	4522	5054	6250	1770	5667	7733
Berlin	9743	2185	4567		3910	7376	4376	5977	3194	4402	8036	5077	1453	5500	7305	1078	4560	574	5782	6128	9919	6037
Bombay	8154	5967	2964	3910		9273	1041	5134	6297	8054	4503	8383	4814	2673	8020	2991	6866	4462	8701	3148	6097	9722
Buenos Aires	6931	5417	11974	7376	9273		10242	4270	4208	5596	9127	5928	5963	11463	7558	7568	7759	6918	6118	11042	7234	4633
Calcutta	7183	6549	2024	4376	1041	10242		6026	7148	7981	3744	8050	5521	1534	7037	3646	6326	4954	8148	2189	5547	9495
Cape Town	9064	5854	8045	5977	5134	4270	6026		4509	8449	6947	9327	5076	7372	11532	5219	10330	6005	9969	7525	6412	8511
Cape Verde Is.	10246	1499	7763	3194	6297	4208	7148	4509		4066	10664	4975	1762	8539	8311	3507	5911	2731	5772	9221	10856	4857
Chicago	6557	3093	6592	4402	8054	5596	7981	8449	4066		9346	920	4258	7790	4244	5476	2305	3950	1745	8128	9668	1673
Darwin	3843	10209	3728	8036	4503	9127	3744	6947	10664	9346		8557	9265	2642	5355	7390	7105	8598	7835	1979	1964	9081
Denver	5653	3991	6348	5077	8383	5928	8050	9327	4975	920	8557		5122	7465	3338	6154	1831	4688	831	7661	8759	1434
Gibraltar	10676	1249	6009	1453	4814	5963	5521	5076	1762	4258	9265	5122		6828	8075	1874	5273	1094	5936	7483	10798	5629
Hong Kong	5591	7572	1226	5500	2673	11463	1534	7372	8539	7790	2642	7465	6828		5537	4980	5634	5981	7240	693	4607	8776
Honolulu	2604	7180	5067	7305	8020	7558	7037	11532	8311	4244	5355	3338	8075	5537		8104	2815	7226	2557	5296	5513	3781
Istanbul	10175	2975	4379	1078	2991	7568	3646	5219	3507	5476	7390	6154	1874	4980	8104		5498	1551	6843	5659	9088	7102
Juneau	5415	4526	4522	4560	6866	7759	6326	10330	5911	2305	7105	1831	5273	5634	2815	5498		4418	1842	5869	8035	3219
London	9789	1527	5054	574	4462	6918	4954	6005	2731	3950	8598	4688	1094	5981	7226	1551	4418		5439	6667	10501	5541
Los Angeles	4828	4794	6250	5782	8701	6118	8148	9969	5772	1745	7835	831	5936	7240	2557	6843	1842	5439		7269	7931	1542
Manila	4993	8250	1770	6128	3148	11042	2189	7525	9221	8128	1979	7661	7483	693	5296	5659	5869	6667	7269		3941	8829
Melbourne	3113	12101	5667	9919	6097	7234	5547	6412	10856	9668	1964	8759	10798	4607	5513	9088	8035	10501	7931	3941		8422
Mexico City	5449	4385	7733	6037	9722	4633	9495	8511	4857	1673	9081	1434	5629	8776	3781	7102	3219	5541	1542	8829	8422	
Moscow	9116	3165	3597	996	3131	8375	3447	6294	3982	4984	7046	5485	2413	4439	7033	1088	4534	1549	6068	5130	8963	6688
New Orleans	6085	3524	7314	5116	8865	4916	8803	8316	4194	833	9545	1082	4757	8480	4207	6171	2905	4627	1673	8724	9275	934
New York	7242	2422	6823	3961	7794	5297	7921	7801		713	9959	1631	3627	8051	4959	5009	2854	3459	2451	8493	10355	2085
Nome	5438	4954	3428	4342	5901	8848	5271	10107	6438	3314	6235	2925	5398	4547	3004	5101	1094	4381	2876	4817	7558	4309
Oslo	9247	2234	4360	515	4130	7613	4459	6494	3444	4040	8022	4653	1791	5337		1518	4045	714	5325	6016	9926	5706
Panamá	6514	3778	8906	5849	9742	3381	10114	7014	3734	2325	10352	2636	4926	10084	5245	6750	4460	5278	3001	10283	9022	1495
Paris	9990	1659	5101	542	4359	6877	4889	3841	2666	4133	8575	4885	964	5956	7434	1401	4628	213	5601	6673	10396	5706
Port Said	10485	3391	4584	1747	2659	7362	3506	4590	3672	6103	7159	6819	2179	4975	8738	693	6215	2154	7528	5619	8658	7671
Québec	7406	2240	6423	3583	7371	5680	7481	7857	3355	878	9724	1752	3383	8650	5000	4644	2660	3101	2579	8124	10497	2454
Reykjavik	8678	1777	4903	1479	5191	7099	5409	7111	3248	2954	8631	3596	2047	6031	6084	2558	3268	1171	4306	6651	10544	4622
Rio de Janeiro	8120	4428	10768	6144	8257	1218	9376	3769	3040	5296	9960	5871	4775	10995	8190	6395	7598	5772	6296	11254	8186	4770
Rome	10475	2125	5047	734	3843	6929	4496	5249	2772	4808	8190	5561	1034	5768	8022	854	5247	887	6326	6457	9934	6353
San Francisco	4786	4872	5902	5657	8392	6474	7809	10241	5921	1858	7637	949	5936	6894	2392	6700	1525	5355	347	6963	7854	1885
Seattle	5222	4501	5396	5041	7741	6913	7224	10199	5714	1737	7619	1021	5462	6471	2678	6063	899	4782	959	6641	8186	2337
Shanghai	5399	7229	662	5215	3133	12197	2112	8059	8443	7053	3142	6698	6646	772	4934	4959	4869	5710	6477	1152	5005	8039
Singapore	5850	8326	2774	6166	2429	9864	1791	6016	8700	9365	2075	9063	7231	1652	6710	5373	7235	6744	8767	1479	3761	10307
Tokyo	4656	7247	1307	5538	4188	11400	3186	9071	8589	6303	3367	5795	6988	1796	3850	5556	4011	5938	5470	1863	5089	7035
Valparaíso	6267	5678	11774	7795	10037	761	10993	4998	4649	5268	8961	5452	6408	11607	6793	8172	7271	7263	5527	10930	6998	4053
Vienna	10010	2291	4639	328	3718	7368	4259	5671	3147	4694	7974	5383	1386	5429	7626	783	4895	772	6108	6120	9792	6306
Washington, D.C.	7066	2667	6922	4167	7988	5216	8088	7894	3486	597	9923	1494	3822	8148	4829	5216	2834	3665	2300	8560	10173	1878
Wellington	2062	11269	6698	11265	7677	6260	7042	7019	10363	8349	3310	7516	12060	5853	4708	10663	7475	11682	6714	5162	1595	6899
Winnipeg	6283	3389	5907	4286	7644	6297	7424	9054	4556	714	8684	798	4435	7096	3806	5361	1597	3918	1525	7414	9319	2097
Zanzibar	9892	5323	5803	4309	2855	6421	3859	2346	4635	8358	6409	9221	4103	5414	10869	3312	8795	4604	10021	5763	6802	9484

Air Distances given in statute miles

Moscow, Russia	New Orleans, U.S.A.	New York, U.S.A.	Nome, Alaska, U.S.A.	Oslo, Norway	Panamá, Panama	Paris, France	Port Said, Egypt	Québec, Canada	Reykjavik, Iceland	Rio de Janeiro, Brazil	Rome, Italy	San Francisco, U.S.A.	Seattle, U.S.A.	Shanghai, China	Singapore, Singapore	Tokyo, Japan	Valparaíso, Chile	Vienna, Austria	Washington, D.C., U.S.A.	Wellington, New Zealand	Winnipeg, Canada	Zanzibar, Tanzania	
9116	6085	7242	5438	9247	6514	9990	10485	7406	8678	8120	10475	4786	5222	5399	5850	4656	6267	10010	7066	2062	6283	9892	Apia
3165	3524	2422	4954	2234	3778	1659	3391	2240	1777	4428	2125	4872	4501	7229	8326	7247	5678	2291	2667	11269	3389	5323	Azores Islands
3597	7314	6823	3428	4360	8906	5101	4584	6423	4903	10768	5047	5902	5396	662	2774	1307	11774	4639	6922	6698	5907	5803	Beijing
996	5116	3961	4342	515	5849	542	1747	3583	1479	6114	734	5657	5041	5215	6166	5538	7795	328	4167	11265	4285	4309	Berlin
3131	8865	7794	5901	4130	9742	4359	2659	7371	5191	8257	3843	8392	7741	3133	2429	4188	10037	3718	7988	7677	7644	2855	Bombay
8375	4916	5297	8848	7613	3381	6877	7362	5680	7099	1218	6929	6474	6913	12197	9864	11400	761	7368	5216	6260	6297	6421	Buenos Aires
3447	8803	7921	5271	4459	10114	4889	3506	7481	5409	9376	4496	7809	7224	2112	1791	3186	10993	4259	8088	7042	7424	3859	Calcutta
6294	8316	7801	10107	6494	7014	5841	4590	7857	7111	3769	5249	10241	10199	8059	6016	9071	4998	5671	7894	7019	9054	2346	Cape Town
3982	4194	3355	6438	3444	3734	2666	3672	3355	3248	3040	2772	5921	5714	8443	8700	8589	4649	3147	3486	10363	4556	4635	Cape Verde Is.
4984	833	713	3314	4040	2325	4133	6103	878	2954	5296	4808	1858	1737	7053	9365	6303	5268	4694	597	8349	714	8358	Chicago
7046	9545	9959	6235	8022	10352	8575	7159	9724	8631	9960	8190	7637	7619	3142	2075	3367	8961	7974	9923	3310	8684	6409	Darwin
5485	1082	1631	2925	4653	2636	4885	6819	1732	3596	5871	5561	949	1021	6698	9063	5795	5452	5383	1494	7516	798	9921	Denver
2413	4757	3627	5398	1791	4926	964	2179	3383	2047	4775	1034	5936	5462	6646	7231	6988	6408	1386	3822	12060	4435	4103	Gibraltar
4439	8480	8051	4547	5337	10084	5956	4975	7650	6031	10995	5768	6894	6471	772	1652	1796	11607	5429	8148	5853	7096	5414	Hong Kong
7033	4207	4959	3004	6784	5245	7434	8738	5000	6084	8190	8022	2392	2678	4934	6710	3850	6793	7626	4829	4708	3806	10869	Honolulu
1088	6171	5009	5101	1518	6750	1401	693	4644	2558	6395	854	6700	6063	4959	5373	5556	8172	783	5216	10663	5361	3312	Istanbul
4534	2905	2854	1094	4045	4460	4628	6215	2660	3268	7598	5247	1525	899	4869	7235	4011	7271	4895	2834	7475	1597	8795	Juneau
1549	4627	3459	4381	714	5278	213	2154	3101	1171	5772	887	5355	4782	5710	6744	5938	7263	772	3665	11682	3918	4604	London
6068	1673	2451	2876	5325	3001	5601	7528	2579	4306	6296	6326	347	959	6477	8767	5470	5527	6108	2300	6714	1525	10021	Los Angeles
5130	8724	8493	4817	6016	10283	6673	5619	8124	6651	11254	6457	6963	6641	1152	1479	1863	10930	6120	8560	5162	7414	5763	Manila
8963	9275	10355	7558	9926	9022	10396	8658	10497	10544	8186	9934	7854	8186	5005	3761	5089	6998	9792	10173	1595	9319	6802	Melbourne
6688	934	2085	4309	5706	1495	5706	7671	2454	4622	4770	6353	1885	2337	8039	10307	7035	4053	6306	1878	6899	2097	9484	Mexico City
	5756	4662	4036	1016	6711	1541	1710	4242	2056	7179	1474	5868	5199	4235	5238	4650	8792	1044	4883	10297	4687	4270	Moscow
5756		1171	3937	4795	1603	4788	6756	1534	3711	4796	5439	1926	2101	7720	10082	6858	4514	5385	966	7794	1418	8754	New Orleans
4662	1171		3769	3672	2231	3622	5590	439	2576	4820	4273	2571	2408	7357	9630	6735	5094	4224	205	8946	1281	7698	New York
4036	3937	3769		3836	5541	4574	5745	3489	3366	8586	5082	2547	1976	3784	6148	2983	8360	4657	3792	7383	2599	8209	Nome
1016	4795	3672	3836		5691	832	2211	3263	1083	6482	1243	5181	4591	5020	6246	5221	7914	859	3870	10974	3854	4803	Oslo
6711	1603	2231	5541	5691		5382	7146	2659	4706	3294	5903	3322	3651	9324	11687	8423	2943	6026	2080	7433	2998	8245	Panamá
1541	4788	3622	4574	832	5382		1975	3235	1380	5703	682	5441	4993	5752	6671	6033	7251	644	3828	11791	4118	4396	Paris
1710	6756	5590	5745	2211	7146	1975		5250	3227	6244	1317	7394	6759	5132	5088	5842	8088	1429	5796	10249	6032	2729	Port Said
4242	1534	439	3489	3263	2659	3235	5250		2189	5125	3943	2642	2353	6981	9097	6417	5504	3858	610	9228	1199	7443	Québec
2056	3711	2576	3366	1083	4706	1380	3227	2189		6118	2044	4199	3614	5559	7160	5472	7225	1805	2800	10724	2804	5757	Reykjavik
7179	4796	4820	8586	6482	3294	5703	6244	5125	6118		5684	6619	6891	11340	9774	11535	1855	6136	4797	7349	6010	5589	Rio de Janeiro
1474	5439	4273	5082	1243	5903	682	1317	3943	2044	5684		6240	5659	5677	6232	6124	7420	463	4435	11524	4803	3712	Rome
5868	1926	2571	2547	5181	3322	5441	7394	2642	4199	6619	6240		678	6132	8479	5131	5876	5988	2442	6739	1504	9958	San Francisco
5199	2101	2408	1976	4591	3651	4993	6759	2353	3614	6891	5639	678		5703	8057	4777	6230	5376	2329	7242	1150	9359	Seattle
4235	7720	7357	3784	5020	9324	5752	5132	6981	5559	11340	5677	6132	5703		2377	1094	11650	5270	7442	6054	6350	5971	Shanghai
5238	10082	9630	6148	6246	11687	6671	5088	9097	7160	9774	6232	8479	8057	2377		3304	10226	6036	9834	5292	8685	4480	Singapore
4650	6858	6735	2983	5221	8423	6033	5842	6417	5472	11535	6124	5131	4777	1094	3304		10635	5679	6769	5760	5575	7040	Tokyo
8792	4514	5094	8360	7914	2943	7251	8088	5504	7225	1855	7420	5876	6230	11650	10226	10635		7783	4977	5785	5931	7184	Valparaíso
1044	5385	4224	4657	850	6026	644	1429	3858	1805	6136	463	5988	5376	5270	6036	5679	7783		4429	11278	4604	3983	Vienna
4883	966	205	3792	3870	2080	3828	5796	610	2800	4797	4435	2442	2329	7442	9834	6769	4977	4429		8745	1243	7884	Washington, D.C.
10297	7794	8946	7383	10974	7433	11791	10249	9228	10724	7349	11524	6739	7242	6054	5292	5760	5785	11278	8745		8230	8122	Wellington
4687	1418	1281	2599	3854	2998	4118	6032	1199	2804	6010	4803	1504	1150	6350	8685	5575	5931	4604	1243	8230		8416	Winnipeg
4270	8754	7698	8209	4803	8245	4396	2729	7443	5757	5589	3712	9958	9359	5971	4480	7040	7184	3983	7884	8122	8416		Zanzibar

Passport and Foreign Travel Information

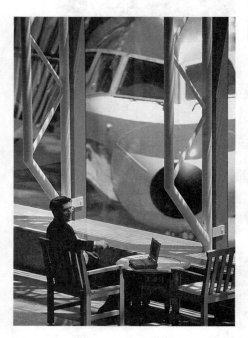

United States Passport

Apply for your passport at least 30 to 60 days before you take a trip abroad. It will save possible delay. And you won't need to go through the procedure too often since an adult's passport is valid for ten years, and a minor's (under age 18) may be used for five years.

Where To Apply

1. A U.S. State Department Passport Agency, (Boston, Chicago, Honolulu, Houston, Los Angeles, Miami, New Orleans, New York City, Philadelphia, San Francisco, Seattle; Stamford, Connecticut; and Washington, D.C.)
2. Ask at your local courthouse or post office for the nearest accepting Federal or State Clerk of Court or designated post office. These are located in most County Seats and in larger municipalities.
3. If overseas, the nearest U.S. Embassy, Consulate General, or Consulate.

How To Apply

If you possess a previous U.S. Passport showing you as bearer and issued less than twelve years ago but after your eighteenth birthday, you may apply for a new passport by mail. Obtain a DSP-82 "Application for Passport by Mail" from one of the places listed under "Where to Apply." Read carefully the instructions on the back of the form. Obtain two new photographs which meet the requirements specified here; then mail the completed application together with your two photographs, your previous passport, and a check or money order for the renewal fee of $55 to the address noted on the form. Persons under 18 years old must apply in person.

If you do not meet the requirements outlined in the previous paragraph or this is your first passport, you must apply in person. You must also have with you proof of citizenship, proof of identity, and photographs as specified below.

Qualifications

The following qualifying documents must be presented with your DSP-11 "Passport Application":
1. Proof of citizenship: Previous passport, certified birth certificate, report of birth abroad of U.S. citizen, or certificate of naturalization or citizenship.
2. Proof of identity: Recent passport, certificate of naturalization or of citizenship, valid driver's license, or government identification card. These may be supplemented as necessary by the affidavit of an accompanying witness who has known you at least two years and who bears identification as defined here.
3. Photographs: Two duplicate prints taken within six months of when you apply for passport. Prints may be black and white or color, must measure exactly 2 inches by 2 inches edge to edge; full head and face centered on a plain, light background with headsize 1 to 1³/₈ inches from bottom of chin to top of hair. Wear normal attire; do not wear a hat or dark glasses. Ordinary snapshot, vending machine, self-developing, or acetate-base prints are not acceptable.

Fees

Passport fees: first-time applicants $55 + $10 execution fee; renewal $55; 5-year passport (minors) $30 + $10 execution fee.

Visas

Visa requirements vary from country to country and according to the length and purpose of your visit. Some countries require a visa for a U.S. citizen; others do not. For general information write for the brochure "Foreign Entry Requirements," Consumer Information Center, Dept. 361C, Pueblo, CO 81009. Also available from local passport agencies. (See "Where To Apply.") Cost $0.50.

Health

Under the International Health Regulations, a country may require an International Certificate of Vaccination only against yellow fever. A smallpox vaccination is not required by any country. No immunizations are required to return to the United States. Anti-malarial and other preventive measures are advisable for some travelers; check with your health care provider or local health department. You should also be sure that any recommended immunizations, such as polio, diptheria, tetanus, or influenza, are up to date.

Businesspersons planning foreign travel should determine what health insurance coverage, if any, they should have while outside the United States. Medicare does not cover health care costs outside the U.S. and its territories except under limited circumstances in Canada and Mexico.

If you become ill upon return to the United States, inform your physician of your recent travel abroad. For more information, see "Health Information for International Travel," U.S. Government Printing Office, Washington, D.C. 20402.

Tips for Foreign Travel

☐ Make two photocopies of your passport identification page. Leave one copy at home, and carry the other copy with you in a separate place from your passport. This will facilitate replacement if your passport is stolen or lost.

☐ Leave a copy of your itinerary with family or friends at home so that you can be notified in case of an emergency.

☐ You should call the State Department's Citizens Emergency Center at 202/647-5225 for information on the areas to be visited. Stay aware of events in the country you are visiting.

☐ When traveling in disturbed or remote areas, or residing abroad, you should register and keep in touch with the nearest American embassy or consulate.

☐ Familiarize yourself with local laws and customs of the countries in which you are traveling. While in a foreign country, you are subject to its laws.

☐ Avoid conspicuous clothing and expensive jewelry and do not carry excessive amounts of money or unnecessary credit cards. And, do not leave luggage unattended in public areas or accept packages from strangers.

☐ In order to avoid violating local laws, deal only with authorized agents when exchanging money or purchasing souvenirs.

☐ Contact the nearest U.S. consul if you get into trouble.

Quick Travel Guide for Selected Countries

Entry requirements and travel advisories are subject to change. Travelers are advised to contact a travel agent, the State Department, a passport office, and/or the embassy of the destination for definitive travel information. In Islamic countries, when appearing in public, women should cover their arms, legs, and, in some places, their heads. Holidays for which a date is not given change from year to year; contact the country's embassy for exact dates.

Country	Argentina	Australia	Austria	Bahamas
	Capital: Buenos Aires *Intl Dialing Code:* 54 *Consulate Phone:* 202/939-6400 *Currency:* Peso *Languages:* Spanish, English, Italian, German, French	*Capital:* Canberra *Intl Dialing Code:* 61 *Consulate Phone:* 202/797-3000 *Currency:* Dollar *Languages:* English, indigenous	*Capital:* Wien (Vienna) *Intl Dialing Code:* 43 *Consulate Phone:* 202/895-6700 *Currency:* Schilling *Language:* German	*Capital:* Nassau *Intl Dialing Code:* 809 *Consulate Phone:* (202) 319-2660 *Currency:* Dollar *Languages:* English, Creole
City Codes	Buenos Aires 1, Córdoba 51, La Plata 21, Mendoza 61, Rosario 41	Adelaide 8, Brisbane 7, Canberra 6, Melbourne 3, Sydney 2	Graz 316, Linz 732, Wien 1	
Climate	Climate ranges from hot, subtropical lowlands of the north to cold and rainy in the south. January in Buenos Aires is like Washington, D.C., in July; July is like San Francisco in January.	Arid to semiarid; temperate in the south and east; tropical in the north; most of southern Australia has warm summers and mild winters (seasons are reversed from North America).	Cold winters with frequent rain in the lowlands and snow in the mountains; cool summers with occasional showers.	Tropical marine.
Clothing	Lightweight cottons are advisable for the north; woolens are needed during the winters and year-round in the extreme south. Dress is more formal than in the U.S. Shorts are not universally acceptable.	Wear lightweight clothing year-round in the temperate regions; during the winter, warmer clothes and an overcoat are required. Casual clothing is usually appropriate.	Clothing needs and tastes are about the same as the northeastern United States. Bring sweaters and light woolens for possible cool spells in the summer. Many restaurants in Vienna have dress codes.	Lightweight clothing is worn year-round. Beachwear should be confined to resort areas. Daytime dress is casual; evenings, clothes are more formal.
Entry Requirements	Passport, visa	Passport, visa, ticket to leave, sufficient funds	Passport	Proof of citizenship, ticket to leave
Holidays	New Year's Day, Jan. 1; Maundy Thursday; Good Friday; Labor Day, May 1; National Day, May 25; Flag Day, June 20; Independence Day, July 9; Anniversary of San Martín's Death, Aug. 17; Columbus Day, Oct. 12; Immaculate Conception, Dec. 8; Christmas Day, Dec. 25	New Year's Day, Jan. 1; Australia Day, late January; Good Friday; Holy Saturday; Easter Monday; ANZAC Day, Apr. 25; Queen's Birthday, June; Christmas Day, Dec. 25; Boxing Day, Dec. 26	New Year's Day, Jan. 1; Epiphany, Jan. 6; Easter Monday; Labor Day, May 1; Ascension Day; Whitmonday; Corpus Christi; Assumption Day, Aug. 15; National Day, Oct. 26; All Saints' Day, Nov. 1; Feast of the Immaculate Conception, Dec. 8; Christmas Day, Dec. 25; St. Stephen's Day, Dec. 26	New Year's Day, Jan. 1; Good Friday; Easter Monday; Whitmonday; Labor Day, early June; Independence Day, July 10; Emancipation Day, early Aug.; Discovery Day, Oct. 12; Christmas Day, Dec. 25; Boxing Day, Dec. 26
Special Notes	Tapwater is safe.			Hurricane season is from June to November. Water is potable but saline, and many people use bottled water. Mosquitos and sand flies may be a problem.

Country	Belgium	Brazil	Canada	Chile
	Capital: Bruxelles (Brussels) *Intl Dialing Code:* 32 *Consulate Phone:* 202/333-6900 *Currency:* Franc *Languages:* Dutch (Flemish), French, German	*Capital:* Brasília *Intl Dialing Code:* 55 *Consulate Phone:* 202/745-2700 *Currency:* Cruzeiro *Languages:* Portuguese, Spanish, English, French	*Capital:* Ottawa *Intl Dialing Code:* 1 *Consulate Phone:* 202/682-1740 *Currency:* Dollar *Languages:* English, French	*Capital:* Santiago *Intl Dialing Code:* 56 *Consulate Phone:* 202/785-1746 *Currency:* Peso *Languages:* Spanish
City Codes	Antwerpen 3, Bruxelles 2, Gent 91, Liège 41	Belo Horizonte 31, Brasília 61, Rio de Janeiro 21, São Paulo 11		Concepción 41, Santiago 2, Valparaiso 32
Climate	Mild winters with little snow; cool summers; rainy, humid, cloudy.	In most of the country, days range from warm to hot; rainy season from November to February; cool winters in the extreme south; seasons are reversed from North America.	Varies from temperate in the south to subarctic and arctic in the north.	Climate ranges from desert in the north to cool and damp in the south; summers are dry and hot with cool nights; winters are cold and rainy. Seasons are reversed from North America.
Clothing	Clothing and shoe needs in Belgium are about the same as for the Pacific Northwest. Raincoat, umbrella, and low-heeled, thick-soled walking shoes are necessary.	Spring or summer clothes are appropriate year-round.	Lightweight clothes for summer months with a sweater for cool evenings; heavy clothing for winter months.	Sweaters are useful for cool summer nights; a jacket or coat is needed in the winter. Shorts should not be worn outside resort areas.
Entry Requirements	Passport, ticket to leave, sufficient funds	Passport, visa, ticket to leave; yellow fever and other inoculations recommended	Proof of citizenship	Passport, business visa or tourist card; difficult to enter and exit by car
Holidays	New Year's Day, Jan. 1; Easter Monday; Labor Day, May 1; Ascension Day; Whitmonday; National Day, July 21; Assumption Day, Aug. 15; All Saints' Day, Nov. 1; Armistice Day, Nov. 11; Christmas Day, Dec. 25	New Year's Day, Jan. 1; Carnival, Feb./Mar.; Good Friday; Tiradentes Day, Apr. 21; Labor Day, May 1; Corpus Christi; Independence Day, Sept. 7; Nossa Senhora de Aparecida, Oct. 12; Proclamation of the Republic, Nov. 15; Christmas Day, Dec. 25	New Year's Day, Jan. 1; Good Friday; Easter Monday; Victoria Day, mid-May; Dominion Day, July 1; Civic Holiday, early Aug.; Thanksgiving, Oct. 12; Remembrance Day, Nov. 11; Christmas Day, Dec. 25; Boxing Day, Dec. 26	New Year's Day, Jan. 1; Good Friday; Labor Day, May 1; Battle of Iquique, May 21; Corpus Christi; St. Peter's and Paul's Day; Assumption Day, Aug. 15; Day of the Army, Sept. 10; National Liberation Day, Sept. 11; Independence Day, Sept. 18; Columbus Day, Oct. 12; All Saints' Day, Nov. 1; Immaculate Conception, Dec. 8; Christmas Day, Dec. 25
Special Notes	Tapwater is potable.	Street crime is common in Brazil's larger cities. Tapwater is not safe for consumption. Carefully prepared and thoroughly cooked foods are safe for consumption.		Do not eat unwashed fruits and vegetables. Tapwater is generally potable except after occasional floods. Accustom yourself gradually to tap water by using bottled water initially. Smog is prevalent in Santiago.

Country	China (excluding Taiwan)	Colombia	Costa Rica	Czech Republic
	Capital: Beijing (Peking) *Intl Dialing Code:* 86 *Consulate Phone:* 202/328-2517 *Currency:* Yuan *Languages:* Chinese dialects	*Capital:* Santa Fe de Bogotá *Intl Dialing Code:* 57 *Consulate Phone:* 202/387-8338 *Currency:* Peso *Language:* Spanish	*Capital:* San Jose *Intl Dialing Code:* 506 *Consulate Phone:* 202/234-2945 *Currency:* Colón *Language:* Spanish	*Capital:* Praha (Prague) *Intl Dialing Code:* 42 *Consulate Phone:* 202/274-9100 *Currency:* Koruna *Languages:* Czech, Slovak
City Codes	Beijing 10, Fuzhou 591, Guangzhou (Canton) 20; Jinan 531, Nanjing 791, Shanghai 21	Barranquilla 58, Bogotá 1, Cali 2, Medellín 4		Brno 5, Ostrava 69, Pizeň 19, Praha 2
Climate	Extremely diverse; tropical in the south to subarctic in the north.	Tropical along the coast and eastern plains; cooler in the highlands.	Tropical; rainy season from May to November; dry season from December to April.	Cool, pleasant summers; cold, cloudy, humid winters.
Clothing	In the north, lightweight clothing is required for the summer and heavy woolens for the harsh winters. In the south, tropical clothing is suitable for summer and spring-like clothing is worn in the winter. Clothing should be casual but conservative.	Knits and lightweight woolens are suitable in Bogotá. Tropical clothing is worn in the lowlands.	Spring-weight clothing, with a sweater for cool evenings, is recommended. Beachwear should be confined to resorts.	Bring rainwear and light or heavy woolens depending on the season. Casual but conservative dress is appropriate.
Entry Requirements	Passport, visa; inoculations recommended	Passport	Passport, ticket to leave, sufficient funds	Passport
Holidays	New Year's Day, Jan. 1; Chinese New Year, Jan. or Feb.; Labor Day, May 1, National Day, Oct. 1	New Year's Day, Jan. 1; Epiphany, Jan. 6; St. Joseph's Day, Mar. 19; Maundy Thursday; Good Friday; Labor Day, May 1; Ascension Day; Corpus Christi; Feast of the Sacred Heart; St. Peter and Paul Day; Independence Day, July 20; Battle of Boyaca, Aug. 7; Assumption Day, Aug. 15; Columbus Day, Oct. 12; All Saints' Day, Nov. 1; Independence of Cartagena, Nov. 11; Immaculate Conception, Dec. 8; Christmas Day, Dec. 25	New Year's Day, Jan. 1; St. Joseph's Day, Mar. 19; Maundy Thursday; Good Friday; Anniversary of the Battle of Rivas, Apr. 11; Labor Day, May 1; Corpus Christi; Annexation of Guanacaste, July 5; Our Lady of the Angels, Aug. 2; Assumption Day, Aug. 15; Independence Day, Sept. 15; Columbus Day, Oct. 12; Immaculate Conception, Dec. 8; Christmas Day, Dec. 25	New Year's Day, Jan. 1; Easter Monday; Labor Day, May 1; National Liberation Day, May 9; Christmas Day, Dec. 25; Boxing Day, Dec. 26
Special Notes	Travel to most of Tibet and many other areas is restricted without special permission. Tours can be extremely strenuous. Use bottled water.	Because of sporadic guerilla activity, travel in certain areas may by hazardous. Tapwater is not safe, and food should be prepared carefully.	Drinking water in major San Jose hotels and restaurants is purified; outside the capital drinking water should be purified.	Tapwater is usually safe.

Country	Denmark	Egypt	Finland	France
	Capital: København (Copenhagen) *Intl Dialing Code:* 45 *Consulate Phone:* 202/234-4300 *Currency:* Krone *Language:* Danish	*Capital:* Al-Qāhirah (Cairo) *Intl Dialing Code:* 20 *Consulate Phone:* 202/895-5400 *Currency:* Pound *Language:* Arabic	*Capital:* Helsinki *Intl Dialing Code:* 358 *Consulate Phone:* 202/298-5800 *Currency:* Markka *Languages:* Finnish, Swedish	*Capital:* Paris *Intl Dialing Code:* 33 *Consulate Phone:* 202/944-6000 *Currency:* Franc *Languages:* French
City Codes		Al-Iskandarīyah (Alexandria) 3, Al-Qāhirah 2, Aswan 97, Asyūt 88		Bordeaux 56, Lyon 7, Marseille 91, Nice 93, Paris 1, Toulouse 61
Climate	Humid and overcast; mild, windy winters; cool, sunny summers.	Desert; hot, dry summers with moderate winters.	Cold winters; mild summers. Helsinki's winter climate is similar to Boston's.	Cool winters and mild summers inland; mild winters and hot summers along the Mediterranean.
Clothing	Woolen clothes are worn most of the year. Lightweight clothes may be required in the summer.	Lightweight summer clothing is needed for the summer; light woolens for the winter and cool evenings. Casual dress is appropriate, but revealing clothing should be avoided.	Warm outdoor clothing for winter and light woolens for summer are necessary.	Clothing needs are similar to those in Washington, D.C.
Entry Requirements	Passport, ticket to leave, sufficient funds	Passport, visa, sufficient funds; inoculations recommended	Passport, ticket to leave, sufficient funds	Passport
Holidays	New Year's Day, Jan. 1; Thurs.–Mon. surrounding Easter; Prayer Day; Ascension Day; Constitution Day, June 5; Christmas Day, Dec. 25; Boxing Day, Dec. 26	Union Day, Feb. 22; Ramadan; Sinai Liberation Day, Apr. 25; Labor Day, May 1; Evacuation Day, June 18; Islamic New Year; Revolution Day, July 23; Prophet's Birthday; Armed Forces Day, Oct. 6; Suez Day, Oct. 24; Victory Day, Dec. 23	New Year's Day, Jan. 1; Epiphany; Good Friday; Easter; Easter Monday; May Day Eve, Apr. 30; May Day, May 1; Ascension Day; Whitsunday; Whitmonday; Midsummer's Day; All Saints' Day; Independence Day, Dec. 6; Christmas Day, Dec. 25	New Year's Day, Jan. 1; Easter Monday; Labor Day, May 1; Ascension Day; Whitmonday; Bastille Day, July 14; Assumption Day, Aug. 15; All Saints' Day, Nov. 1; Armistice Day, Nov. 11; Christmas Day, Dec. 25
Special Notes		Water in Cairo and Alexandria is generally safe, but milk should be boiled. Negotiate the fares with taxi drivers before entering the taxi.	Tapwater is potable.	

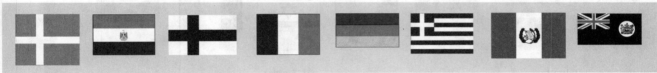

Country	Germany	Greece	Guatemala	Hong Kong
	Capital: Berlin (designated), Bonn (de facto) *Intl Dialing Code:* 49 *Consulate Phone:* 202/298-4000 *Currency:* Mark *Language:* German	*Capital:* Athínai (Athens) *Intl Dialing Code:* 30 *Consulate Phone:* 202/939-5800 *Currency:* Drachma *Language:* Greek	*Capital:* Guatemala *Intl Dialing Code:* 502 *Consulate Phone:* 202/745-4952 *Currency:* Quetzal *Languages:* Spanish, indigenous	*Capital:* Victoria (Hong Kong) *Intl Dialing Code:* 852 *Consulate Phone:* 202/462-1340 *Currency:* Dollar *Languages:* Chinese (Cantonese), English
City Codes	Berlin 30, Bonn 228, Essen 201, Frankfurt am Main 69, Hamburg 40, München (Munich) 89	Athínai 1, Iráklion 81, Lárisa 41, Piraiévs 1, Thessaloníki 31	Guatemala 2, all other cities 9	
Climate	Cool, cloudy, wet winters and summers; high relative humidity.	Mild, wet winters; hot, dry summers.	Hot and humid in the lowlands; cooler in the highlands.	Cool, humid winters; hot, rainy summers.
Clothing	Germany is cooler than much of the United States, especially in summer. Lightweight summer clothing is seldom needed. Very warm clothing is needed in winter.	Lightweight clothing from May–September; woolens from October–April.	Spring- or summer-weight clothing is needed most of the year; woolens are practical November through February.	Cottons and rainwear are advisable for the summer; warmer clothes are needed for the winter. Sports clothes are good for daytime; evenings, clothes are more formal.
Entry Requirements	Passport, ticket to leave, sufficient funds	Passport	Passport, business visa or tourist card; inoculations recommended	Passport, visa (for stays of more than 1 month), ticket to leave, sufficient funds
Holidays	New Year's Day, Jan. 1; Good Friday; Easter Monday; Labor Day, May 1; Ascension Day; Whitmonday; Day of Unity, June 17; Repentance Day, Nov. 16; Christmas Day, Dec. 25; Boxing Day, Dec. 26	New Year's Day, Jan. 1; Epiphany, Jan. 6; Independence Day, Mar. 25; Good Friday; Easter Monday; Labor Day, May 1; Pentecost; Assumption Day, Aug. 15; Ochi Day, Oct. 28; Christmas Day, Dec. 25	New Year's Day, Jan. 1; Maundy Thursday; Good Friday; Holy Saturday; Labor Day, May 1; Army Day, June 30; Assumption Day, Aug. 15; Independence Day, Sept. 15; Revolution Day, Oct. 20; All Saints' Day, Nov. 1; Christmas Eve, Dec. 24; Christmas Day, Dec. 25; New Year's Eve, Dec. 31	New Year's Day, Jan. 1; Chinese New Year, Jan. or Feb.; Good Friday; Easter Monday; Queen's Birthday, late June; Liberation Day, Aug.; Christmas Day, Dec. 25; Boxing Day, Dec. 26
Special Notes	All water and food is safe. Telecommunications in former East Germany remain poor.	Drinking water is safe in Athens and most resorts. Wash fruit before eating.	Tapwater is not potable, and fruits and vegetables should be prepared carefully.	

Country	Hungary	India	Indonesia	Ireland
	Capital: Budapest	*Capital:* New Delhi	*Capital:* Jakarta	*Capital:* Dublin
	Intl Dialing Code: 36	*Intl Dialing Code:* 91	*Intl Dialing Code:* 62	*Intl Dialing Code:* 353
	Consulate Phone: 202/362-6730	*Consulate Phone:* 202/939-7000	*Consulate Phone:* 202/775-5200	*Consulate Phone:* 202/462-3939
	Currency: Forint	*Currency:* Rupee	*Currency:* Rupiah	*Currency:* Pound (punt)
	Language: Hungarian	*Languages:* English, Hindi, Telugu, Bengali, indigenous	*Languages:* Indonesian, Javanese, Sundanese, Madurese, other indigenous	*Languages:* English, Irish Gaelic
City Codes	Budapest 1, Debrecen 5, Győr 96, Miskole 46	Bangalore 80, Bombay 22, Calcutta 33, Madras 44, New Delhi 11	Bandung 22, Jakarta 21, Medan 61, Semarang 24, Surabaya 31	Cork 21, Dublin 1, Galway 91, Waterford 51
Climate	Cold, cloudy, humid winters; warm, pleasant summers.	Varies from tropical monsoon in the south to temperate in the north. Summers are very hot in most of India.	Tropical; hot, humid; more moderate in the highlands; rainy season from November to April.	Humid and overcast; mild winters; cool summers.
Clothing	Lightweight clothing is needed for the summer and heavy woolens for the winter.	Summer clothing is suitable year-round in the south. In the north, light-weight woolens are necessary from mid-December to mid-February. Women should wear modest, loose-fitting clothing.	Lightweight cotton clothes are worn year-round, often with two changes a day. Women should dress conservatively.	Medium- to heavy-weight clothing is worn most of the year.
Entry Requirements	Passport	Passport, visa, ticket to leave; inoculations recommended	Passport, visa (for stays of more than 60 days); inoculations recommended	Passport, ticket to leave, sufficient funds
Holidays	New Year's Day, Jan. 1; National (Liberation) Day, Apr. 4; Easter Monday; Labor Day, May 1; Constitution Day, Aug. 20; October Revolution Day, Nov. 7; Christmas Day, Dec. 25; Boxing Day, Dec. 26	Republic Day, Jan. 26; Holi; Independence Day, Aug. 15; Dashara; Mahatma Gandhi's Birthday, Oct. 2; Diwali; Christmas Day, Dec. 25	New Year's Day, Jan. 1; Good Friday; Ramadan and Id al-Fitr; Ascension Day; Hijra; Independence Day, Aug. 17; Prophet's Birthday; Christmas Day, Dec. 25	New Year's Day, Jan. 1; St. Patrick's Day, Mar. 17; Good Friday; Easter Monday; Bank Holiday, early June; Bank Holiday, early August; Bank Holiday, late October; Christmas Day, Dec. 25; St. Stephen's Day, Dec. 26
Special Notes	Tapwater in Budapest is potable. Avoid unpasteurized milk and food products that lack preservatives.	Political unrest makes travel to West Bengal, Jammu and Kashmir, and the Punjab potentially dangerous. Permits are required for many restricted areas. Tapwater is unsafe throughout India. In hotels and restaurants, drink only bottled or carbonated water and avoid ice cubes.	Increasing numbers of thefts have been reported on public transportation, especially in Jakarta and Bali. Sanitation is adequate to excellent in Indonesia's international hotels, but caution should be exercised outside major cities.	Tapwater is potable.

Country	Israel	Italy	Jamaica	Japan
	Capital: Yerushalayim (Jerusalem)	*Capital:* Roma (Rome)	*Capital:* Kingston	*Capital:* Tōkyō
	Intl Dialing Code: 972	*Intl Dialing Code:* 39	*Intl Dialing Code:* 809	*Intl Dialing Code:* 81
	Consulate Phone: 202/364-5500	*Consulate Phone:* 202/328-5500	*Consulate Phone:* 202/452-0660	*Consulate Phone:* 202/939-6700
	Currency: Shekel	*Currency:* Lira	*Currency:* Dollar	*Currency:* Yen
	Languages: Hebrew, Arabic, Yiddish	*Language:* Italian	*Languages:* English, Creole	*Language:* Japanese
City Codes	Hefa (Haifa) 4, Ramat Gan 3, Tel Aviv-Yafo 3, Yerushalayim 2	Firenze 55, Genova 10, Milano 2, Napoli 81, Palermo 91, Roma 6, Venezia 41		Kyōto 75, Nagoya 52, Naha 98, Ōsaka 6, Sapporo 11, Tōkyō 3, Yokohama 45
Climate	Temperate; hot and dry in desert areas; cooler and more rainy in December through March.	Predominantly Mediterranean climate; alpine in the far north; hot and dry in the south.	Tropical; hot, humid; temperatures are more moderate in the interior highlands.	Varies from tropical in the south to cool temperate in the north.
Clothing	Clothing and shoe needs are about the same as for the American southwest. Dress at religious sites should be appropriately modest.	Woolens and sweaters are practical for most of the year; cottons are recommended for the hot summers.	Summer clothes are suitable year-round. The evenings can be chilly, especially from November to March, and light wraps or sweaters are recommended. Dress is informal, but swimsuits should be worn only at the beach.	Lightweight clothing is worn in the summer throughout the country. Medium- to heavy-weight clothing is needed for the winter. Very heavy clothing is needed for the mountains.
Entry Requirements	Passport	Passport	Passport, business visa, ticket to leave, sufficient funds	Passport, ticket to leave
Holidays	Purim; Passover; Independence Day; Yom Kippur; Rosh Hashanah; Tabernacles; Hanukkah	New Year's Day, Jan. 1; Epiphany, Jan. 6; Easter Monday; Liberation Day, Apr. 25; Labor Day, May 1; Ascension Day; Anniversary of the Republic, June 2; Assumption Day, Aug. 15; All Saints' Day, Nov. 1; Immaculate Conception Day, Dec. 8; Christmas Day, Dec. 25; St. Stephen's Day, Dec. 26	New Year's Day, Jan 1; Ash Wednesday; Good Friday; Easter Monday; Labor Day, May 23; Independence Day, early Aug.; National Heroes' Day, late Oct.; Christmas Day, Dec. 25; Boxing Day, Dec. 26	New Year's, Dec. 28–Jan. 3; Adult's Day, Jan. 15; National Foundation Day, Feb. 11; Vernal Equinox Day, Mar. 21; Constitution Day, May 3; Children's Day, May 5; Respect for the Aged Day, Sept. 15; Autumnal Equinox Day, Sept.; Health and Sports Day, Oct. 10; Culture Day, Nov. 3; Labor Thanksgiving Day, Nov. 23; Emperor's Birthday, Dec. 23
Special Notes	Travel to the West Bank and Gaza Strip is potentially dangerous and may be restricted. Travel only in daylight hours and stay on established roads and paths. Do not take public buses; avoid bus stops. Tapwater is potable. All stores and banks are closed from 12:30 on Friday to Sunday morning.	Tapwater is safe. Meat, fruit, vegetables and shellfish should be well prepared.	Hurricane season is from June to November. Crime is a serious problem in Kingston. Municipal water supplies are potable. Fruits and vegetables are safe.	Drinking water, fruits, and vegetables are safe.

Country	Kazakhstan	Kenya	Luxembourg	Malaysia
	Capital: Almaty (Alma-Ata) *Intl Dialing Code:* 7 *Consulate Phone:* 202/333-4507 *Currency:* Tenge *Languages:* Kazakh	*Capital:* Nairobi *Intl Dialing code:* 254 *Consulate Phone:* 202/387-6101 *Currency:* Shilling *Languages:* English, Swahili, indigenous	*Capital:* Luxembourg *Intl Dialing Code:* 352 *Consulate Phone:* 202/265-4171 *Currency:* Franc *Languages:* French, Luxembourgish, German	*Capital:* Kuala Lumpur *Intl Dialing Code:* 60 *Consulate Phone:* 202/328-2700 *Currency:* Ringgit *Languages:* Malay, Chinese dialects, English, Tamil
City Codes	Almaty 3272	Kisumu 35, Mombasa 11, Nairobi 2, Nakuru 37		Ipoh 5, Johor Baharu 7, Kajang 3, Kuala Lumpur 3
Climate	Widely variable temperatures with hot summers and cold winters; milder temperatures in the southeast; rain in the mountains.	Varies from tropical along the coast to arid in the interior. Rainy seasons are from March to June and from October to December.	Mild winters, cool summers.	Tropical; hot summers and winters; heavy summer rainfall, moderate winter rainfall.
Clothing	Light cottons are needed for the hot summer days; warm woolens for winter wear.	Light- and medium-weight clothing is worn most of the year. Sweaters and light raincoats are needed during the rainy season. Some restaurants have evening dress codes.	Fall and light winter clothing is worn. Some restaurants have evening dress codes.	Lightweight clothing is suitable for the tropical climate, except in the high-land resort areas.
Entry Requirements	Passport, visa, ticket to leave	Passport, visa, ticket to leave; cholera and other inoculations recommended	Passport, ticket to leave, sufficient funds	Passport, ticket to leave, sufficient funds
Holidays	New Year's Day, Jan. 1; Ramadan; Navroos, late Mar.; Labor Day, May 1; Independence Day, Dec. 16; Christmas Day, Dec. 25	New Year's Day, Jan. 1; Ramadan and Id al-Fitr; Good Friday; Easter Monday; Madaraka Day, June 1; Kenyatta Day, Oct. 20; Independence Day, Dec. 12; Christmas Day, Dec. 25; Boxing Day, Dec. 26	New Year's Day, Jan. 1; Easter Monday; May Day, May 1; Ascension Day; Whitmonday; National Day, June 23; Assumption Day, Aug. 15; All Saints' Day, Nov. 1; Christmas Day, Dec. 25; St. Stephen's Day, Dec. 26	Chinese New Year, Jan. or Feb.; Ramadan and Id al-Fitr; Labor Day, May 1; Wesak Day, May 30; Monarch's Day, June 1; Id al-Adha; National Day, Aug. 31; Prophet's Birthday; Diwali; Christmas Day, Dec. 25
Special Notes	Tapwater is not potable. Air transportation is sometimes disrupted. For stays of more than three days, travelers must register with OVIR. To register, present a letter of invitation and a health certificate showing negative results on an HIV test given within the preceding 30 days.	Avoid tapwater and unwashed fruits outside the capital. Anti-malarial drugs are recommended.		Tapwater in cities is considered safe. Malaria is a problem in rural areas, and anti-malarial pills are recommended.

Country	Mexico	Netherlands	New Zealand	Norway
	Capital: Ciudad de México (Mexico City) *Intl Dialing Code:* 52 *Consulate Phone:* 202/736-1000 *Currency:* Peso *Languages:* Spanish, indigenous	*Capital:* Amsterdam (designated), The Hague (seat of government) *Intl Dialing Code:* 31 *Consulate Phone:* 202/244-5300 *Currency:* Guilder *Language:* Dutch	*Capital:* Wellington *Intl Dialing Code:* 64 *Consulate Phone:* 202/328-4800 *Currency:* Dollar *Languages:* English, Maori	*Capital:* Oslo *Intl Dialing Code:* 47 *Consulate Phone:* 202/333-6000 *Currency:* Krone *Languages:* Norwegian, Lapp
City Codes	Acapulco 74, Cancún 988, Chihuahua 14, Ciudad de México 16, Monterrey 83, Puebla 22, Tijuana 66	Amsterdam 20, Rotterdam 10, 's-Gravenhage (The Hague) 70, Utrecht 30	Auckland 9, Christchurch 3, Dunedin 3, Hamilton 7, Wellington 4	
Climate	Varies from tropical to desert; cooler at higher elevations. Guadalajara and Mexico City are pleasant year-round. Monterrey, the Yucatan Peninsula, and desert areas are very hot in the summer.	Mild winters, cool summers.	Temperate; wet, windy, cool; warm summers; mild winters; seasons are reversed from North America.	Temperate along coast, colder interior; rainy year-round on west coast.
Clothing	Wear tropical clothing in desert areas and lowlands. In Mexico City and other mountainous areas, medium-weight clothing is comfortable. Shorts are worn only on the beaches.	Clothing needs are similar to those of Seattle, Washington. Some restaurants have evening dress codes.	Warm clothing is comfortable most of the year. Raincoats are essential.	Lightweight clothing and light woolens are worn in the summer, and heavy clothing is needed in the winter.
Entry Requirements	Proof of citizenship, business visa or tourist card no longer recommended.	Passport which must be valid for six months or more when entering the country, ticket to leave	Passport, ticket to leave, sufficient funds	Passport, ticket to leave, sufficient funds
Holidays	New Year's Day, Jan. 1; Constitution Day, Feb. 5; Birthday of Benito Juárez, Mar. 21; Maundy Thursday; Good Friday; Holy Saturday; Labor Day, May 1; Battle of Puebla, May 5; President's Message Day, Sept. 1; Independence Day, Sept. 16; Columbus Day, Oct. 12; Day of the Dead, Nov. 1–2; Revolution Anniversary, Nov. 20; Guadalupe Day, Dec. 12; Christmas Day, Dec. 25	New Year's Day, Jan. 1; Good Friday; Easter Monday; Queen's Birthday, Apr. 30; Ascension Day; Whitmonday; Christmas Day, Dec. 25; Boxing Day, Dec. 26	New Year's Day, Jan. 1; New Zealand Day, Feb. 6; Good Friday; Easter Monday; Queen's Birthday, June; Labor Day, late Oct.; Christmas Day, Dec. 25; Boxing Day, Dec. 26	New Year's Day, Jan. 1; Maundy Thursday; Good Friday; Easter Monday; May Day, May 1; Constitution Day, May 17; Ascension Day; Whitmonday; Christmas Day, Dec. 25; Boxing Day, Dec. 26
Special Notes	Tapwater is not safe. Cooked food is safe to eat; raw vegetables are not. Avoid ice cubes.	Tapwater is safe.		Tapwater is potable.

	Peru	Philippines	Poland	Portugal
Country	*Capital:* Lima *Intl Dialing Code:* 51 *Consulate Phone:* 202/833-9860 *Currency:* Inti *Languages:* Quechua, Spanish, Amara	*Capital:* Manila *Intl Dialing Code:* 63 *Consulate Phone:* 202/467-9300 *Currency:* Peso *Languages:* English, Pilipino, Tagalog	*Capital:* Warszawa (Warsaw) *Intl Dialing Code:* 48 *Consulate Phone:* 202/234-3800 *Currency:* Zloty *Language:* Polish	*Capital:* Lisboa (Lisbon) *Intl Dialing Code:* 351 *Consulate Phone:* 202/328-8610 *Currency:* Escudo *Language:* Portuguese
City Codes	Arequipa 54, Callao 1, Chiclayo 74; Cuzco 84; Lima 1, Trujillo 44	Bocolod 34, Cebu 32, Davao 82, Iloilo 33, Manila 2	Gdańsk 58, Katowice 32, Lódź 42, Poznań 61, Kraków 12, Warszawa 22	Coimbra 39, Lisboa 1, Porto 2, Setúbal 65
Climate	Varies from tropical in the east to dry desert in the west; winters are damp; seasons are reversed from those in North America.	Hot and humid; cooler in mountainous areas.	Cold, cloudy, moderately severe winters with frequent precipitation; mild summers with frequent showers and thundershowers.	Mild, damp winters; hot, dry summers; climate is more moderate along the coast.
Clothing	Medium-weight clothing is suitable in the winter; in summer, wear light-weight clothing. Fashions are similar to those in the U.S., but shorts should be worn only in resort areas.	Cotton and other lightweight clothing is worn all year. If traveling to the popular mountain resorts in northern Luzon, light sweaters are appropriate. Some restaurants have evening dress codes.	Spring-weight clothing is worn in the summer and heavy clothing in the winter. Rainwear is advisable through-out the year.	Wear summer clothing during the temperate sunny days and cool nights. Fall-weight clothing and a topcoat or warm raincoat are appropriate for winter. A rain hat or umbrella is rec-ommended. Swimsuits should be con-fined to the beach.
Entry Requirements	Passport, business visa, ticket to leave; hepatitis inoculations recommended	Passport, ticket to leave	Passport	Passport
Holidays	New Year's Day, Jan. 1; Maundy Thursday; Good Friday; Labor Day, May 1; St. Peter and St. Paul's Day, June 29; Independence Days, July 28, 29; Santa Rosa Day, Aug. 30; National Dignity Day, early Oct.; All Saints' Day, Nov. 1; Immaculate Conception, Dec. 8; Christmas Eve, Dec. 24; Christmas Day, Dec.25	New Year's Day, Jan. 1; Maundy Thursday; Good Friday; Labor Day, May 1; Independence Day, June 12; Philippine-American Friendship Day, July 4; All Saints' Day, Nov. 1; Boni-facio Day, Nov. 30; Christmas Day, Dec. 25; Rizal Day, Dec. 30	New Year's Day, Jan. 1; Easter Monday; Labor Day, May 1; Corpus Christi; National Day, July 22; All Saints' Day, Nov. 1; Christmas Day, Dec. 25; Boxing Day, Dec. 26	New Year's Day, Jan. 1; Shrove Tuesday; Good Friday; Anniversary of the Revolution, Apr. 25; Labor Day, May 1; Portugal Day, June 10; Corpus Christi; Assumption Day, Aug. 15; Republic Day, Oct. 5; All Saints' Day, Nov. 1; Independence Day, Dec. 1; Immaculate Conception, Dec. 8; Christmas Day, Dec. 25
Special Notes	Terrorism is prevalent in rural Peru, and a cholera epidemic makes fruits and vegetables unsafe. water is potable in major cities.	Do not drink untreated or unboiled water outside Manila. Rebel activity in some areas makes travel potentially dangerous.		Tapwater is potable year-round in large cities and in outlying areas during rainy seasons. Bottled spring water is available.

	Puerto Rico	Russia	Singapore	South Africa
Country	*Capital:* San Juan *Intl Dialing Code:* 1 *Currency:* U.S. dollar *Language:* Spanish	*Capital:* Moskva (Moscow) *Intl Dialing Code:* 7 *Consulate Phone:* 202/298-5700 *Currency:* Ruble *Languages:* Russian, Tatar	*Capital:* Singapore *Intl Dialing Code:* 65 *Consulate Phone:* 202/537-3100 *Currency:* Dollar *Languages:* Chinese (Mandarin), English, Malay, Tamil	*Capital:* Pretoria (administrative), Cape Town (legislative), Bloemfontein (judicial) *Intl Dialing Code:* 27 *Consulate Phone:* 202/232-4400 *Currency:* Rand *Languages:* Afrikaans, English, Xhosa, Zulu, Swazi, other indigenous
City Codes		Moskva 095, Nižnij Novgorod (Gorky) 8312, St. Petersburg 182		Bloemfontein 51, Cape Town 21, Durban 31, Johannesburg 11, Pretoria 12
Climate	Mild, little seasonal temperature variation.	Mostly temperate to arctic continental; winters vary from cold in the west to frigid in Siberia; summers range from hot in the south to cool along the Arctic coast.	Tropical; hot, humid, rainy.	Mostly semiarid; subtropical along coast; sunny days, cool nights. Seasons are reversed from North America.
Clothing	Lightweight clothing is worn through-out the year with a sweater or jacket for cooler evenings. Some restaurants have evening dress codes.	Clothing requirements are the same as in the northern U.S. although the weather tends to be cooler. Public buildings, hotels, and homes are well heated. Hot weather occurs from June through August.	Light cotton clothing is worn through-out the year. An umbrella is needed. Some restaurants have evening dress codes.	Clothing suitable for central and southern California is appropriate for South Africa's mild climate. Many restaurants have evening dress codes.
Entry Requirements	Proof of citizenship	Passport, visa	Passport which must be valid for six months or more when entering the country, ticket to leave, sufficient funds	Passport which must be valid for six months or more when entering the country, ticket to leave, sufficient funds
Holidays	New Year's Day, Jan 1; Epiphany, Jan. 6; De Hostos' Birthday, Jan. 11; Martin Luther King's Birthday, Jan. 15; Presi-dents' Day, Feb.; Emancipation Day, Mar. 22; De Diego's Birthday, Apr. 16; Memorial Day, late May; Independence Day, July 4; Muñoz Rivera's Birthday, July 17; Constitution Day, July 25; Barbosa's Birthday, July 27; Labor Day, early Sept.; Columbus Day, early Oct; Veteran's Day, Nov. 11; Discovery of Puerto Rico, Nov. 19; Thanksgiving, late Nov.; Christmas Day, Dec. 25	New Year's Day, Jan. 1; International Women's Day, Mar. 8; Labor Days, May 1, 2; Victory Day, May 9; Constitution Day, Oct. 7	Chinese New Year, Jan. or Feb.; Ramadan and Id al-Fitr; Good Friday; Labor Day, May 1; Wesak Day, May; National Day, Aug. 9; Diwali; Christ-mas Day, Dec. 25	New Year's Day, Jan. 1; Founder's Day, Apr. 6; Good Friday; Easter Monday; Ascension Day; Republic Day, May 31; Settler's Day, early Sept.; Kruger Day, Oct. 10; Day of the Covenant, Dec. 16; Christmas Day, Dec. 25; Boxing Day, Dec. 26
Special Notes	Hurricane season is from June to November.	Avoid tapwater, especially in St. Petersburg, and drink bottled water. Avoid cold foods, such as salads.		The U.S. State Department warns that the political situation in South Africa is potentially dangerous. Drinking water is generally safe, but avoid bathing in lakes or streams. Anti-malarial pills are recommended in rural areas.

Country	South Korea	Spain	Sweden	Switzerland
	Capital: Sŏul (Seoul)	*Capital:* Madrid	*Capital:* Stockholm	*Capital:* Bern
	Intl Dialing Code: 82	*Intl Dialing Code:* 34	*Intl Dialing Code:* 46	*Intl Dialing Code:* 41
	Consulate Phone: 202/939-5600	*Consulate Phone:* 202/452-0100	*Consulate Phone:* 202/467-2600	*Consulate Phone:* 202/745-7900
	Currency: Won	*Currency:* Peseta	*Currency:* Krona	*Currency:* Franc
	Language: Korean	*Languages:* Spanish (Castilian), Catalan, Galician, Basque	*Language:* Swedish	*Languages:* German, French, Italian, Romansch
City Codes	Inch'ŏn 32, Pusan 51, Sŏul 2, Taegu 53	Barcelona 3, Madrid 1, Sevilla 54, Valencia 6	Göteborg 31, Malmö 40, Stockholm 8, Uppsala 18, Västerås 21	Basel 61, Bern 31, Genève 22, Lausanne 21, Lucerne 41, Zürich 1
Climate	Temperate, with rainfall heavier in summer than winter.	Interior has hot, clear summers and cold winters; coast has moderate, cloudy summers and cool winters.	Temperate in the south with cold, cloudy winters and cool, partly cloudy summers; subarctic in the north.	Varies with altitude; cold, cloudy, snowy winters; cool to warm, cloudy, humid summers with occasional showers.
Clothing	Clothing requirements are similar to those of the eastern U.S. Dress is more conservative than in the U.S.	Clothes suitable for the Washington, D.C., climate are recommended. Slacks are worn in public, but shorts are not. Sweaters and raincoats are advisable.	Lightweight clothing is used in the summer, with heavy clothing for winter.	Light woolens may be worn in the summer and heavy winter clothing in the winter.
Entry Requirements	Passport, visa, ticket to leave	Passport	Passport, ticket to leave, sufficient funds	Passport
Holidays	New Year, Jan 1–3; Lunar New Year, Jan. or Feb.; Independence Day, Mar. 1; Buddha's Birthday, May; Memorial Day, June 6; Constitution Day, July 17; Liberation Day, Aug. 15; Chusok (Thanksgiving), Aug or Sept.; Armed Forces Day, Oct. 1; Foundation Day, Oct. 3; Korean Alphabet Day, Oct. 9; Christmas Day, Dec. 25	New Year's Day, Jan. 1; Epiphany, Jan. 6; St. Joseph's Day, Mar. 19; Good Friday; May Day, May 1; Corpus Christi; St. John's Day, June 24; St. James' Day, July 25; Assumption Day, Aug. 15; National Day, Oct. 12; All Saints' Day, Nov. 1; Constitution Day, Dec. 6; Immaculate Conception, Dec. 8; Christmas Day, Dec. 25	New Year's Day, Jan. 1; Good Friday; Easter Monday; Labor Day, May 1; Ascension Day; Whitmonday; Midsummer's Day, late June; All Saints' Day, early Nov.; Christmas Day, Dec. 25; Boxing Day, Dec. 26	New Year's, Jan. 1, 2; Good Friday; Easter Monday; Ascension Day; Whitmonday; Labor Day, May 1; National Day, Aug. 1; Christmas Day, Dec. 25; Boxing Day, Dec. 26
Special Notes	Outside of the major hotels, water is generally not potable.	Drinking water in Madrid is safe. Use bottled water elsewhere. Peel all fruit.	Tapwater is potable, and dairy products pure.	

Country	Taiwan	Tanzania	Thailand	Trinidad and Tobago
	Capital: T'aipei	*Capital:* Dar es Salaam	*Capital:* Krung Thep (Bangkok)	*Capital:* Port of Spain
	Intl Dialing Code: 886	*Intl Dialing Code:* 255	*Intl Dialing Code:* 66	*Intl Dialing Code:* 809
	Consulate Phone: None; for passport and visa requirements, call TECRO at 202/895-1800	*Consulate Phone:* 202/939-6125	*Consulate Phone:* 202/944-3600	*Consulate Phone:* 202/467-6490
	Currency: Dollar	*Currency:* Shilling	*Currency:* Baht	*Currency:* Dollar
	Languages: Chinese dialects	*Languages:* English, Swahili, indigenous	*Languages:* Thai, indigenous	*Languages:* English, Hindi, French, Spanish
City Codes	Kaohsiung 7, T'ainan 6, T'aipei 2	Dar es Salaam 51, Dodoma 61, Mwanza 68, Tanga 63	Bangkok 2, Chiang Mai 53, Krung Thep 2, Nakhon Sawan 56, Ubon Ratchathani 45	
Climate	Chilly, damp winters; hot, humid summers; rainy season from June to August, often cloudy.	Varies from tropical along the coast to temperate in the highlands; rainy season from November to April; dry season from May to October.	Tropical; dry, cooler winters; warm, rainy, cloudy summers; southern isthmus is always hot and humid.	Tropical; dry season from January to May.
Clothing	In winter, light jackets and sweaters are recommended; in summer, lightweight garments are essential. An umbrella is useful year-round.	Lightweight, tropical clothing is worn year-round. In the cooler season, a light wrap is useful in the evening. Conservative dress is required. Bring sunglasses and a hat.	Lightweight, washable clothing is comfortable and practical for Bangkok's tropical climate. In northern Thailand, a jacket or sweater is needed during the cool season. Swimwear should be worn only on the beach.	Summer-weight clothing is worn year-round. Beachwear should be confined to the beach. Restaurants may have evening dress codes.
Entry Requirements	Passport which must be valid for six months or more when entering the country, visa, ticket to leave	Passport, visa, ticket to leave; cholera inoculations highly recommended. yellow fever inoculations required	Passport, ticket to leave; yellow fever inoculation required if you have been to Africa after 1992, other inoculations recommended	Passport, ticket to leave
Holidays	Founding of the Republic, Jan. 1; Chinese New Year, Jan. or Feb.; Youth Day, Mar. 29; Tomb-sweeping Day, Apr. 5; Confucius's Birthday, Sept. 28; National Day, Oct. 10; Taiwan Restoration Day, Oct. 25; Chiang Kaishek's Birthday, Oct. 31; Dr. Sun Yat-Sen's Birthday, Nov. 12; Constitution Day, Dec. 25	Zanzibar Revolution Day, Jan. 12; CCM Day, Feb. 5; Good Friday; Easter Monday; Ramadan and Id al-Fitr; Union Day, Apr. 26; Peasants' Day, July 7; Hijra; Prophet's Birthday; Independence Day, Dec. 9; Christmas, Dec. 25	New Year's Day, Jan. 1; Songkran Festival, Apr. 13; Coronation Day Anniversary, May 5; Visakhja Puja, May; Buddhist Lent, June or July; Queen's Birthday, Aug. 12; Chulalongkorn Day, Oct. 23; King's Birthday, Dec. 5; New Year's Eve, Dec. 31	New Year's Day, Jan. 1; Ramadan and Id al-Fitr; Good Friday; Easter Monday; Whitmonday; Corpus Christi; Labor Day, June 19; Discovery Day, early Aug.; Independence Day, Aug. 31; Republic Day, Sept. 24; Diwali (Festival of Lights); Christmas Day, Dec. 25; Boxing Day, Dec. 26
Special Notes	Drinking water is safe at T'aipei's major hotels, but when dining elsewhere, drink only hot or bottled water. High pollen counts and air pollution can contribute to asthma.	Tapwater is not potable. Water should be boiled and filtered and fruits and vegetables carefully prepared. Do not swim or paddle in lakes or streams. Anti-malarial drugs are recommended. Do not go barefoot.	Thailand has an extremely strict anti-narcotics law that provides for severe sentences, including sentences in excess of 20 years for drug traffickers. Avoid tap water, raw milk, ice cream, uncooked meats, and unwashed raw fruits and vegetables.	Hurricane season is from June to November. Tapwater is safe but do not drink water from an unknown source. Wash fruits and vegetables carefully.

TERCRO T'aipei Economic and Cultural Representative Office

Country	Turkey	Ukraine	United Arab Emirates	United Kingdom
	Capital: Ankara *Intl Dialing Code:* 90 *Consulate Phone:* 202/659-8200 *Currency:* Lira *Languages:* Turkish, Kurdish, Arabic	*Capital:* Kyyiv (Kiev) *Intl Dialing Code:* 38 *Consulate Phone:* 202/333-7507 *Currency:* Hryvnia *Language:* Ukrainian	*Capital:* Abū Zaby (Abu Dhabi) *Intl Dialing Codes:* 971 *Consulate Phone:* 202/338-6500 *Currency:* Dirham *Languages:* Arabic, English, Farsi, Hindi, Urdu	*Capital:* London *Intl Dialing Code:* 44 *Consulate Phone:* 202/462-1340 *Currency:* Pound sterling *Languages:* English, Welsh, Gaelic
City Codes	Adana 322, Ankara 312, Istanbul 212 or 216, Izmir 232	Kharkiv (Kharkov) 0572, Kyyiv 044, Odessa 0482	Abū Zaby 2, Al-'Ayn 3, Ash-Shāriqah 6, Dubayy 4, 'Ujmān 6	Belfast 1232, Birmingham 121, Cardiff 1222, Glasgow 141, Liverpool 151, London 171 or 181, Manchester 161
Climate	Mild, wet winters; hot, dry summers. Climate is more severe in the interior.	Temperate; cool, pleasant summers and mild to cold winters; southern regions warmer with winter temperatures seldom dropping to freezing.	Desert; hot and dry; cooler in the eastern mountains and during the winter.	Temperate; mild winters; cool summers; cloudy with rainfall in all seasons.
Clothing	Summer requires lightweight clothing in the northern areas and tropical clothing in the south. Warm woolens are necessary for the winter months.	Medium- and lightweight clothing with a sweater or jacket for cool evenings is appropriate in summer months; woolens are needed for winter wear.	Lightweight attire is necessary during the summer. From mid-October through April, spring or fall clothing is suitable. Everyone should dress modestly.	Fall and winter clothing is needed from about September through April; spring and summer clothing is useful the rest of the year. Always bring a raincoat and umbrella. Some restaurants have dress codes.
Entry Requirements	Passport, visa	Passport, visa; inoculations recommended	Passport, visa, ticket to leave	Passport, ticket to leave
Holidays	New Year's Day, Jan. 1; Ramadan and Id al-Fitr; National Sovereignty Day, Apr. 23; Spring Day, May 1; Youth Day, May 19; Constitution Day, May 27; Id al-Adha; Victory Day, Aug. 30; Republic Day, Oct. 29	New Year's Day, Jan. 1; Orthodox Christmas Day, Jan. 7; International Women's Day, Mar. 8; Labor Day, May 1; Victory Day, May 9; Independence Day, Aug. 24	New Year's Day, Jan. 1; Ramadan and Id al-Fitr; Id al-Adha; Hijra; National Day, Dec. 2; Christmas Day, Dec. 25	New Year's Day, Jan. 1; Good Friday; Easter Monday; May Day, early May; Spring Bank Holiday, late May; Summer Bank Holiday, late August; Christmas Day, Dec. 25; Boxing Day, Dec. 26
Special Notes	Tapwater should be avoided.	Credit cards and traveler's checks are accepted only in foreign-run shops and restaurants. Travelers' facilities are not highly developed. Energy cutbacks may affect heat and hot water supplies and make transportation, other than by train, unreliable. Do not drink tapwater.	Water is potable.	Traffic moves on the left on British roads.

Country	United States	Venezuela	Vietnam	Zimbabwe
	Capital: Washington, D.C. *Intl Dialing Code:* 1 *Currency:* Dollar *Languages:* English, Spanish	*Capital:* Caracas *Intl Dialing Code:* 58 *Consulate Phone:* 202/342-2214 *Currency:* Bolivar *Languages:* Spanish, indigenous	*Capital:* Ha Noi *Intl Dialing Code:* 84 *Consulate Phone:* 202/861-0737 *Currency:* Dong *Languages:* Vietnamese, French, Chinese, Khmer, indigenous	*Capital:* Harare *Intl Dialing Code:* 263 *Consulate Phone:* 202/332-7100 *Currency:* Kwacha *Languages:* English, ChiShona, SiNdebele
City Codes		Barquisimeto 51, Caracas 2, Maracaibo 61, Valencia 41	Danang 51, Ha Noi 4, Ho Chi Minh City 8	Bulawayo 9, Harare 4, Mutare 20
Climate	Mostly temperate, but varies from tropical to arctic; arid to semiarid in west.	Tropical; hot, humid; more moderate in the highlands; rainy season from May to November.	Tropical; hot temperatures in April and May; rainy season June through October; cooler evening temperatures November through March.	Tropical; moderated by altitude; rainy season from November to March.
Clothing	Clothing ranges from very lightweight to very heavy, depending on the region and time of year.	Spring-weight clothing is appropriate in Caracas. Elsewhere temperatures vary with altitude from tropics to freezing. Many restaurants have dress codes. Shorts should be worn only on the beach.	Lightweight clothing is worn year-round; take a sweater or jacket for cooler evenings in the northern highlands.	Light, summer apparel is appropriate from October to May. Fall or spring clothing is suitable the rest of the year. Some urban restaurants have dress codes.
Entry Requirements	Passport, visa	Passport, business visa or tourist card, ticket to leave	Passport, visa	Passport, ticket to leave, sufficient funds, yellow fever inoculations recommended
Holidays	New Year's Day, Jan. 1; Martin Luther King's Birthday, Jan. 15; Presidents' Day, late Feb.; Memorial Day, late May; Independence Day, July 4; Labor Day, early Sept.; Columbus Day, early Oct.; Veteran's Day, Nov. 11; Thanksgiving Day, late Nov.; Christmas Day, Dec. 25	New Year's Day, Jan. 1; Carnival; Maundy Thursday; Good Friday; Holy Saturday; Declaration of Independence Day, Apr. 19; Labor Day, May 1; Battle of Carabobo, June 24; Independence Day, July 5; Bolivar's Birthday, July 24; Columbus Day, Oct. 12; Christmas Eve, Dec. 24; Christmas Day, Dec. 25	Tet; Liberation Day, Apr. 30; Labor Day, May 1; National Day, Sept. 2; Christmas Day, Dec. 25	New Year's Day, Jan. 1; Good Friday; Easter Monday; Independence Day, Apr. 18; Worker's Day, early May; Africa Day, May 25; Heroes' Days, Aug. 11–12; Christmas Day, Dec. 25; Boxing Day, Dec. 26
Special Notes		Tapwater should be boiled and vegetables carefully prepared.	Water is not potable; avoid ice cubes. Fruits should be peeled and vegetables cooked. Anti-malarial tablets are recommended. Petty crime can be a problem in Ho Chi Minh City. Use pedicabs only if the hotel orders them for you.	Sporadic violence is not uncommon; travel in rural areas is not advised. Tapwater is safe in all urban areas but not in rural areas. Anti-malarial tablets are recommended in rural areas.

Weights, Measures, and Formulas

Measures

Linear

1 inch = 2.540 centimeters
1 foot = .305 meter
1 yard = .914 meter
1 mile = 1.609 kilometers
1 meter = 39.37 inches
1 meter = 3.28 feet = 1.094 yards
1 kilometer = .621 mile
1 mile = 1,760 yards = 5,280 feet
1 yard = 36 inches = 3 feet
1 foot = 12 inches
1 span = 9 inches
1 hand = 4 inches
1 mile = 8 furlongs
1 furlong = 220 yards
1 nautical mile (knot) =1.152 statute
    miles = 1.853 kilometers

Distance

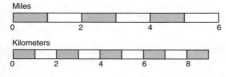

Miles to Kilometers: Multiply number of miles
    by 1.6
Kilometers to Miles: Multiply number of kilo
    meters by .6

Speed

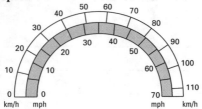

30 mph is maximum speed limit in most U.S.
    towns. The metric equivalent is 50 km/h.
50 mph is maximum speed limit on many rural
    two-lane roads in U.S. In metric, 80 km/h.
65 mph is maximum speed limit on many U.S.
    interstate highways. In metric, 105 km/h.
60 mph is maximum speed allowed on access-
    controlled highways in Canada. The metric
    equivalent is 100 km/h.

Square/Area

1 sq. inch = 6.451 sq. centimeters
1 sq. foot = .093 sq. meter
1 sq. yard = .836 sq. meter
1 sq. centimeter = .155 sq. inch
1 sq. meter = 10.764 sq. feet = 1.196 sq. yards
1 sq. foot = 144 sq. inches
1 sq. yard = 9 sq. feet
An acre is equal to a square, the side of which is
    208.7 feet.
1 acre = 4,840 sq. yards = 43,560 sq. feet
1 sq. mile = 640 acres
1 sq. mile = 2.59 sq. kilometers
1 sq. kilometer = .386 sq. mile

Cubic/Volume

1 cu. inch = 16.387 cu. centimeters
1 cu. foot = .028 cu. meter
1 cu. yard = .765 cu. meter
1 cu. centimeter = .061 cu. inch
1 cu. meter = 35.314 cu. feet
1 cu. meter = 1.303 cu. yards
1 cu. yard = 27 cu. feet
1 cu. foot = 1,728 cu. inches
1 cord of wood = 4 x 4 x 8 feet = 128 cu. feet

Dry Measure (U.S.)

1 bushel = 1.245 cu. feet = 2,150.42 cu inches
1 bushel = 4 pecks = 32 quarts = 64 pints
1 peck = 8 quarts = 16 pints

Liquid Measure (U.S.)

1 pint = 16 ounces = .473 liter
1 quart = 2 pints = 32 ounces
1 quart = .946 liter
1 gallon = 4 quarts = 3.785 liters
1 liter = 1.057 quarts

Liquid Measurement

The Imperial/Canadian gallon is based on the
Imperial quart, which is approximately one-
fifth larger than the U.S. quart. *The following
measurements are approximate for easy
conversion.*
1 Imperial gallon = 4.5 liters
1 Imperial gallon = 1.2 U.S. gallons
1 liter = .22 Imperial gallon
5 Imperial gallons = 6 U.S. gallons

Miscellaneous

1 great gross = 12 gross = 144 dozen
1 gross = 12 dozen = 144 units
1 dozen = 12 units
1 score = 20 units
1 quire = 24 sheets
1 ream = 20 quires = 480 sheets
1 ream printing paper = 500 sheets

Clothing Size Equivalents

Men's Suits and Overcoats

American: 36, 38, 40, 42, 44, 46
British: 36, 38, 40, 42, 44, 46
European: 46, 48, 51, 54, 56, 59

Women's Suits and Dresses

American: 8, 10, 12, 14, 16, 18
British: 10, 12, 14, 16, 18, 20
European: 38, 40, 42, 44, 46, 48

Shirts

American: 14, $14^1/_2$, 15, $15^1/_2$, 16, $16^1/_2$, 17
British: 14, $14^1/_2$, 15, $15^1/_2$, 16, $16^1/_2$, 17
European: 36, 37, 38, 39, 41, 42, 43

Men's Shoes

American: $7^1/_2$, 8, $8^1/_2$, $9^1/_2$, $10^1/_2$, $11^1/_2$
British: 7, $7^1/_2$, 8, 9, 10, 11
European: $40^1/_2$, 41, 42, 43, $44^1/_2$, 46

Women's Shoes

American: 6, $6^1/_2$, 7, $7^1/_2$, 8, $8^1/_2$
British: $4^1/_2$, 5, $5^1/_2$, 6, $6^1/_2$, 7
European: $37^1/_2$, 38, 39, $39^1/_2$, 40, $40^1/_2$

Weights

Avoirdupois

1 ounce = 28.35 grams
1 pound = .453 kilograms = 16 ounces
1 gram = .035 ounce
1 kilogram = 2.205 pounds
1 short ton = 2,000 pounds
1 short ton = .907 metric tons
1 long ton = 2,240 pounds
1 long ton = 1.016 metric tons
1 stone = 14 pounds

Troy

1 ounce = 20 pennyweights = 48 grains
1 pound = 12 ounces = 5,760 grains
1 carat = 3.086 grains
1 pennyweight = 24 grains = .05 ounce
1 grain troy = 1 grain avoirdupois =
    1 grain apothecaries' weight

Temperature

Fahrenheit to Celsius:
    Subtract 32 from the number of Fahrenheit,
    then multiply by 5/9.
Celsius to Fahrenheit:
    Multiply the number of Celsius by 9/5 and
    add 32.

Mathematical Formulas

Diameter of Circle:
circumference divided by 3.1416

Circumference of a Circle:
diameter multiplied by 3.1416

Area of Circle:
square of radius multiplied by 3.1416 or square
    of diameter multiplied by .7854

Area of Triangle:
base multiplied by $1/_2$ of height

Area of Paralellogram (including square):
base multiplied by height

Surface Area of Sphere:
square of diameter multiplied by 3.1416

Volume of Sphere:
cube of diameter multiplied by .52

Volume of Prism or Cylinder:
area of base multiplied by height

Volume of Pyramid or Cone:
area of base multiplied by $1/_3$ of height

Amount of Simple Interest:
principal multiplied by rate of interest multiplied
    by time (in terms of years or fractions thereof)

Personal Information

Name _____

    Address _____

    _____

    _____

    Home Telephone (   ) _____

    Home FAX (   ) _____

Company _____

    Address _____

    _____

    Telephone (   ) _____

    Company FAX (   ) _____

Passport No. _____

    Expiration Date _____

Driver's License No. _____

    Expiration Date _____

    Auto Model and Year _____

    VIN _____

    License Plate _____

    Emergency Road Service _____

    Number _____

    Telephone _____

In case of emergency, notify:

    Name _____

    Relationship _____

    Address _____

    _____

    Telephone (   ) _____

    FAX (   ) _____

Emergency Medical Instructions

    . _____

    Blood Type _____

    Allergies _____

    Prescriptions _____

Glasses / Contact Lens Prescriptions

    _____

Physician _____

    Office Telephone (   ) _____

Pharmacist _____

    Telephone (   ) _____

Dentist _____

    Telephone (   ) _____

Miscellaneous Information _____

    Bank _____

    Telephone (   ) _____

    FAX (   ) _____

    Religious Affiliation _____

Other

    Name _____

    _____

    Name _____

    _____

    Name _____

    _____

    Name _____

    _____

    Name _____

Insurance Policies

Policy Type	Company	Policy Number	Agent Telephone
_____	_____	_____	( ) _____
_____	_____	_____	( ) _____
_____	_____	_____	( ) _____
_____	_____	_____	( ) _____